Corfu
& the Ionians

Sally Webb

D0958433

LONELY PLANET PUBLICATIONS
Melbourne • Oakland • London • Paris

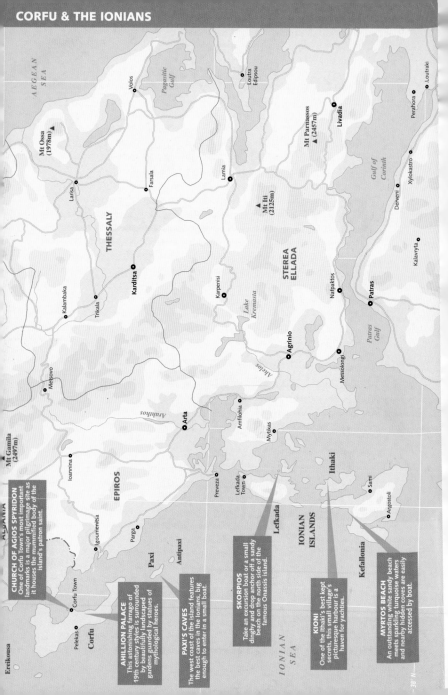

AEGEAN SEA

Volos

Pagasitic Gulf

Loutra Edipsou

Loutraki

Perahora

Mt Parnassos ▲ (2457m)

Livadia

Mt Ossa (1978m) ▲

Larisa

Farsala

Lamia

Mt Iti (2125m)

Gulf of Corinth

Xylokastro

Derveni

THESSALY

Kalambaka

Trikala

Karditsa

Karpenisi

STEREA ELLADA

Lake Kremasta

Nafpaktos

Patras

Kalavryta

Metsovo

Arahthos

Arta

Agrinio

Ahelos

Messolongi

Patras Gulf

Mt Gamila (2497m)

Ioannina

EPIROS

Amfilohia

Mytikas

Preveza

Lefkada Town

Lefkada

Ithaki

Sami

Igoumenitsa

Parga

Antipaxi

Paxi

IONIAN ISLANDS

Kefallonia

Argostoli

ALVANIA

Ereikousa

Pelekas

Corfu Town

Corfu

IONIAN SEA

CHURCH OF AGIOS SPYRIDON
One of Corfu Town's most important landmarks is a major thoroughfare often as it houses the mummified body of the island's patron saint.

AHILLION PALACE
This astonishing farrago of 19th century styles is surrounded by beautifully landscaped gardens guarded by statues of mythological heroes.

PAXI'S CAVES
The west coast of the island features the best caves in the Ionians, big enough to enter in a small boat.

SKORPIOS
Take an excursion boat or a small dinghy and drop anchor off a sandy beach on the north side of the famous Onassis island.

KIONI
One of the Ithaki's best kept secrets, this small village's picturesque harbour is a haven for yachties.

MYRTOS BEACH
An outstanding white sandy beach meets sparkling turquoise waters and nearby hidden coves are easily accessed by boat.

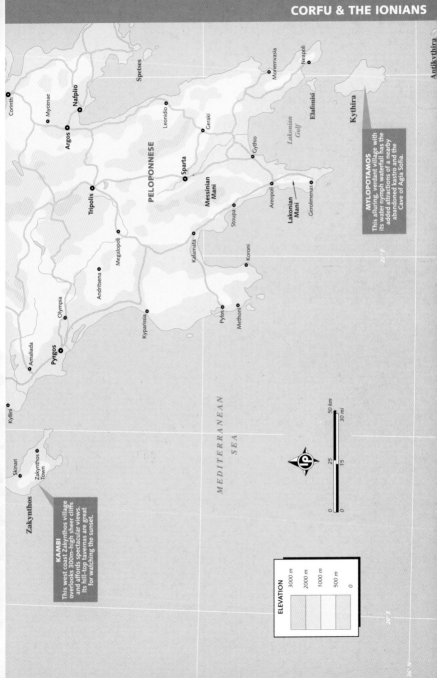

CORFU & THE IONIANS

KAMBI
This west coast Zakynthos village overlooks 300m-high sheer cliffs and affords spectacular views. Its hill-top tavernas are great for watching the sunset.

MYLOPOTAMOS
This alluring, verdant village with its water nymph waterfall has the added attractions of a nearby abandoned kastro and the Cave of Agia Sofia.

PELOPONNESE

Zakynthos

Skinari
Zakynthos Town

Kyllini
Amaliada
Pyrgos
Olympia
Andritsena
Megalopoli
Kyparissia
Pylos
Methoni
Koroni
Kalamata
Stoupa
Tripolis
Sparta
Messinian Mani
Lakonian Mani
Areopoli
Gerolimenas
Gythio
Geraki
Leonidio
Argos
Mycenae
Nafplio
Corinth
Spetses
Monemvasia
Neapoli
Elafonisi
Kythira
Antikythira

Lakonian Gulf

MEDITERRANEAN SEA

ELEVATION
3000 m
2000 m
1000 m
500 m
0

0   25   50 km
0   15   30 mi

22° E
23° E
36° N

Corfu & the Ionians
1st edition – April 2000

Published by
Lonely Planet Publications Pty Ltd A.C.N. 005 607 983
192 Burwood Rd, Hawthorn, Victoria 3122, Australia

Lonely Planet Offices
Australia PO Box 617, Hawthorn, Victoria 3122
USA 150 Linden St, Oakland, CA 94607
UK 10a Spring Place, London NW5 3BH
France 1 rue du Dahomey, 75011 Paris

Photographs
Many of the images in this guide are available for licensing from
Lonely Planet Images.
email: lpi@lonelyplanet.com.au

Front cover photograph
Smugglers Cove situated at the Gulf of St Georgios, Zakynthos Island,
Ionian Islands. (Chris Christo)

ISBN 1 86450 073 5

text & maps © Lonely Planet 2000
photos © photographers as indicated 2000

Printed by Colorcraft Ltd, Hong Kong

Contents – Text

PAXI & ANTIPAXI

LEFKADA & ITS SATELLITES

ITHAKI

KEFALLONIA

Contents – Maps

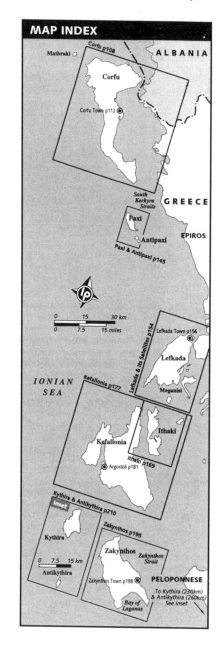

MAP INDEX

Mathraki

Corfu p108

ALBANIA

Corfu

Corfu Town p112

South
Kerkyra
Straits

GREECE

Paxi

Antipaxi

EPIROS

Paxi & Antipaxi p145

0   15   30 km
0   7.5   15 miles

Lefkada & its Satellites p154

Lefkada Town p156

Lefkada

IONIAN
SEA

Kefallonia p177

Meganisi

Ithaki

Kefallonia

Ithaki p169

Argostoli p181

Kythira & Antikythira p210

Inset

Zakynthos p195

Kythira

Zakynthos

Zakynthos
Strait

0   7.5   15 km

Antikythira

Zakynthos Town p198

PELOPONNESE

To Kythira (230km)
& Antikythira (260km)
See inset

Bay of
Laganas

The Author

Sally Webb

Sally was born and brought up in Melbourne but has spent many years living in both the UK and Italy and has travelled widely in Europe, the USA and Asia. In a former life she was an art historian, having studied at Melbourne University and at the Courtauld Institute of Art in London from where she graduated in 1990 with an MA in Art History. She moved to Italy in 1994 and became a journalist and travel writer.

After five years in Italy, where she worked for the Rome-based *Wanted in Rome*, Sally returned to Australia and is currently based in Sydney, having swapped cobblestoned streets and ancient ruins for skyscrapers and harbour views.

Sally is a regular contributor to *Australian Gourmet Traveller* and has written for other publications in the USA, Italy and Australia, including the *Qantas Club* magazine and Ansett Airline's *Vive*. Sally has worked as an author/co-author on Lonely Planet's *Rome, Italy, Mediterranean Europe* and *New South Wales* guides, and is currently eating her way around Melbourne and Sydney for the *Out to Eat* series.

FROM THE AUTHOR

Thanks to Nickolaos Momouris and especially to Lia Mathioudakis at Corfu's EOT for information and contacts, and to Panos Aronis for doing the impossible and finding me accommodation on Paxi in high season. Spiros Anemogiannis in Longos, Paxi, demonstrated why Greek hospitality and helpfulness has become the stuff of legend. Thanks also to Aemon Ryan at Hertz in Kefallonia and Geoff Harvey at Drive Away in Australia.

Paul Hellander gave me some extremely helpful advice and information and editor Craig MacKenzie made the production process trouble-free. I thank them both.

Like Odysseus, my travels had their moments. A huge thank you to my family for keeping in contact when I most needed it, and also to Adrian Arena, Lucy Carruthers, Celia Bockmuehl, Jennie Funk and Sari Taddei. I am indebted to Mark Banning-Taylor and Karen Freeman for storing my work in progress, for accommodation in London and for their valued friendship. My greatest thanks goes to my dear friend Orla Guerin, whose wonderful company in Kefallonia and Lefkada – as well as on many other odysseys of life – was nothing short of a delight.

This Book

From the Publisher

The editing of this book was coordinated by Craig MacKenzie. He was assisted by Susannah Farfor. The coordinating designer was Jacqui Saunders who was assisted by Rachel Imeson. Paul Hellander's knowledge of the Greek language was invaluable. Maria Vallianos produced the cover and Jim Miller produced the back cover map. Martin Harris, Trudi Canavan, Margaret Jung and Sarah Jolly produced the illustrations. Thanks also to Quentin Frayne from Lonely Planet's phrasebooks department and QuarkXPress manager Tim Uden.

Foreword

ABOUT LONELY PLANET GUIDEBOOKS

The story begins with a classic travel adventure: Tony and Maureen Wheeler's 1972 journey across Europe and Asia to Australia. Useful information about the overland trail did not exist at that time, so Tony and Maureen published the first Lonely Planet guidebook to meet a growing need.

From a kitchen table, then from a tiny office in Melbourne (Australia), Lonely Planet has become the largest independent travel publisher in the world, an international company with offices in Melbourne, Oakland (USA), London (UK) and Paris (France).

Today Lonely Planet guidebooks cover the globe. There is an ever-growing list of books and there's information in a variety of forms and media. Some things haven't changed. The main aim is still to help make it possible for adventurous travellers to get out there – to explore and better understand the world.

At Lonely Planet we believe travellers can make a positive contribution to the countries they visit – if they respect their host communities and spend their money wisely. Since 1986 a percentage of the income from each book has been donated to aid projects and human rights campaigns.

Updates Lonely Planet thoroughly updates each guidebook as often as possible. This usually means there are around two years between editions, although for more unusual or more stable destinations the gap can be longer. Check the imprint page (following the colour map at the beginning of the book) for publication dates.

Between editions up-to-date information is available in two free newsletters – the paper *Planet Talk* and email *Comet* (to subscribe, contact any Lonely Planet office) – and on our Web site at www.lonelyplanet.com. The *Upgrades* section of the Web site covers a number of important and volatile destinations and is regularly updated by Lonely Planet authors. *Scoop* covers news and current affairs relevant to travellers. And, lastly, the *Thorn Tree* bulletin board and *Postcards* section of the site carry unverified, but fascinating, reports from travellers.

Correspondence The process of creating new editions begins with the letters, postcards and emails received from travellers. This correspondence often includes suggestions, criticisms and comments about the current editions. Interesting excerpts are immediately passed on via newsletters and the Web site, and everything goes to our authors to be verified when they're researching on the road. We're keen to get more feedback from organisations or individuals who represent communities visited by travellers.

> Lonely Planet gathers information for everyone who's curious about the planet – and especially for those who explore it first-hand. Through guidebooks, phrasebooks, activity guides, maps, literature, newsletters, image library, TV series and Web site we act as an information exchange for a worldwide community of travellers.

Research Authors aim to gather sufficient practical information to enable travellers to make informed choices and to make the mechanics of a journey run smoothly. They also research historical and cultural background to help enrich the travel experience and allow travellers to understand and respond appropriately to cultural and environmental issues.

Authors don't stay in every hotel because that would mean spending a couple of months in each medium-sized city and, no, they don't eat at every restaurant because that would mean stretching belts beyond capacity. They do visit hotels and restaurants to check standards and prices, but feedback based on readers' direct experiences can be very helpful.

Many of our authors work undercover, others aren't so secretive. None of them accept freebies in exchange for positive write-ups. And none of our guidebooks contain any advertising.

Production Authors submit their raw manuscripts and maps to offices in Australia, USA, UK or France. Editors and cartographers – all experienced travellers themselves – then begin the process of assembling the pieces. When the book finally hits the shops, some things are already out of date, we start getting feedback from readers and the process begins again ...

WARNING & REQUEST

Things change – prices go up, schedules change, good places go bad and bad places go bankrupt – nothing stays the same. So, if you find things better or worse, recently opened or long since closed, please tell us and help make the next edition even more accurate and useful. We genuinely value all the feedback we receive. Julie Young coordinates a well travelled team that reads and acknowledges every letter, postcard and email and ensures that every morsel of information finds its way to the appropriate authors, editors and cartographers for verification.

Everyone who writes to us will find their name in the next edition of the appropriate guidebook. They will also receive the latest issue of *Planet Talk*, our quarterly printed newsletter, or *Comet*, our monthly email newsletter. Subscriptions to both newsletters are free. The very best contributions will be rewarded with a free guidebook.

Excerpts from your correspondence may appear in new editions of Lonely Planet guidebooks, the Lonely Planet Web site, *Planet Talk* or *Comet*, so please let us know if you *don't* want your letter published or your name acknowledged.

Send all correspondence to the Lonely Planet office closest to you:

Australia: PO Box 617, Hawthorn, Victoria 3122
USA: 150 Linden St, Oakland, CA 94607
UK: 10A Spring Place, London NW5 3BH
France: 1 rue du Dahomey, 75011 Paris

Or email us at: talk2us@lonelyplanet.com.au

For news, views and updates see our Web site: www.lonelyplanet.com

HOW TO USE A LONELY PLANET GUIDEBOOK

The best way to use a Lonely Planet guidebook is any way you choose. At Lonely Planet we believe the most memorable travel experiences are often those that are unexpected, and the finest discoveries are those you make yourself. Guidebooks are not intended to be used as if they provide a detailed set of infallible instructions!

Contents All Lonely Planet guidebooks follow roughly the same format. The Facts about the Destination chapters or sections give background information ranging from history to weather. Facts for the Visitor gives practical information on issues like visas and health. Getting There & Away gives a brief starting point for researching travel to and from the destination. Getting Around gives an overview of the transport options when you arrive.

The peculiar demands of each destination determine how subsequent chapters are broken up, but some things remain constant. We always start with background, then proceed to sights, places to stay, places to eat, entertainment, getting there and away, and getting around information – in that order.

Heading Hierarchy Lonely Planet headings are used in a strict hierarchical structure that can be visualised as a set of Russian dolls. Each heading (and its following text) is encompassed by any preceding heading that is higher on the hierarchical ladder.

Entry Points We do not assume guidebooks will be read from beginning to end, but that people will dip into them. The traditional entry points are the list of contents and the index. In addition, however, some books have a complete list of maps and an index map illustrating map coverage.

There may also be a colour map that shows highlights. These highlights are dealt with in greater detail in the Facts for the Visitor chapter, along with planning questions and suggested itineraries. Each chapter covering a geographical region usually begins with a locator map and another list of highlights. Once you find something of interest in a list of highlights, turn to the index.

Maps Maps play a crucial role in Lonely Planet guidebooks and include a huge amount of information. A legend is printed on the back page. We seek to have complete consistency between maps and text, and to have every important place in the text captured on a map. Map key numbers usually start in the top left corner.

> Although inclusion in a guidebook usually implies a recommendation we cannot list every good place. Exclusion does not necessarily imply criticism. In fact there are a number of reasons why we might exclude a place – sometimes it is simply inappropriate to encourage an influx of travellers.

Introduction

The seven main Ionian islands are Corfu, Paxi, Kefallonia, Zakynthos, Ithaki, Lefkada and Kythira. The first six are dotted down the west coast of Greece; Kythira (and its satellite Antikythira) dangles off the southern tip of the Peloponnese.

The islands differ from other island groups and, geographically, are less quintessentially Greek. More reminiscent of Corfu's neighbour Italy, not least in light, their colours are mellow and green compared with the stark, dazzling brightness of the Aegean.

If we are to believe Homer, the islands were important during Mycenaean times; however, no magnificent palaces or even modest villages from that period have been revealed, although Mycenaean tombs have been unearthed. Ancient history lies buried beneath many tonnes of earthquake rubble – seismic activity has been constant on all Ionian islands, including Kythira.

According to Homer, Odysseus' kingdom consisted not only of Ithaca (Ithaki) but also encompassed Kefallonia, Zakynthos and Lefkada. Ithaca has long been controversial. Classicists and archaeologists in the 19th century concluded that Homer's Ithaca was modern Ithaki, his Sami was Sami on Kefallonia, and his Zakynthos was today's Zakynthos, which sounded credible. But in the early 20th century German archaeologist Wilhelm Dorpfeld put a spanner in the works by claiming that Lefkada was ancient Ithaca, modern Ithaki was ancient Sami and Kefallonia was ancient Doulichion. His theories have now fallen from favour with everyone except the people of Lefkada.

The islands' geographical position meant that they were continually at the mercy of foreign invaders. The Corinthians settled there in the 8th century BC, and the islands were under Roman protection from 229 BC until 395 AD. The islands were nominally part of the Byzantine Empire for eight centuries, during which time they were subjected to attacks from and control by various northern raiders including Vandals, Goths, Saracens, Normans and Angevins.

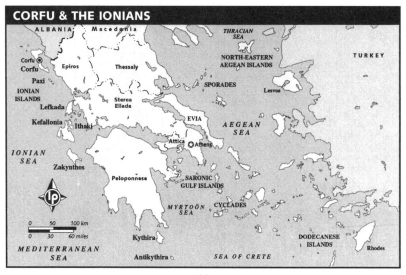

11

The Venetians ruled for around 400 years and influenced the appearance and culture of the islands considerably.

French occupancy under Napoleon, a brief Russian interlude and an oppressive British protectorate all left their mark, as did massive aerial bombing campaigns during WWII when the Italians and later the Germans occupied the islands.

The islands saw a great deal of emigration after WWII and again following the earthquakes of 1948 and 1953 which devastated the region.

But while Greeks left, the foreign invasion has never really stopped. With the exception of difficult-to-get-to Kythira, and to a lesser extent expensive Paxi and mountainous and unsettled Ithaki, none of the islands has been spared mass tourism. Parts of Corfu, Lefkada, Kefallonia and Zakynthos have been ruined by the construction of purpose-built apartment blocks and hotels which are packed to the brim with package tourists from northern Europe in summer but then close down to remain ugly blights on the landscape for the rest of the year. Tourism is predominantly of the sun and sand variety, enhanced by reliable weather, magnificent sandy beaches and crystal clear Ionian waters. Watersports enthusiasts don't have to look far to find something to suit them – from swimming to scuba diving, snorkelling, windsurfing, waterskiing or parasailing.

Those who do make the effort to get away from the crowds – perhaps by walking into the hills or olive groves, driving into the mountains, taking a small motorised dinghy to a hidden cove, or best of all by setting sail in the fabled Ionian waters – will be richly rewarded. It is only then that the countless centuries of history, legend and myth which long have attracted travellers and invaders really make themselves apparent.

Facts about the Ionians

HISTORY
Mythical Beginnings & Prehistoric Culture

The origin of the name Ionian is obscure. It is not, as often believed, connected with Ion, the son of Apollo, who according to mythology, was the founder of Ionia in Asia Minor. Instead, the name is thought to derive from the goddess Io, one of Zeus' countless paramours. To protect Io from the wrath of his jealous wife Hera, Zeus transformed the beautiful Io into a white heifer. Hera, too clever by half, asked Zeus to give her the cow. Io, in the form of the heifer, escaped, fleeing to the waters now known as the Ionian Sea. She kept swimming until she reached Egypt, where Zeus turned his lover back into a human.

Archaeological evidence on Corfu and Kefallonia indicates that the region was inhabited in the Palaeolithic period (early Stone Age, 70,000-50,000 BC). It is believed that the islands were settled by people from Illyria (present day Albania), although there is also evidence that they were linked to the Apulian civilisation from southern Italy.

Bronze Age

Of the three dominant Bronze Age powers in the Mediterranean – the Cycladic, the Minoan and the Mycenaean civilisations – the Ionians had their closest connections with the latter two.

There was a significant amount of trade between the Ionians and the Minoans (3000-1100 BC) on Crete. Wood from the *abies cephalonica*, the fir tree unique to Kefallonia, was used to build the palace of Knossos. However the two cultures were never linked.

The Ionians were close to Mycenaean culture (1900-1100 BC), the first great civilisation on the Greek mainland. Mycenaean civilisation was characterised by independent city-states such as Corinth, Pylos, Tiryns and, the most powerful of them all, Mycenae (150km from modern day Patras and a short hop from the Ionians).

If we are to believe Homer, the islands were important during Mycenaean times; Mycenaean tombs have been found on Kefallonia, Zakynthos and Lefkada, and there was a Mycenaean colony on Kythira. However, no magnificent palaces or even modest villages from that period have been revealed; ancient history lies buried beneath tonnes of earthquake rubble.

City-States to Roman Protection

From the 9th until the 4th century BC Greece was made up of independent city-states, namely Athens, Sparta and Corinth, which were constantly involved in power struggles. They actively sought out new colonies in the western Mediterranean, in particular Magna Graecia (southern Italy and Sicily), for which the Ionians were convenient stepping stones.

The most important colony on the Ionians at the time was Kerkyra (near modern day Corfu Town) established by the mighty city-state of Corinth in 734 BC. The Corinthians also set up colonies on Greece's Ionian coast and on the island of Lefkada. Over time Kerkyra defined itself as a major naval force, while Kefallonia, blessed with protected harbours, was established as a trading post between the eastern and western Mediterranean regions.

Thanks to its strategic position and increasing wealth and ambition, it wasn't long before Kerkyra started founding its own colonies, often rivalling Corinth. In 664 Corfu staged a successful revolt against Corinth, which was allied to Sparta, and became an ally of Sparta's archenemy, Athens. This alliance provoked Sparta into challenging Athens, thus precipitating the Peloponnesian Wars, which raged from 431 to 404 BC.

Naval forces from Corfu, Kefallonia, Zakynthos and Kythira participated in the Athenian expedition to Sicily which attempted to capture Syracuse, one of Corinth's greatest allies. The expedition was not successful, with Athens and her allies suffering a catastrophic defeat.

The wars left Corfu and the Ionians depleted, as they did all participants, and Corfu became little more than a staging post for whoever happened to be holding sway in Greece.

The subsequent period for the Ionians was confused. The city-states declined due to the rise of Macedon, geographically the modern nome, or province, of Macedonia and an area which is still contested today. Under Philip II of Macedon and his son Alexander the Great, the northern kingdom rose to become the greatest power in the Mediterranean, extending its territories south into Thrace and the rest of Greece, including the Ionians.

The Macedonians focused on conquests in the east and during Alexander's 13-year reign the empire was extended into Persia, Egypt and parts of India. However, much less attention was given to Greece's western frontier, where the Ionians were being threatened by Illyrian pirates. The problem had become so severe that in the 3rd century BC Corfu had to appeal for help from outside. A force of Greeks that came to Corfu's rescue was defeated at Paxi, but help was at hand with the arrival of 200 ships from Rome, which was developing as the new power in the western Mediterranean. By the end of the 3rd century BC, Corfu had placed herself under Roman protection, and eventually Rome incorporated all the Ionian islands into the province of Achaea. From 215 to 146 BC the Romans continued their Greek campaign. The new territories then became a battleground as Roman generals fought for supremacy. The Ionians witnessed their second famous naval battle in 31 BC, off Cape Actium when Octavian was victorious over Mark Antony and Cleopatra and consequently became Rome's first emperor, assuming the title Augustus, meaning the Grand One.

For the next 300 years, Greece, as the Roman province of Achaea, experienced an unprecedented period of peace, the Pax Romana. The Romans allowed their new colonies a certain amount of autonomy with regards to language, religion and law. They had always venerated Greek art, literature and philosophy, and aristocratic Romans sent their offspring to the many schools in Athens. Indeed, the Romans adopted most aspects of Hellenistic culture, spreading its unifying traditions throughout their empire.

Byzantine Empire

In 324 Emperor Constantine I (also known as Constantine the Great), a Christian convert, transferred the capital of the empire from Rome to Byzantium, a city on the western shore of the Bosphorus, which was renamed Constantinople (present day İstanbul). This was as much due to insecurity in Italy itself as to the growing importance of the wealthy eastern regions of the empire. By the end of the 4th century, the Roman Empire was formally divided into a western and eastern half. While Rome went into terminal decline, the eastern capital grew in wealth and strength, long outliving its western counterpart (the Byzantine Empire lasted until the capture of Constantinople by the Turks in 1453).

Due to their geographical position on the outer edge of the Byzantine empire, the Ionian islands did not enjoy any constant defence and life for the islanders was anything but stable. They were invaded by a succession of foreign raiders, including the Huns, Vandals, Ostrogoths, Slavs and Bulgars, although each time the Byzantines would manage to wrestle the islands back into their control.

The Normans

It is one of the ironies of history that the demise of the Byzantine Empire was accelerated not by invasions of infidels from the east, nor barbarians from the north, but by fellow Christians from the west – the Frankish crusaders.

Following their occupation of much of southern Italy, the Normans, led by Robert Guiscard, landed at Corfu in 1081 and occupied the rest of the islands until 1083. The islands were to be used as bases from where Guiscard could launch attacks on mainland

Greece. Ultimately, though, Guiscard had his sights set on Constantinople itself.

This was the first of several such incursions into the Ionian region by the crusaders on their way to Asia Minor. The stated mission of the crusades was to liberate the Holy Land from the Muslims, but in reality they were driven as much by greed as by religious fervour. By the time the First Crusade was launched in 1095, the Franks had already made substantial gains in Italy at the empire's expense and the rulers of Constantinople were understandably nervous about giving the crusaders safe passage on their way to Jerusalem.

Meanwhile skirmishes in the Ionians continued. The Normans were defeated by the Byzantines, assisted by their Venetian allies, in a great sea battle off the coast of Corfu in the first half of the 12th century. The Venetians then struck a bargain with Constantinople giving them the right to free trade anywhere along the coast of Greece.

Ever persistent, the Normans returned to the Ionian archipelago in the 1140s. In 1149 Corfu was recaptured by the Byzantines with the aid of the Venetians, who were fast increasing their trade privileges as spoils of the battles. An aristocratic Italian, Matteo Orsini, was installed by the Normans as a sort of diplomatic representative in the southern Ionian. Orsini declared the islands of Kefallonia, Ithaki and Zakynthos as a mini-kingdom, the 'County Palatine of Kefallonia'. The region remained in a fluctuating state of semi-autonomous allegiance until the early 13th century.

Venetians, Latin Princes & Angevins

The Fourth Crusade in 1204 proved that the Byzantines had plenty to fear from the Venetians. The crusaders struck a deal with Venice, whose relationship with the Byzantines had become increasingly sour over the preceding century, and was able to persuade the crusaders that Constantinople presented richer pickings than Jerusalem.

Constantinople was sacked in 1204 and the crusaders installed Baldwin of Flanders as head of the short-lived Latin Empire of Constantinople. Much of the Byzantine Empire was partitioned into feudal states ruled by self-styled 'Latin' (mostly Frankish) princes. Greece now entered one of the most tumultuous periods of its history. The Byzantines fought to regain their lost capital and to keep the areas they had managed to hold on to (the so-called Empire of Nicaea, south of Constantinople in Asia Minor), while the Latin princes fought among themselves to expand their territories.

In her share of the spoils, Venice claimed all the Greek islands, including the Ionians. Matteo Orsini acquiesced to giving up his County Palatine of Kefallonia to the Venetians. They took three more years to claim Corfu, then under the control of a Genoese pirate, Leone Vetrano. He had gained public support from his Corfiot subjects who were less than enchanted with the Venetians' sacking of Constantinople. However, in 1212 Corfu, Paxi and Lefkada aligned themselves with the Byzantine despotate of Epiros on the mainland, ruled by Michael Angelos Comnenus, which occupied the west coast of Greece and part of Albania. Realising the importance of the Ionians, the despotate sought to win the islanders' support by offering lucrative tax arrangements. With the Venetians in a weak position, the County Palatine also aligned itself with the despotate of Epiros, which was increasingly gaining in strength.

In 1258 the Normans asserted their strength once again when Corfu was captured by Manfred, who was the son of the half-Norman, half-German king Frederick II and heir to the Norman kingdom of Sicily.

Manfred's presence in the Ionians was short-lived, despite his marriage to the daughter of Despot Michael of Epiros. He returned to Italy to defend his inheritance from the French house of Anjou, which, with papal support, had captured Sicily. He died in his attempts, and the Angevins claimed the kingdom of Naples and Sicily. As a result, in 1267, the Ionians passed into the control of Charles I of Anjou.

Constantinople had been reclaimed by the Byzantines with assistance from the Empire of Nicaea. For Charles I, the Ionians represented a useful base for his intended conquest of the Byzantine capital.

Back in Sicily, spurred by the events known as the Sicilian Vespers in March 1282, the Angevins were ousted from power. The citizens of Palermo declared an independent republic, endorsing Peter of Aragon as king, and effectively separated themselves from the Neapolitan mainland to bring themselves under Spanish rule. In the ensuing years the Aragonese attempted to take Corfu and the other islands several times, but the Angevin defences held strong. Their rule, with power administered through a viceroy in Corfu and Paxi and by the Orsini family in Kefallonia, Ithaki and Zakynthos, established a feudal kingdom throughout the islands. It lasted until the Angevin dynasty lost its potency through a series of family struggles and the Venetians again asserted their claim to the islands.

Venetian Rule

By the second half of the 14th century Venice had become the undisputed sea power in the Mediterranean. Corfiot aristocrats and landowners had begun to recognise where the power in the region lay and in 1386 the island offered itself to Venice. In turn, Venice allowed the island some sort of freedom in the areas of religion and education, and retained the Angevins' feudal system.

After the fall of Constantinople to the Ottomans in 1453 Greece once again became a battleground, this time fought over by the Turks and Venetians. With the exception of Lefkada, the Ionian islands were the only part of Greece which never became fully part of the Ottoman Empire.

In 1483 the southern Ionians were captured by the Turks. The occupation wasn't to last long; Venetian and Spanish forces liberated these islands in 1499 and placed all seven under the control of Venice. Much effort and money was dedicated to the islands' protection and defence, particularly when other Venetian outstations were falling to the Ottomans. A significant proportion of the Venetian naval fleet, as well as Venice's supreme military commander,

The Golden Book

Venetian rule of the Ionians brought with it political systems similar to those in the lagoon city itself. As in Venice, the Ionian islands were ruled by a number of favoured aristocratic families. The family names of the titled islanders were inscribed in a registry, the so-called *Libro d'Oro* (Golden Book). On Corfu the book listed 112 families who effectively controlled the administration of the islands. Members of the *Libro d'Oro* formed the general assembly which elected a governing council of 150 citizens, who in turn appointed the public administrators. The Turkish siege of Corfu in 1537 resulted in many noble families being wiped out. Wealthy merchants were then elevated to fill the vacancies in the *Libro d'Oro*.

An entry in the *Libro d'Oro* meant that the families had the right to partake of refreshments at Corfu's Liston (see under Corfu Town in the Corfu chapter), which was the only place in all of Greece reserved exclusively for the aristocracy.

When the French under Napoleon took control of the islands in 1797 jubilant crowds gathered in the streets of the island capitals to celebrate the end of the oppressive and unjust social order. The Golden Books were publicly incinerated in the streets.

However the tradition had established itself and Golden Books were produced up until the beginning of the 20th century.

was based at Corfu – poised to head east in battle should the need arise.

The Venetians ruled for four centuries on a mercantile and feudal basis. The Ionians flourished and Venice reaped significant economic rewards from the various island industries of wine, currants, silk and cotton. The towns of Corfu, Argostoli, Lefkada and Zakynthos were transformed by distinctive Venetian architecture. The Venetians turned natural harbours into functioning ports, constructed houses and cisterns, and introduced olive trees to the islands, most notably on Corfu and Paxi, where island farmers were paid handsomely for every 100 trees that they planted.

Although Italian was used as the official language of the islands, most Greek residents continued to speak their native tongue. In a sense the Ionians became the last outpost of Hellenic culture, unaffected by the Muslim influence of the Ottomans, and many artists, writers and patriots took refuge there.

The islands were still subject to continual attacks by the Turks. In 1537 they took siege of Corfu, ravaging the island but failing to take the Old Fortress in Corfu Town and the Angelokastro in the north-west of the island.

Lefkada oscillated between the Venetians and the Ottomans before finally being taken into Venetian control in 1684.

A second Turkish siege on Corfu was quashed in 1716. By this time the Ionians were Venice's last overseas possession, but the feudal society had broken down with town-based nobles neglecting their rural estates and the well being of their peasant workers. Over the ensuing eight decades Venice gave less and less attention – and funding – to the islands. The public coffers ran dry, education virtually ground to a halt and soldiers went unpaid and unfed.

French Occupation

The French revolution of 1789 gave fresh encouragement to freedom movements throughout Europe. In Greece the Filiki Eteria (Friendly Society) was working towards an overthrow of Ottoman rule. The message of the society spread quickly and branches opened throughout Greece. The leaders believed that armed force was the only effective means of liberation, and made generous monetary contributions to the freedom fighters. They recruited in the Ionian islands and overseas.

After Napoleon took Venice in 1797, it wasn't long before the French exerted their influence on the Ionian islands. They turned the social order on its head and embarked on an ambitious building program in Corfu until Napoleon's demise in 1814. However they were far from welcome, with a total disregard for local customs and traditional lifestyles.

In 1799 a combined Russian-Turkish fleet captured the islands. It was supported by Ali Pasha, the despot of Epiros, who proceeded to set up his own power base in Greece in defiance of the Ottoman sultan. In negotiations with the British, it was agreed that Ali Pasha would be given Lefkada, close to his territory, in exchange for providing force against the French. The British subsequently reneged on their agreement, realising that to give away Lefkada to Ali Pasha would have turned the islanders against the British and could have been disastrous at such a delicate time.

The Russians established the independent Septinsular Republic, protecting the islands from both the French and the ambitious Ali Pasha. Although there was a certain amount of civil unrest when dissatisfied peasants rebelled against the aristocrats who had been granted control of the islands, it was the first time in almost 400 years that the Greeks had some measure of self-rule and can be seen as a precursor to the War of Independence. Under the Treaty of Tilsit, the Russians gave the islands back to France in 1807.

British Protectorate

With the fall of Napoleon in 1814, the future of the Ionians was unsure. A local politician Ioannis Kapodistrias, who had negotiated with both the British and the Russians, and had been credited with playing a major role in the defence of Lefkada from Ali Pasha, helped foster a deal whereby the islands would be part of a British protectorate maintaining a level of local autonomy. The Ionian State was established in 1815 and lasted until 1864.

British rule was oppressive. The typical British colonial superiority exhibited by the first High Commissioner, Sir Thomas Maitland, was echoed by almost all his successors and made the Brits less than universally popular. On a more positive note, the British constructed roads, bridges, schools and hospitals, established trade links and developed agriculture and industry. They also introduced their own judicial and educational systems and set up a university, the

King Tom & Co

The first high commissioner of the Ionian State was Sir Thomas Maitland who held the position from 1815 till his death in 1824. Everyone hated him – the British referred to him as 'King Tom' while the Greeks gave him the less flattering nickname of 'the Abortion'. He insisted that the Ionians remain neutral during the War of Independence and he disarmed and imprisoned the freedom fighters, and ordered the execution of some of them. Despite his unpopularity, Maitland did help to reactivate the islands' flagging economy, using the funds gained to start an ambitious but necessary construction program of roads and public buildings.

His successor, Sir Frederick Adam, was unpopular for different reasons, and virtually bankrupted the islands with his excesses. He and his Corfiot wife – who was endowed with a particularly prominent moustache – established a glittering cultural circle which included the Zantiot poet, Dionysos Solomos, who had moved to Corfu.

Sir Howard Douglas, high commissioner from 1835 to 1841, was one of the more popular men in the role. He is credited with establishing the National Ionian Bank and implementing a system of loans to agricultural producers. It was he who insisted that all his officials learn modern Greek.

Further autonomy was given to the islands under Lord Seaton, high commissioner from 1843 to 1848, who believed that the Ionians should be united with Greece. He established free elections in the islands and also encouraged a free press. Although his intentions were honourable, his actions backfired as the pro-British factions said that he was allowing the Greeks too much power while the pro-Greek caucus branded the British as oppressors.

Subsequent commissioners included Sir Henry Ward, Sir John Young and even Lord Gladstone who performed the role for a couple of weeks before being recalled to Britain where he became prime minister. The last high commissioner was Sir Henry Stow who was almost as unpopular as King Tom and operated in a tyrannical fashion until the islands were given back to Greece in 1862.

Ionian Academy. However, the nationalistic fervour in the rest of Greece soon reached the Ionian islands.

The War of Independence

On the mainland, Ali Pasha launched a private rebellion against the sultan in 1820. This gave the Greeks the opportunity they had been waiting for. On 25 March 1821, Bishop Germanos of Patras signalled the beginning of the War of Independence when he hoisted the Greek flag at the monastery of Agias Lavras in the Peloponnese. Fighting broke out almost simultaneously across most of Greece and the occupied islands, with the Greeks making big early gains.

The War of Independence all but bypassed the Ionians. Under the British Protectorate, the islands were forced to remain neutral, and known members of the Filiki Eteria were arrested. Some were executed.

The fighting was particularly savage. Within a year the Greeks had captured the fortresses of Monemvasia, Navarino (modern Pylos) and Nafplio in the Peloponnese, and Messolongi, Athens and Thiva (Thebes). Greek independence was proclaimed at Epidaurus on 13 January 1822.

Western powers were reluctant to intervene, fearing the consequences of creating a power vacuum in south-eastern Europe, where the Turks still controlled much territory. Help came from the philhellenes (literally, lovers of Greece and Greek culture) – aristocratic young men, recipients of a classical education, who saw themselves as the inheritors of a glorious civilisation and were willing to fight to liberate its oppressed descendants. These philhellenes included Shelley, Goethe, Schiller, Victor Hugo, Alfred de Musset and Lord Byron. Byron arrived in Messolongi – an important centre of resistance – in January 1824 and died three months later of pneumonia.

By 1827 the Turks had captured Modon (Methoni) and Corinth, and recaptured

Navarino, Messolongi and Athens. Eventually the western powers intervened, and a combined Russian, French and British fleet destroyed the Turkish-Egyptian fleet in the Bay of Navarino in October 1827. Sultan Mahmud II defied the odds and proclaimed a holy war, prompting Russia to send troops into the Balkans to engage the Ottoman army. Fighting continued until 1829 when, with Russian troops at the gates of Constantinople, the sultan accepted Greek independence by the Treaty of Adrianople.

Birth of the Greek Nation

The Greeks had been busy organising the independent state they proclaimed several years earlier. In April 1827 they elected Ioannis Kapodistrias as their first president. He was a Corfiot who had been the foreign minister of Tsar Alexander I. Nafplio, in the Peloponnese, was selected as the capital.

Amid ensuing anarchy, Britain, France and Russia again intervened and declared that Greece should become a monarchy and

that the throne should be given to a non-Greek so that they would not be seen to be favouring one Greek faction. A fledgling kingdom was now up for grabs among the offspring of the crowned heads of Europe, but no-one exactly ran to fill the empty throne. Eventually the 17-year-old Prince Otto of Bavaria was chosen, arriving in Nafplio in January 1833. The new kingdom (established by the London Convention of 1832) consisted of the Peloponnese, Sterea Ellada, the Cyclades and the Sporades.

King Otho (as his name became) got up the nose of the Greek people from the moment he set foot on their land. He arrived with a bunch of upper class Bavarian cronies, to whom he gave the most prestigious official posts, and he was just as autocratic as Kapodistrias. Otho moved the capital to Athens in 1834.

Patience with his rule ran out in 1843 when demonstrations in the capital, led by the War of Independence leaders, called for a constitution. Otho mustered a National

The First President

One of Corfu's most famous sons, Ioannis Kapodistrias (often also referred to as John Capodistrias) was born in 1776. Originally from Istria, his family moved to Corfu in the 14th century. The family name was inscribed in the *Libro d'Oro* (Golden Book) from 1471.

Kapodistrias went to university in Italy, studying medicine at Padua. He practised as a doctor on the island and worked in a Turkish military hospital during the Russian offensive. It was during this time that he met Count Mocenigo, a Venetian-Zantiot minister who was the governor of the Russian protected Septinsular Republic. Kapodistrias was appointed his secretary in 1802.

During the second French occupation of Corfu, Kapodistrias left the island in disgust and joined the Russian foreign service, rising to become the foreign minister of Tsar Alexander I. He retired in 1822 and devoted the rest of his life to the struggle for Greek independence.

Kapodistrias aimed to develop a viable model for the emerging Greek state, taking into account the protagonists from the independence struggle. With his Russian past, Kapodistrias believed in a strong, centralised government. He wanted to recreate the autonomous Septinsular Republic that had emerged briefly under the Russians in 1799, but realised that the other interested powers, namely the British and Austrians (who by then controlled Venice) would never let it happen. Instead he campaigned for a British protectorate, with some level of local autonomy.

In April 1827 he was elected as the first president of independent Greece. Although he was good at enlisting foreign support, his aristocratic upbringing made him anything but the people's man. Despite his best diplomatic efforts he was unable to quell the squabbling among the various independence factions. His autocratic manner at home was unacceptable to many of the leaders of the War of Independence, particularly the Maniot chieftains from the Peloponnese who had always been a law unto themselves, and he was assassinated in 1831.

Assembly which drafted a constitution calling for parliamentary government consisting of a lower house and a senate. Otho's cronies were whisked out of power and replaced by War of Independence freedom fighters, who bullied and bribed the populace into voting for them.

The Great Idea

By the mid-19th century the people of the new Greek nation were no better off materially than they had been under the Ottomans, and it was amid this climate of despondency that the Megali Idea (Great Idea) of a new Greek Empire was born. This empire was to include all the lands that had once been under Greek influence and have Constantinople as its capital. Otho enthusiastically embraced the idea, which increased his popularity no end. The Greek politicians, however, did not; they sought ways to increase their own power in the face of Otho's autocratic rule.

By the end of the 1850s, most of the stalwarts from the War of Independence had been replaced by a new breed of university graduates (Athens University had been founded in 1837). In 1862 they staged a bloodless revolution and deposed the king. But they weren't quite able to set their own agenda, because in the same year Britain returned the Ionian islands to Greece, and in the general euphoria the British were able to push forward young Prince William of Denmark, who became King George I (the Greek monarchy retained its Danish links from that time). The seven Ionian islands were given to him as a symbolic coronation gift in 1864. From that time on the history of the Ionians was once again aligned with the rest of Greece.

George I's 50 year reign brought stability to the troubled country, beginning with a new constitution in 1864, which established the power of democratically elected representatives and pushed the king further towards a ceremonial role.

The 1880s brought the first signs of economic growth: the country's first railway lines and paved roads were constructed; the Corinth Canal (begun in 62 AD!) was completed, enabling Piraeus to become a major Mediterranean port; and the merchant navy grew rapidly.

The Great Idea reared its head again in 1897 with another uprising in Crete. The hot-headed prime minister Theodoros Deligiannis responded by declaring war on Turkey and sending help to Crete. A Greek attempt to invade Turkey in the north proved disastrous – it was only through the intervention of the great powers that the Turkish army was prevented from taking Athens.

Crete was placed under international administration. Day-to-day government of the island was gradually handed over to Greeks, and in 1905 the president of the Cretan assembly, Eleftherios Venizelos, announced Crete's union *(enosis)* with Greece, although this was not recognised by international law until 1913. Venizelos became prime minister of Greece in 1910 and was the country's leading politician until his republican sympathies brought about his downfall in 1935.

The Balkan Wars

Although the Ottoman Empire was in its death throes at the beginning of the 20th century, it was still clinging onto Macedonia. It was a prize sought by the newly formed Balkan countries of Serbia and Bulgaria, as well as by Greece, leading to the Balkan Wars. The first, in 1912, pitted all three against the Turks; the second, in 1913, pitted Serbia and Greece against Bulgaria. The outcome was the Treaty of Bucharest (August 1913), which greatly expanded Greek territory by adding the southern part of Macedonia, part of Thrace, another chunk of Epiros, and the North-East Aegean Islands, as well as recognising the union with Crete.

In March 1913, King George was assassinated by a lunatic and his son Constantine became king.

WWI & Smyrna

King Constantine, who was married to the sister of the German emperor, insisted that Greece remain neutral when WWI broke out in August 1914. As the war dragged on, the Allies (Britain, France and Russia) put increasing pressure on Greece to join forces with them against Germany and Turkey. They made promises which they couldn't hope to fulfil, including land in Asia Minor. Venizelos favoured the Allied cause, placing him at loggerheads with the king. Tensions between the two came to a head in 1916, and Venizelos set up a rebel government, first in Crete and then in Thessaloniki, while the pressure from the Allies eventually persuaded Constantine to leave Greece in June 1917. He was replaced by his more amenable second son, Alexander.

Greek troops served with distinction on the Allied side, but when the war ended in 1918 the promised land in Asia Minor was not forthcoming. Venizelos took matters into his own hands and, with Allied acquiescence, landed troops in Smyrna (present day İzmir) in May 1919 under the guise of protecting the half a million Greeks living in that city (just under half its population). With a firm foothold in Asia Minor, Venizelos now planned to push home his advantage against a war-depleted Ottoman Empire. He ordered his troops to attack in October 1920 (just weeks before he was voted out of office). By September 1921, the Greeks had advanced as far as Ankara.

The Turkish forces were commanded by Mustafa Kemal (later to become Atatürk), a young general who also belonged to the Young Turks, a group of army officers pressing for western-style political reforms. Kemal first halted the Greek advance outside Ankara in September 1921 and then routed them with a massive offensive the following spring. The Greeks were driven out of Smyrna and many of the Greek inhabitants were massacred. Mustafa Kemal was now a national hero, the sultanate was abolished and Turkey became a republic.

The outcome of the failed Greek invasion and the revolution in Turkey was the Treaty of Lausanne in July 1923. This gave eastern Thrace and the islands of Imvros and Tenedos to Turkey, while the Italians kept the Dodecanese (which they had temporarily acquired in 1912 and would hold until 1947).

The treaty also called for a population exchange between Greece and Turkey to prevent any future disputes. The Great Idea, which had been such an enormous drain on the country's finances over the decades, was at last laid to rest. Almost 1.5 million Greeks left Turkey and almost 400,000 Turks left Greece. The exchange put a tremendous strain on the Greek economy and caused great hardship for the individuals concerned. Many Greeks abandoned a privileged life in Asia Minor for one of extreme poverty in shantytowns in Greece.

The Republic of 1924-35

The arrival of the refugees coincided with, and compounded, a period of political instability unprecedented even by Greek standards. In October 1920, King Alexander died from a monkey bite, resulting in the restoration of his father, King Constantine. Constantine identified himself too closely with the war against Turkey, and abdicated after the fall of Smyrna. He was replaced by his first son, George II, but George was no match for the group of army officers who seized power after the war. A republic was proclaimed in March 1924 amid a series of coups and counter-coups.

A measure of stability was attained with Venizelos' return to power in 1928. He pursued a policy of economic and educational reforms, but progress was inhibited by the Great Depression. His anti-royalist Liberal Party began to face a growing challenge from the monarchist Popular Party, culminating in defeat at the polls in March 1933. The new government was preparing for the restoration of the monarchy when Venizelos and his supporters staged an unsuccessful coup in March 1935. Venizelos was exiled to Paris, where he died a year later. In November 1935 King George II was restored to the throne by a rigged plebiscite, and he installed the right-wing General Ioannis Metaxas as prime minister. Metaxas came from one of Kefallonia's oldest families. Nine months later, Metaxas assumed dictatorial powers with the king's consent under the pretext of preventing a communist-inspired republican coup.

WWII

Metaxas' grandiose vision was to create a Third Greek Civilisation based on its glorious ancient and Byzantine past, but what he actually created was more like a Greek version of the Third Reich. He exiled or imprisoned opponents, banned trade unions and the KKE (Kommunistiko Komma Ellados, the Greek Communist Party), imposed press censorship, and created a secret police force and a fascist-style youth movement. Metaxas is best known, however, for his reply of *ohi* (no) to Mussolini's request to allow Italians to traverse Greece at the beginning of WWII, thereby maintaining Greece's policy of strict neutrality. The Italians invaded Greece, but were driven back into Albania.

As part of his plans to resurrect the mighty Roman Empire, Mussolini had plans to re-establish an Ionian State under Italian protection. The Italian occupation of the islands during WWII was reasonably peaceful. Many of the islanders had Italian blood and still spoke the language. The problems arose in 1943 when Mussolini was deposed in Italy and the Italian government surrendered to the allies. The islands were subsequently on the receiving end of a vicious German aerial bombing campaign, especially on Corfu and Kefallonia. In an atrocious incident on Kefallonia, lyrically retold (albeit with a bit of artistic licence) by Louis de Bernières in *Captain Corelli's Mandolin*, the surviving Italian soldiers and resistance fighters (more than 5000 officers and troops) surrendered to the Germans, who promptly executed them and then burnt the bodies to hide the evidence.

A prerequisite of Hitler's plan to invade the Soviet Union was a secure southern flank in the Balkans. The British, realising this, asked Metaxas if they could land troops in Greece. He gave the same reply as he had given the Italians, but died suddenly in January 1941. The king replaced him with the more timid Alexandros Koryzis, who agreed to British forces landing in Greece and then committed suicide when German troops marched through Yugoslavia and invaded Greece on 6 April 1941. The defending Greek, British, Australian and New Zealand troops were seriously outnumbered, and the whole country was under Nazi occupation within a month. King George II and his government went into exile in Egypt. The civilian population suffered appallingly during the occupation, many dying from starvation. The Nazis rounded up more than half the Jewish population and transported them to death camps, including 5000 Corfiot Jews.

Numerous resistance movements sprang up. The three dominant ones were ELAS (Ellinikos Laïkos Apeleftherotikos Stratos), EAM (Ethnikon Apeleftherotikon Metopon) and EDES (Ethnikos Dimokratikos Ellinikos Syndesmos). Although ELAS was founded by communists, not all of its members were left-wing, whereas EAM consisted of Stalinist KKE members who had lived in Moscow in the 1930s and harboured ambitions of establishing a postwar communist Greece. EDES consisted of right-wing and monarchist resistance fighters. These groups fought against one another with as much venom as they fought the Germans.

By 1943 Britain had begun speculating on the political complexion of postwar Greece. Winston Churchill wanted the king back and was afraid of a communist takeover, especially after ELAS and EAM formed a coalition and declared a provisional government in the summer of 1944. The Germans were pushed out of Greece in October 1944, but the communist and monarchist resistance groups continued to fight one another.

Civil War

On 3 December 1944, the police fired on a communist demonstration in Syntagma Square. The ensuing six weeks of fighting between the left and the right were known as the Dekemvriana (events of December), the first round of the civil war, and only the intervention of British troops prevented an ELAS-EAM victory. An election held in March 1946 and boycotted by the communists was won by the royalists, and a rigged plebiscite put George II back on the throne.

In October, the left-wing Democratic Army of Greece (DAG) was formed to resume the fight against the monarchy and its British supporters.

Under the leadership of Markos Vafiadis, the DAG swiftly occupied a large swathe of land along Greece's northern border with Albania and Yugoslavia.

By 1947, the US had replaced Britain as Greece's 'minder' and the civil war had developed into a setting for the new Cold War as the Americans fought to contain the spread of Soviet influence in Europe. Inspired by the Truman Doctrine, the US poured in cash and military hardware to shore up the anti-communist coalition government. Communism was declared illegal and the government introduced its notorious Certificate of Political Reliability (proof that the carrier was not left-wing), which remained valid until 1962 and without which Greeks couldn't vote and found it almost impossible to get work.

US aid did little to improve the situation on the ground. The DAG continued to be supplied through the communist states to the north, and by the end of 1947 large chunks of the mainland were under its control, as well as some of the islands.

The tide began to turn the government's way early in 1949 when the DAG was forced out of the Peloponnese, but the fighting dragged on in the mountains of Epiros until October 1949, when Yugoslavia fell out with the Soviet Union and cut the DAG's supply lines. Vafiadis was assassinated by a group of his Stalinist underlings after the fall of the DAG's last major stronghold in the Grammos Mountains, and the remnants of his army capitulated.

If this was a victory, there was nothing to celebrate. The country was in an almighty mess, both politically and economically. More Greeks had been killed in the three years of bitter civil war than in WWII; a quarter of a million people were homeless, many thousands more had been taken prisoner or exiled, and the DAG had taken some 30,000 Greek children from northern Greece to Eastern bloc countries for indoctrination.

Emigration

The sense of despair left by the civil war became the trigger for a mass exodus. Almost a million Greeks headed off in search of a better life elsewhere, primarily to Australia, Canada and the USA.

In the Ionians there was further impetus for emigration after the devastating earthquakes of 1953 (see under Geography later in this chapter). So much damage was done that it would have been impossible to rebuild everything from scratch. With the aid of favourable long-term loans, islanders from Kefallonia, Lefkada and Zakynthos were encouraged to emigrate; they were lent the boat fare, with two years to pay it back, and set off to the new world (predominantly to Australia).

Reconstruction & the Cyprus Issue

A general election was held in 1950. The system of proportional representation resulted in a series of unworkable coalitions, and the electoral system was changed to majority voting in 1952 – which excluded the communists from future governments. The next election was a victory for the newly formed right-wing Ellinikos Synagermos (Greek Rally) party.

Greece joined NATO in 1951, and in 1953 the US was granted the right to operate sovereign bases. Intent on maintaining a right-wing government, the US gave generous aid and even more generous military support. Living standards improved during the 1950s, but Greece remained a poor country.

Cyprus occupied centre stage in Greece's foreign affairs, and has remained close to it to this day. Since the 1930s, Greek Cypriots (four-fifths of the island's population) had demanded union with Greece, while Turkey had maintained its claim to the island ever since the British occupied it in 1914 (it became a British crown colony in 1925). After an outbreak of communal violence between Greek and Turkish Cypriots in 1954, Britain stated its intention to make Cyprus an independent state.

The right-wing Greek Cypriot EOKA (National Organisation of Cypriot Freedom

Fighters) took up arms against the British, but Greece and Turkey finally accepted independence in 1959. Cyprus duly became a republic the following August.

Back in Greece, Georgos Papandreou, a former Venizelos supporter, founded the broadly based EK (Centre Union) in 1958, but an election in 1961 returned the ERE (National Radical Union), Konstantinos Karamanlis' new name for the Greek Rally party, to power for the third time in succession. Papandreou accused the ERE of rigging the ballot – probably true, but the culprits were almost certainly right-wing, military-backed groups (rather than Karamanlis) who feared communist infiltration if the EK came to power. Political turmoil followed, culminating in the murder, in May 1963, of Grigorios Lambrakis, deputy of the communist EDA (Union of the Democratic Left). This was too much for Karamanlis, who resigned and left the country.

Despite the ERE's sometimes desperate measures to stay in power, an election in February 1964 was won by the EK. Papandreou wasted no time in implementing a series of radical changes. He freed political prisoners and allowed exiles to come back to Greece, reduced income tax and the defence budget, and increased spending on social services and education. Papandreou's victory coincided with King Constantine II's accession to the Greek throne, and with a renewed outbreak of violence in Cyprus, which erupted into a full-scale civil war before the UN intervened and installed a peacekeeping force.

The Colonels' Coup

The right in Greece was rattled by Papandreou's tolerance of the left, fearing that this would increase the EDA's influence. The climate was one of mutual suspicion between the left and the right, each claiming that the other was plotting a takeover. Finally, Papandreou decided the armed forces needed a thorough overhaul, which seemed fair enough, as army officers were more often than not the perpetrators of conspiracies. King Constantine refused to cooperate with this, and Papandreou resigned. Two years of ineffectual interim govern-

ments followed before a new election was scheduled for May 1967.

The election was never to be. A group of army colonels led by Georgos Papadopoulos and Stylianos Patakos staged a coup on 21 April 1967. King Constantine tried an unsuccessful counter-coup in December, after which he fled the country. A military junta was established with Papadopoulos as prime minister.

The colonels imposed martial law, abolished all political parties, banned trade unions, imposed censorship, and imprisoned, tortured and exiled thousands of Greeks who opposed them. Suspicions that the coup had been aided by the CIA remain conjecture, but criticism of the coup, and the ensuing regime, was certainly not forthcoming from the CIA or the US government. In June 1972 Papadopoulos declared Greece a republic (confirmed by a rigged referendum in July) and appointed himself president.

In November 1973 students began a sit-in at Athens' Polytechnic college in protest against the junta. On 17 November, tanks stormed the building, injuring many and killing at least 20. On 25 November, Papadopoulos was deposed by the thuggish Brigadier Ioannidis, head of the military security police.

The following July, desperate for a foreign policy success to bolster the regime's standing, Ioannidis decided it was time to play the Cyprus card. He hatched a wild scheme to assassinate President Makarios and unite Cyprus with Greece. The scheme went disastrously wrong after Makarios got wind of the plan and escaped. The junta installed Nikos Sampson, a former EOKA leader, as president, and Turkey reacted by invading the island.

The junta quickly removed Sampson and threw in the towel, but the Turks continued to advance until they occupied the northern third of the island, forcing almost 200,000 Greek Cypriots to flee their homes for the safety of the south.

After the Colonels

The army now called Karamanlis from Paris to clear up the mess in Greece. An election was arranged for November 1974 (won handsomely by Karamanlis' New Democracy party), and the ban on communist parties was lifted. Andreas Papandreou (son of Georgos) formed PASOK (the Panhellenic Socialist Union), and a plebiscite voted 69% against restoration of the monarchy.

Karamanlis' New Democracy (ND) party won the election in 1977, but his personal popularity began to decline. One of his biggest achievements before accepting the largely ceremonial post of president was to engineer Greece's entry into the European Community (now the European Union), which involved jumping the queue ahead of other countries who had waited patiently to be accepted. On 1 January 1981 Greece became the 10th member of the EC.

The Socialist 1980s

Andreas Papandreou's PASOK party was successful in the election of October 1981 with 48% of the vote, giving Greece its first socialist government.

PASOK came to power with an ambitious social program and a promise to close US air bases and withdraw from NATO.

After seven years in government, these promises remained unfulfilled (although the US military presence was reduced); unemployment was high and reforms in education and welfare had been limited. Women's issues fared better, though: the dowry system was abolished, abortion legalised, and civil marriage and divorce were implemented. The crunch came in 1988 when Papandreou's love affair with air hostess Dimitra Liani (whom he subsequently married) hit the headlines, and PASOK became embroiled in a financial scandal involving the Bank of Crete.

In July 1989 an unlikely coalition of conservatives and communists took over to implement a *katharsis* (campaign of purification) to investigate the scandal. In September it ruled that Papandreou and four of his ministers be tried for embezzlement, telephone tapping and illegal grain sales. Papandreou's trial ended in January 1992 with his acquittal on all counts.

The 1990s

An election in 1990 brought the ND back to power with a majority of only two seats, and with Konstantinos Mitsotakis as prime minister. Intent on redressing the country's pressing economic problems – high inflation and high government spending – the government imposed austerity measures, including a wage freeze for civil servants and steep increases in public utility costs and basic services. The government also cracked down on tax evasion which is still so rife it's described as the nation's favourite pastime.

The austerity measures sparked off a series of strikes in the public sector in mid-1990, and again in 1991 and 1992. The government's problems were compounded by an influx of Albanian refugees and the dispute over the use of the name Macedonia for the southern republic of former Yugoslavia.

By late 1992 corruption allegations were being made against the government. It was claimed that Cretan-born Mitsotakis had a large, secret collection of Minoan art, and in mid-1993 there were allegations of government telephone tapping. Former Mitsotakis supporters began to cut their losses – in June 1993 Antonis Samaras, the ND's former foreign minister, founded the Political Spring party and called upon ND members to join him. So many of them joined that the ND lost its parliamentary majority and its capacity to govern.

An early election was held in October, which Andreas Papandreou's PASOK party won with 47% of the vote against 39% for ND and 5% for Political Spring. Through the majority voting system, this translated into a handsome parliamentary majority for PASOK.

Papandreou's final spell at the helm was dominated by speculation about his heart condition and general poor health. Papandreou was rarely sighted outside his villa at Kifissia, where he lived surrounded by his ministerial coterie of family and friends. He was finally forced to step down in early 1996 after another bout of ill-health, and his death on 26 June marked the end of an era in Greek politics.

Papandreou's departure produced a dramatic change of direction for PASOK, with the party abandoning his left-leaning politics and electing economic reformer Costas Simitis as prime minister. The new leader had been an outspoken critic of Papandreou and had been sacked as industry minister four months previously. He surprised many by calling a snap poll in September 1996, and campaigned hard in support of his Mr Clean image. He was rewarded with almost 42% of the vote, enough for a comfortable parliamentary majority.

Simitis belongs to much the same school of politics as Britain's Tony Blair. Since he took power, PASOK policy has shifted right to the extent that it now agrees with the opposition New Democracy on all major policy issues. His government has focused almost exclusively on the push for further integration with Europe, which has meant more tax reform and more austerity measures – as dictated by European Union (EU) bosses in Brussels. This hasn't gone down well with the electorate, and it's rare for a day to pass without a protest of some sort. Simitis has stuck to his guns, though, and Greece appears on track to join the euro band in early 2000 – despite the disruption to the economy resulting from the 1999 NATO war against Serbia.

Recent Foreign Policy

Greece's foreign policy is dominated by its extremely sensitive relationship with Turkey, its giant Muslim neighbour to the east. These two uneasy NATO allies seem to delight in niggling each other, and are constantly attempting to upstage each other in an ongoing war of one-upmanship. Incidents which might appear trivial to the outsider frequently bring the two to the brink of war – most recently after Turkish journalists symbolically replaced the Greek flag on the tiny rocky outcrop of Imia (Kardak to the Turks) in February 1996. Both sides poured warships into the area before being persuaded to calm down.

The Kurdish rebellion in eastern Turkey has been a constant source of friction. Many Greeks empathise with the Kurds as a fel-low people fighting for freedom from Turkish tyranny – much like their own War of Independence fighters. Greece has often been accused of secretly aiding the Kurds, and the Simitis government wound up with egg all over its face when Turkish secret agents captured Kurdish leader Abdullah Ocalan in Kenya in early 1999. The circumstances remain confused, but Ocalan was captured after he was spotted at the Greek embassy in Nairobi.

The massive earthquake which devastated the İzmit area of western Turkey on 17 August 1999 sparked a remarkable turnaround in relations between the warring neighbours. According to geologists, the quake moved Turkey 1.5m closer to Greece. It had the same effect on the Greek people, who urged their government to join the rescue effort. Greek teams were among the first on the scene, where they were greeted as heroes. The Turks were quick to return the favour after the Athens quake which followed on 7 September 1999. While Turkey remains the top priority, Greece has also had its hands full in recent years coping with events to the north precipitated by the break up of former Yugoslavia and the collapse of the communist regimes in Albania and Romania.

The first crisis to arise from the break up of Yugoslavia was sparked by the former Yugoslav republic of Macedonia's attempt to become independent Macedonia. This prompted an emotional outburst from Greece, which argued that the name 'was, is, and always will be' Greek. Greece was able to persuade its EU partners to recognise Macedonia only if it changed its name, which is how the independent acronym of FYROM (Former Yugoslav Republic of Macedonia) came into being.

The wars in Croatia and Bosnia had little political impact on Greece, but the country found itself in an impossible position during the 1999 NATO war against Serbia over Kosovo. The Greek public, already strongly sympathetic towards their fellow Orthodox Christian Serbs in the battle against the Muslim Albanian Kosovars, was outraged when NATO bombing began. Americans bore the brunt of anti-NATO demonstrations, violent at first, that lasted throughout the war. Although Thessaloniki was used as a shipment point for NATO equipment, Greece played no active part in the war (unlike Turkey).

The war probably affected the Ionians more than other parts of Greece thanks to their geographical proximity to the war zone; tourism, on which the islands depend, was down compared with previous years.

GEOGRAPHY

The Ionian islands are anchored in the Ionian Sea off the western coast of Greece. Corfu and Paxi are regarded as the Northern Ionian islands; Lefkada, Kefallonia, Ithaki and Zakynthos are the Southern Ionian islands. Together these islands cover an area of 2307 sq km.

The island of Kythira, historically (although no longer politically) linked with the other islands, is situated south of the Laconian Peninsula of the Peloponnese.

There are also many islands and islets which are satellites of the main islands: Ereikousa, Mathraki, Othoni and two other uninhabited islands off Corfu's north-west coast; Antipaxi off Paxi; Meganisi, Madouri, Skorpidi, Skorpios, Kalamos, Kastos, Sparti, Thilia, Petalou and Kythros between Lefkada and the mainland; and Antikythira south of Kythira.

With the exception of Kythira, all of the Ionians are mountainous. The highest mountain in the Ionians is Mt Enos on Kefallonia which rises to 1627m. The protected east coasts of the islands tend to slope gently into the sea, and have consequently seen the majority of tourism development. The west coasts are often rocky and inaccessible, with cliffs soaring up to 200m above the sea. But the best sandy beaches can be found along the islands' west coasts, often accessible only by boat.

Seismic activity in the region has caused inestimable losses and damage over the centuries. The islands of Kefallonia, Ithaki and Zakynthos all sit above the meeting point of three tectonic plates – the Eurasian plate, which supports Italy, parts of northern Greece

How do You Spell Ionian?

Inconsistencies in the transliteration of the Greek language mean that each of the Ionian islands has more than one spelling variant. Corfu, for example, is also known as Kerkyra or Corcyra. Paxi is sometimes spelt Paxoi or the anglicised Paxos, and Antipaxi often referred to as Andipaxi. Lefkada is known as Lefkas, Lefkata and even Leucas. Ithaki is often referred to by its ancient name of Ithaca or as Itaca. Kefallonia enjoys the most variants in spelling – from Cephallonia to Cephalonia, Kefalonia, Kefalinia and Kefallinia. Zakynthos is also known as Zante, and Kythira often spelt Kithera, or Kythera. Antikythira also goes by the name Andikythira.

and the Balkans; the Turkish-Hellenic plate, which supports southern Greece and the Aegean, Turkey and Cyprus; and the African plate which carries most of the southern Mediterranean. Seismic activity is caused by the tension between the constantly moving plates, with major earthquakes occurring only a few times each century.

Lefkada suffered badly in the 1948 earthquake, and Lefkada, Kefallonia, Ithaki and Zakynthos were virtually flattened by the earthquakes of August 1953, a series of 113 tremors and aftershocks. Over 600 people were killed during the earthquakes and an estimated 70% of buildings were destroyed. Many villages were totally wiped out.

CLIMATE

The Ionian islands receive a great amount of rain and consequently the vegetation, with the exception of the more exposed Kythira, is more luxuriant than on other islands.

The Ionian islands can be extremely hot in summer. The average temperature in Corfu in July and August is around 32°C, but it is not unusual to have days on end where the mercury soars to 40°C and above. July and August are almost entirely dry. The Ionians do not experience the *meltemi*, which is a strong wind that acts as a natural air-conditioning system for the eastern coast

CORFU

Elevation - 2m/6ft

KYTHIRA

Elevation - 167m/548ft

of mainland Greece (including Athens) and the Aegean Islands. In the northern Ionian Sea the *maistro* wind brings a breath of fresh air to Corfu and Paxi.

Winters are mild, with the wet season beginning in late October and finishing in early April. The average temperature in December and January is 15°C. Corfu has the nation's highest rainfall, averaging 240mm in December.

Kythira, located off the southern tip of the Peloponnese, has a much drier climate, similar to that of the Aegean islands. The average temperature in July and August is 25°C.

ECOLOGY & ENVIRONMENT

Greece is belatedly becoming environmentally conscious; regrettably, it is often a case of closing the gate after the horse has bolted. Environmental education has begun in schools, but it will be some time before community attitudes change.

Deforestation and soil erosion are problems that go back thousands of years, the main culprits being olive cultivation and goats, but firewood gathering, shipbuilding, housing and industry have all taken their toll. In classical times Homer wrote of Kefallonia's 'wooded peaks' and of 'forested Zakynthos'. These forests were cut down long ago to clear land for agriculture and later, under the Venetians, for shipbuilding.

In the Ionians the greatest environmental hazard is mass tourism. You can see the worst of this in the ghastly purpose-built resorts of southern Corfu, Zakynthos and parts of Kefallonia and Lefkada, where once beautiful landscapes and beaches have been forever blighted by unsightly, tasteless apartment blocks, built with revenue rather than aesthetics in mind.

The Ionians put themselves on the environmental map in the early 1980s when the battles to save the endangered monk seal and loggerhead turtle began (see Endangered Species under Flora & Fauna later in this chapter).

Solar energy is used for water heating and other power needs and solar panels are a common sight on all the Ionian islands.

Fortunately the Ionians are yet to reach the dire straits that other parts of the country are in with regard to rubbish. Dirty beaches would scare tourists away, so there are now good sewerage and drainage systems in most areas and the beaches and water are regarded as the cleanest in Europe. On the whole the roads in the Ionians are reasonably litter free – you'll immediately notice the difference if you drive for any length of time on the mainland. But don't be surprised if you see evidence of indiscriminate waste disposal, such as an entire kitchen discarded in the middle of nowhere, at the top of a mountain road. Education has only come so far.

FLORA & FAUNA
Flora

Vegetation on the Ionians combines elements of the tropical with forests that could be northern European: exotic orchids as well as wild flowers emerge below spring snowlines, and eucalypts and acacias share soil with plane, oak and maple trees.

The Ionian islands have a different biological clock from the rest of Europe or America. As early as January the first daffodils and crocuses make their appearance, and by Easter the majority of wild flowers are in full bloom. Spring flowers include anemones, white cyclamens, irises, lilies, poppies, gladioli, tulips, daisies and many more.

Early summer sees the yellow flowers of Spanish broom, as well as the stunning bougainvillea in shades of bright pink, rich magenta, vivid red and deep purple, and the oleander in white and every shade of pink. Camomile, campanula and anemones can also be seen.

Not surprisingly the punishing heat of the Ionian summer wreaks havoc with plant life, but the autumn rains encourage a regeneration of the blooms in what is known as the Ionian second spring, when the dwarf cyclamens, crocuses and a variety of wild flowers appear.

Trees and shrubs common in the Ionians include umbrella pines, cypresses, mastic trees, laurels, privet and myrtle. There are also several varieties of oak – namely the Holm Oak and the Kerm Oak – which grow as large shrubs.

Fruit trees, both wild and cultivated, abound. Almonds, walnuts and pomegranates can often be found near olive groves or in domestic gardens. The ubiquitous olive is perhaps the most common tree in the Ionians, literally covering Paxi (and a fair portion of the other islands as well). Over 60% of the trees covering Corfu are olives, many of them hundreds of years old.

Herbs can be found all over the islands. Walkers will find their olfactory senses stimulated by the scent of wild rosemary, oregano, thyme, sage and myrtle.

Australian eucalypts can also be seen in the Ionians, although they are even more common in the Peloponnese and Crete, where they were used in tree-planting programs from the 1920s onwards.

Fauna

The Ionian islands are extraordinarily rich in bird life, with both resident breeding birds and migrating birds on their way through the islands from Africa to Europe in spring (and back in autumn). The best time of day to go bird-watching is either early morning or in the evening, and take your binoculars.

The usual Mediterranean small birds – wagtails, tits, warblers, bee-eaters, finches, larks, swallows, flycatchers, thrushes and chats – can be found in olive groves, woods and forests and in agricultural and scrubby areas. Housemartins and starlings are very common summer visitors. Birds of prey in the Ionians include peregrine falcons and kestrels and, especially in more remote areas, buzzards, griffons, Egyptian vultures and golden eagles.

The lakes and saltpans of Corfu and Lefkada are conveniently located in the migratory paths of many birds, attracting herons, egrets and marsh harriers.

Mammals such as foxes, squirrels, rats and mice are common throughout the Ionians, as are hedgehogs and bats. The nature reserve on Mt Enos on Kefallonia is home to a handful of wild horses, known as the Ainos mountain horses. They are the descendants of a group of tamed horses let loose in the 1920s and 30s.

The waters around Paxi are the best places to spot dolphins, although they are becoming rarer. You can get more information about dolphins from the Greek Society for the Protection & Study of Dolphins & Cetaceans (☎ 01-572 6612, fax 265 9917, email delphis@hol.gr), Imitou 50, Peristeri 121 32, Athens.

The Ionians have their fair share of reptiles and amphibians, including the Balkan green lizard, the Balkan wall lizard (found especially on Kefallonia and Zakynthos) and the gecko. The line-up of snakes includes adders, grass snakes and the only poisonous one, the horned-nose viper, a short snake with zigzag markings.

There are over 40 species of butterfly and moth. The most colourful of these is the scarce swallowtail (yellow with black markings), the large two-tailed pasha (which has an 8cm wingspan), the southern white admiral and the long-tailed blue. Other insects prevalent in the islands are cicadas, mosquitoes, flies, bees and wasps.

Endangered Species

Europe's rarest mammal, the monk seal *(Monachus monachus)*, used to be very common in the Mediterranean, but is now on the brink of extinction in Europe – it survives in slightly larger numbers in the Hawaiian Islands. There are only about 400 left in Europe, half of which live in Greece. There are about 40 in the Ionian Sea and the

Save our Seals

The Mediterranean monk seal is the rarest of all the seal species and one of the six most endangered mammals in the world. It belongs to the same genus as the Hawaiian and Caribbean monk seals. The latter is now believed to be extinct, since none has been sighted since the 1950s.

Monk seals *(Monachus monachus)* have been in existence for around 15 million years, and in ancient times were so abundant that Homer wrote of herds of them lying on beaches. There is also mention of them in the works of Plutarch, Pliny and Aristotle. It is estimated that in the 15th century around 5000 of the seals lived around the coasts of Spain, France, Portugal, Italy, Albania, Egypt, Israel, Turkey, Algeria and the Lebanon. Numbers have declined drastically in the last 100 years and the present population now stands at around 400 individuals, about half of which live in Greece. There are small numbers in Madeira and Italy, but the second largest colony lives in the Atlantic, off the coast of north-west Africa, entirely cut off from the rest.

In the past the seals were hunted for their skin and oil, and were killed by fishers because they ate the fish caught in nets. Nowadays they are threatened by marine pollution – oil spills and the numerous pesticides that end up in the sea. But the greatest threat is from disturbance by humans. Before the days of mass tourism the seals would haul themselves onto gently sloping sandy beaches to give birth, where they and their young were safe from rough waves. Then, as remote beaches became exploited by the tourist industry, the seals abandoned them and resorted to quiet coastal caves fronted by a patch of sand. However, these caves are now also becoming tourist attractions. Unfortunately, the births take place between May and November which coincides with the tourist season. A seal usually only has one pup at a time. The pup remains on land until it is weaned six to eight weeks later. If a female is frightened by the presence of tourists she may miscarry or abandon her helpless pup.

Tourism has driven the monk seal from Sardinia, Sicily and Corsica. To prevent the same happening in Greece it is imperative that tourists do not visit remote sea caves –the last safe refuge of the seal. If the necessary measures are not taken the species could become extinct within 25 years. If you are lucky enough to see a monk seal, keep a distance from it and keep quiet, to make your presence felt as little as possible. Sadly, drachma-hungry boat captains and excursion organisers offer day trips from various locations on Kefallonia to the caves used by the monk seals. These excursions should be avoided.

The Hellenic Society for the Study & Protection of the Monk Seal (☎ 01-522 2888, fax 522 2450), Solomou 53, Athens 104 32, has a seal rescue centre on Alonnisos, and the Worldwide Fund for Nature (WWF) funds a seal watch led by Dimitris Panos (☎ 0671-31 114) at Fiskardo, Kefallonia.

MARTIN HARRIS

rest are found in the Aegean. These sensitive creatures are particularly susceptible to human disturbance, and now live only in isolated coastal caves. The majority of reported seal deaths are the result of accidental trapping, but the main threat to their survival is the continuing destruction of habitat. Tourist boats are major culprits. The Hellenic Society for the Study & Protection of the Monk Seal (☎ 01-522 2888, fax 522 2450), Solomou 53, Athens 104 32, has a seal rescue centre on Alonnisos, and the Worldwide Fund for Nature (WWF) funds a seal watch project on Zakynthos. (See the boxed text 'Save our Seals'.)

The waters around Zakynthos are also home to the last large sea turtle colony in Europe, that of the loggerhead turtle *(Caretta caretta)*. The loggerhead also nests in smaller numbers on the Peloponnese and on Crete. The Sea Turtle Protection Society of Greece (☎/fax 01-523 1342, email stps@compulink.gr), Solomou 57, Athens 104 32, runs monitoring programs and is always looking for volunteers. (See the boxed text 'At Loggerheads in the Ionians' in the Zakynthos chapter.)

The Adouin's gull is the rarest seabird in Greece, and is threatened by rapidly increasing numbers of its competitors, a scarcity of breeding sites and depletion of fish stocks. A program is under way in Kythira and on other islands in the Dodecanese, the Cyclades and the Sporades to protect the species. Information can be obtained from the Hellenic Ornithological Society (☎/fax 01-381 1271), Benaki 53, Athens 106 81.

National Parks
On Kefallonia, the Mt Enos National Park was founded in 1962 to protect the forest of Kefallonian firs *(abies cephalonica)* which are particular to the area. It also encompasses nearby Mt Roudi. There is a network of forest paths for walkers and hikers, but little else in the way of facilities.

After many years of effort by conservationists, a National Marine Park has now been established on Zakynthos in the Bay of Laganas area. Its aim is to protect the nesting beaches of the loggerhead turtles. Severe boating restrictions have been put in place and some of the six nesting beaches in the area are off limits from dusk till dawn.

GOVERNMENT & POLITICS
The Region of the Ionian Islands is one of 13 administrative regions in Greece. It comprises the larger prefectures of Corfu, Lefkada, Kefallonia-Ithaki and Zakynthos, as well as the smaller Diapondia Islands (Othoni, Ereikousa and Mathraki), Paxi, and Meganisi, Kastos, Kalamos and other satellites of Lefkada. The capital of the region and the administrative assembly is in Corfu Town.

The head of the Region of the Ionian Islands, the Secretary General, is appointed by the Greek Government. Each of the four prefectures has an elected governor and an elected mayor. Elections are held every four years. The Region of the Ionian Islands is responsible for the implementation of government policy within its area. It is also responsible for the realisation of works financed by the Community Support Framework which is co-financed by the EU.

Kythira is classified as part of the Attica region, and is administered from Piraeus.

ECONOMY
The economy of the Ionian islands has changed during the last 20 years from a traditionally agricultural economy to one based on services directly or indirectly related to tourism. The agricultural sector diminished between 1981 and 1991, though it is still a significant part of the islands' economy. Employment in the agricultural sector covers approximately 38%, while employment in services is 46% of total employment. It is estimated that over 20,000 people are employed in the tourism industry.

As a proportion of Gross National Income (GNI), tourism represents 64%, agriculture is 21%, light industry and crafts represent 15%. The GNI per capita is 44% of the EU average and 88% of the Greek average. On a European level, the Ionian islands do not fair well; they are in 166th position out of the 179 EU-defined regions as regards the GNI, and the average income is 43.7% of the EU average.

The Ionian islands have the third highest flow of tourists (after the south Aegean and Crete), and tourism in the region represents 11% of tourist activity in the whole country. Development in the region is closely linked to tourism. Local authorities are trying to extend the traditional summer season (May to September) by encouraging related activities such as sailing, golf and culture.

Agricultural products include very high quality olive oil, wine, cumquats, honey and fish.

The NATO war against Serbia in 1999 had a negative effect on tourism in the Ionians, with many international tour operators and local hospitality industry workers reporting more vacancies than usual in high season.

Greece appears on track for the second phase of European monetary union in 2000.

POPULATION & PEOPLE

According to the last census taken in 1991, the population of the Ionian islands – with the exclusion of Kythira – stands at 193,734 people.

Corfu is the most populous island with 107,592 people. (Corfu is also the third most populous island in Greece.) The population of Kefallonia is 32,474. Zakynthos has 32,557 inhabitants and Lefkada 21,111. Between 1971 and 1981 the population of Lefkada and Kefallonia decreased dramatically due to emigration. However, during the same period the population in Corfu increased by 7%. In the decade 1981-91 the population in Zakynthos increased by 9.1%, in Corfu by 6% and in Kefallonia by 3.2%. During the same period the population in Lefkada decreased.

Kythira has a population of 3100, including 70 people who live on Antikythira.

EDUCATION

Education in Greece is free at all levels of the state system, from kindergarten to tertiary. Primary schooling begins at the age of six, but most children attend a state-run kindergarten from the age of five. Private

kindergartens are popular with those who can afford them. Primary school classes tend to be larger than those in most European countries – usually 30 to 35 children. Primary school hours are short (8 am to 1 pm), but children get a lot of homework.

At 12, children enter the *gymnasio*, and at 15 they may leave school, or enter the *lykeio*, from where they take university-entrance examinations. Although there is a high percentage of literacy, many parents and pupils are dissatisfied with the education system, especially beyond primary level. The private sector therefore flourishes, and even relatively poor parents struggle to send their children to one of the country's 5000 *frontistiria* (intensive coaching colleges) to prepare them for the very competitive university-entrance exams. Parents complain that the education system is badly underfunded. The main complaint is about the lack of modern teaching aids in both gymnasio and lykeio.

Grievances reached a peak in 1991, when lykeio students staged a series of sit-ins in schools throughout the country, and organised protest marches. In 1992, gymnasio pupils followed suit, and the government responded by making proposals that called for stricter discipline and a more demanding curriculum. More sit-ins followed, and in the end the government changed its plans and is still reassessing the situation.

ARTS
Architecture, Painting & Sculpture

The best examples of early artistic activity in the Ionians can be found in Corfu's small but impressive Archaeological Museum, the Lefkada Archaeological Museum and the Zakynthos Museum. However, centuries of occupation and pirating in the area, combined with continual damage from earthquakes, mean that there are precious few traces of antiquity.

Mycenaean tombs have been found on Kefallonia, Lefkada and Zakynthos and there was a Mycenaean colony on Kythira. Typical Mycenaean artefacts include gold masks, diadems, cups, dress ornaments, carved ivory and seal-stones, and pottery.

Bell tower, Church of Panagia, Hora, Kythira

Corfu Island, from New Citadel

Church near Kaladi Beach, Kythira

Church of Agios Spyridon, Corfu Town

Church of Agios Iason and Agios Sosipater, Kanoni Peninsula, Corfu

Olive-wood carvings, fruit and vegetables, postcards and posters can be bought in Corfu Old Town.

Examples also exist of Corfiot pottery production in the so-called Geometric style, following the production of ruling Corinth. The pottery from this period is distinguished by geometric patterning, often in bands or panels, and with stylised animal friezes.

Under Corinthian influence, there was a great deal of artistic activity as well as construction. On Corfu's Kanoni Peninsula, ruins of magnificent monuments from this period include a circular cenotaph of Menecrates and several Doric temples. Decorative elements from these constructions are on display in Corfu's Archaeological Museum and include the famous Gorgon Medusa frieze and a carved stone lion that sat atop the Menecrates temple. Both show the Corinthian artistry of the period at its peak.

The Archaic period (6th to 5th centuries BC) saw the influence of Corinth with the first large stone temples and the earliest life-size marble statues. Athens took over from Corinth in pottery production using red clay with a high iron content, which contrasted strongly against the glossy black surface. Vases and pots were decorated with scenes from Greek mythology.

There was a flourishing artistic school on Corfu towards the end of the Archaic period which had its own style, and was not influenced by Corinth. Corfiot pottery production reached its height in the late 6th century BC and the first half of the 5th. Subsequently artistic production in the Ionians followed that of Athens.

During the Classical period (480 BC until the death of Alexander the Great in 323 AD) naturalism was being achieved for the first time in European art. There was an obsession with the human figure and with drapery. Sculptors sought ideal proportions for the human figure, and the nude female figure first appeared in the 4th century BC as Aphrodite. Very little free-standing bronze sculpture from this period survives anywhere in Greece – although the Roman copies in marble are a good indication of what the originals were like. It was at this time that many temples were built. Any that

once stood in the Ionians have long since been reduced to rubble by natural forces (including earthquakes) or human pillaging.

During the Hellenistic period (323-31 BC) sculpture often showed greater realism than in the classical period. It was able to express suffering and old age, and delighted in the grotesque. Portraiture also came into its own in sculpture and on coins. Gold was also used to make exquisite jewellery.

In the Hellenistic and Roman period Athens continued to produce marble sculpture, largely for export. From the mid-3rd century BC, the Ionians were under the control of Rome.

During the Byzantine period churches were built in the Byzantine style, with a central dome supported by four arches on piers and flanked by vaults, with smaller domes in the four corners and three apses to the east. The churches were usually decorated with frescoes on a dark-blue ground showing figures of Christ, the evangelists, scenes from the Life of Christ, and the saints. In the later centuries the scenes involve more detailed narratives, including cycles of the life of the Virgin and the miracles of Christ. Thanks to earthquakes in the region, very few such buildings or their decorations survive on the Ionians.

Much artistic activity during this period and later involved the prolific production of icons. After the Ottoman conquest of Constantinople and mainland Greece, many Byzantine painters and intellectuals headed for Crete which, like the Ionians, was occupied by the Venetians. But in 1669 Crete too fell to the Turks, and many of these artists moved to the Ionians, before continuing their journey to Italy.

Their arrival in Corfu, Zakynthos and Kefallonia sparked the emergence of what became known as the Ionian school. The taste in the Ionians was quite different to the rest of Greece. Whereas Greek icons of the period followed a strict iconography and formal symbolism, the western Renaissance had abandoned such rigid rules centuries before. The Greek artists had to rapidly absorb the tastes of the previous Angevin and current Venetian rulers for a more western-style art.

The founder of the school was Kalamata-born Panagiotis Doxaras (1662-1729) who had migrated to Zakynthos as a boy and became apprenticed to an icon-painter. His works can be seen in the church of Agios Dimitrios in Lefkada Town as well as in the Public Library of Lefkada's Collection of Post-Byzantine Icons, and in the Zakynthos museum. His son Nikolaos Doxaras worked in a similar style. Nikolas Koutzouzis (1714-1811) was another follower. A priest who produced works in a dramatic baroque style, he created a scandal on Zakynthos when he depicted himself as part of the religious imagery. Another priest called Kandounis managed to incorporate the worst Italian rococo excesses, including flushed looking Madonnas, into his works.

Stunning icons by some of the best Cretan artists of the period who relocated to the Ionians, including Michael Damaskinos (1530-92), Emanuel Tzanes (1610-90) and Theodoros Poulakis, were produced on Corfu, and can be seen in Corfu's Byzantine Museum.

After the War of Independence, Greece continued with the neoclassical style dominant in Western European architecture and sculpture at the turn of the century, thus providing a sense of continuity with its ancient past.

With the German Otho on the Greek throne, the Munich school of art, working in the traditions of classicism and romanticism, was the main influence on Greek painters after independence. During the 19th century, however, Greek artists trained in various centres of Europe, including Rome and Paris. Andreas Kriezis specialised in portraits and nautical themes, and Dionysios Tsokos and Theodoros Vryzakis often focused on the War of Independence. Nikiphoros Lytras, Konstantinos Volanakis and Nicholas Gyzis, in the second half of the century, chose genre scenes and their paintings became more pictorial than descriptive. Gyzis' historical paintings were more visionary, coinciding with the fascination with the Great Idea of the Greek empire. The settings, costumes and historical subjects of many of these 19th century paintings express Greek conditions at the time. Corfu's Municipal Art Gallery contains several history paintings relevant to the Ionians.

The English painter and writer Edward Lear, of *The Owl and the Pussy-Cat* fame, spent some time in Greece in the mid-19th century. His watercolours of the Ionian islands are some of the best depictions of how these landscapes once appeared. At the start of the 20th century, Corfiot artist George Samartzis worked in a style influenced by French postimpressionism.

From the first decades of the 20th century artists like Konstantinos Parthenis and Konstantinos Kaleas and later George Bouzianis were able to use the heritage of the past and at the same time assimilated various developments in modern art. Notable modern painters in the Ionians include the Corfiots Nikos Venturas (1899-1990), an engraver, and Papa Aglaia (1904-84) who produced striking abstract works.

Weaving and embroidery were substantial cottage industries throughout the Ionians. The town of Karya on Lefkada is still noted for its production of embroidered linens and lace work, and a small museum in the village traces the history of the craft through the historical memorabilia of the island's most famous embroiderer.

Workshops on Corfu have been producing ceramic tableware since the 18th century. These objects were distributed and sold throughout the Ionian islands and on the Greek mainland. In the 19th century these workshops produced everyday household objects such as water pitchers and storage jars for oil and wine as well as more decorative pieces. Zakynthos potters specialised in making ceramic tiles and bricks. Woodcarving and metal work have achieved rather less prominence. Wooden chests and icon screens and sanctuary doors in churches were often elaborately carved and there was a folk tradition of carved figures on ships' prows. The silversmiths produced liturgical vessels and crosses, ornate Gospel covers and icon frames, many of which can still be seen *in situ* in the larger churches throughout the Ionians.

Dance

The folk dances of today derive from the ritual dances performed in ancient Greek temples. One of these dances, the *syrtos*, is depicted on ancient Greek vases, and there are references to dances in Homer's works.

Many Greek folk dances, including the syrtos, are performed in a circular formation; in ancient times, dancers formed a circle in order to seal themselves off from evil influences.

Each region of Greece has its own dances, but one dance you'll see performed everywhere is the *kalamatianos*, originally from Kalamata in the Peloponnese. It's the dance in which dancers stand in a row with their hands on one another's shoulders.

Popular dances in the Ionians were influenced by those of Crete and the Peloponnese, and include the *ballos, mermingas, girouzatos, divaratikos* and *vaskopoules* as well as the syrtos.

Zakynthian folk dances are some of the most interesting in Greece. Many of them were introduced to the island by Greek refugees or Italians during the period of Venetian rule. They are performed during celebrations for saints days and weddings. The *yiaryitos* is a variation on the Cretan crane dance. It is often performed together with the *galiantra,* an Italian dance. Another Italian dance adopted by the Zakynthians is the *manfrena*. When Zakynthians dance the syrtos, they do it at a slower pace than in other parts of Greece. The *stavrotos,* however, is danced at a lively pace and is accompanied by *tambourioniakara,* a percussion instrument.

Music

Singing and the playing of musical instruments have also been an integral part of life in Greece since ancient times. There has been a great deal of cross-fertilisation over the centuries. Greek music has been influenced by Italy, Turkey, the Balkans and the Middle East, all of whom were influenced by the Byzantines who were in turn influenced by the ancient Greeks.

Ceramic figurines holding musical instruments resembling harps and flutes date back

MARGARET JUNG

The mandolin-like *bouzouki* – a traditional Greek musical instrument

to 2000 BC. Musical instruments of ancient Greece included the lyre, lute, *piktis* (pipes), *kroupeza* (a percussion instrument), *kithara* (a stringed instrument), *aulos* (a wind instrument), *barbitos* (similar to a violin cello) and the *magadio* (similar to a harp).

If ancient Greeks did not have a musical instrument to accompany their songs, they imitated the sound of one. It is believed that unaccompanied Byzantine choral singing derived from this custom.

The *bouzouki*, which you will hear in the Ionians and everywhere else in Greece, is a mandolin-like instrument similar to the Turkish *saz* and *baglama*. It is one of the main instruments of *rembetika* music – the Greek equivalent of the American Blues, to which much of current Greek pop owes its origins.

Rembetika was popularised by the refugees from Asia Minor and performed in *tekedes* (hashish dens) in seedy areas of cities and ports. It had themes concerning hashish and prison life. In the late 1930s, Metaxas' censorship meant that such themes disappeared from recordings of rembetika, but continued clandestinely in some tekedes. This polarised the music, and the recordings, stripped of their 'meaty' themes and language, became insipid and bourgeois; recorded rembetika even adopted another name – *Laïko tragoudi* – to disassociate it from its illegal roots. Although WWII brought a halt to recording, a number of composers emerged at this time. They included Apostolos Kaldaras, Yiannis Papaïoanou, Georgos Mitsakis and Manolis Hiotis; one of the greatest female rembetika singers, Sotiria Bellou, also appeared at this time.

During the 1950s and 1960s rembetika became increasingly popular, but less and less authentic. Much of the music was glitzy and commercialised, although the period also produced two great composers of popular music (including rembetika) in Mikis Theodorakis and Manos Hatzidakis. The best of Theodorakis' work is the music which he set to the poetry of Seferis, Elytis and Ritsos.

During the junta years, many rembetika clubs were closed down, but interest in genuine rembetika revived in the 1980s – particularly among students and intellectuals. There are now a number of rembetika clubs in Athens.

Italian music directly influenced the emergence of folk songs on Kefallonia and Zakynthos, notably the *arekia*, *kantades* and *serenades*, which are quite distinct from the traditional eastern-influenced rembetika. The arekia is a short song, which originates from Lixouri on Kefallonia. It was created by the fishermen who gathered in tavernas after a day at sea. It is sung by a single male voice, and every interpretation is different. The name arekia comes from the Italian *ad orecchio* (by ear). It is often quiet and reflective, taking the form of a love ballad or a lament for absent friends and family. The kantades which can still be heard at various restaurants and tavernas on Zakynthos, are descended from opera and are often love songs, although they can also be comedies. Accompanied by a guitar, the kantades are usually sung by groups of three or four men. The serenades were traditionally sung by courting men to their objects of desire after nightfall in the alleyways of Kefallonian towns.

Since independence, Greece has followed mainstream developments in classical music. You'll also find all the main forms of western popular music. Rock, particularly heavy metal, seems to have struck a chord with young urban Greeks.

Few Greek performers have hit it big on the international scene. The best known are Demis Roussos, the larger than life singer who spent the 1980s strutting the world stage clad in his caftan, and the US-based techno wizard Yanni.

Literature

The first, and greatest, ancient Greek writer was Homer, author of the *Iliad* and *Odyssey*, set in the Ionian islands. Nothing is known of Homer's life – where or when he lived, or whether, as it is alleged, he was blind. The historian Herodotus thought Homer lived in the 9th century BC, and no scholar since has proved nor disproved this.

In the 5th century BC, Herodotus became the author of the first historical work about western civilisation. His highly subjective account of the Persian Wars has, however, led him to be regarded as the 'father of lies' as well as the 'father of history'. The historian Thucydides (5th century BC) was more objective, but took a high moral stance. He wrote an account of the Peloponnesian Wars, and also the famous *Melian Dialogue*, which chronicles the talks between the Athenians and Melians prior to the Athenian siege of Melos.

Pindar (c518-438 BC) is regarded as the pre-eminent lyric poet of ancient Greece. He was commissioned to recite his odes at the Olympic Games. The greatest writers of love poetry were Sappho (6th century BC) and Alcaeus (5th century BC), both of whom lived on Lesvos. Sappho's poetic descriptions of her affections for other women gave rise to the term 'lesbian'. Ironically she threw herself to her death off a cliff on Lefkada out of unrequited love for a man.

In Byzantine times, poetry, like all of the arts, was of a religious nature. During Ottoman rule, poetry was inextricably linked with folk songs, which were not written down but passed on by word of mouth. Many of these songs were composed by the klephts, and told of the harshness of life in the mountains and of their uprisings against the Turks.

Dionysios Solomos (1798-1857) and Andreas Kalvos (1796-1869), who were both born on Zakynthos, are regarded as the first modern Greek poets. Solomos' work was heavily nationalistic and his *Hymn to Freedom* became the Greek national anthem. At this time there were heated debates among writers, politicians and educators about whether the official language should be Demotiki or Katharevousa. Demotic was the spoken language of the people and Katharevousa was an artificial language loosely based on Ancient Greek. Almost all writers favoured Demotic, and from the time of Solomos, most of them wrote only in that language.

Lefkada was the birthplace of two great national poets, Aristotelis Valaoritis (1824-79), who owned an island off Nydri, and Angelos Sikelianos (1884-1951). Sikelianos wrote vibrant lyrical poetry and advocated progressive theories, including the 'Delphic Idea' of learning and the arts, to revive the mythic passion and power of ancient Greece. Together with his American wife Eva, he sought to create an international Delphic centre and university and a permanent festival of the arts, which did in fact take place (supported by his personal funds) in 1927 and 1930.

The best known 20th century Greek poets are George Seferis (1900-71), who won the Nobel Prize for literature in 1963, and Odysseus Elytis (1911-96), who won the same prize in 1979. Seferis drew his inspiration from the Greek myths, whereas Elytis' work is surreal. Angelos Sikelianos (1884-1951) was another poet who drew inspiration from ancient Greece, particularly Delphi. His poetry is highly evocative, and includes incantatory verses emulating the Delphic oracle. Yiannis Ritsos is another highly acclaimed Greek poet; his work draws on many aspects of Greece – its landscape, mythology and social issues. The most celebrated 20th century Greek novelist is Nikos Kazantzakis.

Drama

Drama in Greece can be dated back to the contests staged at the Ancient Theatre of Dionysos in Athens during the 6th century BC for the annual Dionysia festival. During one of these competitions, Thespis left the ensemble and took centre stage for a solo performance regarded as the first true dramatic performance. The term 'thespian' for actor derives from this event.

Aeschylus (525-456 BC) is the so-called 'father of tragedy'; his best known work is the *Oresteia* trilogy. Sophocles (c496-406 BC) is regarded as the greatest tragedian. He is thought to have written over 100 plays, but only seven major works survive.

These include *Ajax, Antigone, Electra, Trachiniae* and his most famous play, *Oedipus Rex*. His plays dealt mainly with tales from mythology and had complex plots. Sophocles won first prize 18 times at the Dionysia festival, beating Aeschylus in 468 BC, whereupon Aeschylus went off to Sicily in a huff.

Euripides (c485-406 BC), another famous tragedian, was more popular than either Aeschylus or Sophocles because his plots were considered more exciting. He wrote 80 plays of which 19 are extant (although one, *Rhesus*, is disputed). His most famous works are *Medea, Andromache, Orestias* and *Bacchae*. Aristophanes (c427-387 BC) wrote comedies – often ribald – which dealt with topical issues. His play *The Wasp* ridicules Athenians who resorted to litigation over trivialities; *The Birds* pokes fun at Athenian gullibility; and *Plutus* deals with the unfair distribution of wealth.

You can often see plays by the ancient Greek playwrights at various festivals in the Ionians and in other parts of Greece. See individual island chapters and Public Holidays & Special Events in the Facts for the Visitor chapter.

SOCIETY & CONDUCT
Traditional Culture

Like other parts of Greece, the Ionians are steeped in traditional customs. Namedays, weddings and funerals all have great significance. On someone's nameday an open-house policy is adopted and refreshments are served to well-wishers who stop by with gifts. Weddings are highly festive occasions, with dancing, feasting and drinking sometimes continuing for days.

Tourism has played a role in the disappearance of some island culture in the Ionians. For many, the lure of the tourist drachma is more important than maintaining traditional values, and the original essence of some places – predominantly beach resorts – has been drowned by commercialism. Once sleepy fishing ports have been tarted up to attract yachties or daytrippers with cash to burn. But it is probably just as well, as the fishers could not hope to

Namedays

Namedays, not birthdays, are celebrated in Greece. Great significance is attached to the name given to a child, and the process of choosing a name follows fairly rigid conventions. The idea of a child being given a name just because the parents like the sound of it is unknown in Greece. Even naming a child after someone as a mark of respect or admiration is unusual. That so many children were named Vyronis (the Greek form of Byron) was a measure of the tremendous gratitude the Greeks felt for the philhellene Lord Byron.

Children are never named after parents, but the eldest son in a family is often called after his paternal grandfather, and the eldest daughter after her paternal grandmother. Names are usually of religious origin. Each island or area in Greece has a patron saint, and people living in that area often name a child after its patron saint.

The patron saint of Corfu is Agios Spyridon and it seems as if about half of the men who were born there are called Spyridon (often shortened to Spyros). Exceptions to this custom occur if a family is not religious – quite a rarity in Greece. A nonreligious family will often give its offspring a name derived from ancient Greece or mythology. Socrates, Aristotle, Athena and Aphrodite are popular.

Each saint has a special feast day. A person's nameday is the feast day of the saint after which they were named. On someone's nameday, open house is held and a feast is laid on for the friends and neighbours who call. They will give a small gift to the person whose nameday it is, but there is less emphasis on the giving of presents than there is in birthday celebrations.

If you meet someone in Greece on their nameday, the customary greeting is 'chronia polla!', which means 'many years!'.

make a living from what they catch in these fished-out seas. The best place to experience traditional culture is in inland mountain villages. Regardless of tourism, every island has religious and secular festivities that haven't changed for hundreds of years. Kythira remains unspoilt and out of the Ionians is the island which best retains its traditional culture.

Greeks tend to be more superstitious than other Europeans. Tuesday is considered an unlucky day because on that day the Byzantine Empire fell to the Ottomans. Many Greeks will not sign an important transaction, get married or begin a trip on a Tuesday. Greeks also believe in the 'evil eye', a superstition prevalent in many Middle Eastern countries. If someone is the victim of the evil eye, then bad luck will befall them. The bad luck is the result of someone's envy, so one should avoid being too complimentary about things of beauty, especially newborn babies. To ward off the evil eye, Greeks often wear a piece of blue glass, resembling an eye, on a chain around their necks.

Dos & Don'ts

The Greeks' reputation for hospitality is not a myth, although it's a bit harder to find these days, especially on the tourism ravaged Ionians. However, it is not unheard of for a traveller to be invited into a stranger's home for coffee or a meal.

If you are invited out for a meal with Greeks, you are their guest; the bill is not shared as in northern European countries, but paid by the host.

When drinking wine it is the custom to only half fill the glass. It is bad manners to empty the glass, so it must be constantly replenished. When visiting someone you will be offered coffee; again, it is bad manners to refuse. You will also be given a glass of water and perhaps a small serve of preserves. It is the custom to drink the water, then eat the preserves and then drink the coffee.

Personal questions are not considered rude in Greece, and if you react as if they are you will be the one causing offence. You will be inundated with queries about your age, salary, marital status etc. Expect commiserations if you are over 25 and unmarried!

If you go into a *kafeneio*, taverna, or shop, the customary greeting to the waiters or assistants is '*kalimera'* (good day) or '*kalispera'* (good evening) – likewise if you meet someone in the street.

You may have come to Greece for sun, sand and sea, but if you want to bare all, other than on a designated nude beach, remember that Greece is a traditional country, so take care not to offend the locals.

Treatment of Animals

The Greek attitude to animals depends on whether the animal is a cat or not. It's definitely cool to be a cat. Even the mangiest-looking stray can be assured of a warm welcome and a choice titbit on approaching the restaurant table of a Greek. Most other domestic animals are greeted with a certain indifference. You don't see many pet dogs, or pets of any sort for that matter.

The main threat to animal welfare is hunting. Greek hunters are notorious for blasting anything that moves, and millions of animals are killed during the long 'open' season, from 20 August to 10 March, which encompasses the bird migratory period.

RELIGION

About 98% of Greeks belong to the Greek Orthodox Church. Most of the remainder are either Roman Catholic, Jewish or Muslim.

The Greek Orthodox Church is closely related to the Russian Orthodox Church and together they form the third largest branch of Christianity. Orthodox, meaning 'right belief', was founded in the 4th century by Constantine the Great, who was converted to Christianity by a vision of the Cross.

By the 8th century, there were a number of differences of opinion between the pope in Rome and the patriarch of Constantinople, as well as increasing rivalry between the two. One dispute was over the wording of the Creed. The original Creed stated that the Holy Spirit proceeds 'from the Father', which the Orthodox Church adhered to, whereas Rome added 'and the Son'. Another bone of contention concerned the celibacy of the clergy. Rome decreed priests had to be celibate; in the Orthodox Church, a priest could marry before he became ordained. There were also differences in fasting – in the Orthodox Church, not only was meat forbidden during Lent, but also wine and oil.

By the 11th century these differences had become irreconcilable, and in 1054 the pope and the patriarch excommunicated one another. Ever since, the two have gone their own ways as the (Greek/Russian) Orthodox Church and the Roman Catholic Church.

During Ottoman times membership of the Orthodox Church was one of the most important criteria in defining a Greek, regardless of where he or she lived. The church was the principal upholder of Greek culture and traditions.

Religion is still integral to life in the Ionians, and the year is centred on the festivals of the church calendar. Most Greeks, when they have a problem, will go into a church and light a candle to the saint they feel is most likely to help them. Hundreds of tiny churches are dotted around the islands. Most have been built by individual families in the name of their selected patron saint as thanksgiving for God's protection.

If you wish to look around a church, you should dress appropriately. Women should wear skirts that reach below the knees and cover their shoulders, and men should wear long trousers and have their arms covered. Regrettably, many churches are kept locked nowadays, but it's usually easy enough to locate caretakers, who will be happy to open them up for you.

LANGUAGE

Greek (spoken with a songful accent due to the influence of Italian) is the official language of Corfu and the Ionians, and the only effective means of communication. Though Italian may be spoken by some of the older folk, and English is widely spoken in areas of high tourism – and also because of a large proportion of expats residing there – you'd be wise to arm yourself with a few Greek words and phrases. The Language chapter at the back of this book can get you started – for a more comprehensive guide to the language, get a copy of Lonely Planet's *Greek phrasebook*.

Facts for the Visitor

TOP 10 HIGHLIGHTS

1 Chartering a yacht to see the Ionians at their best
2 Swimming in the almost phosphorescent turquoise water of the Ionian Sea
3 Sitting outside a kafeneio (cafe) in a traditional, unspoilt Kytherian village, watching the world go by or playing backgammon
4 Sipping a glass of ouzo and nibbling on fresh grilled octopus by the sea
5 Watching the sunset at Pelekas in Corfu
6 Renting a motorised dinghy and exploring difficult-to-get-to beaches and coves
7 Drinking a caffe frappé or a tsin tsin birra in the elegant Liston in Corfu Town
8 Visiting Corfu's Archaeological Museum and Zakynthos' Neo-Byzantine Museum
9 Listening to lyrical Zantiot kantades
10 Tasting and buying local produce – Robola wine, honey and olive oil

SUGGESTED ITINERARIES

One of the most difficult aspects of travel is organising an itinerary. The following list provides a choice of one, two and three-week itineraries. Unless you have plenty of time – or plan your trip well – you probably won't be able to get to Kythira in the same trip as Corfu.

One week

Northern Ionians Spend two days in Corfu Town; explore the narrow streets of the old town and visit the museums. Spend one night in Paleokastritsa or Lakones; walk the path between the two, visit Moni Theotokou and Angelokastro, and have a meal at one of the restaurants on the Lakones-Makrades road. Spend two days at a west coast resort and catch a sunset at Pelekas, or head to the Diapondia Islands. Visit Lake Korission, Issos beach and surrounds. Spend one or two nights on Paxi.

Southern Ionians Spend one day and night on Lefkada, explore the capital and relax on a west coast beach. Overnight on Meganisi. Spend two days on Ithaki, visiting Vathy's museums and the villages of Anogi, Frikes and Kioni. Have two days in Fiskardo on Kefallonia (in the high season stay elsewhere and visit on a day trip), to see Assos village and Myrtos Beach. Spend one day in Sami to visit the nearby caves, or a day in Argostoli visiting Lourdata Beach.

Two weeks

Combine the above itineraries, but allow an extra day for Corfu Town, visiting the Ahillion Palace, and an extra day for the Diapondia Islands, and perhaps an extra night on Lefkada. Spending only one day in Fiskardo may enable you to include Kythira – you may find it the greatest surprise in the Ionians.

Three weeks

Follow the two-week itinerary, allowing an extra day on Corfu to visit Durrell territory in the pretty north-east, staying in Kalami. Then head for Kythira (it might take you a good day or so to get there) and spend the rest of your trip there, including an overnight stay on remote Antikythira.

PLANNING
When to Go

Spring and autumn are the best times to visit the Ionians. Winter is pretty much a dead loss outside the major towns. Most of the Ionians' tourist infrastructure goes into hibernation from November until the beginning of April – hotels and restaurants are closed and bus and ferry services are either drastically reduced or plain cancelled. Kythira has a very short season and things wind down in early September.

The cobwebs are dusted off in time for Easter, when the first tourists start to arrive. Conditions are perfect between Easter and mid-June, when the weather is pleasantly warm in most places, but not too hot; beaches and ancient sites are relatively uncrowded; public transport operates on close to full schedules; and accommodation is cheaper and easy to find.

Mid-June until the end of August is the high season. It's party time on the islands and everything is in full swing. It's also very hot – in July and August the mercury can soar to 40°C (over 100°F) in the shade just about anywhere in the country; the beaches are crowded, the sites are swarming with tour groups and in many places accommodation is booked solid.

The season starts to wind down after August and conditions are ideal once more until the shutdown at the end of October.

Maps

Unless you are going to trek or drive, the free maps given out by the EOT (the Greek National Tourist Organisation) will probably suffice, although they are not 100% accurate. On islands where there is no EOT office there are usually tourist maps for sale for around 400 dr but, again, these are not always very accurate.

The best maps are published by the Greek company Road Editions, in conjunction with the Hellenic Army Geographical Service. There is a wide range of maps to suit various needs, starting with a 1:500,000 map of Greece.

Motorists should check the company's blue-cover Greek island series which features maps of Corfu, Lefkada, Kefallonia and Ithaca, and Zakynthos; maps of Kythira, Paxi and Antipaxi are, apparently, in the pipeline. The scale of these maps ranges from 1:50,000 for Lefkada, 1:60,000 for Zakynthos, 1:70,000 for Kefallonia and Ithaki, and 1:100,000 for Corfu.

Even the smallest roads and villages are clearly marked, and the distance indicators are spot-on – important when negotiating your way around the backblocks. These maps are widely available in bookshops and minimarkets all over the Ionian islands and cost around 1200 dr to 1500 dr. They are also available in other countries from larger bookshops with extensive travel sections.

The maroon-cover 1:250,000 map of the Peloponnese also covers Kythira, and is essential for those driving across the Peloponnese to either Gythio or Neapoli, the two mainland ports serving Kythira.

What to Bring

Sturdy shoes or trainers are essential for walking along cliff-top paths. Sandals are the most comfortable footwear for the beach or when it is really hot.

A day-pack is useful for the beach, and for sightseeing or trekking. A compass is essential if you are going to trek in remote areas, as is a whistle, which you can use should you become lost or disorientated. A torch (flashlight) might come in handy during occasional power cuts. If you like to fill a washbasin or bathtub (a rarity in Greece), bring a universal plug as Greek bathrooms rarely have plugs.

Many camping grounds have covered areas where tourists without tents can sleep in summer, so you can get by with a lightweight sleeping bag and foam bedroll. Whether or not you are going to self-cater, a plastic food container, plate, cup, cutlery, bottle opener, water container and an all-purpose knife are useful, not only for picnics, but for food you take with you on long boat trips.

You will require only light clothing – preferably cotton – during summer months. During spring and autumn you'll need a light sweater or jacket in the evening. In winter take a heavy jacket or coat, warm sweaters, winter shoes or boots, and an umbrella.

In summer a sun hat and sunglasses are essential (see the Health section later in this chapter). Sunscreen creams are expensive, as are moisturising and cleansing creams. Film is not expensive, especially in larger towns and tourist areas, but the stock tends to hang around for a while in remoter areas.

If you read a lot, it's a good idea to bring along a few disposable paperbacks to read and swap.

TOURIST OFFICES

Tourist information is handled by the Greek National Tourist Organisation, known by the initials GNTO abroad and EOT (Ellinikos Organismos Tourismou) throughout Greece.

Local Tourist Offices

The address of the EOT's head office (☎ 01-331 0561/62, fax 325 2895, email gnto@eexi .gr) is Amerikis 2, Athens 105 64.

EOT offices are thin on the ground in the Ionians. There are EOT offices only on Corfu and on Kefallonia. There are no tourist offices on Paxi, Lefkada, Ithaki, Zakynthos or Kythira. Most EOT staff speak English. The Corfu office has some local information (including ferries) and a handful of glossy brochures. Some have absolutely nothing to offer except an apology. Some commercial tourism offices or local travel agents in the island capitals and larger resorts can give limited advice, but often their main preoccupation is to entice people onto their organised tours.

Tourist Offices Abroad

GNTO offices abroad include:

Australia (☎ 02-9241 1663/64/65) 51 Pitt St, Sydney NSW 2000
Austria (☎ 1-512 5317/18) Opernring 8, Vienna A-10105
Belgium (☎ 2-647 5770) 172 Ave Louise Louizalaan, B-1050 Brussels
Canada (☎ 416-968 2220) 1300 Bay St, Toronto, Ontario M5R 3K8
Denmark (☎ 3-325 332) Vester Farimagsgade 1, 1606 Copenhagen
France (☎ 01-42 60 65 75) 3 Ave de l'Opéra, Paris 75001
Germany
  Frankfurt: (☎ 69-237 735) Neue Mainzer-strasse 22, 60311Frankfurt
  Munich: (☎ 40-454 498) Pacellistrasse 5, W 80333 Munich 2
  Hamburg: (☎ 30-217 6262) Abteistrasse 33, 20149 Hamburg 13
  Berlin: Wittenbergplatz 3A, 10789 Berlin 30
Israel (☎ 23-517 0501) 5 Shalom Aleichem St, Tel Aviv 61262
Italy
  Rome: (☎ 06-474 4249) Via L Bissolati 78-80, Rome 00187
  Milan: (☎ 02-860 470) Piazza Diaz 1, 20123 Milan
Japan (☎ 03-350 55 911) Fukuda Building West, 5F 2-11-3 Akasaka, Minato-Ku, Tokyo 107
Netherlands (☎ 020-625 4212/13/14) Leidse-straat 13, Amsterdam NS 1017
Norway (☎ 2-426 501) Ovre Slottsgate 15B, 0157 Oslo 1
Sweden (☎ 8-679 6480) Birger Jarlsgatan 30, Box 5298 S, 10246 Stockholm
Switzerland (☎ 01-221 0105) Loewenstrasse 25, CH 8001 Zurich
UK (☎ 020-7499 4976) 4 Conduit St, London W1R ODJ
USA
  New York: (☎ 212-421 5777) Olympic Tower, 645 5th Ave, New York, NY 10022

Chicago: (☎ 312-782 1084) Suite 600, 168 North Michigan Ave, Chicago, Illinois 60601
Los Angeles: (☎ 213-626 6696) Suite 2198, 611 West 6th St, Los Angeles, California 92668

Tourist Police

The tourist police work in cooperation with the regular Greek police and EOT. Each tourist police office has at least one member of staff who speaks English. Hotels, restaurants, travel agencies, tourist shops, tourist guides, waiters, taxi drivers and bus drivers all come under the jurisdiction of the tourist police. If you think that you have been ripped off by any of these, report it to the tourist police and they will investigate. If you need to report a theft or loss of passport, then go to the tourist police first, and they will act as interpreters between you and the regular police. The tourist police also fulfil the same functions as the EOT and municipal tourist offices, dispensing maps and brochures, and giving information on transport. They can often help you to find accommodation.

VISAS & DOCUMENTS
Passport

To enter Greece you need a valid passport or, for EU nationals, travel documents (ID cards). You must produce your passport or EU travel documents when you register in a hotel or pension in Greece. You will find that many accommodation proprietors will want to keep your passport during your stay. This is not a compulsory requirement; they need it only long enough to take down the details.

Visas

The list of countries whose nationals can stay in Greece for up to three months without a visa includes Australia, Canada, all EU countries, Iceland, Israel, Japan, New Zealand, Norway, Switzerland and the USA. Other countries included are Cyprus, Malta, the European principalities of Monaco and San Marino and most South American countries. The list changes so contact Greek embassies for the full list.

Those not included can expect to pay about US$20 for a three month visa.

Turkish-Occupied North Cyprus Greece will refuse entry to travellers whose passport indicates that they have visited Turkish-occupied North Cyprus since November 1983. This can be overcome if, upon entering North Cyprus, you ask the immigration officials to stamp a piece of paper (loose-leaf visa) rather than your passport. If you enter North Cyprus from the Greek Republic of Cyprus (only possible for a day visit), an exit stamp is not put into your passport.

Visa Extensions If you wish to stay in Greece for longer than three months, apply at a consulate abroad or at least 20 days in advance to the Aliens Bureau (☎ 01-770 5711), Leoforos Alexandras 173, Athens. Take your passport and four passport photographs along. You may be asked for proof that you can support yourself financially, so keep all your bank exchange slips (or the equivalent from a post office). These slips are not always automatically given – you may have to ask for them. The Aliens Bureau is open 8 am to 1 pm on weekdays. Elsewhere in Greece apply to the local police authority. You will be given a permit which will authorise you to stay in the country for a period of up to six months.

Most travellers get around this by visiting Bulgaria or Turkey for a brief time and then re-entering Greece.

Travel Insurance
A travel insurance policy to cover theft, loss and medical problems is a good idea. The policies handled by STA Travel and other student travel organisations are usually good value. There is a wide variety of policies available; check the small print.

Some policies specifically exclude 'dangerous activities' which can include scuba diving, motorcycling, even trekking. A locally acquired motorcycle licence is not valid under some policies.

You may prefer a policy that pays doctors or hospitals direct rather than you having to pay on the spot and claim later. If you have to claim later make sure you keep all documentation. Some policies ask you to call back (reverse charges) to a centre in your home country where an immediate assessment of your problem is made.

Check that the policy covers ambulances or an emergency flight home.

Driving Licence & Permits
Greece recognises all national driving licences, provided the licence has been held for at least one year. It also recognises an International Driving Permit, which should be obtained before you leave home.

Hostel Cards
A Hostelling International (HI) card is of no use in the Ionians. The only place it might come in handy is if you are passing through Athens and want to use the Athens International Youth Hostel.

Student & Youth Cards
The most widely recognised form of student ID is the International Student Identity Card (ISIC). Holders qualify for half-price admission to museums and ancient sites and for discounts at some budget hotels and hostels. You are strongly advised to get the card *before* coming to the Ionians as the package tourism-oriented travel agents on the islands do not issue them. See the boxed text 'Student Cards'.

There are no student discounts on domestic flights (unless linked to an international flight), and none to be had on buses, ferries or trains either. Students will, however, find some good deals on international air fares.

Photocopies
The hassles created by losing your passport, travellers cheques and other important documents can be reduced considerably if you take the precaution of taking photocopies. It is a good idea to have photocopies of the passport pages that cover personal details, issue and expiry date and the current entry stamp or visa. Other documents worth photocopying are airline tickets, credit cards, driving licence and your insurance details.

Student Cards

An ISIC (International Student Identity Card) is a plastic ID-style card displaying your photograph. These cards are widely available from budget travel agencies (take along proof that you are a student). In Athens you can get one from the International Student & Youth Travel Service (ISYTS; ☎ 01-323 3767), 2nd floor, Nikis 11.

Some travel agencies in Greece offer discounts on organised tours to students. However, there are no student discounts for travel within Greece (although Olympic Airways gives a 25% discount on domestic flights which are part of an international flight). Turkish Airlines (THY) gives 55% student discounts on its international flights. THY has flights from Athens to Istanbul and Izmir. Most ferries to Cyprus, Israel and Egypt from Piraeus give a 20% student discount and a few of the services between Greek and Italian ports do so also. If you are under 26 but not a student, the Federation of International Youth Travel Organisation (FIYTO) card gives similar discounts.

Many budget travel agencies issue FIYTO cards including London Explorers Club, 33 Princes Square, Bayswater, London W2 (☎ 020-7792 3770); and SRS Studenten Reise Service, Marienstrasse 23, Berlin (☎ 030-2 83 30 93).

You should also keep a record of the serial numbers of your travellers cheques, and cross them off as you cash them.

This emergency material should be kept separate from the originals, so that hopefully they won't both get lost (or stolen) at the same time. Leave an extra copy with someone at home just in case.

There is another option for storing details of your vital travel documents before you leave – Lonely Planet's online Travel Vault. Storing details of your important documents in the vault is safer than carrying photocopies. It's the best option if you travel in a country with easy Internet access. Your password-protected travel vault is accessible online at any time.

You can create your own travel vault for free at www.ekno.lonelyplanet.com.

EMBASSIES & CONSULATES
Greek Embassies & Consulates
The following is a selection of Greek diplomatic missions abroad:

Albania (☎ 42-34 290/91) Rruga Frederik Shiroka, Tirana
Australia (☎ 02-6273 3011) 9 Turrana St, Yarralumla, Canberra ACT 2600
Bulgaria (☎ 92-946 1027) San Stefano 33, Sofia 1504
Canada (☎ 613-238 6271) 76-80 Maclaren St, Ottawa, Ontario K2P OK6

Cyprus (☎ 02-441 880/81) Byron Boulevard 8-10, Nicosia
Denmark (☎ 33-11 4533) Borgergade 16, 1300 Copenhagen K
Egypt (☎ 02-355 1074) 18 Aisha el Taymouria, Garden City, Cairo
France (☎ 01-47 23 72 28) 17 Rue Auguste Vacquerie, 75116 Paris
Germany (☎ 228-83010) An Der Marienkapelleb 10, 53 179 Bonn
Ireland (☎ 01-676 7254)1 Upper Pembroke St, Dublin 2
Israel (☎ 03-605 5461) 47 Bodenheimer St, Tel Aviv 62008
Italy (☎ 06-854 9630) Via S Mercadante 36, Rome 00198
Japan (☎ 03-340 0871/72) 3-16-30 Nishi Azabu, Minato-ku, Tokyo 106
Netherlands (☎ 070-363 87 00) Koninginne-gracht 37, 2514 AD, The Hague
New Zealand (☎ 04-473 7775) 5-7 Willeston St, Wellington
Norway (☎ 22-44 2728) Nobels Gate 45, 0244 Oslo 2
South Africa (☎ 12-437 351/52) 995, Pretorius Street, Arcadia, Pretoria 0083
Spain (☎ 01-564 4653) Avenida Doctor Arce 24, Madrid 28002
Sweden (☎ 08-663 7577) Riddargatan 60, 11457 Stockholm
Switzerland (☎ 31-951 0814) Postfach, 3000 Berne 6, Kirchenfeld
Turkey (☎ 312-436 8860) Ziya-ul-Rahman Caddesi 9-11, Gaziosmanpasa 06700, Ankara
UK (☎ 020-7229 3850) 1A Holland Park, London W11 3TP

USA (☎ 202-939 5818) 2221 Massachusetts Ave NW, Washington DC 20008

Embassies & Consulates in the Ionians

All foreign embassies in Greece are in Athens and its suburbs, while the following consulates are in Corfu Town:

Belgium (☎ 0661-24 404) Alexandras 44
Denmark (☎ 0661-35 698) Ethnikis Antistasseos 4
France (☎ 0661-26 312) Iakanou Polyla 22
Germany (☎ 0661-31 453) Guilford Street 52
Ireland (☎ 0661-32 469) Kapodistriou 20a
Italy (☎ 0661-37 351) Alexandras 10
Netherlands (☎ 0661-39 900) Idromeneu 2
Norway (☎ 0661-39 667) Donzelot 9
Sweden (☎ 0661-31 386) Scaramanca Square 7
UK (☎ 0661-30 055) Menekratou 1

Generally speaking, your own country's embassy won't be much help in emergencies if the trouble you're in is remotely your own fault. Remember that you are bound by Greek laws. Your embassy will not be sympathetic if you end up in jail after committing a crime locally, even if such actions are legal in your own country.

In genuine emergencies you might get some assistance, but only if other channels have been exhausted. For example, if you need to get home urgently, a free ticket home is exceedingly unlikely – the embassy would expect you to have insurance. If you have all your money and documents stolen, it might assist with getting a new passport, but a loan for onward travel is out of the question.

CUSTOMS

There are no longer duty-free restrictions within the EU. This does not mean, however, that customs checks have been dispensed with: random searches are still made for drugs.

Upon entering the country from outside the EU, customs inspection is usually cursory for foreign tourists. There may be spot checks, but you probably won't have to open your bags. A verbal declaration is usually all that is required.

You may bring the following into Greece duty-free: 200 cigarettes or 50 cigars; 1L of spirits or 2L of wine; 50g of perfume; 250mL of eau de Cologne; one camera (still or video) and film; a pair of binoculars; a portable musical instrument; a portable radio or tape recorder; a typewriter; sports equipment; and dogs and cats (with a veterinary certificate).

Importation of works of art and antiquities is free, but they must be declared on entry, so that they can be re-exported. Import regulations for medicines are strict; if you are taking medication, make sure you get a statement from your doctor before you leave home. It is illegal, for instance, to take codeine (present in many extra-strong pain relievers) into Greece without an accompanying doctor's certificate.

An unlimited amount of foreign currency and travellers cheques may be brought into Greece. But if you intend to leave the country with foreign banknotes over US$1000, you must declare the sum upon entry.

Restrictions apply to the importation of sailboards into Greece. See the Activities section later in this chapter for more details.

It is strictly forbidden to export antiquities (anything over 100 years old) without an export permit. This crime is second only to drug smuggling in the penalties imposed. (The place to apply for an export permit is the Antique Dealers & Private Collections Section, Archaeological Service, Polygnotou 13, Athens.) It is an offence to remove even the smallest article from an archaeological site.

Vehicles

Cars can be brought into Greece for four months without a carnet; only a green card (international third party insurance) is required. Your vehicle will be registered in your passport when you enter Greece in order to prevent you leaving the country without it.

MONEY
Currency

The unit of currency in Greece is the drachma (dr). Coins come in denominations of five, 10, 20, 50 and 100 dr. Banknotes come in 100, 200, 500, 1000, 5000 and 10,000 dr.

Exchange Rates

country	unit		drachma
Albania	1 lekë	=	2.48 dr
Australia	A$1	=	214 dr
Canada	C$1	=	227 dr
euro	€1	=	330 dr
France	1FF	=	50.37 dr
Germany	DM1	=	169 dr
Ireland	IR£1	=	420 dr
Italy	L1000	=	0.17 dr
Japan	¥100	=	322 dr
Netherlands	f1	=	150 dr
New Zealand	NZ$1	=	172 dr
United Kingdom	UK£1	=	532 dr
United States	US$1	=	329 dr

Warning It's all but impossible to exchange Turkish lira in Greece. The only place you can change them is at the head office of the National Bank of Greece, Panepistimiou 36, Athens – and it'll give only about 75% of the going international rate.

Exchanging Money

Banks will exchange all major currencies in either cash, travellers cheques or Eurocheques. The best known travellers cheques in Greece are Thomas Cook and American Express (AmEx). While a passport is required to change travellers cheques, it is not needed for cash.

Commission charged on the exchange of banknotes and travellers cheques varies not only from bank to bank but from branch to branch. It's less for cash than for travellers cheques. For travellers cheques the commission is 350 dr for up to 20,000 dr; 450 dr for amounts between 20,000 dr and 30,000 dr; and a flat rate of 1.5% on any amounts over 30,000 dr.

Post offices can exchange banknotes – but not travellers cheques – and charge less commission than banks. Many travel agencies and hotels will also change money and travellers cheques at bank rates, but their commission charges are higher.

If there is a chance that you may apply for a visa extension, make sure you receive, and keep hold of, a bank exchange slip after each transaction.

Cash Nothing beats cash for convenience – or for risk. If you lose it, it's gone for good and very few travel insurers will come to your rescue. Those that will, normally limit the amount to about US$300. It's best to carry no more cash than you need for the next few days, which means working out your likely needs when you change travellers cheques or withdraw cash from an ATM.

It's also a good idea to set aside a small amount of cash, say US$50, as an emergency stash.

Travellers Cheques The main reason to carry travellers cheques rather than cash is the protection they offer against theft. They are, however, losing popularity as more and more travellers opt to put their money in a bank at home and withdraw it at ATMs as they go along.

AmEx, Visa and Thomas Cook cheques are all widely accepted and have efficient replacement policies. Maintaining a record of the cheque numbers and recording when you use them is vital when it comes to replacing lost cheques. Keep this record separate from the cheques themselves. US dollars are a good currency to use.

ATMs ATMs (automatic teller machines) are to be found in almost every town large enough to support a bank – and certainly in most tourist areas. If you've got Master-Card or Visa/Access, there are plenty of places to withdraw money.

Most ATMs also accept Cirrus and Maestro cards.

AFEMs (Automatic Foreign Exchange Machines) are common in the main towns in the Ionians and occasionally can be found in the larger tourist resorts. They take all the major European currencies, Australian and US dollars and Japanese yen, and are useful in an emergency. They charge a hefty commission, though.

Credit Cards The great advantage of credit cards is that they allow you to pay for major items without carrying around great wads of cash. Credit cards are now an accepted part of the commercial scene just about everywhere in Greece. They can be used to pay for a wide range of goods and services such as upmarket meals and accommodation, car hire and souvenir shopping.

If you are not familiar with the card options, ask your bank to explain the workings and relative merits of the various schemes: cash cards, charge cards and credit cards. Ask whether the card can be replaced in Greece if it is lost or stolen.

The main credit cards are MasterCard, Visa (Access in the UK) and Eurocard, all of which are widely accepted in Greece. They can also be used as cash cards to draw drachma from the ATMs of affiliated Greek banks in the same way as at home. Daily withdrawal limits are set by the issuing bank. Cash advances are given in local currency only. Credit cards can be used to pay for accommodation in all the smarter hotels. Some C class hotels will accept credit cards, but D and E class hotels rarely do. Most upmarket shops and restaurants accept credit cards. However it is never a good idea to rely on the establishment taking credit cards, so always check first.

The main charge cards are AmEx and Diner's Club Card, which are widely accepted throughout tourist areas but unheard of elsewhere.

International Transfers If you run out of money or need more for whatever reason, you can instruct your bank back home to send you a draft. Specify the city and the bank as well as the branch that you want the money sent to. If you have the choice, select a large bank and ask for the international division. Money sent by electronic transfer should reach you within 24 hours.

Security
The safest way of carrying cash and valuables (passport, travellers cheques, credit cards etc) is a favourite topic of travel conversation. The simple answer is that there is no foolproof method. The general principle is to keep things out of sight. The front pouch belt, for example, presents an obvious target for a would-be thief – only marginally less inviting than a fat wallet bulging from your back pocket.

The best place is under your clothes in contact with your skin where, hopefully, you will be aware of an alien hand before it's too late. Most people opt for a money-belt, while others prefer a leather pouch hung around the neck. Another possibility is to sew a secret stash pocket into the inside of your clothes. Whichever method you choose, put your valuables in a plastic bag first – otherwise they will get soaked in sweat as you wander around in the heat. After a few soakings, they will end up looking like they've been through the washing machine.

Costs
Greece is still a cheap country by northern European standards, but it is no longer dirt-cheap and the Ionians are certainly not the cheapest part of Greece.

A rock-bottom daily budget would be 7000 dr. This would mean hitching, camping, staying away from bars, and only occasionally eating in restaurants or taking ferries. Allow at least 12,000 dr per day if you want your own room and plan to eat out regularly as well as travelling about and seeing the sights. You will still need to do a fair bit of self-catering.

If you really want a holiday with comfortable rooms and restaurants all the way then you will need closer to 20,000 dr per day. Note that these budgets are for individuals. Couples sharing a double room can get by on less.

Prices vary quite a lot between islands, particularly for accommodation. In high season prices can double. Charming fishing villages tend to be expensive, but you can find cheaper deals in the less attractive resorts where there is plenty of purpose-built accommodation.

Paxi is expensive regardless of where you stay. Lefkada is generally good value, as is Kythira off season.

Museums Most small museums charge up to 500 dr and major sites and museums cost between 1200 dr and 2000 dr. Museums and sites are free on Sunday from 1 November to the end of March, as well as on 6 March, 18 April, 18 May, 5 June and the last weekend in September.

Admission to sites and museums is free all year for anyone under 18, card-carrying EU students and teachers, and journalists. Students from outside the EU qualify for a 50% discount with their International Student Identification Card (ISIC), while pensioners (over 65) from EU countries also pay half-price.

Tipping & Bargaining

In restaurants the service charge is included in the bill but it is the custom to leave a small amount. The practice is often just to round off the bill. Likewise for taxis – a small amount is appreciated.

Bargaining is not as widespread in Greece as it is farther east. The prices in most shops are clearly marked and are non-negotiable. The same applies to restaurants and public transport. It is always worth bargaining over the price of hotel rooms or *domatia* (the Greek equivalent of the British B&B, minus the breakfast), especially if you are intending to stay a few days. You may get short shrift in peak season, but prices can drop dramatically in the off season. Souvenir shops and market stalls are other places where your negotiating skills will come in handy. If you feel uncomfortable about haggling, walking away can be just as effective – you can always go back.

POST & COMMUNICATIONS

Post offices *(tahydromio)* are easily identifiable by means of the yellow signs outside. Regular post boxes are also yellow. The red boxes are for express mail only.

Postal Rates

The postal rate for postcards and airmail letters to destinations within the EU is 170 dr for up to 20g and 270 dr for up to 50g. To other destinations the rate is 200 dr up to 20g and 300 dr for up to 150g. Post within Europe takes five to eight days and to the USA, Australia and New Zealand, nine to 11 days. Some tourist shops also sell stamps, but with a 10% surcharge.

Express mail costs an extra 400 dr and should ensure delivery in three days within the EU – use the special red post boxes. Valuables should be sent registered post, which costs an extra 350 dr.

Sending Mail

Do not wrap a parcel until it has been inspected at a post office. Take the parcel to the parcel counter of a regular post office.

Receiving Mail

You can receive mail poste restante (general delivery) at the main post offices in Corfu Town, Lefkada Town, Argostoli and Zakynthos Town. The service is free of charge, but you are required to show your passport. Ask senders to write your family name in capital letters and underline it, and to mark the envelope 'poste restante'.

It is a good idea to ask the post office clerk to check under your first name as well if letters you are expecting cannot be located. After one month, uncollected mail is returned to the sender. If you are about to leave a town and expected mail hasn't arrived, ask at the post office to have it forwarded to your next destination, c/o poste restante.

Parcels are not delivered in Greece; they must be collected from the parcel counter of a post office.

Telephone

The Greek telephone service is maintained by the public corporation known as Organismos Tilepikoinonion Ellados, which is always referred to by the acronym OTE (pronounced O-tay). The system is modern and efficient.

Public telephones all use phonecards, which cost 1000 dr for 100 units, 1800 dr for 200 units, 4200 dr for 500 units, and 8200 dr for 1000 units. The 100-unit cards are widely available at *periptera* (street kiosks), corner shops and tourist shops; the others can be bought at OTE offices.

The phones are easy to operate and can be used for local, long distance and international calls. The 'i' at the top left of the push-button dialling panel brings up the operating instructions in English. Don't remove your card before you are told to do so or you will wipe out the remaining credit. Local calls cost one unit per minute.

It is possible to use various national card schemes, such as Telstra Australia's Telecard, to make international calls. You will still need a phonecard to dial the scheme's access number, which will cost you one unit, and the time you spend on the phone is also charged at local call rates.

International calls can also be made from OTE offices. A counter clerk directs you to a cubicle equipped with a metered phone, and payment is made afterwards.

Villages and the remote islands without OTE offices almost always have at least one metered phone for international and long distance calls – usually in a shop, kafeneio or taverna.

Another option is the periptero. Almost every periptero has a metered telephone which can be used for local, long distance and direct dial international calls. There is a small surcharge, but it is less than that charged by hotels.

Reverse charge (collect) calls can be made from an OTE office. The time you have to wait for a connection can vary considerably, from a few minutes to two hours. If you are using a private phone to make a reverse charge call, dial the operator (domestic ☎ 151, international ☎ 161).

To call overseas direct from Greece, dial the Greek overseas access code (☎ 00), followed by the country code for the country you are calling, then the local area code (dropping the leading zero if there is one) and then the number. (Note that for calls to Italy the leading zero of the area code should be retained.)

The table below lists some country codes and per-minute charges:

country	code	cost per minute
Australia	61	236 dr
France	33	183 dr
Germany	49	183 dr
Ireland	353	183 dr
Italy	39	183 dr
Japan	81	319 dr
Netherlands	31	183 dr
New Zealand	64	319 dr
Turkey	90	183 dr
UK	44	183 dr
USA & Canada	1	236 dr

Off-peak rates are 25% cheaper. They are available to Africa, Europe, the Middle East and India between 10 pm and 6 am; to the Americas between 11 pm and 8 am; and to Asia and Oceania between 8 pm and 5 am.

To call Greece, the international access code is ☎ 30.

Fax & Telegraph
Most post offices have fax machines; telegrams can be sent from any OTE office.

Email & Internet Access
Greece was slow to embrace the wonders of the Internet, but is now striving to make up for lost time. There has also been a huge increase in the number of hotels and businesses using email, and these addresses have been listed throughout this book.

Internet cafes are springing up in the major towns in the Ionians, and are listed under the Information section for towns and resorts where available.

There are also several Internet service providers who can provide short term local accounts for those travelling with a laptop and needing local access. Try Forthnet (www.forthnet.gr) or OTE (www.otenet.gr).

INTERNET RESOURCES
Predictably enough, there has recently been a huge increase in the number of Web sites providing information about Greece. Almost all of these are general sites relating to the whole of the country – often with sections on the Ionians.

The Ionian islands regional authorities have their own Web site at www.ionianislands.gr. The site offers general historical and tourist information, with separate sections for each of the islands (except

Kythira). An added feature is that you can listen to Greek music while you check the site! EOT has a site at www.areianet.gr /infoxenios/GNTO which has practical information and advice for tourists.

For information on all of Greece, check the *500 Links to Greece* site at www .viking1.com/corfu/link.htm. It has links to a huge range of sites covering everything from accommodation to Zeus. The Web site www.all-hotels.gr proudly claims that it lists every one of the 7500 hotels and holiday apartment complexes in Greece, including all of those in the Ionians.

The address www.greektravel.com takes you to an assortment of interesting and informative sites on Greece by Matt Barrett. The Greek Ministry of Culture (www.culture .gr) has put together an excellent site with loads of information about museums and ancient sites. Other sites include www .gogreece.com/travel and www.aegean.ch. You'll find more specialist Web sites listed throughout the book.

Lonely Planet has its own Web site (www.lonelyplanet.com) which gives a summary on travelling to the Ionians, postcards from other travellers and the Thorn Tree bulletin board, where you can ask questions before you go or dispense advice when you get back. The subWWWay section links you to other Web travel resources.

BOOKS

Most books are published in different editions by different publishers in different countries. As a result, a book might be a hardcover rarity in one country while it's readily available in paperback in another.

Fortunately, bookshops and libraries search by title or author, so your local bookshop or library is in the best position to advise you on the availability of the following recommendations.

Lonely Planet

Lonely Planet's *Greece* guide is now in its fourth edition and includes coverage of Corfu and the Ionians. The Lonely Planet guides to both *Mediterranean Europe* and *Western Europe* also include coverage of

Greece, as does *Europe on a shoestring.* The regional titles *Greek Islands*, *Crete, Crete Condensed* and *Cyprus* were published at the same time as this guide. The *Greek phrasebook* is very helpful.

Author Katherine Kizilos vividly evokes Greece's landscapes, people and politics in her book *The Olive Grove: Travels in Greece*. She explores the islands and borderlands of her father's homeland, and life in her family's village in the Peloponnese mountains. The book is part of the Journeys travel literature series.

Guidebooks

The ancient Greek traveller Pausanias is acclaimed as the world's first travel writer. *The Guide to Greece* was written in the 2nd century AD. Umpteen editions later, it is now available in English in paperback. For archaeology buffs, the *Blue Guides* are hard to beat. They go into tremendous detail about all the major sites, and many of the lesser known ones. The *Blue Guide to Greece* includes coverage of the Ionians.

The Second Book of Corfu Walks: The Road to Old Corfu by long time Corfu resident Hilary Whitton Paipeti lists 23 walks and four mountain bike tours on the island, and is of great use to anyone wanting to get off the beaten track. By the same author is *In the Footsteps of Lawrence Durrell and Gerald Durrell in Corfu 1935-39*, a small guide to the various places on Corfu where the Durrells spent so much time, and which they described so well in their writings.

Travel

The English painter and writer Edward Lear, of *The Owl and the Pussy-Cat* fame, spent some time in Greece in the mid-19th century. His watercolours of the Ionian islands are some of the best depictions of how these landscapes once appeared. *The Corfu Years*, a journal of his life in the Ionians, *Journeys of a Landscape Painter* and *A Cretan Diary* are worth a read.

Lawrence Durrell, who spent an idyllic childhood on Corfu, is the best known of the 20th century philhellenes. His evocative book *Prospero's Cell* is a diary of his life on Corfu in the late 1930s. It forms the first part of a trilogy on life in the Greek islands, which includes *Reflections on a Marine Venus*, about Rhodes, and *Bitter Lemons*, set in Cyprus. *Spirit of Place* is a collection of writings about Corfu and the Ionians, and includes accounts of Durrell's return visit to the islands after WWII. Durrell's coffee-table book *The Greek Islands* is one of the most popular books of its kind.

My Family and Other Animals by Lawrence's brother Gerald is a hilarious account of the Durrell family's chaotic and wonderful life on Corfu, packed with anecdotes and descriptions of the landscape as it once was and the island's wildlife.

The Colossus of Maroussi by Henry Miller is now regarded as a classic. Although it was written in Paris, Miller relates his travels in Greece at the outbreak of WWII with feverish enthusiasm. His voyage included a sojourn with the Durrell family in Kalami, and his is a unique observation of Corfu, the islanders and the Durrells themselves.

Terence Spencer's *Fair Greece, Sad Relic: Literary Philhellenism from Shakespeare to Byron* looks at the work of the English writers, poets and travellers who came, saw and recorded with their pens Greece from the fall of Constantinople to the early 19th century.

People & Society

Although none of the following books are specifically about the Ionians, the information about Greek culture and society will be of interest to all travellers. *The Cyclades, or Life Amongst the Insular Greeks* by James Theodore Bent (first published 1885) is still the greatest English-language book about the Greek islands. It relates the experiences of the author and his wife while travelling around the Cyclades in the late 19th century. The book is now out of print, but the Hellenic Book Service may have a second-hand copy; see under Bookshops later in this chapter.

Time, Religion & Social Experience in Rural Greece by Laurie Kain Hart is a fascinating account of village traditions, many

of which are alive and well beneath the tourist veneer.

Portrait of a Greek Mountain Village by Juliet du Boulay is in a similar vein, based on the author's experiences in an isolated village.

Another book which will whet your appetite for a holiday in Greece is *Hellas: A Portrait of Greece* by Nicholas Gage.

Vanishing Greece by Clay Perry, with an introduction by Patrick Leigh Fermor, is a large and expensive book with magnificent photographs of the landscapes and people of rural Greece. However, the sad message of the book is that the rural culture of Greece, little changed since Homer's time, is fast vanishing.

History & Mythology

A Traveller's History of Greece by Timothy Boatswain & Colin Nicholson gives the layperson a good general reference on the historical background of Greece, from Neolithic times to the present day. *Modern Greece: A Short History* by CM Woodhouse is in a similar vein, although it has a right-wing bent. It covers the period from Constantine the Great to 1990.

Mythology was an intrinsic part of life in ancient Greece, and some knowledge of it will enhance your visit. One of the best publications on the subject is *The Greek Myths* by Robert Graves (two volumes) which relates and interprets the adventures of the main gods and heroes worshipped by the ancient Greeks. Maureen O'Sullivan's *An Iconoclast's Guide to the Greek Gods* presents entertaining and accessible versions of the myths.

There are many translations around of Homer's *Iliad* and *Odyssey*, which tell the story of the Trojan War and the subsequent adventures of Odysseus (known as Ulysses in Latin). The translations by EV Rieu are among the best.

One of the best commentaries on Homer is M I Finley's *The World of Odysseus* which examines the identity of Homer, when his *Odyssey* and *Iliad* were written, and the society that these classical figures would have lived in.

Women in Athenian Law and Life by Roger Just is the first in-depth study of the role of women in ancient Greece. *The Argonautica Expedition* by Theodor Troev encompasses Greek mythology, archaeology, travel and adventure. It relates the voyage undertaken by the author and his crew in the 1980s following in the footsteps of Jason and the Argonauts.

Mary Renault's novels provide an excellent feel for ancient Greece. *The King Must Die* and *The Bull from the Sea* are vivid tales of Minoan times. *Mistras and Byzantine Style and Civilisation* by Sir Steven Runciman and *Fourteen Byzantine Rulers* by Michael Psellus are both good introductions to Greece's Byzantine Age.

Poetry

Sappho: A New Translation by Mary Bernard is the best translation of this great ancient poet's works. According to legend Sappho threw herself off a cliff at Cape Lefkada on the island of Lefkada out of unrequited love.

Collected Poems by George Seferis, *Selected Poems* by Odysseus Elytis and *Collected Poems* by Constantine Cavafy are all excellent translations of Greece's greatest modern poets.

Novels

English writer Louis de Bernières has become almost a cult figure following the success of *Captain Corelli's Mandolin*, which tells the emotional story of a young Italian army officer sent to the island of Kefallonia during WWII. The enormous success of the novel has even been credited with a slight increase in tourism on Kefallonia, and you don't have to look far to find a tourist clutching a well thumbed copy.

In Russell Hoban's mystery, *The Medusa Frequency*, the protagonist enters the underworld through an olive tree in Paxi. The rest of the action takes place within a computer.

The most well known and widely read Greek author is the Cretan writer Nikos Kazantzakis, whose novels are full of drama and larger-than-life characters. His most famous works are *The Last Tempta-tion*, *Zorba the Greek*, *Christ Recrucified* and *Freedom or Death*. The first two have been made into films.

Although not directly related to the Ionian islands, there are plenty of engaging accounts of expatriates settling in Greece. Australian writer Gillian Bouras writes of living in Greece in *A Foreign Wife* and *Aphrodite and the Others*. Fellow Australian Beverley Farmer has two collections of beautifully written short stories, *Home Time* and *Milk*, many of which are about foreigners endeavouring to make their home in Greece.

The Australian journalists George Johnston and Charmian Clift wrote several books with Greek themes during their 19 years as expatriates, including Johnston's novel *The Sponge Divers*, set on Kalymnos, and Clift's autobiographical *A Mermaid Singing*, which is about their experiences on Hydra.

Botanical Field Guides

The Flowers of Greece & the Aegean by William Taylor & Anthony Huxley is the most comprehensive field guide to Greece, and includes descriptions of flora found in the Ionians. Also worth consulting are books by George Sfikas, a Greek writer, naturalist and mountaineer, including *Wildflowers of Greece*, *Trees & Shrubs of Greece* and *Medicinal Plants of Greece*.

Children's Books

Robin Lister's retelling of *The Odyssey* is aimed at children aged 10 to 12, but makes compelling listening for younger children when read aloud.

The Greek publisher Malliaris-Paedia puts out a good series of books on the myths, retold in English for young readers by Aristides Kesopoulos. The titles are *The Trojan War and the Wanderings of Odysseus, The Gods of Olympus and the Lesser Gods, The Labours of Hercules, Theseus and the Voyage of the Argonauts* and *Heroes and Mythical Creatures*.

Bookshops

There are no specialist English or foreign-language bookshops in the Ionians, but most major towns and tourist resorts have bookshops or general stores that sell some foreign-language books.

It's important to note that imported books are expensive – normally two to three times the recommended retail price in the UK and the USA.

In Corfu Town, the Xenoglosso Bookshop, G Markora 45, has a range of English-language books including novels and a few travel guides.

The Greek publisher Efstathiadis specialises in English translations of books by Greek authors as well as books about Greece by foreign authors.

Abroad, the best bookshop for new and second-hand books about Greece, written in both English and Greek, is the Hellenic Book Service (☎ 020-7267 9499, fax 7267 9498), 91 Fortress Rd, Kentish Town, London NW5 1AG. It stocks almost all of the books recommended here.

Many hotels have small collections of second-hand books to read or swap.

FILMS

A movie of the bestselling novel *Captain Corelli's Mandolin* by Louis de Bernières was due to be shot in early 2000. The film will star Nicholas Cage and will be filmed on location near Sami in Kefallonia. The islands of Ithaki and Corfu will also be used as locations for their historic buildings, none of which were left standing on Kefallonia as a result of the devastating 1953 earthquakes.

James Bond came to the Ionians too. The sandy, rocky dunes behind the beach at Issos on the south-western coast of Corfu were used as a location for *For Your Eyes Only*.

After the filming had finished the crew donated the set to the locals for use as a beach kiosk or information booth; they promptly dismantled it to use as building materials.

Corfu Town's elegant Liston arcade featured briefly in the epic holocaust documentary *Shoah* by Claud Lanzman as the backdrop for the rounding up of Corfiot Jews by the Nazis during WWII.

NEWSPAPERS & MAGAZINES

Greeks are great newspaper readers. There are 15 daily newspapers, of which the most widely read are *Ta Nea*, *Kathimerini* and *Eleftheros Typos*.

The main English-language newspapers are the daily (except Monday) *Athens News* (250 dr) which carries Greek and international news, and the weekly *Hellenic Times* (300 dr), with predominantly Greek news. In addition to these, there's the Athens edition of the *International Herald Tribune* (350 dr) which includes an eight page English-language edition of the Greek daily *Kathimerini*. All are widely available in towns and major resorts in the Ionians. You'll find the *Athens News* electronic edition on the Internet at athensnews.dolnet.gr. The site archives date back to 1995.

Atlantis (1000 dr) is a glossy monthly magazine with articles on politics, travel and the arts.

Foreign newspapers are also widely available, although only between April and October in smaller resort areas. They generally arrive one day after publication. You'll find all the British and other major European dailies, as well as international magazines such as *Time*, *Newsweek* and the *Economist*.

In Corfu, a monthly English language magazine, *The Corfiot*, is available from newsstands for 500 dr. It contains news and feature articles about Corfu and listings of interesting cultural events. It also publishes classified ads, including job offers. Corfu Town also has a free bilingual (Greek and English) magazine called *Liston* which can be found in various shops in the town and has limited information and listings of cafes, bars and restaurants.

RADIO & TV

Greece has two state-owned radio channels, ET 1 and ET 2. ET 1 runs three programs; two are devoted to popular music and news, while the third plays mostly classical music. It has a news update in English at 7.30 am from Monday to Saturday, and at 9 pm from Monday to Friday. It can be heard on 91.6 MHz and 105.8 MHz on the FM band, and

729 KHz on the AM band. ET 2 broadcasts mainly popular music.

Western music fans can check Radio Gold (105 FM), which plays mainly music from the 60s, or Kiss FM (90.9 FM), which plays a mixture of rock and techno.

The best short-wave frequencies for picking up the BBC World Service are:

GMT	frequency
3 to 7.30 am	9.41 MHz (31m band)
	6.18 MHz (49m band)
	15.07 MHz (19m band)
7.30 am to 6 pm	12.09 MHz (25m band)
	15.07 MHz (19m band)
6.30 to 11.15 pm	12.09 MHz (25m band)
	9.41 MHz (31m band)
	6.18 MHz (49m band)

As far as Greek TV is concerned, quantity rather than quality is the operative word. There are nine TV channels and various pay-TV channels. All the channels show English and US films and soapies with Greek subtitles. A bit of channel surfing will normally turn up something in English.

VIDEO SYSTEMS

If you want to record or buy video tapes to play back home, you won't get a picture unless the image registration systems are the same. Greece uses PAL, which is incompatible with the North American and Japanese NTSC system. Australia and most of Europe uses PAL.

PHOTOGRAPHY & VIDEO

Because of the brilliant sunlight in summer, you'll get better results using a polarising lens filter. As elsewhere in the world, developing film is a competitive business. Most places charge around 80 dr per print, plus a 400 dr service charge.

Properly used, a video camera can give a fascinating record of your holiday. As well as videoing the obvious things – sunsets, spectacular views – remember to record some of the ordinary everyday details of life in the region. Often the most interesting things occur when you're actually intent on filming something else.

Make sure you keep the batteries charged, and have the necessary charger, plugs and transformer for the country you are visiting.

Film & Equipment

Major brands of film are widely available, although they can be expensive in smaller towns. Expect to pay about 1500 dr for a 36 exposure roll of Kodak Gold ASA 100; less for other brands. You'll find all the gear you need in the photography shops of major towns in the Ionians.

It is possible to obtain video cartridges easily in large towns and cities, but make sure you buy the correct format. It is usually worth buying at least a few cartridges duty-free to start off your trip.

Restrictions & Etiquette

Never photograph a military installation or anything else that has a sign forbidding photography.

Flash photography is not allowed inside churches, and it's considered taboo to photograph the main altar.

Greeks usually love having their photos taken but always ask permission first. The same goes for video cameras, probably even more annoying and offensive for the locals than a still camera.

TIME

Greece is two hours ahead of GMT/UTC and three hours ahead on daylight-saving time, which begins on the last Sunday in March, when clocks are put forward one hour. Daylight saving ends on the last Sunday in September.

So, when it is noon in Corfu it is also noon in İstanbul, 10 am in London, 11 am in Rome, 2 am in San Francisco, 5 am in New York and Toronto, 8 pm in Sydney and 10 pm in Auckland.

ELECTRICITY

Electricity is 220V, 50 cycles. Plugs are the standard continental type with two round pins and all hotel rooms have power points while most camping grounds have supply points.

WEIGHTS & MEASURES

Greece uses the metric system. Liquids – especially barrel wine – are often sold by weight rather than volume eg 959g of wine is equivalent to 1000mL.

Remember that, like other continental Europeans, Greeks indicate decimals with commas and thousands with points.

LAUNDRY

There are laundrettes in some of the larger towns in the Ionians, which are listed in the individual island chapters. They charge from 2000 dr to 2500 dr to wash and dry a load whether you do it yourself or have it service-washed. Hotel and room owners will usually provide you with a washtub if requested.

TOILETS

Most places in the Ionians have western-style toilets, especially hotels and restaurants which cater for tourists. You'll occasionally come across Asian-style squat toilets in older houses, kafeneia and public toilets.

Public toilets are a rarity, except at airports and bus and train stations. Cafes are the best option if you get caught short, but you'll be expected to buy something for the privilege.

One rather unpleasant peculiarity of the Greek plumbing system is that it can't handle toilet paper; apparently the pipes are too narrow. Whatever the reason, anything larger than a postage stamp seems to cause a problem; flushing away tampons and sanitary napkins is guaranteed to block the system. Toilet paper etc should be placed in the small bin provided in every toilet.

HEALTH

Travel health depends on your predeparture preparations, your day-to-day health care while travelling and how you handle any medical problem or emergency that does develop. While the list of potential dangers can seem quite frightening, few travellers experience more than upset stomachs.

Refer to Travel Insurance under Visas & Documents earlier in this chapter for information on health insurance.

Medical Kit Check List

Following is a list of items you should consider including in your medical kit – consult your pharmacist for brands available in your country.

- [ ] **Aspirin or paracetamol (acetaminophen in the USA)** – for pain or fever
- [ ] **Antihistamine** – for allergies, eg, hay fever; to ease the itch from insect bites or stings; and for the prevention of motion sickness
- [ ] **Cold and flu tablets, throat lozenges and nasal decongestant**
- [ ] **Multivitamins** – consider for long trips, when dietary vitamin intake may be inadequate
- [ ] **Antibiotics** – consider including these if you're travelling well off the beaten track; see your doctor, as they must be prescribed, and carry the prescription with you
- [ ] **Loperamide or diphenoxylate** –'blockers' for diarrhoea
- [ ] **Prochlorperazine or metaclopramide** – for nausea and vomiting
- [ ] **Rehydration mixture** – to prevent dehydration, which may occur, for example, during bouts of diarrhoea; particularly important when travelling with children
- [ ] **Insect repellent, sunscreen, lip balm and eye drops**
- [ ] **Calamine lotion, sting relief spray or aloe vera** – to ease irritation from sunburn and insect bites or stings
- [ ] **Antifungal cream or powder** – for fungal skin infections and thrush
- [ ] **Antiseptic (such as povidone-iodine)** – for cuts and grazes
- [ ] **Bandages, Band-Aids (plasters) and other wound dressings**
- [ ] **Water purification tablets or iodine**
- [ ] **Scissors, tweezers and a thermometer** – note that mercury thermometers are prohibited by airlines

Warning Codeine, which is commonly found in headache preparations, is banned in Greece; check labels carefully, or risk prosecution. There are strict regulations that apply to the importation of medicines into Greece, so obtain a certificate from your doctor which outlines any medication you may have to carry into the country with you.

Health Preparations

Make sure you're healthy before you start travelling. If you are embarking on a long trip make sure your teeth are OK.

If you wear glasses take a spare pair and your prescription.

If you require a particular medication take an adequate supply, as it may not be available locally. Take the prescription or, better still, part of the packaging showing the generic rather than the brand name (which may not be locally available), as it will make getting replacements easier.

Immunisations

No jabs are required for travel to Greece but a yellow fever vaccination certificate is required if you are coming from an infected area. There are, however, a few routine vaccinations that are recommended. These should be recorded on an international health certificate, available from your doctor or government health department. Don't leave your vaccinations until the last minute as some require more than one injection. Recommended vaccinations include:

Tetanus & Diphtheria Boosters are necessary every 10 years and proper protection is highly recommended.

Polio A booster of either the oral or injected vaccine is required every 10 years to maintain immunity after childhood vaccination. Polio is still prevalent in many developing countries.

Hepatitis A The most common travel-acquired illness that can be prevented by vaccination. Protection can be provided in two ways – either with the antibody gamma globulin or with the vaccine Havrix 1440. Havrix 1440 provides long-term immunity (possibly more than 10 years) after an initial injection and a booster at six to 12 months. Gamma globulin is a ready-made antibody, which should be given as close as possible to departure because it is at its most effective in the first few weeks after administration; the effectiveness tapers off gradually between three and six months.

Rabies Pretravel rabies vaccination involves having three injections over 21 to 28 days and should be considered by those who will spend a month or longer in a country where rabies is common, especially if they are cycling, handling animals, caving, travelling to remote areas, or for children (who may not report a bite). If someone who has been vaccinated is bitten or scratched by an animal they will require two booster injections of vaccine; those not vaccinated will require more.

Basic Rules

Care in what you eat and drink is the most important health rule; stomach upsets are the most likely travel health problem (30 to 50% of travellers in a two week stay experience this) but the majority of these upsets will be relatively minor. Don't become paranoid; trying the local food is part of the experience of travel, after all.

Avoid climatic extremes: keep out of the sun when it's hot, dress warmly when it's cold. You can avoid insect bites by covering bare skin when insects are around, by screening windows or beds and by using insect repellents.

Seek local advice: if you're told the water is unsafe due to some form of sea creature like jellyfish, don't go in. In situations where there is no information, discretion is the better part of valour. However the Ionian sea is relatively free of such creatures. Sharks have been sighted off the western coast of Lefkada – but very rarely.

Food & Water Tap water is safe to drink in the Ionians, but most people drink bottled still mineral water. You might experience mild intestinal problems if you're not used to copious amounts of olive oil; however, you'll get used to it and current research says it's good for you.

If you don't vary your diet, are travelling hard and fast and missing meals, or simply lose your appetite, you can soon start to lose weight and place your health at risk. Fruit and vegetables, readily available all over the Ionians, are good sources of vitamins. Eat plenty of grains (including rice) and bread. If your diet isn't well balanced or if your food intake is insufficient, it's a good idea to take vitamin and iron pills.

In hot weather make sure you drink enough – don't rely on feeling thirsty to indicate when you should drink. Not needing to urinate or very dark yellow urine is a danger sign. Always carry a water bottle with you on long trips.

Excessive sweating can lead to loss of salt and muscle cramping. Salt tablets are not a good idea as a preventative, but in places where salt is not used much adding salt to food can help.

Everyday Health Normal body temperature is 37°C or 98.6°F; more than 2°C (4°F) higher indicates a high fever. The normal adult pulse rate is 60 to 100 per minute (children 80 to 100, babies 100 to 140). You should know how to take a temperature and a pulse rate. As a general rule the pulse increases about 20 beats per minute for each degree C (2°F) rise in fever.

Respiration (breathing) rate is also an indicator of illness. Between 12 and 20 breaths per minute is normal for adults and older children (up to 30 for younger children, 40 for babies). People with a high fever or serious respiratory illness (such as pneumonia) breathe more quickly than normal. More than 40 shallow breaths a minute may indicate pneumonia.

Environmental Hazards

Sunburn By far the biggest health risk in the Ionians comes from the intensity of the sun. You can get sunburnt surprisingly quickly, even through cloud. Use a sunscreen and take extra care to cover areas which don't normally see sun. A hat helps, as does zinc cream or some other barrier cream for your nose and lips. Calamine lotion is good for mild sunburn. Greeks claim that yogurt applied to sunburn is soothing. Remember to protect your eyes with good-quality sunglasses.

Prickly Heat Prickly heat is an itchy rash caused by excessive perspiration trapped under the skin. Keeping cool, bathing often, drying the skin and using a mild talcum

powder or even resorting to air-conditioning may help until you acclimatise.

Heat Exhaustion Dehydration or salt deficiency can cause heat exhaustion. Take time to acclimatise to high temperatures, and drink sufficient liquids. Wear loose clothing and a broad-brimmed hat. Do not do anything too physically demanding.

Salt deficiency is characterised by fatigue, lethargy, headaches, giddiness and muscle cramps and in this case salt tablets may help. Vomiting or diarrhoea can deplete your liquid and salt levels.

Heat Stroke This serious and sometimes fatal condition can occur if the body's heat-regulating mechanism breaks down and the body temperature rises to dangerous levels. Long, continuous periods of exposure to high temperatures can leave you vulnerable to heat stroke. You should avoid excessive alcohol consumption or strenuous activity when you first arrive in a hot climate.

The symptoms are feeling unwell, not sweating very much or at all and a high body temperature (39 to 41°C or 102 to 106°F). Where sweating has ceased the skin becomes flushed and red. Severe, throbbing headaches and lack of coordination will also occur, and the sufferer may be confused or aggressive. Eventually the victim will become delirious or convulse. Hospitalisation is essential, but in the interim get victims out of the sun, remove their clothing, cover them with a wet sheet or towel and then fan continually. Give fluids, if they are conscious.

Fungal Infections Fungal infections are more frequent in hot weather and are most likely to occur on the scalp, between the toes (athlete's foot) or fingers, in the groin and on the body (ringworm). You get ringworm (a fungal infection, not a worm) from infected animals or by walking on damp areas like shower floors.

To prevent fungal infections wear loose, comfortable clothes, avoid artificial fibres, wash frequently and dry carefully. If you do get an infection, wash the infected area daily with a disinfectant or medicated soap and water, and dry well. Apply an antifungal cream or powder (tolnaftate). Expose the infected area to air or sunlight as much as possible and wash all towels and underwear in hot water as well as changing them often.

Hypothermia Too much cold is just as dangerous as too much heat, particularly if it leads to hypothermia. Although everyone associates Greece with heat and sunshine, the high mountainous regions can be cool, even in summer. Keeping warm while trekking in mountainous regions in spring and autumn can be as much of a problem as keeping cool in the lower regions during summer.

Hypothermia occurs when the body loses heat faster than it can produce it and the core temperature of the body falls. It is surprisingly easy to progress from very cold to dangerously cold due to a combination of wind, wet clothing, fatigue and hunger, even if the air temperature is above freezing. It is best to dress in layers; silk, wool and some of the newer artificial fibres all insulate well. A hat is important, as a lot of heat is lost through the head. A strong and waterproof outer layer is essential, as keeping dry is vital. Carry basic supplies, including food containing simple sugars to generate heat quickly and lots of fluid to drink. A space blanket should always be carried in cold environments.

Symptoms of hypothermia are exhaustion, numb skin (particularly toes and fingers), shivering, slurred speech, irrational or violent behaviour, lethargy, stumbling, dizzy spells, muscle cramps and violent bursts of energy. Irrationality may take the form of sufferers claiming they are warm and trying to take off their clothes.

To treat mild hypothermia, first get the person out of the wind and/or rain, remove their clothing if it's wet and replace it with dry, warm clothing. Give them hot liquids – not alcohol – and some high-kilojoule, easily digestible food. Do not rub victims; it's better to allow them to slowly warm themselves. This should be enough to treat the early stages of hypothermia. The early recognition and treatment of mild hypothermia is the only way to prevent severe hypothermia, which is a critical condition.

Motion Sickness Sea sickness can be a problem. Although noted for calm waters, ideal for sailing holidays, the Ionian can be unpredictable and gets very rough when the *maistro* wind blows.

If you are prone to motion sickness, eat lightly before and during a trip, and try to find a place that minimises disturbance – near the wing on aircraft, close to midships on boats, near the centre on buses. Fresh air usually helps; reading and cigarette smoke don't. Commercial motion-sickness preparations, which can cause drowsiness, have to be taken before the trip commences; when you're feeling sick it's too late. Ginger (available in capsule form) and peppermint (including mint-flavoured sweets) are natural preventatives.

Infectious Diseases

Diarrhoea Simple things like a change of water, food or climate can all cause a mild bout of diarrhoea, but a few rushed toilet trips with no other symptoms is not indicative of a major problem.

Dehydration is the main danger with any diarrhoea, particularly in children or the elderly as dehydration can occur quite quickly. Under all circumstances *fluid replacement* (at least equal to the volume being lost) is the most important thing to remember. Weak black tea with a little sugar, soda water, or soft drinks allowed to go flat and diluted 50% with clean water are all good.

Hepatitis Hepatitis is a general term for inflammation of the liver. It is a common disease worldwide. The symptoms are fever, chills, headache, fatigue, feelings of weakness and aches and pains, followed by loss of appetite, nausea, vomiting, abdominal pain, dark urine, light-coloured faeces, jaundiced (yellow) skin and the whites of the eyes may turn yellow. **Hepatitis A** is transmitted by contaminated food and drinking water. The disease poses a real threat to the western traveller. You should seek medical advice, but there is not much you can do apart from resting, drinking lots of fluids, eating lightly and avoiding fatty foods. People who have had hepatitis should avoid alcohol for some time after the illness, as the liver needs time to recover. **Hepatitis E** is transmitted in the same way, and can be very serious in pregnant women.

There are almost 300 million chronic carriers of **Hepatitis B** in the world. The disease is spread through contact with infected blood, blood products or body fluids; for example, through sexual contact, unsterilised needles and blood transfusions, or contact with blood via small breaks in the skin. Other risk situations include having a shave, tattoo, or having your body pierced with contaminated equipment. The symptoms of type B may be more severe and may lead to long-term problems. **Hepatitis D** is spread in the same way, but the risk is mainly in shared needles.

Hepatitis C can lead to chronic liver disease. The virus is spread by contact with blood – usually via contaminated transfusions or shared needles.

Tetanus This potentially fatal disease is found worldwide. It is difficult to treat but is preventable with immunisation.

Rabies Rabies is a fatal viral infection and is caused by a bite or scratch by an infected animal. It's rare, but it's found in Greece. Dogs are noted carriers as are monkeys and cats. Any bite, scratch or even lick from a warm-blooded, furry animal should be cleaned immediately and thoroughly. Scrub with soap and running water, and then clean with an alcohol or iodine solution. If there is any possibility that the animal is infected medical help should be sought immediately. Even if the animal is not rabid, all bites should be treated seriously as they can become infected or can result in tetanus. A rabies vaccination is now available and should be considered if you are in a high risk category eg if you intend to explore

caves (bat bites can be dangerous), work with animals, or travel so far off the beaten track that medical help is more than two days away.

Sexually Transmitted Diseases Sexual contact with an infected sexual partner spreads these diseases. While abstinence is the only 100% preventative, using condoms is also effective. Gonorrhoea, herpes and syphilis are among these diseases; sores, blisters or rashes around the genitals, discharges or pain when urinating are common symptoms. In some STDs, such as wart virus or chlamydia, symptoms may be less marked or not observed at all in women. Syphilis symptoms eventually disappear completely but the disease continues and can cause severe problems in later years. The treatment of gonorrhoea and syphilis is with antibiotics.

There are numerous other sexually transmitted diseases, for most of which effective treatment is available. There is no cure for herpes.

HIV/AIDS Infection with the human immunodeficiency virus (HIV) may lead to acquired immune deficiency syndrome (AIDS), which is a fatal disease. Any exposure to blood, blood products or body fluids may put the individual at risk. The disease is often transmitted through sexual contact or dirty needles – vaccinations, acupuncture, tattooing and body piercing can be potentially as dangerous as intravenous drug use.

If you do need an injection, ask to see the syringe unwrapped in front of you, or take a needle and syringe pack with you. Fear of HIV infection should never preclude treatment for serious medical conditions.

Insect-Borne Diseases

Typhus Tick typhus is a problem from April to September in rural areas, particularly areas where animals congregate. Typhus begins with a fever, chills, headache and then muscle pains, followed a few days later by a body rash. There is often a large painful sore at the site of the bite and nearby lymph nodes are swollen and painful. There is no vaccine available. The best protection is to check your skin carefully after walking in danger areas such as long grass and scrub. A strong insect repellent can help, and serious walkers in tick areas should consider having their boots and trousers impregnated with benzyl benzoate and dibutylphthalate. (See Cuts, Bites & Stings later in this chapter for information about ticks.)

Lyme Disease Lyme disease is a tick-transmitted infection which may be acquired throughout Europe. The illness usually begins with a spreading rash at the site of the bite and is accompanied by fever, headache, extreme fatigue, aching joints and muscles and mild neck stiffness. If untreated, these symptoms usually resolve over several weeks but over subsequent weeks or months disorders of the nervous system, heart and joints may develop. The response to treatment is best early in the illness. The longer the delay, the longer the recovery period.

Cuts, Bites & Stings

Skin punctures can easily become infected in hot climates and may be difficult to heal. Treat any cut with an antiseptic such as povidone-iodine. Where possible avoid bandages and Band-Aids, which can keep wounds wet.

Although there are a lot of bees and wasps in Greece, their stings are usually painful rather than dangerous. Calamine lotion or sting relief spray will give relief and ice packs will reduce the pain and swelling.

Snakes Always wear boots, socks and long trousers when walking through undergrowth where snakes may be present. Don't put your hands into holes and crevices, and be careful when collecting firewood.

Snake bites do not cause instantaneous death and antivenenes are usually available. Keep the victim calm and still, wrap the bitten limb tightly, as you would for a sprained ankle, and then attach a splint to immobilise it. Then seek medical help, if possible with the dead snake for identification. Don't attempt to catch the snake if there is even a re-mote possibility of being bitten again. Tourniquets and sucking out the poison are now comprehensively discredited.

Jellyfish, Sea Urchins & Weever Fish Watch out for sea urchins around rocky beaches; if you get some of their needles embedded in your skin, olive oil will help to loosen them. If they are not removed they will become infected. Be wary also of jelly fish, particularly during the months of September and October. Although they are not lethal in the Ionians, their stings can be painful. Dousing in vinegar will deactivate any stingers which have not 'fired'. Calamine lotion, antihistamines and analgesics may reduce the reaction and relieve the pain. Much more painful than either of these, but thankfully much rarer, is an encounter with the weever fish. It buries itself in the sand of the tidal zone with only its spines protruding, and injects a painful and powerful toxin if trodden on. Soaking your foot in very hot water (which breaks down the poison) should solve the problem. It can cause permanent local paralysis in the worst instance.

Bedbugs & Lice Bedbugs live in various places, but particularly in dirty mattresses and bedding. Spots of blood on bedclothes or on the wall around the bed can be read as a suggestion to find another hotel. Bedbugs leave itchy bites in neat rows. Calamine lotion or sting relief spray may help.

All lice cause itching and discomfort. They make themselves at home in your hair, your clothing or in your pubic hair. You catch lice through direct contact with infected people or by sharing combs, clothing and the like. Powder or shampoo treatment will kill the lice and infected clothing should then be washed in very hot water.

Leeches & Ticks Leeches may be present in damp conditions. They attach themselves to your skin to suck your blood. Trekkers often get them on their legs or in their boots. Salt or a lighted cigarette end will make them fall off. Do not pull them off, as the bite is then more likely to become infected.

An insect repellent may keep them away. You should always check your body if you have been walking through a potentially tick-infested area as ticks can cause skin infections and other more serious diseases.

Women's Health
Antibiotic use, synthetic underwear, sweating and contraceptive pills can lead to fungal vaginal infections, especially when travelling in hot climates. Fungal infections are characterised by a rash, itch and discharge and can be treated with a vinegar or lemon-juice douche, or with yogurt. Nystatin, miconazole or clotrimazole pessaries or vaginal cream are the usual treatment. Maintaining good personal hygiene and using loose-fitting clothes and cotton underwear may help prevent these infections.

Sexually transmitted diseases are a major cause of vaginal problems. Symptoms include a smelly discharge, painful intercourse and sometimes a burning sensation when urinating. Medical attention should be sought and male sexual partners must also be treated. For more details see Sexually Transmitted Diseases earlier in this chapter. Besides abstinence, the best thing is to practise safer sex using condoms.

Hospital Treatment
Citizens of EU countries are covered for free treatment in public hospitals within Greece on presentation of an E111 form. Inquire at your national health service or travel agent in advance. Emergency treatment is free to all nationalities in public hospitals. In an emergency, dial ☎ 166. There is at least one doctor on every island in the Ionians (most hotels and travel agents will have a list) and the larger towns have hospitals. Pharmacies can dispense medicines which are available only on prescription in most European countries, so you can consult a pharmacist for minor ailments.

All this sounds fine, but although medical training is of a high standard in Greece, the health service is badly underfunded and one of the worst in Europe. Hospitals are overcrowded, hygiene is not always what it should be and relatives are expected to bring in food for the patient – which could be a problem for a tourist. Conditions and treatment are better in private hospitals, which are expensive. All this means that a good health insurance policy is essential.

WOMEN TRAVELLERS
Women travellers should encounter no problems in the Ionians. The crime rate remains relatively low, and solo travel is probably safer than in most European countries. This does not mean that you should be lulled into complacency; bag snatching and rapes do occur, although violent offences are rare.

Restaurants are quite comfortable with giving solo women a table for one, and you get fewer stares than you would doing the same thing in Italy, for example. Most hotel rooms and domatia have twin beds. In the low season you will probably pay a single rate, although in the high season you might be forced to pay the full price for a double room.

The biggest nuisance to foreign women travelling alone are the guys the Greeks have nicknamed *kamaki*. The word means 'fishing trident' and refers to the kamaki's favourite pastime, 'fishing' for foreign women. You'll find them wherever there are lots of tourists; generally young, smooth-talking guys who aren't in the least bashful about sidling up to foreign women in the street. They can be very persistent, but they are a hassle rather than a threat. Be firm, but polite. They will soon leave you alone – then they'll head for the next 'fish'.

The majority of Greek men treat foreign women with respect and are genuinely helpful. Often however, they will find it strange that a woman is travelling alone, unaccompanied by a husband, relative or friend. Although Greece is still a fairly conservative country, Greek women are as modern as their counterparts in the rest of Western Europe. Except in the smallest isolated villages the evening *volta* (stroll) as a showpiece for unmarried daughters no longer exists. Young Greek women hold good jobs, leave their villages to study or work, live with their boyfriends etc.

GAY & LESBIAN TRAVELLERS

In a country where the church still plays a prominent role in shaping society's views on issues such as sexuality, it should come as no surprise that homosexuality is generally frowned upon – especially outside the major cities. While there is no legislation against homosexual activity, it certainly pays to be discreet and to avoid open displays of togetherness.

This has not prevented Greece from becoming an extremely popular destination for gay travellers. There is no overt gay scene in the Ionians, although homosexuality is accepted in the livelier resorts which attract a young crowd.

Other parts of Greece are perhaps more appealing to gay travellers. The town of Eressos on the island of Lesvos (Mytilini), birthplace of the lesbian poet Sappho, has become something of a place of pilgrimage for lesbians. Athens has a busy gay scene, as does Thessaloniki. Mykonos has long been famous for its gay bars, beaches and general hedonism, while Paros (and Antiparos), Rhodes, Santorini and Skiathos all have their share of gay hang-outs.

The *Spartacus International Gay Guide*, published by Bruno Gmünder (Berlin), is widely regarded as the leading authority on the gay travel scene. The Greek section has been given a thorough overhaul for the 1998/99 edition, and it contains a wealth of information on gay venues everywhere from Alexandroupolis to Xanthi.

There's also stacks of information on the Internet. *Roz Mov* at www.geocities.com /WestHollywood/2225/index.html, is a good place to start. It has pages on travel info, gay health, the gay press, organisations, events and legal issues – and links to lots more sites. Gayscape has a useful site at www.jwpublishing.com/gayscape.gre.html with lots of links.

The main gay rights organisation in Greece is the Elladas Omofilofilon Kommunitas (☎ 01-341 0755, fax 883 6942, email eok@nyx.gr) upstairs at Apostolou Pavlou 31 in the Athens suburb of Thisio. There are no gay organisations based in the Ionians.

DISABLED TRAVELLERS

If mobility is a problem and you wish to visit the Ionians, the hard fact is that most hotels, museums and ancient sites are not wheelchair accessible. An exception is Corfu's excellent Archaeological Museum which has full wheelchair access. Beaches can also be a problem.

Your trip needs careful planning, so get as much information as you can before you go. The British-based Royal Association for Disability and Rehabilitation (RADAR) publishes a useful guide called *Holidays & Travel Abroad: A Guide for Disabled People*, which gives a good overview of facilities available to disabled travellers in Europe. Contact RADAR (☎ 020-7250 3222, fax 7250 0212, email radar@radar.org.uk) at 12 City Forum, 250 City Road, London EC1V 8AF.

If you are planning to take a package holiday, the operator should be able to provide full details about the accessibility of accommodation and transport.

Lavinia Tours (☎ 031-23 2828, fax 21 9714) at Egnatia 101 (PO Box 111 06), Thessaloniki 541 10, specialises in arranging tours for disabled travellers. Managing director Eugenia Stravropoulou has travelled widely both in Greece and abroad in her wheelchair.

SENIOR TRAVELLERS

Card-carrying EU pensioners can claim a range of benefits such as reduced admission charges at museums and ancient sites and discounts on trains.

TRAVEL WITH CHILDREN

Greece is a safe and relatively easy place to travel with children. It's especially easy if you're staying by the beach or at a resort hotel.

If you're travelling around, the main problem is a shortage of decent playgrounds and other recreational facilities.

Don't be afraid to take children to the ancient sites. Many parents are surprised by how much their children enjoy them.

Hotels and restaurants are very accommodating when it comes to meeting the needs of children, although highchairs are a rarity outside resorts. The service in restaurants is normally very quick, which is great when you've got hungry children on your hands.

Fresh milk is readily available in large towns and tourist areas, but you'll do better trying to buy it yourself rather than relying on restaurants or bars, which seem to prefer to use tinned condensed or heat-treated milk. Supermarkets and minimarkets are the best place to look. Formula is available everywhere.

Mobility is an issue for parents with very small children. Strollers (pushchairs) are fine in the main towns of the Ionians and resorts. However, they are hopeless on the beach, on rough stone paths and up steps, and a curse when getting on/off buses and ferries. Backpacks or front pouches are the best options.

Travel on ferries and buses is free for children under four. They pay half-price up to the age of 10 (ferries) and 12 (buses). Full fares apply otherwise. On domestic flights, you'll pay 10% of the fare to have a child under two sitting on your knee. Kids aged two to 12 pay half-price.

USEFUL ORGANISATIONS

ELPA (☎ 01-779 1615), the Greek automobile club, has its headquarters on the ground floor of Athens Tower, Messogion 2-4, Athens 115 27. ELPA offers reciprocal services to members of national automobile associations on production of a valid membership card. If your vehicle breaks down, dial ☎ 104.

The UK-based Friends of the Ionian (☎ 01298-70131, email info@foi.u-net.com), 24 Bath Road, Buxton SK17 6HH, aims to improve the quality of tourism in the Ionians by extending the length of the season to reduce the enormous pressure on resorts and coasts, and offering tourists alternatives to the beach. The group also focuses on local environmental issues. It is funded by membership.

It produces various pamphlets (500 dr) with historical and ecological information as well as some well researched self-guided trails on Paxi, Ithaki and Zakynthos. These

are available from travel agents in the featured areas.

DANGERS & ANNOYANCES
Theft

Crime, especially theft, is low in Greece, but unfortunately it is on the increase. The vast majority of thefts from tourists are still committed by other tourists; the biggest danger of theft is probably in dormitory rooms in hostels and at camp sites. So make sure you do not leave valuables unattended in such places.

If you are staying in a hotel room, and the windows and door do not lock securely, just ask for your valuables to be locked in the hotel safe – hotel proprietors are happy to do this.

LEGAL MATTERS
Drugs

Greek drug laws are the strictest in Europe. Greek courts make no distinction between possession and pushing. Possession of even a small amount of marijuana is likely to land you in jail.

BUSINESS HOURS

Banks are open 8 am to 2 pm Monday to Thursday, and 8 am to 1.30 pm Friday. Some banks in larger towns also open between 3.30 and 6.30 pm in the afternoon and on Saturday morning.

Post offices are open 7.30 am to 2 pm Monday to Friday.

The opening hours of OTE offices (for long distance and overseas telephone calls) vary according to the size of the town. In smaller towns they are usually open 7.30 am to 3 pm daily; 6 am until 11 pm in larger towns.

In summer, the usual opening hours for shops are 8 am to 1.30 pm and 5.30 to 8.30 pm on Tuesday, Thursday and Friday, and 8 am to 2.30 pm on Monday, Wednesday and Saturday. Shops open 30 minutes later in winter. These times are not always strictly adhered to. Many shops in tourist resorts are open seven days a week.

Department stores and supermarkets are open 8 am to 8 pm Monday to Friday, 8 am to at least 3 pm on Saturday, but are closed Sunday.

Periptera are open from early morning until late at night. They sell everything from bus tickets to cigarettes.

Museums

Most museums open at 8 or 8.30 am, and close at around 2.30 or 3 pm. Most places are closed on Monday. There are lots of minor archaeological sites which are unenclosed – and therefore always open.

PUBLIC HOLIDAYS & SPECIAL EVENTS

All banks and shops and most museums and ancient sites close on public holidays. National public holidays in Greece are:

New Year's Day	1 January
Epiphany	6 January
First Sunday in Lent	February
Greek Independence Day	25 March
Good Friday	March/April
(Orthodox) Easter Sunday	March/April
Spring Festival/Labour Day	1 May
Feast of the Assumption	15 August
Ohi Day	28 October
Christmas Day	25 December
St Stephen's Day	26 December

On Corfu, St Spyridon's Day on 11 August is an unofficial public holiday, and some businesses, including public offices, are closed.

The Greek year is a succession of festivals and events, some of which are religious, some cultural, others an excuse for a good knees-up, and some a combination of all three. The following is by no means an exhaustive list, but it covers the most important events, both national and regional. If you're in the right place at the right time, you'll certainly be invited to join the revelry. Note that most of the music and dancing part of the celebrations take place the night *before* the festival, not on the actual day.

January

Feast of Agios Vasilios (St Basil) The year kicks off with this festival on 1 January. A church ceremony is followed by the exchanging of gifts, singing, dancing and feasting; the New Year pie *(vasilopitta)* is sliced and the person who gets the slice containing a coin will supposedly have a lucky year.

Epiphany (the Blessing of the Waters) On 6 January, Christ's baptism by St John is celebrated throughout Greece. Seas, lakes, rivers and baptismal fonts are blessed and crosses immersed in them.

February-March

Carnival The Greek carnival season is the three weeks before the beginning of Lent (the 40 day period before Easter, which is traditionally a period of fasting). The carnivals are ostensibly Christian pre-Lenten celebrations, but many derive from pagan festivals. There are many regional variations, but fancy dress, feasting, traditional dancing and general merrymaking prevail. The best carnival celebrations in the Ionians are in Zakynthos and Kefallonia. On Shrove Monday, the Monday before Ash Wednesday (the first day of Lent), people take to the hills throughout Greece to have picnics and fly kites.

March

Independence Day The anniversary of the hoisting of the Greek flag by Bishop Germanos at Moni Agias Lavras is celebrated on 25 March with parades and dancing. Germanos' act of revolt marked the start of the War of Independence. Independence Day coincides with the Feast of the Annunciation, so it is also a religious festival.

March-April

Easter The most important festival in the Greek Orthodox religion. Emphasis is placed on the Resurrection rather than on the Crucifixion, so it is a joyous occasion. The festival commences on the evening of Good Friday with the *perifora epitavios*, when a shrouded bier (representing Christ's funeral bier) is carried through the streets to the local church. This moving candlelit procession can be seen in towns and villages throughout the Ionians. The Resurrection Mass starts at 11 pm on Saturday night. At midnight, packed churches are plunged into darkness to symbolise Christ's passing through the underworld. The ceremony of the lighting of candles which follows is the most significant moment in the Orthodox year, for it symbolises the Resurrection. Its poignancy and beauty are spellbinding. If you are in the Ionians at Easter you should endeavour to attend this ceremony, which ends with the setting off of fireworks and candlelit processions through the streets. The

A packed beach and the moorings at Paleokastritsa, Corfu

The ornately decorated interior and statuary of the Ahillion Palace, Corfu

Secluded swimming area at Cape Drastis, near Sidhari, Corfu

Panoramic view of Corfu Town from the New Fortress

Part of the circular harbour at the resort village of Kassiopi, Corfu

Coastline near Sidhari, Corfu, a springboard to the Diapondia Islands

Lenten fast ends on Easter Sunday with the cracking of red-dyed Easter eggs and an outdoor feast of roast lamb followed by Greek dancing. The day's greeting is *Hristos anesti* ('Christ is risen'), to which the reply is *Alithos anesti* ('Truly He is risen'). On both Palm Sunday (the Sunday before Easter) and Easter Sunday, St Spyridon (the mummified patron saint of Corfu) is taken out for an airing and joyously paraded through Corfu Town. He is paraded again on 11 August.

Feast of Agios Georgos (St George) The feast day of St George, Greece's patron saint, and patron saint of shepherds, takes place on 23 April or the Tuesday following Easter (whichever comes first), and is celebrated especially in rural communities.

May

May Day On the first day of May there is a mass exodus from towns to the country. During picnics, wildflowers are gathered and made into wreaths to decorate houses.

Ionian Day The anniversary of the Ionian islands' union with Greece (in 1864) is commemorated on 21 May with wreath-laying, marches and military parades.

June

Navy Week The festival celebrates the long relationship between the Greek and the sea with events in fishing villages and ports throughout the country.

Feast of St John the Baptist This feast day on 24 June is widely celebrated. Wreaths made on May Day are kept until this day, when they are burned on bonfires.

August

St Spyridon's Day Corfu celebrates St Spyridon on 11 August every year, as well as on Palm Sunday, Easter Saturday and the first Sunday in November. A gold casket containing the mummified patron saint of Corfu is joyously paraded through Corfu Town. The streets are jam-packed with people, marching bands, religious and civic leaders and anyone and everyone.

Assumption Greeks celebrate Assumption Day (15 August) with family reunions. The whole population seems to be on the move either side of the big day, so it's a good time to avoid public transport. Accommodation may be hard to come by in larger towns, as it is snapped up by Greeks visiting their relatives. All the islands have major festivities for the occasion, the most bizarre of which is probably the phenomenon of the Virgin's snakes in Markopoulo on Kefallo-

nia. Small snakes whose heads are marked with a cross appear in and around the village during the first half of the month and are collected by the locals; on 15 August in a special ceremony they are released. Originally the snakes just happened to appear in the village streets, entered the church and disappeared near the icon of the Panagia Fidon (Virgin of the Snakes). Sceptics, and natural historians, would argue that the church and village are on the natural migratory path of the snakes.

September

Genesis tis Panagias (Virgin's Birthday) This day is celebrated on 8 September throughout Greece with religious services and feasting.

Exaltation of the Cross This is celebrated on 14 September throughout Greece with processions and hymns.

October

Ohi (No) Day Metaxas' refusal to allow Mussolini's troops free passage through Greece in WWII is commemorated on 28 October with remembrance services, military parades, folk dancing and feasting.

December

Christmas Day Although not as important as Easter, Christmas is still celebrated with religious services and feasting. Nowadays much western influence is apparent, including Christmas trees, decorations and presents.

Summer Festivals & Performances

There are cultural events throughout the Ionians in summer.

Corfu's Festival has classical music performances and other events and takes place in September. Paxi hosts a classical music festival in September which attracts Greek and international performers. Concerts are held in Longos and other parts of the island.

The island of Ithaki hosts a theatre competition for young playwrights in June and a music contest featuring emerging Greek composers in July.

Lefkada's international festival of folklore, language and arts takes place from June to August. There is a variety of cultural events, including music and dance from all over the world. The festival was launched just after WWII and aims to encourage international cultural exchange and understanding. In 1999 the festival was expanded to include events over a longer period of time all over the island, not just in Lefkada Town.

Kefallonia gathers Greek and foreign choirs, symphony orchestras and folk dance groups for its International Choral Music Festival held on the Lixouri Peninsula from August to September. Wine is also celebrated on Kefallonia at the Robolo Festival in Omala in September.

Zakynthos comes alive, culturally speaking, in August with a variety of cultural events under the title Zakyntheia, and the wine flows freely for the annual wine festival at the end of the month.

ACTIVITIES
Windsurfing
Windsurfing is the most popular water sport in Greece. Vasiliki on Lefkada is regarded as one of the best windsurfing beaches in Europe, and according to some, Vasiliki is one of the best places in the world to learn the sport.

You'll find sailboards for hire almost everywhere. Hire charges range from 2000 dr to 3000 dr an hour, depending on the gear. If you are a novice, most places that rent equipment also give lessons.

Sailboards may only be brought into Greece if a Greek national residing in Greece guarantees that it will be taken out again. To find out the procedure for arranging this, contact the Hellenic Windsurfing Association (☎ 01-323 0330), Filellinon 7, Athens.

Water-Skiing
Islands with water-ski centres are Corfu, Paxi, Lefkada, Zakynthos and Kythira. These are listed in the individual island chapters.

Snorkelling & Diving
Snorkelling is enjoyable just about anywhere along the coast of Greece. Especially good places are Paleokastritsa on Corfu, various beaches on the east coasts of Zakynthos and Lefkada. Equip yourself with a mask, snorkel and some fins and you're away. Snorkelling gear can be bought all over the islands.

However, diving is another matter. Any kind of underwater activity using breathing apparatus is strictly forbidden other than under the supervision of a diving school. This is to protect the antiquities in the depths of the Ionian and Aegean seas. There are diving schools on the islands of Corfu, Zakynthos and Kefallonia. The GNTO in your country can give you a list of diving schools.

Trekking & Walking
There are a number of companies running organised treks. One of the biggest is Trekking Hellas (☎ 01-323 4548, fax 325 1474, email trekking@compulink.gr), Filellinon 7, Athens 105 57. You'll find more information at its Web site, www.trekking.gr. In 1999 it was running seven-day Ionian islands 'adventure' treks to Ithaki and Kastos, departing from Athens or Preveza, passing through Astakos, involving sea travel in an inflatable rubber dinghy and accommodation in local hotels or camping on the beach.

The Ionians lend themselves to walking, and it's a great way to get off the beaten track. You are unlikely to get into danger as settlements or roads are never far away. You will encounter a variety of paths. *Kalderimi* are cobbled or flagstone paths which link settlements and date back to Byzantine times. Sadly, many have been bulldozed to make way for roads. Donkey paths are a feature of all of the Ionians but many of these have now been widened and some even asphalted over.

Hilary Whitton Paipeti's *Second Book of Corfu Walks* (see Guidebooks earlier in this chapter) has a huge range of trails to follow. The Friends of the Ionian (see Useful Organisations earlier in this chapter) produces walking maps for the islands of Paxi, Ithaki and Zakynthos.

COURSES
Language
If you are serious about learning the language, an intensive course at the start of your stay is a good way to go about it.

Corfu's Ionian University runs courses in Modern Greek and Greek Civilisation in July and August. Details are available from the Secretariat of the Ionian University (☎ 0661-22 993/94) at Megaron Kapodistria 49, Corfu Town.

WORK
Permits
EU nationals don't need a work permit, but they need a residency permit if they intend to stay longer than three months. Nationals of other countries are supposed to have a work permit.

English Teaching
If you're looking for a permanent job, the most widely available option is to teach English. A TEFL (Teaching English as a Foreign Language) certificate or a university degree is an advantage but not essential. In the UK, look through the *Times Educational Supplement* or Tuesday's edition of the *Guardian* newspaper – in other countries, contact the Greek embassy.

Another possibility is to find a job teaching English once you are in the Ionians. There are language schools in Corfu Town, Argostoli on Kefallonia, Zakynthos Town and Lefkada Town. Strictly speaking, you need a licence to teach in these schools, but many will employ teachers without one. The best time to look around for such a job is late summer, before the academic year begins.

Bar & Hostel Work
The bars of the Ionian islands could not survive without foreign workers and there are plenty of summer jobs up for grabs every year. The pay is not fantastic, but you get to spend a summer in the islands. April/May is the time to go looking. Travellers hotels such as the Pink Palace in Agios Godios, Corfu are other places that regularly employ foreign workers.

Volunteer Work
The Hellenic Society for the Study & Protection of the Monk Seal (☎ 01-522 2888, fax 522 2450), Solomou 53, Athens 106 82, and the Sea Turtle Protection Society of Greece (☎/fax 01-384 4146, email stps@compulink.gr), Solomou 35, Athens 106 82, both use volunteers for their monitoring programs on the Ionian islands. See the Kefallonia and Zakynthos chapters for more details.

Other Work
There are sometimes jobs advertised in the classifieds of English-language newspapers such as *The Corfiot*, or you can place an advertisement yourself. EU nationals can also make use of the OAED (Organismos Apasholiseos Ergatikou Dynamikou), the Greek National Employment Service, in their search for a job. The OAED has offices throughout Greece.

The seasonal harvest work seems to be monopolised by migrant workers from Albania, and is no longer a viable option for travellers.

ACCOMMODATION
There is a range of accommodation available in Greece to suit every taste and pocket. All places to stay are subject to strict price controls set by the tourist police. By law, a notice must be displayed in every room, which states the category of the room and the price charged in each season. The price includes a 4.5% community tax and 8% value-added tax (VAT).

Accommodation owners may add a 10% surcharge for a stay of less than three nights, but this is not mandatory. A mandatory charge of 20% is levied if an extra bed is put into a room. During July and August, accommodation owners will charge the maximum price, but in spring and autumn, prices will drop by up to 20%, and perhaps by even more in winter. These are the times to bring your bargaining skills into action.

Rip-offs rarely occur, but if you suspect you have been exploited by an accommodation owner, report it to either the tourist police or regular police and they will act swiftly.

Camping
There are plenty of camping grounds in the Ionians; Corfu has 12 of them, there are

four on Lefkada, one on Kefallonia and two on Zakynthos. A few are operated by the EOT, but most are privately run. Very few are open outside the high season (April to October). The Greek National Tourism Organisation produces a directory, *Camp in Greece*, with detailed description of all camp sites in the country, including directions on how to find them, facilities on site, pitches, greenery and beaches nearby. The Panhellenic Camping Association (☎/fax 01-362 1560), Solonos 102, Athens 106 80, also publishes an annual booklet listing all the camp sites and their facilities.

Camping fees are highest from 15 June to the end of August. Most camping grounds charge from 1200 dr to 1400 dr per adult and 600 dr to 800 dr for children aged four to 12. There's no charge for children aged under four. Tent sites cost from 900 dr per night for small tents, and from 1200 dr per night for large tents. Caravan sites start at around 2500 dr.

Between May and mid-September it is warm enough to sleep out under the stars, although you will still need a lightweight sleeping bag to counter the pre-dawn chill. It's a good idea to have a foam pad to lie on and a waterproof cover for your sleeping bag.

Freelance (wild) camping is illegal, but the law is not always strictly enforced. If you do decide to take a chance on this, make sure you are not camping on private land, and clear up all rubbish when you leave. If you are told to move by the police, do so without protest, as the law is occasionally enforced. Freelance camping is more likely to be tolerated on islands that don't have camp sites. It's wise to ask around before freelance camping anywhere in Greece.

Apartments
Self-contained family apartments are available in some hotels and domatia. There are also a number of purpose-built apartments, particularly on the islands, available for either long or short term rental. Prices vary considerably according to the amenities offered. The tourist police may be able to help

in larger towns. In smaller villages and resorts, ask in a kafeneio or travel agent.

Domatia
Domatia are the Greek equivalent of the British B&B, minus breakfast. Once upon a time domatia comprised little more than spare rooms in the family home which could be rented out to travellers in summer; nowadays, many are purpose-built appendages to the family house. Some come complete with fully equipped kitchens. Standards of cleanliness are generally high. The decor runs the gamut from cool grey marble floors, coordinated pine furniture, pretty lace curtains and tasteful pictures on the walls, to so much kitsch you are almost afraid to move in case you break an ornament.

Domatia remain a popular option for budget travellers. They are classified A, B or C. Expect to pay from 4000 dr to 9000 dr for a single, and 6000 dr to 15,000 dr for a double, depending on the class, whether bathrooms are shared or private, the season and how long you plan to stay. Domatia are found on all of the Ionian islands. Many domatia are officially open only between April and October.

From June to September domatia owners are out in force, touting for customers. They often greet buses and boats, shouting 'Room, room!' and often carrying photographs of their rooms. In peak season, it can prove a mistake not to take up an offer – but be wary of owners who are vague about the location of their accommodation. 'Close to town' can turn out to be way out in the sticks. If you are at all dubious, insist they show you the location on a map.

Hostels
There are no hostels in the Ionian islands.

Traditional Settlements
Traditional settlements are old buildings of architectural merit that have been renovated and converted into tourist accommodation. There are some terrific places among them, but they are expensive – most are equivalent in price to an A or B class hotel. The best one in the Ionians is in Fiskardo on Kefallonia.

Pensions

Pensions in Greece are virtually indistinguishable from hotels. They are classed A, B or C. An A class pension is equivalent in amenities and price to a B class hotel, a B class pension is equivalent to a C class hotel and a C class pension is equivalent to a D or E class hotel.

Hotels

Hotels in Greece are divided into six categories: deluxe, A, B, C, D and E. Hotels are categorised according to the size of the room, whether or not they have a bar, and the ratio of bathrooms to beds, rather than standards of cleanliness, comfort of the beds and friendliness of staff – all elements which may be of greater relevance to guests.

As one would expect, deluxe, A and B class hotels have many amenities, private bathrooms and constant hot water. C class hotels have a snack bar, rooms have private bathrooms, but hot water may only be available at certain times of the day. The D class hotels may or may not have snack bars, most rooms will share bathrooms, but there may be some with private bathrooms, and they may have solar-heated water, which means hot water is not guaranteed. The E classes do not have a snack bar, bathrooms are shared and you may have to pay extra for hot water – if it exists at all.

Prices are controlled by the tourist police and the maximum rate that can be charged for a room must be displayed on a board behind the door of each room. The classification is not often much of a guide to price. Rates in D and E class hotels are generally comparable with domatia. You can pay anywhere from 10,000 dr to 20,000 dr for a single in high season in C class and 15,000 dr to 25,000 dr for a double. Prices in B class range from 15,000 dr to 25,000 dr for singles, and from 25,000 dr to 35,000 dr for doubles. A class prices are not much higher.

FOOD

The food of the Ionians is linked to the islands' history. Corfu, for example, which was never occupied by the Turks, retains traditional recipes of Italian, Spanish and ancient Greek derivations. Pasta features prominently on menus throughout the island, although in the tourism-oriented world of today, this could fairly be passed off as catering to the vast number of Italian tourists who descend on the island each year in high summer.

Traditional Corfiot food is still served in many tavernas and restaurants on the island. Casserole cooking has always been popular. *Pastitsada* derives from the Venetian *spezzatino*. It is made from layered pasta (usually macaroni), beef or veal and tomato filling, with bechamel sauce, paprika, cinnamon and cheese topping. Cloves and garlic are sometimes used. Another favourite Corfiot dish is *sofrito*. It contains veal (sometimes beef or lamb) cooked slowly in white sauce with olive oil, wine vinegar, garlic, parsley and onion with generous dashings of white pepper. At its best, and freshly cooked, the meat is tender and flavoursome. If it has been sitting around for a few days it is somewhat less appealing. *Bourdeto* is a hot casserole of fish with tomatoes, paprika and cayenne.

If you visit Kefallonia, sampling *kreatopita* (Kefallonian meat pie) is a must. It is a delicious combination of tender lamb cooked with onions, rice, potatoes, carrots and tomatoes topped with layers of filo pastry (see boxed text 'Kreatopita – Kefallonian Meat Pie'). Some other Kefallonian specialities include *skordalia*, garlic infused mashed potatoes, and *bakaliaropita*, a fish pie made of cod. Kefallonian cheese and dairy products are among the best in the archipelago.

The British cannot be credited with introducing many great culinary secrets to the Ionians.

One possible exception is *tsin tsin birra* or ginger beer, which can still be found in the cafes on the Liston in Corfu Town. The nonalcoholic drink is made in the traditional way using the finest ingredients of grated ginger, lemon juice, lemon oil, water and sugar. The liquid mixture is brewed in large cauldrons and is best drunk fresh. Historically it was stored in small stone bottles stoppered with marbles.

Kreatopita – Kefallonian Meat Pie

You won't have to hunt too hard to find this popular and tasty dish on the menus of tavernas and restaurants in Kefallonia. There are slight variations – some people make it with goat's meat and the ingredients can differ slightly. There's a bit of shopping and chopping to do but otherwise it's really quite simple, so there's no reason you can't make it at home too.

- one leg of lamb, with the meat cut into small pieces (keep the bones for stock)
- ¼ cup olive oil
- one onion, chopped
- three potatoes, parboiled and diced
- one large (or two small) carrots, parboiled and diced
- three cups cooked rice
- two tablespoons tomato purée
- one cup feta cheese, crumbled
- ½ cup parsley, chopped
- one tablespoon dried oregano
- three cloves garlic, chopped
- three sprigs fresh mint, chopped
- one tablespoon cinnamon
- salt and freshly ground black pepper
- juice of one lemon
- grated peel of one lemon
- 16 filo pastry sheets
- eight tablespoons melted butter
- three hard boiled eggs, quartered

Place lamb bones in large saucepan, cover with water and simmer (with lid on) for an hour. Strain, reduce liquid to one cup and reserve. Sprinkle lamb with lemon juice.

Heat the oil in a pan, add the onions and lamb, and saute the meat until the onions are soft but not brown. Empty pan into a large bowl and add the potatoes, carrot, rice, tomato purée, cheese, oregano, garlic, mint, cinnamon, parsley and grated peel. Season with salt and pepper.

Add enough lamb stock to keep the filling moist while the pie bakes.

Grease a large baking tin (approximately 20 x 30 x 8cm). Add a base of eight filo sheets, brushing the melted butter between each sheet, completely covering the base and sides of the pan. Add the filling and spread evenly. Arrange the quartered eggs on top and cover with remaining layers of filo, brushing each layer including the top with melted butter. With a sharp knife, score the top three layers of pastry with large diamond or square shapes.

Bake for 40 to 50 minutes at 325°F (160°C) until pastry has turned a deep golden brown. Remove pie from the oven and let it stand for about 10 minutes, then cut it into diamonds or squares and serve warm.

However, the vast majority of the food you'll find in the Ionians falls under the general banner of Greek cuisine, which does not enjoy a reputation as one of the world's great cuisines. Maybe that's because many travellers have experienced Greek cooking only in tourist resorts. The old joke about the Greek woman who, on summer days, shouted to her husband 'Come and eat your lunch before it gets hot' is based on truth. Until recently, food was invariably served lukewarm – which is how Greeks prefer it. Most restaurants that cater to tourists have now cottoned on to the fact that foreigners expect cooked dishes to be served hot, and improved methods of warming meals (which includes the dreaded microwave) have made this easier. If your meal is not hot, ask that it be served *zesto*, or order grills, which have to be cooked to order. Greeks are fussy about fresh ingredients, and frozen food is rare.

Greeks eat out a lot, regardless of socio-economic status. Enjoying life is paramount to them and a large part of this enjoyment comes from eating and drinking with your friends.

By law, every eating establishment must display a written menu including prices. Bread will automatically be put on your table and usually costs between 100 dr and 200 dr, depending on the restaurant's category.

Where to Eat

The *taverna* is usually a traditional place with a rough-and-ready ambience, although some are more upmarket. The menu is usually displayed in the window or on the door. Some tavernas don't open until 8 pm, and then stay open until the early hours. Some are closed on Sunday.

Psistaria are places that specialise in spit roasts and charcoal-grilled food – usually lamb, pork or chicken, while a *psarotaverna* is a taverna specialising in fish.

An *estiatorio* restaurant is normally more sophisticated than a taverna or psistaria. You'll find damask tablecloths, smartly attired waiters and printed menus at each table with an English translation. Ready-made food is usually displayed in a *bain-marie* and there may also be a charcoal grill.

An *ouzeri* serves ouzo. Greeks believe it is essential to eat when drinking alcohol so, in traditional establishments, your drink will come with a small plate of titbits or *mezedes* (appetisers) – perhaps olives, a slice of feta and some pickled octopus. Ouzeria are becoming trendy and many now offer menus with both appetisers and main courses.

A *galaktopoleio* (literally 'milk shop') sells dairy produce including milk, butter, yogurt, rice pudding, cornflour pudding, custard, eggs, honey and bread. It may also sell home-made ice cream. Look for the sign '*pagoto politiko*' displayed outside. Most have seating and serve coffee and tea. They are inexpensive for breakfast and usually open from very early in the morning until evening.

A *zaharoplasteio* (patisserie) sells cakes (both traditional and western), chocolates, biscuits, sweets, coffee, soft drinks and, possibly, bottled alcoholic drinks. They usually have some seating.

Kafeneia are often regarded by foreigners as the last bastion of male chauvinism in Europe. With bare light bulbs, nicotine-stained walls, smoke-laden air, rickety wooden tables and raffia chairs, they are frequented by middle-aged and elderly Greek men in cloth caps who while away their time fiddling with worry beads, playing cards or backgammon, or engaged in heated political discussion.

It was once unheard of for women to enter a kafeneio but in large cities this situation is changing. In rural areas, Greek women are rarely seen inside kafeneia. When a female traveller enters one, she is inevitably treated courteously and with friendship if she manages a few Greek words of greeting. If you feel inhibited about going into a kafeneio, opt for outside seating. You'll feel less intrusive.

Kafeneia originally only served Greek coffee but now most also serve soft drinks, Nescafé and beer. They are generally fairly cheap, with Greek coffee costing about 150 dr and Nescafé with milk 250 dr or less. Most kafeneia are open all day every day, but some close during siesta time (roughly from 3 to 5 pm).

You'll find plenty of pizzerias, creperies and *gelaterias* (which sell Italian-style ice cream in various flavours). International restaurants are rare although you'll find the odd Chinese restaurant in the most touristy resorts in Corfu and Zakynthos.

Meals

Breakfast Most Greeks have Greek coffee and perhaps a cake or pastry for breakfast. Budget hotels and pensions offering breakfast provide it continental-style (rolls or bread with jam, and tea or coffee) and up-market hotels serve breakfast buffets (western and continental-style).

Otherwise, restaurants and galaktopoleia serve bread with butter, jam or honey; eggs; and the budget travellers' favourite, yogurt *(yiaourti)* with honey. In tourist areas, many menus offer an 'English' breakfast – which means bacon and eggs.

Lunch This is eaten late – between 1 and 3 pm – and may be either a snack or a complete meal. The main meal can be lunch or dinner – or both. Greeks enjoy eating and often have two large meals a day.

Dinner Greeks also eat dinner late. Many people don't start to think about food until about 9 pm, which is why some restaurants don't bother to open their doors until after 8 pm. In tourist areas dinner is often served earlier.

A full dinner in Greece begins with appetisers and/or soup, followed by a main course of either ready-made food, grilled meat, or fish. Only very posh restaurants or those pandering to tourists include western-style desserts on the menu. Greeks usually eat cakes separately in a galaktopoleio or zaharoplasteio.

Greek Specialities
Snacks Favourite Greek snacks include pretzel rings sold by street vendors, *tyropitta* (cheese pie), *bougatsa* (custard-filled pastry), *spanakopitta* (spinach pie) and *sandouits* (sandwiches). Street vendors sell various nuts and dried seeds such as pumpkin for 200 dr to 400 dr a bag. Chestnuts are roasted on the roadsides in winter.

Mezedes In a simple taverna, possibly only three or four mezedes (appetisers) will be offered – perhaps taramasalata (fish-roe dip), tzatziki (yogurt, cucumber and garlic dip), olives and feta (sheep or goat's milk) cheese. Ouzeria and restaurants usually offer wider selections.

Mezedes include *ohtapodi* (octopus), *garides* (shrimp), *kalamaria* (squid), dolmades (stuffed vine leaves), *melitzanos-*

alata (aubergine or eggplant dip) and *mavromatika* (black-eyed beans). Hot mezedes include *keftedes* (meatballs), *fasolia* (white haricot beans), *gigantes* (lima beans), *loukanika* (little sausages), tyropitta, spanakopitta, *bourekaki* (tiny meat pie), *kolokythakia* (deep-fried zucchini), *melitzana* (deep-fried aubergine) and *saganaki* (fried cheese).

It is quite acceptable to make a full meal of these instead of a main course. Three plates of mezedes are about equivalent in price and quantity to one main course. You can also order a *pikilia* (mixed plate).

Soups Soup is a satisfying starter or, indeed, an economical meal in itself with bread and a salad. *Psarosoupa* is a filling fish soup with vegetables, while *kakavia* (Greek bouillabaisse) is laden with seafood and more expensive. *Fasolada* (bean soup) is also a meal in itself. *Avgolemano soupa* (egg and lemon soup) is usually prepared from a chicken stock. If you're into offal, don't miss the traditional Easter soup *mayiritsa* at this festive time.

Salads The ubiquitous (and no longer inexpensive) Greek or village salad, *horiatiki salata*, is a side dish for Greeks, but many drachma-conscious tourists make it a main dish. It consists of tomato, cucumber, peppers, onions, olives and feta cheese, sprinkled with oregano and dressed with olive oil and lemon juice. A tomato salad often comes with onions, cucumber and olives, and, with bread, makes a satisfying lunch. In winter, try the cheaper *radikia salata* (dandelion salad).

Main Dishes The most common main courses are *moussaka* (layers of eggplant or zucchini, minced meat and potatoes topped with cheese sauce and baked), *pastitsio* (baked cheese-topped macaroni and bechamel, with or without minced meat), dolmades and *yemista* (stuffed tomatoes or green peppers). Other main courses include *giouvetsi* (casserole of lamb or veal and pasta), *stifado* (meat stewed with onions), *soutzoukakia* (spicy meatballs in tomato sauce, also known as Smyrna sausages) and *salingaria* (snails in oil with herbs). *Melizanes papoutsakia* is baked eggplant stuffed with meat and tomatoes and topped with cheese, which looks, as its Greek name suggests, like a little shoe. Spicy loukanika is a good budget choice and comes with potatoes or rice. Lamb fricassee, cooked with lettuce, *arni fricassée me maroulia*, is usually filling enough for two to share.

Fish is usually sold by weight in restaurants, but is not as cheap nor as widely available as it used to be. Ironically it is in summer when the fresh fish supplies start thinning out, and if you are in the Ionians in August you will probably be disappointed with the poor selection and poor quality of the fish on offer. Some restaurants in the Ionians import their fish from other parts of Greece or abroad, and in the tackier resort areas, many restaurants serve frozen fish to their culinary indiscriminating clientele.

Calamari (squid), deep-fried in batter, remains a tasty option for the budget traveller at 1000 dr to 1400 dr for a generous serve. Other reasonably priced fish (about 1000 dr a portion) are *marides* (whitebait), sometimes cloaked in onion, pepper and tomato sauce, and *gopes*, which are similar to sardines. More expensive are *ohtapodi* (octopus), *bakaliaros* (cod), *xifias* (swordfish) and *glossa* (sole). Ascending the price scale further are *synagrida* (snapper) and *barbounia* (red mullet). *Astakos* (lobster) and *karabida* (crayfish) are top of the range at about 10,000 dr per kg.

Fish is mostly grilled or fried. More imaginative fish dishes include shrimp casserole and mussel or octopus saganaki (fried with tomato and cheese). Freshwater fish are not widely available in the Ionians.

Desserts Greek cakes and puddings include *baklava* (layers of filo pastry filled with honey and nuts), *loukoumades* (puffs or fritters with honey or syrup), *kataïfi* (chopped nuts inside shredded wheat pastry or filo soaked in honey), *rizogalo* (rice pudding), *loukoumi* (Turkish delight), *halva* (made from semolina or sesame seeds) and *pagoto* (ice cream). Tavernas and restaurants usually only have a few of these on the menu. The best places to go for these delights are galaktopoleia or zaharoplasteia.

Vegetarian Food You won't find many dedicated vegetarian restaurants in the Ionians – or the rest of Greece for that matter. However, nonmeat-eaters shouldn't have too much difficulty, and can easily make a meal out of several vegetarian mezes.

Unfortunately, many vegetable soups and stews are based on meat stocks. Fried vegetables are safe bets as olive oil is always used – never lard. Vegetarians who eat eggs can rest assured that an economical omelette can be whipped up just about anywhere. Salads are cheap, fresh, substantial and very nourishing. Some other options are yogurt, rice pudding, cheese and spinach pies, and nuts. Creperies also offer tasty vegetarian selections.

Lent, incidentally, is a good time for vegetarians because the meat is missing from many dishes.

Fast Food Western-style fast food has arrived in Greece in a big way and the Ionians are no exception. 'Mac' fans may have difficulty locating their favourite burger; the Greek substitute is Goody's, which also has a good salad bar.

It's hard, though, to beat eat-on-the-street Greek offerings. Foremost among them are the *gyros* and the souvlaki. The gyros is a giant skewer laden with slabs of seasoned meat which grills slowly as it rotates and the meat is trimmed steadily from the outside; souvlaki are small individual kebab sticks. Both are served wrapped in pitta bread, with salad and lashings of tzatziki.

Another favourite is *tost*, which is a bread roll cut in half, stuffed with the filling(s) of your choice, buttered on the outside and then flattened in a heavy griddle iron.

Fruit Greece grows many varieties of fruit. Most visitors will be familiar with *syka* (figs), *rodakina* (peaches), *stafylia* (grapes), *karpouzi* (watermelon), *milo* (apples), *portokalia* (oranges) and *kerasia* (cherries).

Many will not, however, have encountered the *frangosyko* (prickly pear). Also known as the Barbary fig, it is the fruit of the opuntia cactus, recognisable by the thick green spiny pads that form its trunk. The fruit are borne around the edge of the pads in late summer and autumn and vary in colour from pale orange to deep red. They are delicious but need to be approached with extreme caution because of the thousands of tiny prickles (invisible to the naked eye) that cover their skin. Never pick one up with your bare hands. They must be peeled before you can eat them. The simplest way to do this is to trim the ends off with a knife and then slit the skin from end to end.

Another fruit that will be new to many people is the *mousmoula* (loquat). These small orange fruit are among the first of summer, reaching the market in mid-May. The flesh is juicy and pleasantly acidic.

Self-Catering Eating out in the Ionians is as much an entertainment as a gastronomic experience, so to self-cater is to sacrifice a lot. But if you are on a low budget you will need to make the sacrifice – for breakfast and lunch at any rate. All towns and villages of any size have supermarkets (or at least a

minimarket), fruit and vegetable stalls and bakeries.

The major towns on each island all have regular street markets. Only in isolated villages is food choice limited. You may only find one all-purpose shop – a *pantopoleio* – which will stock meat, vegetables, fruit, bread and tinned foods.

DRINKS
Nonalcoholic Drinks
Coffee & Tea Greek coffee is the national drink. It is a legacy of Ottoman rule and, until the Turkish invasion of Cyprus in 1974, the Greeks called it Turkish coffee. It is served with the grounds, without milk, in a small cup. Connoisseurs claim there are at least 30 variations of Greek coffee, but most people know only three – *glyko* (sweet), *metrio* (medium) and *sketo* (without sugar).

The next most popular coffee is instant, called Nescafé (which it usually is). Ask for Nescafé *me ghala* (pronounced 'me **ga**-la') if you want it with milk. In summer, Greeks drink Nescafé chilled, with or without milk and sugar – this version is called frappé.

Espresso and filtered coffee, once sold only in trendy cafes, are now also widely available.

Tea is inevitably made with a tea bag.

Nes Frappé

You can hardly miss the forest of straws sprouting from glasses of frothy-topped black liquid at countless street cafes throughout Greece. Nes(café) frappé has almost universally overtaken the traditional Greek (or Turkish) coffee as the nation's favourite beverage. But what could possibly be the attraction of a glass of cold water, flavoured with a spoonful of instant coffee and sugar, processed to resemble a glass of Guinness stout and then chilled with ice cubes?

Nes frappé is not a beverage to be taken in a hurry; it is certainly not a beverage to be drunk for the caffeine hit that you might expect from traditional coffee. Its primary role is that of a 'ticket' to sit at a street cafe in order to idly chat and smoke. Its arrival at the table, however, is treated with almost reverential ceremony. Firstly the imbiber will dutifully stir the ice cubes to ensure that every molecule of Nes frappé is equally chilled, and then the first minuscule sip is taken. It is considered extremely bad form to drink the mixture quickly, so never order one if you intend to quench your thirst in Greek company. The next sip may follow between five and 10 minutes later; in fact, the whole drinking procedure may take up to an hour.

The drink's universal popularity throughout the country and at all times of the year may be a puzzle to observers, for its appeal as a beverage is surely limited. The cafe owners, however, are not complaining – at 500 dr a shot, it is a sure-fire money spinner.

Fruit Juice & Soft Drinks Packaged fruit juices are available everywhere. Fresh orange juice is also widely available, but doesn't come cheap. The products of all the major soft-drink multinationals are available everywhere in cans and bottles, along with local brands.

Milk Fresh milk is easily found at minimarkets and supermarkets – although in smaller villages supplies can run out by the end of the day. A litre costs about 350 dr. UHT milk is available almost everywhere, as is condensed milk.

Water Tap water is safe to drink in Greece, although sometimes it doesn't taste too good. Most people prefer to drink bottled spring water, sold widely in 500mL and 1.5L plastic bottles. If you're happy with tap water, fill a container with it before embarking on ferries or you'll wind up paying through the nose for bottled water. Sparkling mineral water is rare.

Alcoholic Drinks

Beer Beer lovers will find the market dominated by the major northern European breweries. The most popular beers are Amstel and Heineken, both brewed locally under licence. Other beers brewed locally are Henniger, Kaiser, Kronenbourg and Tuborg.

The only local beer is Mythos, launched in 1997 and widely available. It has proved popular with drinkers who find the northern European beers a bit sweet.

Imported lagers, stouts and beers are found in tourist spots such as music bars and discos. You might even spot Newcastle Brown, Carlsberg, Castlemaine XXXX and Guinness.

Supermarkets are the cheapest place to buy beer, and bottles are cheaper than cans. A 500mL bottle of Amstel or Mythos costs about 200 dr (including 25 dr deposit on the bottle), while a 500mL can costs about 260 dr. Amstel also produces a low-alcohol beer and a bock, which is dark, sweet and strong.

Wine According to mythology, the Greeks invented or discovered wine and it has been produced in Greece on a large scale for more than 3000 years.

The modern wine industry, though, is still very much in its infancy. Until the 1950s, most Greek wines were sold in bulk and were seldom distributed any further afield than the nearest town. It wasn't until industrialisation (and the resulting rapid urban growth) that there was much call for bottled wine. Quality control was unheard of until 1969, when appellation laws were introduced as a precursor to applying for membership of the European Community. Wines have improved significantly since then.

Kefallonia is the only important wine producer among the Ionian islands. The Kefallonian Robola de Cephalonie is a superb dry white and one of the best wines in Greece (see boxed text 'Kefallonian Wine'). Corfu produces wines made from the white Kakotrygis and the red Petrokorythos grapes, as well as the Corfiot version of Robola, Kotanitis, Phidia, Mavrodaphne, white Muscat and Martzavi. Other good wines in the region are the local red wine, Thiako, made on Ithaki, Vertzami from Lefkada and Verdea, a white wine, which is produced on Zakynthos.

Some of the most popular and reasonably priced wines from other parts of Greece include Rotonda, Kambas, Boutari, Calliga and Lac des Roches. Boutari's Naoussa is worth looking out for. It's a dry red wine from the Naoussa area of northwest Macedonia.

Retsina For most travellers to Greece retsina (resinated wine) is an acquired taste but sampling it, either in small or large quantities, is an essential part of the experience. This wine, flavoured with pine resin and a speciality of Attica and Central Greece, is also commonly available in most tavernas in the Ionians, and will often be your only choice if you don't want to fork out for a bottle. It is usually at its best when taken from the barrel. The bottled variety can be wicked.

Spirits Ouzo is the most popular aperitif in Greece. Distilled from grape stems and flavoured with anise, it is similar to the

Kefallonian Wine

Wine has been produced in Kefallonia since ancient times, and all of the island's subsequent rulers sought to exploit the potential of Kefallonia's vineyards. Following the Frankish occupiers, the Venetians were so taken by Kefallonian wine that at one point they prohibited the exportation of muscat to anywhere other than Venice.

Charles Napier, one of the earliest British governors of the Ionians, could see the possibilities of a wine industry on the island when he wrote that 'It is to be regretted that some speculator, versed in the mode of making wine in Madeira, or in France, does not settle in Kefallonia. There can be no doubt that he would succeed.'

The wine industry started to be developed in the mid-19th century when a French company set up a wine-making and bottling operation. By 1872, Ernest Toole, a British businessman, was exporting wines to Germany from his own vineyard on the island. In the 20th century, however, the industry went into decline, suffering severely during the two World Wars, and virtually grinding to a halt after the earthquakes of 1953. Since the 1960s there have been constant improvements.

One of the reasons for which Kefallonian wine has always been better than that of the other islands is the persistence of the various viticulturists in growing the Robola variety.

The word Robola is thought to come from the Latin *ribola*, a red wine which was produced during the 14th century in Istria (in the north-eastern corner of Italy). Another etymological theory attributes the name to *roboli*, a chestnut which thrives in the Epirus region, whose timber is used to make barrels where, traditionally, Robola wine ages best.

The white wines produced on Kefallonia are made from Robola, Tsaoussi, Muscat, Zakynthino and Vostilidi grapes, while the reds come from Mavrodaphne and Thiniatiko grapes. Three of these varieties – Robola, Muscat and Mavrodaphne – are classified as appellation of origin wines. The Robola is one of Greece's best white wines and the Robola grapes cover about 1400 hectares of the island.

There are now six wineries on Kefallonia: the Robola Co-operative in Omola, John Kalligas in Kaligata (Livatho), Andreas Vitoratos and Evryviadis Sclavos on the Lixourian Peninsula, the Spyros Kosmetatos-Gentilini winery in Minies (near Argostoli) and Yannikostas Metaxas in Mavrata (near Skala). At most of these you can call in to taste and buy the wines.

TRUDI CANAVAN

Middle Eastern *arak*, Turkish *raki* and French Pernod. Clear and colourless, it turns white when water is added. A 700mL bottle of a popular brand like Ouzo 12, Olympic or Sans Rival costs about 1200 dr in supermarkets. In an ouzeri, a glass costs from 250 dr to 500 dr. It will be served neat, with a separate glass of water to be used for dilution.

The second most popular spirit is Greek brandy, which is dominated by the Metaxa label. Metaxa comes in a wide choice of grades, starting with the three star version – a high-octane product with little finesse. You can pick up a bottle in a supermarket for about 1500 dr. The quality improves as you go through the grades: five star, seven star, VSOP, Golden Age and finally the top-shelf Grand Olympian Reserve (5600 dr). Other reputable brands include Cambas and Votrys.

If you're travelling off the beaten track, you may come across *chipura*. Like ouzo, it's made from grape stems but without the anise. It's an acquired taste, much like Irish poteen – and packs a similar punch. You'll most likely encounter chipura in village kafeneia or private homes.

ENTERTAINMENT
Cinemas
Greeks are keen movie-goers. There are cinemas in the main towns of Corfu, Zakynthos, Kefallonia and Lefkada. Outdoor cinemas are used in some places in summer.

English-language films are usually shown in English with Greek subtitles. Admission ranges from 1000 dr in small-town movie houses to 1800 dr at plush big-city cinemas.

Discos & Music Bars
Discos can be found in big resort areas, though not in the numbers of a decade ago.

Most young Greeks prefer to head for the music bars that have proliferated to fill the void. These bars normally specialise in a particular style of music – Greek, modern rock, 60s rock, techno and, very occasionally, jazz.

Classical Music, Opera, Dance & Theatre
There are various cultural festivals in the Ionians during summer which attract Greek and international performers of classical music, ballet and modern dance and theatre. In addition, both Corfu Town and Argostoli on Kefallonia have theatres which are used year-round for performances.

See Public Holidays & Special Events earlier in this chapter and the individual island chapters.

Traditional Music
Most of the live music you hear around the resorts is tame stuff laid on for the tourists. There are a couple of restaurants in Zakynthos where you can still hear beautiful kantades.

Folk Dancing
Folk dancing is an integral part of all festival celebrations and there is often impromptu folk dancing in tavernas.

SPECTATOR SPORTS
The Ionians are not strong on spectator sports – except via television.

Soccer (football) remains the most popular spectator sport, although basketball is catching up fast following the successes of Greek sides in European club competition in recent years. Greek soccer teams, in contrast, have seldom had much impact on the European club competition, and the national team is the source of constant hair-wrenching. The side's only appearance in the World Cup finals, in the USA in 1994, brought a string of heavy defeats.

The two glamour clubs of Greek soccer are Olympiakos of Piraeus and Panathinaikos of Athens. The capital supplies a third of the clubs in the first division. The season lasts from September to mid-May; cup matches are played on Wednesday night and first division games on Sunday afternoon. Games are often televised. Entry to a match costs around 1500 dr for the cheapest terrace tickets, or 3000 dr for a decent seat. Fixtures and results are given in the *Athens News*.

Olympiakos and Panathinaikos are also the glamour clubs of Greek basketball. Panathinaikos was the European champion in 1996, and Olympiakos followed suit in 1997.

SHOPPING
The best thing to buy as a souvenir of your trip to the Ionians is probably the superb honey and olive oil produced there. Kythira has the best honey and Paxi the best olive oil.

Various shops in Corfu and Paxi sell beautiful objects carved out of olive wood, such as salad bowls and servers, ornaments, even children's toys. Corfu is renowned for its special kumquat liqueur and *mandolato* nougat. Village women still make lace in traditional ways and produce superb hand-embroidered linens on Kefallonia, Lefkada, Zakynthos and other islands. The best places to buy these handicrafts are mountain villages, away from the touristy beach resorts. Kefallonia is famous for its Robola wine. Many visitors leave with jars of quince jam in their luggage.

As in other parts of Greece, ceramics are produced on the Ionians and you can pick up vibrant locally made painted tableware.

It is illegal to buy, sell, possess or export any antiquity in Greece (see Customs earlier in this chapter). However, there are antiques and 'antiques'; a lot of items only a century or two old are regarded as junk, rather than part of the national heritage.

These items include handmade furniture and odds and ends from rural areas and ecclesiastical ornaments from churches. You can also pick up attractive reproduction icons in most larger towns.

Tagari bags are woven wool bags – often brightly coloured – which hang from the shoulder by a rope. Minus the rope, they make attractive cushion covers.

Getting There & Away

AIR

Most travellers arrive in Greece by air, the cheapest and quickest way to get there.

Airports & Airlines

There are international airports at Corfu, Kefallonia, Zakynthos and Preveza (for Lefkada) but these are for charters only – they do not take scheduled international flights. Kythira has a small airport for Olympic Airways domestic flights to and from Athens.

International scheduled flights to Greece are handled mainly by Athens (including all intercontinental traffic) and Thessaloniki. In summer there are domestic connections with Olympic Airways from Athens to Corfu (four daily), Kefallonia (two daily), Zakynthos (one daily and two on Sunday), Preveza (three a week) and Kythira (five a week). These services are less frequent during winter.

Olympic Airways is no longer Greece's only international airline. Cronus Airlines flies direct from Athens to London and Paris, and via Thessaloniki to Cologne, Dusseldorf, Frankfurt and Stuttgart. Air Manos operates cheap charter flights to London and Manchester, and Air Greece flies from Athens to the Italian port of Bari. Air Greece has a daily flight from Corfu to Athens, and flights from Corfu via Athens to Crete, Rhodes, Thessaloniki, Mytilini and Santorini.

Buying Tickets

If you are flying to Greece from outside Europe, the plane ticket will probably be the most expensive item in your travel budget, and buying it can be an intimidating business. There will be a multitude of airlines and travel agents hoping to separate you from your money, so take time to research the options. Start early – some of the cheapest tickets must be bought months in advance, and popular flights tend to sell out early. Beware that in high season the do-mestic flights to the Ionian islands from Athens sell out months in advance, so it's best to book as early as possible.

Discounted tickets fall into two categories – official and unofficial. Official discount schemes include advance-purchase tickets, budget fares, Apex, Super-Apex and a few other variations on the theme. These tickets can be bought from travel agents or direct from the airline. They often have restrictions – advance purchase being the usual one. There might also be restrictions on how long you must be away, such as a minimum of 14 days and a maximum of one year.

Unofficial tickets are simply discounted tickets the airlines release through selected travel agents.

Return tickets can often be cheaper than a one-way ticket. Generally, you can find discounted tickets at prices as low as, or even lower than, Apex or budget tickets. Phone around travel agents for bargains.

Warning

The information in this chapter is particularly vulnerable to change: Prices for international travel are volatile, routes are introduced and cancelled, schedules change, special deals come and go, and rules and visa requirements are amended. Airlines and governments seem to take a perverse pleasure in making price structures and regulations as complicated as possible. You should check directly with the airline or a travel agent to make certain you understand how a fare (and ticket you may buy) works. In addition, the travel industry is highly competitive and there are many lurks and perks.

The upshot of this is that you should get opinions, quotes and advice from as many airlines and travel agents as possible before you part with your hard-earned cash. The details given in this chapter should be regarded as pointers and are not a substitute for your own careful, up-to-date research.

Air Travel Glossary

Cancellation Penalties If you have to cancel or change a discounted ticket, there are often heavy penalties involved; insurance can sometimes be taken out against these penalties. Some airlines impose penalties on regular tickets as well, particularly against 'no-show' passengers.

Courier Fares Businesses often need to send urgent documents or freight securely and quickly. Courier companies hire people to accompany the package through customs and, in return, offer a discount ticket which is sometimes a phenomenal bargain. However, you may have to surrender all your baggage allowance and take only carry-on luggage.

Full Fares Airlines traditionally offer 1st class (coded F), business class (coded J) and economy class (coded Y) tickets. These days there are so many promotional and discounted fares available that few passengers pay full economy fare.

Lost Tickets If you lose your airline ticket an airline will usually treat it like a travellers cheque and, after inquiries, issue you with another one. Legally, however, an airline is entitled to treat it like cash and if you lose it then it's gone forever. Take good care of your tickets.

Onward Tickets An entry requirement for many countries is that you have a ticket out of the country. If you're unsure of your next move, the easiest solution is to buy the cheapest onward ticket to a neighbouring country or a ticket from a reliable airline which can later be refunded if you do not use it.

Open-Jaw Tickets These are return tickets where you fly out to one place but return from another. If available, this can save you backtracking to your arrival point.

Overbooking Since every flight has some passengers who fail to show up, airlines often book more passengers than they have seats. Usually excess passengers make up for the no-shows, but occasionally somebody gets 'bumped' onto the next available flight. Guess who it is most likely to be? The passengers who check in late.

Promotional Fares These are officially discounted fares, available from travel agencies or direct from the airline.

Reconfirmation If you don't reconfirm your flight at least 72 hours prior to departure, the airline may delete your name from the passenger list. Ring to find out if your airline requires reconfirmation.

Restrictions Discounted tickets often have various restrictions on them – such as needing to be paid for in advance and incurring a penalty to be altered. Others are restrictions on the minimum and maximum period you must be away.

Round-the-World Tickets RTW tickets give you a limited period (usually a year) in which to circumnavigate the globe. You can go anywhere the carrying airlines go, as long as you don't backtrack. The number of stopovers or total number of separate flights is decided before you set off and they usually cost a bit more than a basic return flight.

Transferred Tickets Airline tickets cannot be transferred from one person to another. Travellers sometimes try to sell the return half of their ticket, but officials can ask you to prove that you are the person named on the ticket. On an international flight tickets are compared with passports.

Travel Periods Ticket prices vary with the time of year. There is a low (off-peak) season and a high (peak) season, and often a low-shoulder season and a high-shoulder season as well. Usually the fare depends on your outward flight – if you depart in the high season and return in the low season, you pay the high-season fare.

If you are buying a ticket to fly out of Greece, Athens is one of the major centres in Europe for budget air fares.

In Greece, as everywhere else, always remember to reconfirm your onward or return bookings by the specified time – usually it's 72 hours before departure on international flights. If you don't, there's a risk you'll turn up at the airport only to find you've missed your flight because it was rescheduled, or that the airline has given the seat to someone else.

Charter Flights

In summer there are regular charter flights from northern European countries to Corfu, Kefallonia, Zakynthos and Preveza (for Lefkada). Charter flight tickets are for seats left vacant on flights which have been block-booked by package companies. Tickets are cheap but conditions apply. Theoretically, a ticket should be accompanied by an accommodation booking. This is normally circumvented by travel agents issuing accommodation vouchers which are not meant to be used – even if the hotel named on the voucher actually exists. The law requiring accommodation bookings was introduced in the 1980s to prevent budget travellers flying to Greece on cheap charter flights and sleeping rough on beaches or in parks. It hasn't worked.

Charter flight tickets are valid for up to four weeks, and usually have a minimum-stay requirement of at least three days. Sometimes it's worth buying a charter return even if you think you want to stay for longer than four weeks. The tickets can be so cheap that you can afford to throw away the return portion.

The travel section of major newspapers is the place to look for cheap charter deals. More information on charter flights is given later in this chapter under specific point-of-origin headings.

Scheduled Flights & Domestic Connections

If you are flying to the Ionians on a scheduled flight, chances are you'll arrive in Athens (or possibly Thessaloniki) and then take a domestic flight to your final destination. The domestic portion is incorporated into your ticket by your travel agent.

The vast majority of domestic flights are handled by the country's much-maligned national carrier, Olympic Airways, together with its offshoot, Olympic Aviation.

Olympic Airways has offices wherever there are flights, as well as in other major towns. The head office in Athens (☎ 01-966 6666) is at Leoforos Syngrou 96, and its Web site is at www.olympic-airways.gr. Tickets can be purchased at the airport, from Olympic Airways offices or any travel agent.

However, forward planning is advisable as these domestic flights to the Ionians are packed in high season.

Summer Flights between Athens & the Ionian Islands

The following information is for flights from mid-June to late September. Outside these months, the number of flights to the islands drops considerably. Prices are for one-way fares and include domestic airport tax of 3400 dr paid as part of the ticket.

destination	flights/ week	duration	price
Corfu	26	50 mins	20,700 dr
Kefallonia	10	60 mins	17,900 dr
Kythira	6	45 mins	14,400 dr
Preveza (Lefkada)	5	60 mins	13,900 dr
Zakynthos	7	55 mins	17,400 dr

There are also three flights a week from Thessaloniki to Corfu in summer. The journey takes 50 minutes and a one-way fare costs 20,900 dr.

The free-baggage allowance on Olympic Airways domestic flights is 15kg. However, this does not apply when the domestic flight is part of an international journey. The international free-baggage allowance of 20kg is then extended to the domestic sector. This allowance applies to all tickets for domestic travel sold and issued outside Greece. Olympic offers a 25% student discount on domestic flights, but only if the flight is part of an international journey.

There are no inter-island flights between the Ionian islands (see the Getting Around chapter).

Travel Agents

Many of the larger travel agents use the travel pages of national newspapers and magazines to promote their special deals. Before you make a decision, there are a number of questions you need to ask about the ticket. Find out the airline, the route, the duration of the journey, the stopovers allowed, any restrictions on the ticket and – above all – the price. Ask whether the fare quoted includes all taxes and other possible inclusions.

You may discover when you start ringing around that those impossibly cheap flights, charter or otherwise, are not available, but the agency just happens to know of another one that 'costs a bit more'. Or the agent may claim to have the last two seats available for Greece for the whole of July, which they will hold for a maximum of two hours only. Don't panic – keep ringing around.

If you are flying to Greece from the USA, South-East Asia or the UK, you will probably find the cheapest flights are being advertised by obscure agencies whose names haven't yet reached the telephone directory – the proverbial bucket shops. Many such firms are honest and solvent, but there are a few rogues who will take your money and disappear, only to reopen elsewhere a month or two later under a new name. If you feel suspicious about a firm, don't give it all the money at once – leave a small deposit and pay the balance when you get the ticket. If it insists on cash in advance, go somewhere else or be prepared to take a big risk. Once you have booked the flight with the agency, ring the airline to check you have a confirmed booking.

It can be easier on the nerves to pay a bit more for the security of a better known travel agent. Firms such as STA Travel, with offices worldwide, Council Travel in the USA or Travel CUTS in Canada offer good prices to Europe (including Greece), and are unlikely to disappear overnight.

Travel Insurance

The kind of cover you get depends on your insurance and type of ticket, so ask both your insurer and your ticket-issuing agency to explain where you stand. Ticket loss is usually covered.

Buy travel insurance as early as possible. If you buy it just before you fly, you may find you're not covered for such problems as delays caused by industrial action. Make sure you have a separate record of all your ticket details – preferably a photocopy.

Paying for your ticket with a credit card sometimes provides limited travel insurance, and you may be able to reclaim the payment if the operator doesn't deliver.

Travellers with Special Needs

If you've broken a leg, require a special diet, are travelling in a wheelchair, are taking a baby, or whatever, let the airline staff know as soon as possible – preferably when booking your ticket. Check that your request has been registered when you reconfirm your booking (at least 72 hours before departure) and again when you check in at the airport.

Children under two years of age travel for 10% of the standard fare (or free on some airlines) as long as they don't occupy a seat. But they do not get a baggage allowance. 'Skycots' should be provided by the airline if requested in advance. These will take a child weighing up to about 10kg. Olympic Airways charges half-fare for accompanied children aged between two and 12 years, while most other airlines charge two-thirds.

Departure & Airport Taxes

There is an airport tax of 6800 dr on all international departures from Greece. This is paid when you buy your ticket, not at the airport.

The airport tax for domestic flights is 3400 dr, paid as part of the ticket.

The USA

The North Atlantic is the world's busiest long-haul air corridor, and the flight options to Europe (including Greece) are bewildering.

Microsoft's popular Expedia.com Web site at www.expedia.msn.com gives a good overview of the possibilities.

Other sites worth checking are the ITN (www.itn.net) and Travelocity (www.travelocity.com) sites.

The *New York Times*, *LA Times*, *Chicago Tribune* and *San Francisco Chronicle* and *Examiner* all publish weekly travel sections in which you'll find any number of travel agents' advertisements. Both Council Travel (www.counciltravel.com) and STA (www.sta-travel.com) have offices in major cities nationwide.

New York has the most direct flights to Athens. Olympic Airways has at least one flight a day, and Delta Airlines has three a week. Apex fares range from US$960 to US$1600, depending on the season and how long you want to stay away.

Boston is the only other east coast city with direct flights to Athens – on Saturday with Olympic Airways. Fares are the same as for flights from New York.

There are no direct flights to Athens from the west coast. There are, however, connecting flights to Athens from many US cities, either linking with Olympic Airways in New York or flying with one of the European national airlines to its home country, and then on to Athens. These connections usually involve a stopover of three or four hours.

One-way fares can work out very cheap on a stand-by basis. Airhitch (☎ 212-864 2000) specialises in this. It can get you to Europe one way for US$159 from the east coast and US$239 from the west coast, plus tax. Its Web site is www.airhitch.org.

Courier flights are another possibility. The International Association of Air Travel Couriers (☎ 561-582 8320, fax 582 1581) has flights from six US cities to a range of European capitals – but not Athens. Check its Web site at www.courier.org.

Budget travel agents in Greece offer the following one-way fares from Athens (prices do not include airport tax): Atlanta 110,000 dr, Chicago 110,000 dr, Los Angeles 125,000 dr and New York 85,000 dr. The domestic connection will have to be factored in on top of these tickets.

Canada

Olympic Airways has two flights weekly from Toronto to Athens via Montreal. There are no direct flights from Vancouver, but there are connecting flights via Toronto, Amsterdam, Frankfurt and London on Canadian Airlines, KLM, Lufthansa and British Airways.

Travel CUTS (☎ 1-888-838 CUTS) has offices in all major cities and is a good place to ask about cheap deals. You should be able to get to Athens from Toronto and Montreal for about C$1150 or from Vancouver for C$1500. The *Toronto Globe & Mail*, the *Toronto Star*, the *Montreal Gazette* and the *Vancouver Sun* all carry advertisements for cheap tickets.

For courier flights originating in Canada, contact FB On Board Courier Services in Montreal (☎ 514-631 2677). It can get you to London for C$575 return.

At the time of writing, budget travel agencies in Greece were advertising flights to Toronto for 105,000 dr and to Montreal for 100,000 dr, plus airport tax.

Australia

Olympic Airways has two flights weekly from Sydney and Melbourne to Athens. Return fares are normally priced from about A$1799 in low season to A$2199 in high season.

Thai International and Singapore Airlines also have convenient connections to Athens, as well as a reputation for good service. If you're planning on doing a bit of flying around Europe, it's worth checking around for special deals from the major European airlines. Alitalia, KLM and Lufthansa are three likely candidates with good European networks.

STA Travel and Flight Centre are two of Australia's major dealers in cheap fares. The Sunday tabloid newspapers are a good place to look for cheap flights, as well as the travel sections of the *Sydney Morning Herald* and Melbourne's *Age*.

If you're travelling from Greece to Australia, a one-way ticket from Athens to Sydney or Melbourne costs about 180,000 dr, plus airport tax.

New Zealand

There are no direct flights from New Zealand to Athens. There are connecting flights via Sydney, Melbourne, Bangkok and Singapore on Olympic Airways, United Airlines, Qantas Airways, Thai Airways and Singapore Airlines.

The UK

British Airways, Olympic Airways and Virgin Atlantic operate daily flights between London Heathrow and Athens. Pricing is very competitive, with all three offering return tickets for around UK£200 in high season, plus tax. These prices are for midweek departures; you will pay about UK£40 more for weekend departures.

There are connecting flights to Athens from Edinburgh, Glasgow and Manchester.

Greek newcomer Cronus Airlines (☎ 020-7580 3500) flies the London-Athens route five times weekly for UK£210.

The cheapest scheduled flights are with no-frills specialist EasyJet (☎ 0870 6 000 000), which has two Luton-Athens flights daily. One-way fares range from UK£89 to UK£139 in high season, and from a bargain UK£39 to UK£69 at other times. Its Web site is www.easyjet.com.

There are numerous charter flights between the UK and Greece. Typical London-Athens charter fares are UK£79/129 one way/return in the low season and UK£99/189 in the high season. These prices are for advance bookings, but even in high season it's possible to pick up last-minute deals for as little as UK£59/99.

Many travel agencies offer charter flights to the islands as well as to Athens. Most island destinations cost about UK£109/209 in high season.

Charter flights to Greece also fly from Birmingham, Cardiff, Glasgow, Luton, Manchester and Newcastle.

Contact the Air Travel Advisory Bureau (☎ 020-7636 5000) for information about current charter flight bargains; try its Web site at www.atab.co.uk.

London is Europe's major centre for discounted fares. Some of the most reputable agencies selling discount tickets are:

usit **CAMPUS Travel** (☎ 020-7730 3402, www .campustravel.co.uk) 52 Grosvenor Gardens, London SW1
Council Travel (☎ 020-7287 3337, www.council travel.com) 28A Poland St, London W1V 3DB
STA Travel (☎ 020-7361 6161, www.statravel .co.uk) 86 Old Brompton Rd, London SW7
Trailfinders (☎ 020-7937 5400) 215 Kensington High St, London W8

Listings publications such as *Time Out*, the Sunday papers, the *Evening Standard* and *Exchange & Mart* carry advertisements for cheap fares.

The *Yellow Pages* is worth scanning for travel agents' advertisements, and look out for the free magazines and newspapers widely available in London, especially *TNT*, *Footloose*, *Southern Cross* and *LAM* – you can pick them up outside the main train and tube stations.

Some travel agents specialise in flights for students aged under 30 and travellers aged under 26 (you need an ISIC card or an official youth card). Whatever your age, you should be able to find something to suit your budget.

Most British travel agents are registered with ABTA (Association of British Travel Agents). If you have paid for your flight through an ABTA-registered agent who then goes out of business, ABTA will guarantee a refund or an alternative. If an agency is registered with ABTA, its advertisements will usually say so.

If you're flying from Greece to the UK, budget fares start at 25,000 dr to London or 30,000 dr to Manchester, plus airport tax. Domestic connections from the Ionians to Athens will be on top of these tickets.

Continental Europe

Athens is linked to every major city in Europe by either Olympic Airways or the flag carrier of each country.

London is the discount capital of Europe, but Amsterdam, Frankfurt, Berlin and Paris are also major centres for cheap air fares.

Albania Olympic Airways has at least one flight a day from Tirana to Athens (US$224/ 407 one way/return), going via Thessaloniki

(US$171/311) twice weekly. Student discounts of 25% are available.

France Air France (π 0802 802 802) and Olympic Airways (π 01 42 65 92 42) have at least four Paris-Athens flights daily between them. Expect to pay from 2950FF to 3300FF in high season, dropping to about 2100FF at other times.

Cronus Airlines (π 01 47 42 56 77) flies the same route four times weekly. Olympic Airways also has three flights weekly to Athens from Marseille.

Charter flights are much cheaper. You'll pay around 2000FF in high season for a return flight from Paris to Athens. The fare to Athens drops to 1500FF in low season. Reliable travel agents include:

Air Sud (π 01 40 41 66 66) 18 Rue du Pont-Neuf, 75001 Paris
Atsaro (π 01 42 60 98 98) 9 Rue de l'Echelle, 75001 Paris
Bleu Blanc (π 01 40 21 31 31) 53 Avenue de la République, 75011 Paris
Héliades (π 01 53 27 28 21) 24-27 Rue Basfroi, 75011 Paris
La Grâce Autrement (π 01 44 41 69 95) 72 Boulevard Saint Michel, 75006 Paris
Nouvelles Frontières (π 08 03 33 33) 87 Boulevard de Grenelle, 75015 Paris
Planète Havas (π 01 53 29 40 00) 26 Avenue de l'Opéra, 75001 Paris

Germany Atlas Reisewelt has offices throughout Germany and is a good place to start checking prices.

In Berlin, Alternativ Tours (π 030-8 81 20 89), Wilmersdorfer Strasse 94, has discounted fares to just about anywhere in the world. SRS Studenten Reise Service (π 030-28 59 82 64), at Marienstrasse 23 near Friedrichstrasse station, offers special student (under 35) and youth (under 26) fares. Travel agents offering unpublished cheap flights advertise in *Zitty*, Berlin's fortnightly entertainment magazine.

In Frankfurt, try SRID Reisen (π 069-43 01 91), Berger Strasse 118.

The Netherlands Reliable travel agents in Amsterdam include:

Budget Air (π 020-627 12 51) Rokin 34
Malibu Travel (π 020-626 32 20) Prinsengracht 230
NBBS Reizen (π 020-624 09 89) Rokin 66

Following are some typical one-way fares (not including airport tax) from Athens to European destinations:

destination	one-way fare
Amsterdam	57,500 dr
Copenhagen	59,500 dr
Frankfurt	55,000 dr
Geneva	54,000 dr
Hamburg	52,000 dr
Madrid	73,000 dr
Milan	48,000 dr
Munich	55,000 dr
Paris	55,500 dr
Rome	42,000 dr
Zürich	53,500 dr

Turkey

Olympic Airways and Turkish Airlines share the İstanbul-Athens route, with at least one flight a day each. The full fare is US$250 one way. Olympic Airways also flies twice weekly between İstanbul and Thessaloniki (US$190). Students qualify for a 50% discount on both routes.

There are no direct flights from Ankara to Athens; all flights go via İstanbul.

Cyprus

Olympic Airways and Cyprus Airways share the Cyprus-Greece routes. Both airlines have three flights daily from Larnaca to Athens. Cyprus Airways also flies from Paphos to Athens once a week in winter, and twice a week in summer.

Tickets cost about 50,000 dr one way from Athens to Larnaca and Paphos, or 83,000 dr return.

LAND
Greek Mainland/Athens

Bus Arriving in Greece from its neighbouring countries by bus you will end up in either Athens or Thessaloniki, from where you can get connecting Greek KTEL buses to the Ionian islands or the nearest mainland ports

KTEL Bus Services

origin	destination	duration	price	frequency
Athens	Corfu	11 hours	8150 dr	2 daily
Athens	Paxi	8 hours	8150 dr	1 daily
Athens	Lefkada	5½ hours	6200 dr	4 daily
Athens	Kefallonia	8 hours	7500 dr	3 daily
Athens	Ithaki	7 hours	7100 dr	1 daily
Athens	Zakynthos	7 hours	6310 dr	4 daily
Athens	Patras	3 hours	3650 dr	up to 32 daily
Thessaloniki	Corfu	11 hours	8000 dr	1 daily
Igoumenitsa	Preveza	2½ hours	2100 dr	2 daily
Igoumenitsa	Thessaloniki	8 hours	7800 dr	1 daily
Patras	Lefkada	3 hours	3450 dr	2 daily
Patras	Zakynthos	3½ hours	2860 dr	4 daily
Athens	Gythio	5½ hours	4500 dr	4 daily
Athens	Sparta	4½ hours	3450 dr	10 daily
Sparta	Neapoli	4 hours	2350 dr	4 daily

(and then take a ferry). Relevant KTEL bus services are listed in the above table.

All the above fares include ferry tickets where applicable. In high season it is essential to reserve seats in advance.

Train The Ionian islands are most easily reached by the bus network. However if you are arriving in Athens by train, it might be more convenient to continue your journey by rail to Patras, from where you can commence your Ionian island-hopping (for Corfu, Paxi, Lefkada, Ithaki, Kefallonia and Zakynthos). You will need to change at Patras to either a ferry or a KTEL bus continuing to various island destinations. For Kythira, you can take a train from Athens as far as Kalamata (7 hours, 2160 dr, 4 daily), from where you will have to take a KTEL bus to either Gythio or Neapoli (via Sparta) and then the ferry.

There are two very distinct levels of service offered by the Greek Railways Organisation, OSE (Organismos Sidirodromon Ellados): the slow, stopping-all-stations services that crawl around the countryside, and the faster, modern intercity trains that link most major cities.

The slow trains represent the country's cheapest form of public transport. The fares haven't changed for years; 2nd class fares are absurdly cheap, and even 1st class is cheaper than bus travel. The downside is that the trains are painfully slow, uncomfortable and unreliable. The Athens-Patras journey takes five hours and 1st/2nd class tickets cost 2370/1580 dr.

The intercity trains which link the major cities are a much better way to travel. The services are not necessarily express – the Greek terrain is too mountainous for that – but the trains are modern and comfortable. There are 1st and 2nd class smoking/nonsmoking seats and there is a cafe-bar on board.

Ticket prices for intercity services are subject to a distance loading on top of the normal fares. Seat reservations should be made as far in advance as possible, especially in summer. The Athens-Patras trip takes 3½ hours and tickets cost 3970/2980 dr.

Tickets can be bought from train stations. There is a 20% discount on return tickets. You'll find information on fares and schedules on the Hellenic Railways Organisation Web site, www.ose.gr.

There are no trains in the Ionian islands.

Car & Motorcycle Getting to the Ionians by car or motorbike necessarily involves a ferry trip (except in the case of Lefkada which is connected to the mainland by a causeway), so head for the appropriate port.

For Corfu and Paxi, drivers should head for Igoumenitsa. From Athens take either the New National Road via Corinth (a toll highway) or the slower Old National Road which hugs the coast to Rio (9km east of Patras), then take the ferry across the Gulf of Corinth from Rio to Andirio in Sterea Ellada and continue north on the E55 to Igoumenitsa. The Rio-Andirio ferries operate every 15 minutes from 7 am to 11 pm, or every 30 minutes through the night. (Note that in winter severe weather conditions can mean that the Rio/Andirio ferry service stops.)

For Lefkada, follow the same route as for Igoumenitsa, leaving the E55 at Amfilohia where you head for Vonitsa then follow the directions for Lefkada. Having crossed the causeway you arrive in Lefkada Town.

For Kefallonia, you can take a ferry from Patras (to Sami) or from Kyllini (to Poros). From Athens take the New National Road (E95 and E65) via Corinth to Patras. For Kyllini, continue beyond Patras on the New National Road (E55). Kyllini is 13km off the New National Road about halfway between Patras and Pyrgos. If you are going to Zakynthos, you will need to take the ferry from Kyllini.

To get to Kythira, you will need to head to either Gythio or Neapoli in the Peloponnese. Take the E94/E92 out of Athens to Tripolis, then the E961 to Sparta and south to Gythio. For Neapoli, turn off the E961 after Sparta towards Skala, and follow the road signs.

Turkey

Bus The Hellenic Railways Organisation (OSE) operates Athens-İstanbul buses (22 hours) daily, except Wednesday, leaving the Peloponnese train station in Athens at 7 pm and travelling via Thessaloniki and Alexandroupolis. One-way fares are 21,800 dr from Athens, 14,300 dr from Thessaloniki. Students qualify for a 15% discount and children under 12 travel for half-fare.

Buses from İstanbul to Athens leave the Anadolu Terminal (Anatolia Terminal) at the Topkapi *otogar* (bus station) at 10 am daily except Sunday.

Train There are daily trains between Athens and İstanbul (19,000 dr) via Thessaloniki (13,000 dr) and Alexandroupolis (6350 dr). The service is incredibly slow and the train gets uncomfortably crowded. There are often delays at the border and the journey can take much longer than the supposed 22 hours.

You'd be well advised to take the bus. Inter-Rail Passes are valid in Turkey, but Eurail passes are not.

Car & Motorcycle If you are travelling between Greece and Turkey by private vehicle, the crossing points are at Kipi, 43km northeast of Alexandroupolis, and at Kastanies, 139km north-east of Alexandroupolis.

Bulgaria

Bus The OSE operates two Athens-Sofia buses (15 hours, 13,400 dr) daily except Monday, leaving at 7 am and 5 pm. It also operates Thessaloniki-Sofia buses (7½ hours, 5600 dr, three daily).

Train There is an Athens-Sofia train daily (18 hours, 10,330 dr) via Thessaloniki (nine hours, 6700 dr).

Car & Motorcycle The Bulgarian border crossing is at Promahonas, 145km northeast of Thessaloniki and 50km from Serres.

Albania

Bus There is a daily OSE bus between Athens and Tirana (12,600 dr) via Ioannina and Gjirokastër. The bus departs from Athens (Larisis train station) at 7 pm arriving in Tirana the following day at 5 pm. It leaves Ioannina at 7.30 am and passes through Gjirokastër at 10.30 am. On the return trip, the bus departs from Tirana at 7 am. There are buses from Thessaloniki to Korça (Korytsa in Greek) daily at 8 am. The fare is 6600 dr.

Car & Motorcycle If travelling by car or motorcycle, there are two crossing points between Greece and Albania. The main one is 60km north-west of Ioannina. Take the main Ioannina-Konitsa road and turn left at Kalpaki. This road leads to the border town of Kakavia. The other border crossing is at Krystallopigi, 14km west of Kotas on the Florina-Kastoria road. Kapshtica is the closest town on the Albanian side. It is possible to take a private vehicle into Albania, although it's not a great idea, because of security concerns and problems with obtaining spare parts. Always carry your passport in areas near the Albanian border.

Former Yugoslav Republic of Macedonia (FYROM)

Train There are Thessaloniki-Skopje trains (three hours, 4200 dr, two daily), which cross the border between Idomeni and Gevgelija. They leave Thessaloniki at 6 am and 5.30 pm. Both trains continue to the Serbian capital of Belgrade (12 hours, 11,500 dr). The 5.30 pm service goes all the way to Budapest (21 hours, 20,000 dr).

There are no trains between Florina and FYROM, although there may be trains to Skopje from the FYROM side of the border.

Car & Motorcycle There are two border crossings between Greece and FYROM. One is at Evzoni, 68km north of Thessaloniki. This is the main highway to Skopje which continues to Belgrade.

The other border crossing is at Niki, 16km north of Florina. This road leads to Bitola, and continues to Ohrid, once a popular tourist resort on the shores of Lake Ohrid.

Western Europe

Overland travel between Western Europe and Greece is almost a thing of the past. Air fares are so cheap that land transport cannot compete. Travelling from the UK to Greece through Europe means crossing various borders, so check whether any visas are required before setting out.

Bus There are no bus services to Greece from the UK, nor from anywhere else in northern Europe. Bus companies can no longer compete with cheap air fares.

Train Unless you have a Eurail pass or are aged under 26 and eligible for a discounted fare, travelling to Greece by train is prohibitively expensive. For example, the full one way/return fare from London to Athens is UK£265/521, including the Eurostar service from London to Paris.

Greece is part of the Eurail network. Eurail passes can only be bought by residents of non-European countries and are supposed to be purchased before arriving in Europe. They can, however, be bought in Europe as long as your passport proves that you've been there for less than six months. In London, head for the Rail Europe Travel Centre (☎ 08705-848 848), 179 Piccadilly, W1. Sample fares include UK£461 for an adult Eurail Flexipass, which permits 10 days 1st class travel in two months, and UK£323 for the equivalent youth pass.

If you are starting your European travels in Greece, you can buy your Eurail pass from the Hellenic Railways Organisation offices at Karolou 1 and Filellinon 17 in Athens, and at the station in Patras and Thessaloniki.

Greece is also part of the Inter-Rail Pass system, but the pass for those aged over 26 is not valid in France, Italy and Switzerland – rendering it useless if you want to use the pass to get to Greece. Inter-Rail Youth Passes for those under 26 are divided into zones. A Global Pass (all zones) costs UK£259 and is valid for a month. You need to be under 26 on the first day of travel and to have lived in Europe for at least six months.

Car & Motorcycle Before the troubles in the former Yugoslavia began, most motorists driving from the UK to Greece opted for the direct route: Ostend, Brussels, Salzburg and then down the Yugoslav highway through Zagreb, Belgrade and Skopje and crossing the border to Evzoni.

These days most people drive to an Italian port and get a ferry direct to Igoumenitsa (via Corfu) or to Patras on the mainland. Coming from the UK, this means driving through France, where petrol costs and road tolls are exorbitant.

SEA
Mainland Ports

The Peloponnese has several ports of departure for the Ionian islands: Patras for ferries to Kefallonia, Ithaki, Paxi and Corfu; Kyllini for ferries to Kefallonia and Zakynthos, and Piraeus, Neapoli and Gythio for Kythira which is also served from Crete. Epiros has one port, Igoumenitsa, for Corfu and Paxi; and Sterea Ellada has one, Astakos, for Ithaki and Kefallonia.

The following table gives an overall view of the available scheduled domestic ferries to the Ionians from mainland ports (or other major islands) in high season. Further details and inter-island links can be found under each island entry.

Italy

Large ships, known as 'superferries', ply the Ionian to various ports in Italy. From Corfu, ferries depart for Brindisi, Bari, Ancona, Trieste and Venice in Italy. Once a week, a ferry goes from Kefallonia to Brindisi via Igoumenitsa and Corfu. There are ferries to the mainland ports of Igoumenitsa and Patras from the Italian ports of Ancona, Bari, Brindisi, Trieste and Venice.

The ferries can get very crowded in summer. If you want to take a vehicle across it's a good idea to make a reservation. In the UK, reservations can be made on almost all of these ferries at Viamare Travel Ltd (☎ 020-7431 4560, fax 7431 5456, email ferries@viamare.com), 2 Sumatra Rd, London NW6 IPU.

You'll find all the latest information about ferry routes, schedules and services on the Internet. For a good overview try www.ferries.gr. Another useful Web site is the Greek Travel Pages online service at www.gtpnet.com. This interactive site will give you information on all ferry services between the various Ionian islands ports and the mainland and between the Ionians and Italy.

Ticket prices are fixed by the government, and are determined by the distance travelled rather than by the facilities of a particular boat. Ticket prices include embarkation tax, a contribution to NAT (the seaman's union) and 8% VAT.

Classes The large ferries usually have four classes: 1st class has air-conditioned cabins and a posh lounge and restaurant; 2nd class has smaller cabins and sometimes a separate lounge; tourist class gives you a berth in a shared four-berth cabin; and 3rd (deck) class gives you access to a room with 'airline' seats, a restaurant, a lounge/bar and, of course, the deck.

Deck class remains an economical way to travel, while a 1st class ticket can cost almost as much as flying on some routes.

Domestic Ferries from Mainland Ports

origin	destination	duration	price	frequency
Agia Pelagia (Kythira)	Kasteli (Crete)	4½ hours	4000 dr	2 weekly
Astakos	Pisaetos (Ithaki)	3 hours	1300 dr	1 daily
Gythio	Agia Pelagia (Kythira)	2½ hours	1700 dr	2 daily
Igoumenitsa	Corfu	1½ hours	1400 dr	14 daily
Igoumenitsa	Paxi	2 hours	1600 dr	3 weekly
Kyllini	Zakynthos	1½ hours	1400 dr	5 daily
Kyllini	Argostoli (Kefallonia)	2½ hours	2310 dr	2 daily
Kyllini	Poros (Kefallonia)	1¼ hours	1620 dr	4 daily
Neapoli	Agia Pelagia (Kythira)	1 hour	1500 dr	2 daily
Patras	Sami (Kefallonia)	2½ hours	3200 dr	2 daily
Patras	Ithaki	3½ hours	3200 dr	2 daily
Patras	Vathy (Ithaki)	3¾ hours	2900 dr	2 daily
Sagiada	Corfu	45 mins	1100 dr	1 weekly

Fun on the Ferries

Ferry travel can be absolute chaos in high season. No matter how many passengers are already on the ferry, more will be crammed on. Bewildered, black-shrouded grannies are steered through the crowd by teenage grandchildren, children get separated from parents, people stumble over backpacks, dogs get excited and bark – and everyone rushes to grab a seat. As well as birds in cages and cats in baskets there is almost always at least one truck of livestock on board – usually sheep, goats or cattle – vociferously making their presence known.

Greeks travelling deck class usually make a beeline for the indoor lounge/snack bar, while tourists make for the deck where they can sunbathe. There is no such thing as 'deck only' class on domestic ferries, although there is on international ferries.

You'll need strong nerves and lungs to withstand the lounge/snack bar, though. You can reckon on at least two TVs turned up full blast, tuned to different channels and crackling furiously from interference. A couple of other people will have ghetto blasters pumping out heavy metal, and everyone will be engaged in loud conversation. Smoke-laden air adds the final touch to this 'delightful' ambience. Unlike other public transport in Greece, smoking is not prohibited on ferries.

On overnight trips, backpackers usually sleep on deck in their sleeping bags – you can also roll out your bag between the 'airline' seats. If you don't have a sleeping bag, claim an 'airline' seat as soon as you board. Leave your luggage on it – as long as you don't leave any valuables in it. The noise on board usually dies down around midnight so you should be able to snatch a few hours sleep. If you have opted for a cabin, you will be assigned a bed in either a two or four-bed room. You will probably be woken about 1½ hours before the ferry docks by a porter asking for the cabin key – so that you don't disembark taking the key with you. People travelling in campervans have a special 'camping' area on most ferries, equipped with water and electricity connections so that they can 'camp' on board.

The food sold at ferry snack bars ranges from mediocre to inedible, and the choice is limited to packets of biscuits, sandwiches, very greasy pizzas and cheese pies. Most large ferries also have a self-service restaurant where the food is OK and reasonably priced, with main courses starting at around 1500 dr. If you are budgeting, have special dietary requirements, or are at all fussy about what you eat, take food with you.

Inter-island ferries in the Ionians are a simpler affair. The ferries take both cars and foot passengers, and usually have a small deck and saloon area. Travelling with a car on these ferries can be entertaining and requires more than a little fortitude. To embark, you have to reverse your car over a narrow gangway, dodging crazy drivers aiming to get there before you (even if you have both got prebooked tickets), then follow a myriad of indecipherable instructions (in Greek) yelled at you by the boat crew as to where to park your car. The disembarkation process is, fortunately, more straightforward (for one thing you drive off the ferry in a forward direction), although you'll probably have to battle your way through hordes of foot passengers cramming the decks near the exit and blocking your passage to your car.

Children under four travel for free, while children between four and 10 pay half-fare. Full fares apply for children over 10. Unless you state otherwise, when purchasing a ticket, you will automatically be given deck class. As deck class is what most tourists opt for, it is those prices which will be quoted in this book.

Ticket Purchase Given that ferries are prone to delays and cancellations, it's best not to purchase a ticket until it has been confirmed that the ferry is leaving. If you need to reserve a car space, however, you will need to pay in advance. If the service is cancelled you can transfer your ticket to the next available service with that company.

Agencies selling tickets line the waterfront of most ports, but rarely is there one that sells tickets for every boat, and often an agency is reluctant to give you information about a boat it does not sell tickets for. This means you have to check the timetables displayed outside each agency to find out which ferry is next to depart – or ask the port police.

In high season, a number of boats may be due at a port at around the same time, so it is not beyond the realms of possibility that you might get on the wrong boat. The crucial thing to look out for is the name of the boat; this will be printed on your ticket, and in large English letters on the side of the vessel.

If for some reason you haven't purchased a ticket from an agency, makeshift ticket tables are put up beside a ferry about an hour before departure. Tickets can also be purchased on board the ship after it has sailed. If you are waiting at the quay side for a delayed ferry, don't lose patience and wander off. Ferry boats, once they turn up, can demonstrate amazing alacrity – blink and you may miss the boat.

Most of the ferry companies have their own Web sites, including:

Adriatica	www.adriatica.it
ANEK Lines	www.anek.gr
Hellenic Mediterranean Lines	www.hml.it
Minoan Lines	www.minoan.gr
Strintzis	www.strintzis.gr
Superfast	www.superfast.com
Ventouris	www.ventouris.gr

The following ferry services are for high season (July and August), and prices are for one-way deck class. Deck class on these services means exactly that. If you want a reclining, aircraft-type seat, you'll be up for another 10 to 15% on top of the listed fares. Most companies offer discounts for return travel. Prices are about 30% less in the low season.

Ancona to Patras This route has become increasingly popular in recent years. There can be up to three boats daily in summer, and at least one a day year-round.

Superfast Ferries (☎ 071-20 28 05) provides the fastest and most convenient service, but it's also the most expensive. It has boats daily (20 hours, L148,000). Minoan Lines (☎ 071-20 17 08) has ferries to Patras (20 hours, L124,000) via Igoumenitsa (15 hours) daily except Tuesday. ANEK Lines (☎ 071-20 59 99) runs two direct boats weekly (24 hours, L115,000) and three via Igoumenitsa (34 hours). Strintzis (☎ 071-20 10 68) sails direct to Patras (23 hours, L96,000) three times weekly, twice via Igoumenitsa and Corfu.

All ferry operators in Ancona have booths at the *stazione marittima* (ferry terminal) off Piazza Candy, where you can pick up timetables and price lists and make bookings.

Bari to Corfu, Igoumenitsa & Patras
Superfast Ferries (☎ 080-52 11 416) operates daily to Patras (15 hours, L88,000) via Igoumenitsa (9½ hours). Marlines (☎ 080-52 31 824) has daily boats to Igoumenitsa (12 hours, L70,000), while Ventouris (☎ 080-521 7118) goes to Igoumenitsa (13½ hours, L65,000) via Corfu.

Brindisi to Corfu, Igoumenitsa & Patras
The route from Brindisi to Patras (18 hours) via Corfu (nine hours) and Igoumenitsa (10 hours) is the cheapest and most popular of the various Adriatic crossings. There can be up to five boats daily in high season.

Companies operating ferries from Brindisi are: Adriatica di Navigazione (☎ 0831-52 38 25), Corso Garibaldi 85-87, and on the 1st floor of the stazione marittima, where you must go to check in; Five Star Lines (☎ 0831-52 48 69), represented by Angela Gioia Agenzia Marittima, Via F Consiglio 55; Fragline (☎ 0831-59 01 96), Corso Garibaldi 88; Hellenic Mediterranean Lines (☎ 0831-52 85 31), Corso Garibaldi 8; and Med Link Lines (☎ 0831-52 76 67), represented by Discovery Shipping, Corso Garibaldi 49.

Adriatica and Hellenic Mediterranean are the most expensive at around L100,000 for deck class passage to Corfu (7½ hours), Igoumenitsa (nine hours) or Patras (15½ hours), but they are the best. They are also the only lines which accept Eurail passes. You will still have to pay port tax and a high-season loading in summer – usually about L15,000. If you want to use your Eurail pass, it is important to reserve some weeks in advance, particularly in summer. Even with a booking, you must still go to the Adriatica or Hellenic Mediterranean embarkation office in the stazione marittima to have your ticket checked.

The cheapest crossing is with Five Star Lines, which charges L46,000 to either Igoumenitsa (7½ hours) or Patras (15½ hours). Med Link charges L62,000 to Igoumenitsa and L65,000 to Patras, while Fragline charges L68,000 to Corfu and Igoumenitsa. Fares for cars range from L65,500 to L120,000 in the high season, depending on the line.

From 1 July to 19 September, Italian Ferries (☎ 0831-59 03 05), Corso Garibaldi 96, operates a daily high-speed catamaran to Corfu (3¼ hours, L154,000) leaving Brindisi at 2 pm. The service continues to Paxi (4¾ hours, L190,000 dr).

Brindisi to Kefallonia & Zakynthos Hellenic Mediterranean Lines has daily services to the port of Sami on Kefallonia from late June to early September. The trip takes 15 hours and costs L110,000 for deck class. Med Link also stops occasionally at Sami on its Brindisi-Patras run during July and August.

Hellenic Mediterranean Lines stops at Zakynthos (17 hours, L110,000) two or three times weekly in July and August.

Trieste to Patras ANEK Lines (☎ 040-30 28 88), Stazione Marittima di Trieste, has three boats weekly to Patras travelling via Igoumenitsa. The trip takes 37 hours and costs L106,000 for deck class.

Venice to Patras Minoan Lines (☎ 041-27 12 345), Magazzino 17, Santa Marta, has boats from Venice to Patras (40 hours,

L132,000). All services operate via Corfu and Igoumenitsa, and from mid-May until late September two boats weekly call at Kefallonia.

Other Ionian Islands

For inter-island ferries operating between the various Ionian islands, see the Getting Around chapter.

ORGANISED TOURS

If a package holiday of sun, sand and sea doesn't appeal to you, but you would like to holiday with a group, there are quite a few companies that organise special-interest holidays.

There are several UK companies specialising in package holidays to unspoilt areas of the Ionians. They include: Greek Islands Club (☎ 020-8232 9780); Greek Options (☎ 020-7233 5233); and Simply Ionian (☎ 020-8995 9323/1121, email ion ian@simply-travel.com) whose Web site is at www.simply-travel.com.

Sailing holidays are very popular. You don't need to be in a group as most charter companies can accommodate singles or couples who want to join up with others in a flotilla. See under Yachts in the Getting Around chapter.

There are a number of companies running organised treks. One of the biggest is Trekking Hellas (☎ 01-323 4548, fax 325 1474, email trekking@compulink.gr), Filellinon 7, Athens 105 57.

You'll find more information at its Web site, www.trekking.gr. In 1999 it was running seven-day Ionian islands 'adventure' treks to Ithaki and Kastos, departing from Athens or Preveza, passing through Astakos, involving sea travel in an inflatable rubber dinghy and accommodation in local hotels or camping on the beach.

UK-based Explore Worldwide (☎ 0125-234 4161) organises reasonably priced, small-group holidays which include visits to many of Greece's ancient sites – its Web site is www.explore.co.uk.

Getting Around

AIR

There are no direct air services between the Ionian islands. If you want to fly from one island to another, for example from Corfu to Zakynthos, you have to travel via Athens, often with a lengthy wait at Athens airport, or possibly an overnight stay if flight connections are bad. However, flying is a good option if you want to travel from Corfu to Kythira, for example, avoiding two ferry trips and a long overland drive. See Scheduled Flights & Domestic Connections under Air in the Getting There & Away chapter.

If you've got money to burn you might be able to organise (well in advance) a private plane charter from Corfu through the Corfu Flying Club (☎ 0661-34 458 or ☎ 35 983).

BUS

All long-distance buses in Greece, including the Ionians, are operated by regional collectives known as KTEL (Koino Tamio Eispraxeon Leoforion). There are regular KTEL bus services on Corfu, Paxi, Lefkada, Kefallonia, Ithaki and Zakynthos. These are mainly of use to get you from the main port or major island town to outlying areas and beach resorts and back again, but they don't allow much flexibility or opportunity to get off the beaten track. Details of bus services and ticket prices are given in the individual island chapters.

On Corfu, in addition to the KTEL long distance service, there is a network of local buses serving Corfu Town and its environs.

Bus services on Kythira are virtually nonexistent. They operate mainly for the benefit of school children, rather than for tourists. They normally leave the villages very early in the morning and return early in the afternoon.

The main towns on the larger islands usually have a central, covered bus station with seating, waiting rooms, toilets, and a snack bar selling pies, cakes and coffee. In smaller villages and resorts the 'bus station' may be no more than a bus stop outside a *kafeneio*

or taverna which doubles as a ticket office. In remote areas, the timetable may be in Greek only, but most booking offices have timetables in both Greek and Roman script. The timetables usually give both the departure and return times – useful if you are making a day trip. Times are listed using the 24 hour clock system.

There are no classes for the KTEL buses on the Ionian islands, nor are there any useful bus passes. Fares are based on the distances travelled; they are set by the government and are fairly cheap.

Tickets can be bought in advance, but reservations are not necessary unless you are taking the bus for a lengthy journey from an island to Athens or another point on the mainland.

CAR & MOTORCYCLE

Greek roads are a good place to practise your defensive driving techniques and the Ionians are no exception. The country's road fatality rate is the highest in Europe. More than 2000 people die on the roads every year, with overtaking listed as the greatest cause of accidents. Ever stricter traffic laws have had little impact on the toll.

Heart-stopping moments aside, your own car is a great way to explore off the beaten track. If you are planning to visit several of the Ionian islands your own car will give you the flexibility to hop on a ferry to the next island rather than having to rely on both bus and ferry connections.

There are no highways on the Ionians. The road network consists of single carriageway 'major' and 'minor' surfaced roads. The difference between them is often very slight. There are a few dual carriageway sections on major roads, particularly on Corfu and with EU funding the main roads are being improved all the time. There are also plenty of unsurfaced roads easily accessible to normal cars, as well as poor-quality unsurfaced roads that are best left to four wheel drive vehicles.

It's important to get a good road map. The best ones, with place names written in both Greek and Roman letters, are published by Road Editions (see Maps under Planning in the Facts for the Visitor chapter). None of the roads in the Ionians have numbers – you have to follow the directional signs. In general these signs are written in both Greek and Roman letters, but in more remote areas the Roman signs sometimes disappear. It is worth familiarising yourself with the Greek letters so that you can recognise your direction. The frequency of road signs also leaves a lot to be desired. The distances between villages and resorts tend to be quite small.

Motorcycles and mopeds can be a great way to explore the islands, and can be rented from all the larger towns and most resorts. Novices should be particularly careful; dozens of tourists have accidents every year. There are still a lot of gravel roads and a generous number of large and often dangerous potholes.

Cars can be taken on all the ferries that ply between the islands and from the islands to the mainland but tickets are expensive. Some sample prices for small vehicles include: Igoumenitsa-Corfu 14,100 dr, Patras-Kefallonia (Sami) 14,100 dr, Ithaki (Piso Aetos) to Kefallonia (Sami) 2800 dr, Lefkada (Vasiliki) to Ithaki (Frikes) 5650 dr, Kefallonia (Pessada) to Zakynthos (Schinari) 6087 dr, Kyllini to Zakynthos 7600 dr, and Neapoli-Kythira 4800 dr. Tickets must also be purchased for each passenger in the car.

Petrol is expensive, and the further you get from a major town the more it costs. Prices vary from petrol station to petrol station. Super can be found as cheaply as 199 dr per litre at big city discount places, but 225 dr to 235 dr is the normal range. You may pay closer to 245 dr per litre in remote areas. The price range for unleaded (available everywhere) is from 200 dr to 225 dr per litre. Diesel costs about 170 dr per litre.

See under Documents in the Facts for the Visitor chapter for information on licence requirements. See under Useful Organisations in the Facts for the Visitor chapter for information about the Greek automobile club (ELPA).

Warning If you are planning to use a motorcycle or moped, check that your travel insurance covers you for injury resulting from a motorbike accident. Many insurance companies don't offer this cover, so check the fine print!

Road Rules

In Greece, as throughout continental Europe, you drive on the right and overtake on the left. Outside built-up areas, traffic on a main road has right of way at intersections. In towns, vehicles coming from the right have right of way. Seat belts must be worn in front seats, and in back seats if the car is fitted with them. Children under 12 years of age are not allowed in the front seat. It is compulsory to carry a first-aid kit, fire extinguisher and warning triangle, and it is forbidden to carry cans of petrol. Helmets are compulsory for motorcyclists if the motorbike is 50cc or more, although this rule seems to be routinely ignored in the Ionians.

Outside residential areas the speed limit is 120km/h on highways, 90km/h on other roads and 50km/h in built-up areas. The speed limit for motorbikes up to 100cc is 70km/h and for larger motorbikes, 90km/h. On the Ionians you'll probably find yourself driving at much lower speeds to cope with mountain bends and the all-too-common potholes.

Drivers exceeding the speed limit by 20% are liable for a fine of 20,000 dr; and by 40%, 50,000 dr. Other offences and fines include:

illegal overtaking – 100,000 dr
going through a red light – 100,000 dr
driving without a seat belt – 50,000 dr
motorcyclist not wearing a helmet – 50,000 dr
wrong way down one-way street – 50,000 dr
illegal parking – 10,000 dr

A blood-alcohol content of 0.05% is liable to incur a fine of 50,000 dr, and over 0.08% is a criminal offence.

The police can issue traffic fines, but payment cannot be made on the spot – you will be told where to pay.

If you are involved in an accident and no-one is hurt, the police will not be required to write a report, but it is advisable to go to a nearby police station and explain what happened. A police report may be required for insurance purposes. If an accident involves injury, a driver who does not stop and does not inform the police may face a prison sentence.

Rental

Car Rental cars are widely available, but they are more expensive than in most other European countries. Most of the big multinational car hire companies are represented on the larger islands. The smaller islands often have only one car hire outlet.

The multinationals are, however, the most expensive places to hire a car. High-season weekly rates with unlimited mileage start at about 110,000 dr for the smallest models, such as a 900cc Fiat Panda. The rate drops to about 90,000 dr per week in winter. Then there are the optional extras, such as a collision damage waiver of 3300 dr per day (more for larger models), without which you will be liable for the first 1.5 million dr of the repair bill (much more for larger models). Other costs include a theft waiver of at least 1000 dr per day and personal accident insurance. It all adds up to an expensive exercise. The major companies offer much cheaper prebooked and prepaid rates.

Local companies offer some good deals for those prepared to shop around. They are normally more open to negotiation, especially if business is slow. Their advertised rates are about 25% cheaper than those offered by the multinationals.

Some car rental firms have restrictions on taking cars from the mainland onto the islands and vice versa. Local car hire companies on the islands will not let you take the vehicle off the island. If you are planning to island-hop with your vehicle, check all this beforehand.

Unless you pay with a credit card, most hire companies will require a minimum deposit of 20,000 dr per day. See the Getting Around sections of towns and islands for details of places to rent cars.

Another option for those planning to spend some time travelling with a car in the Ionians, the rest of Greece or in other parts of Europe, is car leasing. This usually can be organised only in your country of residence (although not all countries have companies that do it), and represents significant savings on rental rates for periods of a month or more. In Australia, contact Drive Away Holidays. You can check its rates and conditions at www.driveaway.com.au.

The minimum driving age in Greece is 18 years, but most car hire firms require you to be at least 23, although a few will rent vehicles to 21-year-olds.

Motorcycle Mopeds and motorcycles are available for hire wherever there are tourists to rent them. In many cases their maintenance has been minimal, so check the machine thoroughly before you hire it – especially the brakes (you'll need them!).

Motorbikes are a cheap way to travel around. Rates range from 2500 dr to 6000 dr per day for a moped or 50cc motorbike to 6000 dr to 12,000 dr per day for a 250cc motorbike. Out of season these prices drop considerably, so use your bargaining skills. By October it is sometimes possible to hire a moped for as little as 2000 dr per day. Most motorcycle hirers include third party insurance in the price, but it's wise to check this. This insurance will not include medical expenses. Helmets are not always provided.

BICYCLE

Cycling is not huge in the Ionians, which isn't surprising considering the hilly terrain, and it is rare to see groups of cyclists loaded up with panniers hopping from one Ionian island to another.

However, if you have no other means of transport it can be a good way to explore the islands while staying at a single base – but you'll need strong leg muscles. You can hire bicycles in all the larger towns and most beach resorts, but they are not as widely available as cars and motorbikes. Prices range from 1000 dr to 3000 dr per day, depending on the type and age of the bike. Bicycles are carried free on ferries.

HITCHING

Hitching is never entirely safe in any country in the world, and we don't recommend it. Travellers who decide to hitch should understand that they are taking a small but potentially serious risk. People who do choose to hitch will be safer if they travel in pairs and should let someone know where they are planning to go. Greece has a reputation for being a relatively safe place for women to hitch, but it is still unwise to do it alone. It's better for a woman to hitch with a companion, preferably a male one.

Hitching is a more relaxed affair in the Ionians than in other parts of Greece. Locals often flag down a passing car, truck or moped to get a lift into town. If you've missed the last bus, chances are you'll be able to grab a ride with another tourist or local travelling your way. On country roads, it is not unknown for someone to stop and ask if you want a lift even if you haven't stuck a thumb out. You can't afford to be fussy about the mode of transport – it may be a tractor or a spluttering old truck.

If you are on a ferry travelling to one of the islands, it might be worth asking your fellow boat passengers during the journey if any of them are heading to your final destination with space in their cars.

WALKING

You'll see the best of the Ionians if you do a bit of walking. Although many of the beach resorts are now overcrowded and overpopulated in high season, if you make the effort to head away from civilisation you can enjoy secluded, empty beaches, breathtaking views and charming quiet tavernas on mountain roads. In the larger towns and villages, walking is still the best way to see things. Visiting the archaeological sites involves a fair amount of legwork, especially on the island of Ithaki.

There are donkey paths crisscrossing all the islands which make great walking trails. But be prepared, especially in the height of

summer when temperatures soar and there's little shade. See Books in the Facts for the Visitor chapter and the individual island chapters for information about walking guides and maps.

BOAT
Ferry

Island-hopping is the quintessence of a Greek holiday for many. Each of the Ionian islands has a ferry service of some sort, although in winter services to some of the smaller islands are fairly skeletal. Services start to pick up again from April onwards, reaching their height in July and August.

Ferries come in all shapes and sizes, from the giant 'superferries' that work the major routes (such as Italy to Corfu, Igoumenitsa and Patras, Corfu to Patras and Kefallonia – see the Getting There and Away chapter) to the small, ageing open car ferries that chug along the shorter routes. Island-hopping in the Ionians involves more frequent use of the latter.

Mainland Routes Ferries for the Ionian islands leave from the Peloponnese ports of Patras (for Kefallonia, Ithaki, Paxi and Corfu) and Kyllini (for Kefallonia and Zakynthos); from Astakos (for Ithaki and Kefallonia) in Sterea Ellada; and also from Igoumenitsa in Epiros (for Corfu). Ferries for Kythira leave from the Peloponnese ports of Gythio and Neapoli. See the Getting There and Away chapter.

Inter-Island Routes Island-hopping is not as straightforward as with other Greek island groups. For example you can only get from Corfu to Kefallonia on a direct ferry once a week in summer and not at all in winter. The alternative is to take an overnight ferry from Corfu to Patras and then another ferry from Patras to Kefallonia. Similarly, if you are on Ithaki and want to get to Zakynthos the most direct route is to take a ferry to Kefallonia, followed by a 40 minute drive across the island and then another ferry to Zakynthos. Depending on the ferry timetables, this could involve an overnight stay in Kefallonia. If you are

CHRIS CHRISTO

Horse and carriage on a sightseeing tour of Corfu Town

JOHN ELK III

Town Hall Square, Corfu Town

JOHN ELK III

Palace of Saints Michael & George, Corfu Town

The Venetian influence can be seen in Paxi's roadside buildings.

Centuries-old olive grove, Paxi

Fishing village-cum-resort of Longos, Paxi

waiting for bus connections the whole journey is considerably more time consuming.

The table at the foot of this page is a list of inter-island (and intra-island) connections in high season. Bear in mind that the timetables, frequency and sometimes the route varies, depending on the time of year.

Ferry timetables change from year to year and season to season, and ferries are subject to delays and cancellations at short notice due to bad weather, strikes or boats simply conking out. No timetable is infallible – the people to go to for the most up-to-date ferry information are the local port police *(limenarheio)*, whose offices are usually on or near the quay side.

There's lots of information about ferry services on the Internet. Try www.ferries.gr, which has a useful search program and links. The Greek Travel Pages has a useful site on domestic sea services in Greece at www.gtpnet.gr. You type in your point of departure and arrival and the day you want to travel and it lists the options.

Ferries between Corfu, Patras and Kefallonia are operated by Strintzis Lines and online information is available from www.strintzis.gr. Ferries operating between Kefallonia, Ithaki, Lefkada and Astakos on the mainland are operated by Four Islands Ferries. Local ticket agents are listed in the Getting There & Away sections of each island chapter.

Excursion Boats

In addition to the car ferries which ply between the mainland ports and islands, there are a few smaller boats which link one island with another. In the past these boats were always caïques – sturdy old fishing boats – but gradually these are being replaced by new purpose-built boats, which are usually called express or excursion boats. Tickets tend to cost more than those for the large ferries, and in most cases operate only for day trips. Tickets can usually be bought from any travel agent or at the quay.

There are excursion boats that run between Corfu and the Diapondia Islands, Corfu and Paxi, Paxi and Antipaxi, Lefkada and Meganisi, and (sometimes) Ithaki, Meganisi and Kalamos. Ticket prices and frequency are listed in the individual island chapters.

Hydrofoil

Hydrofoils offer a faster alternative to ferries on some routes, particularly to islands close to the mainland. They take half the time, but usually cost twice as much. They do not take cars or motorbikes. Most routes operate only during high season and all are prone to cancellations if the sea is rough. The ride can be bumpy at the best of times.

There is a hydrofoil that runs twice a day between Corfu and Paxi (1 hour, 3500 dr). One of the services daily travels via

Inter-island & Intra-island Connections in High Season

origin	destination	duration	price	frequency
Corfu	Paxi	4 hours	1900 dr	4 weekly
Corfu	Kefallonia	4½ hours	5200 dr	1 weekly
Lefkada (Vasiliki)	Kefallonia (Fiskardo)	1½ hours	940 dr	2 daily
Lefkada (Nydri)	Meganisi	30 mins	not available	4 daily
Lefkada (Nydri)	Ithaki (Frikes)	1¾ hours	940 dr	1 daily
Kefallonia (Fiskardo)	Ithaki (Frikes)	1 hour	480 dr	1 daily
Kefallonia (Fiskardo)	Lefkada (Nidri)	2 hours	1335 dr	1 daily
Kefallonia (Sami)	Ithaki (Pisaetos)	40 mins	480 dr	4 daily
Kefallonia (Sami)	Ithaki (Vathy)	2 hours	1300 dr	1 daily
Ithaki (Pisaetos)	Lefkada (Vasiliki)	2 hours	940 dr	2 daily
Kefallonia (Argostoli)	Kefallonia (Lixouri)	30 mins	310dr	30 daily
Kefallonia (Pessada)	Zakynthos (Skinari)	2 hours	1025 dr	2 daily

Igoumenitsa on the mainland. Minoan Flying Dolphin runs high season services from Piraeus to Kythira (8 hours).

Taxi Boat

Some islands have taxi boats – small speedboats which operate like taxis, transporting people to places that are difficult to get to by land, such as secluded beaches. Ask a local for details – there are usually no timetables. Some owners charge a set price for each person, others charge a flat rate for the boat, and this cost is divided by the number of passengers. Either way, prices are usually quite reasonable.

Yacht

Despite the disparaging remarks among backpackers, yachting is *the* way to see the Ionian islands. Nothing beats the peace and serenity of sailing the open sea, and the freedom of being able to visit remote and uninhabited islands. The Ionian Sea is relatively calm and experts agree that it is the best place in Greece for a sailing holiday. There is little shallow water, plenty of places to anchor, no tides, few currents and no fog.

The east coasts of the islands of Corfu, Paxi, Lefkada, Kefallonia and Ithaki are dotted with protected coves, inlets and small harbours. (Zakynthos has less to offer the sailor, and the open seas around Kythira can get very rough.) Each island has at least one well equipped yacht harbour, with water and electricity connections. In the smaller harbours the locals will tell you when the water or fuel truck is coming around, and where you can go for a hot shower or to do some washing.

The free EOT booklet *Sailing the Greek Seas*, although long overdue for an update, contains lots of information about weather conditions, weather bulletins, entry and exit regulations, entry and exit ports and guidebooks for yachties. You can pick up the booklet at any GNTO/EOT office either abroad or in Greece.

Independent Charter Chances are, if you are reading this guide, that your budget won't cover buying a yacht. There are several other options open to you. You can hire a bare boat (a yacht without a crew) if two crew members have a sailing certificate. Prices start at US$1300 per week for a 28-footer that will sleep six. It will cost an extra US$800 per week to hire a skipper. You will be expected to pay a hefty security deposit of around US$1000 or more; these are expensive pieces of equipment and a hole in the inflatable rubber dinghy could easily gobble up your deposit.

One of Corfu's biggest charterers is Corfu Yachting Centre, Theotokou 120, near the new port. Other yacht charter companies operating in the Ionians include:

Bob & Litsa Sutcliffe (☎/fax 0661-94 104, email boblitsa@ote.net.gr) Hillside, Temploni Village, 49100 Corfu
Just Boats (☎ 0661-90 932, fax 90 837, email root@just_boats.ker.forthnet.gr) Kontokali 49100 Corfu
OCC Yachting (☎ 0661-99 262, ☎ 42 470, email occtravel@compuserve.com) Gouvia Marina, 49100 Corfu. Its Web site is at www.OCCyachting.com
Kavos Moorings (☎ 01-983 8411, ☎ 982 5701, fax 984 3989) 14 Taxiarchon Street, 17455 Kalamaki, Athens

These companies can also organise flotilla holidays. There are many more yacht charter companies in Greece, many of which are located in Piraeus near Athens; the EOT can provide addresses. In Britain, the Yacht Charter Association (☎ 01425-619004) 60 Silverdale, New Milton, Hampshire BH25 7DE, has a list of charter companies and can provide plenty of information. Most companies also offer sailing courses. Travel agents and specialist yachting holiday companies overseas include:

Templecraft Yacht Charters (☎ 01273-695094) 33 Grand Parade, Brighton, UK
The Moorings (☎ 01843-227 140) 188 Northdown Road, Cliftonville, Kent CT9 2QN, UK
Windstar Cruises (☎ 020-7628 7711) Standard House, 15 Bonhill St, London EC2P 2EA, UK
World Expeditions (☎ 01628-74 174) 7 North Road, Maidenhead, Berkshire SL6 1TL, UK
Grecian Holidays (☎ 800-268 6786, fax 416-510 1509) 75 The Donway West, Don Mills, Ontario M3C 2E9, Canada

Greek Island Cruise Center (☎ 800-341 3030) 4321 Lakemoor Drive, Wilmington, NC 28405, USA

Interpac yachts (☎ 888-9992248) 1050 Anchorage Lane, San Diego CA 92106, USA

Documents & Legal Requirements To charter a yacht bareboat (without a skipper), two people must be experienced and qualified sailors. Years of experience can be a substitute for a formal qualification, in which case an affidavit must be prepared and signed. Every charter company will be able to provide you with details.

Only Greek charter boats can be hired in Greece, and they should fly the Greek flag. You will be required to fill in the boat's log book.

Foreign yachts entering Greek waters are required to fly a code flag 'Q' until cleared by the port authorities. This is done at any of the Greek entry ports which have customs, immigration and health authorities, including Gouvia (Corfu), Vathy (Ithaki), Zakynthos Town and Kapsali (Kythira). The yachts are then issued with a transit log for the time spent in Greek waters which has to be returned to the authorities before sailing out of the Greek territory. This log also enables the crew to buy fuel, cigarettes and alcohol duty-free.

Suggested Sailing Itineraries Where you sail depends on which port or marina you leave from (and presumably return to), how long you've got and where you want to go. Most charter companies will spend some time with you planning a tailor-made itinerary and providing information on likely weather conditions and the most convenient supply stations.

For yacht charters from Corfu, for example, most people head either across to the mainland, anchoring at the sleepy fishing village of Sagiada about 20km north of Igoumenitsa, and then down to Paxi, Antipaxi and back. This would be an easy sail for three or four days. A longer holiday might involve sailing down to the southern Ionian to Lefkada or Kefallonia. The port at Fiskardo on Kefallonia is one of the pretti-est in the archipelago. Charters from Kefallonia or Lefkada can take in the island of Ithaki and Lefkada's satellites, including Meganisi and Kalamos. Zakynthos doesn't have much to offer sailors – the other islands are better.

Conditions The weather is ideal for sailing from April to October. The Ionian is blessed with relatively calm waters, there are no tides and few currents. Fog is not a problem. Other than the *maistro*, a light to moderate north-westerly wind that often blows up in the afternoons, there are few hazardous conditions. Weather forecasts and hazard warnings are broadcast on VHF Channel 16, in English and Greek.

Marinas & Supply Stations The main marinas in the Ionians are at Gouvia (Corfu), Lefkada Town and Nidri (Lefkada), Argostoli and Fiskardo (Kefallonia), and Vathi (Ithaki).

In addition there are many small harbours dotted around the Ionians where boats can tie up, take on water and fuel and where there are plenty of facilities – and entertainment – for yachties.

Books & Charts An essential reference for anyone planning to sail the Ionian Sea is Nicholas Elias' *Greece, Sea Guide. All charts/harbours/bays – supply/tourist information*. Volume III covers the Ionian Sea, the Peloponnese and the south and west coast of the mainland. It covers everything from sea depth to supply stations and anchorages on satellite islands. The book costs 20,000 dr and is widely available. In Corfu it can be obtained from the Gouvia Marina and in Corfu Town from Force 5 (☎ 25 051, fax 42 815), Xenofondos Stratigou 34, on the waterfront between new port and old port. Force 5 also sells sailing equipment, clothing, yacht fittings, ropes, compasses and instruments. The book can also be obtained by contacting the author, Nicholas Elias, Marine Aids Producer, 44 Praxitelous, 11674 Glyfada, Greece (www.amedia.com.gr/eagleray).

Another sea atlas, the *Compile Index Chart of Greek Seas* published by the Hellenic

Navy Hydrographic Service, is an indispensable chart of all Greek waters divided into regions. The XEE64 edition has text in English.

Notes to Mariners is published monthly and is available for consultation at all port authorities. It lists any temporary alterations or permanent changes to published sea charts.

Flotilla Holidays Flotilla holidays are a great introduction to sailing or the perfect solution for sailors with some experience who want the security of having an experienced skipper and technician on hand. Often these sailing holidays will include a week's land-based instruction. Generally groups of six to 12 yachts set sail together and follow a preplanned itinerary around the islands, calling in each night at a different port. People often hire a boat in groups of two to six, but there are usually boats for singles or couples to join. There is plenty of port time for those who want to explore the islands, and there is a representative from the company who answers questions, organises social activities such as onshore dinners and solves problems.

Companies specialising in flotilla holidays include:

Sunsail (☎ 023-9221 0345) The Port House, Port Solent, Portsmouth PO6 4TH, UK
Odysseus Yachting Holidays (☎ 01273-695

094) 33 Grand Parade, Brighton BN2 2QA, UK
Sovereign Sailing (☎ 01273-626284) St George's Road, Brighton BN2 1EA, UK
Islands in the Sun Cruises (☎ 800-661 7958) 10441 124 St, Edmonton, Alberta T5N 1R7, Canada

Motor Boats

You can hire dinghies with outboard motors on almost all the islands, and these places are indicated in the various island chapters, although they are available only on the protected eastern coasts of the islands.

Motor boats are fun, easy to operate (you will be given a lesson on how the engine works before you set off) and give you an enormous amount of freedom as well as the possibility to reach secluded corners of the islands.

There are restrictions as to where you can take the boats but the boat rental outlet will provide you with a map and directions.

Prices vary depending on the location and the season but boats usually cost around 10,000 dr to 12,000 dr per day with petrol on top. Discounts are usually offered for rentals of a few days or more, although you will have to return the boat to its mooring point at the end of each day. Travel agents in most resorts will tell you where you can hire the boats.

Mainland Ports

IGOUMENITSA Ηγουμενίτσα
☎ 0665 • pop 6800

Once a sleepy little outpost, the west coast port of Igoumenitsa (ih-goo-meh-**nit**-sah), 100km from Ioannina, is where you get ferries to Corfu and Italy. It is growing quickly thanks to its strategic position as an important port to Western Europe from the southern Balkans and Middle East. There is little of interest, but if you are travelling by ferry and using Igoumenitsa as your Greek entry or exit point, then you are likely to be spending some time here, if only to have a meal or wait for a boat or bus. Ferries leave in the morning and evening, so you may not have to stay overnight.

There is a very pleasant beach and taverna at **Drepanos**, about 6km north of town, if you feel like a relaxing swim and a meal.

Orientation

Ferries for Corfu and Italy leave from three separate quays quite close to one another on the waterfront of Ethnikis Antistasis. Ferries for Corfu and Paxi depart from just north of the new port. Ferries to Ancona and Venice (in Italy) depart from the new port on the south side of town; those for Brindisi and Bari (in Italy) use the old port in front of the main shipping offices.

For the bus station, turn left from the ferry quays, walk along Ethnikis Antistasis, turn right into 23 Fevrouariou – look out for the sign – and turn left into Kyprou two blocks inland. The bus station is a little way on the left.

Information

The main EOT office (☎ 22 227), in the old port area, is open 7 am to 2.30 pm daily. There is also an EOT booth just outside the arrivals area of the new port. The post office and OTE are next to each other on Evangelistrias. Currency exchange machines and ATMs are available at the Commercial and National banks. The tourist police and regular police (☎ 22 222) are together on the main road near the port entrance. The port police are beside the ferry quays.

Places to Stay & Eat

Campers might head for *Il Sole Mare* on the south side of town, or if you have independent transport, there is a quiet camp site at *Drepanos Beach*, 6km north of town. There are also *domatia* around the new port. Look for signs.

Budget hotels are in short supply. The D class *Egnatia (☎ 23 648, fax 23 63, Eleftherias 2)* has comfortable singles/doubles for 8500/11,500 dr with bathroom. Turn right from the bus station and walk 100m. You will see it across the square on your left. The C class *Hotel Oscar (☎ 23 338, fax 23 557, Agion Apostolon 149)* opposite the new port arrivals area has reasonable rooms for 8000/10,000 dr.

The C class *Hotel Aktaion (☎/fax 22 330, Agion Apostolon 27)* on the waterfront between the Corfu ferry quay and the old port, costs 12,000/16,000 dr.

Bilis (☎ 26 214, Agion Apostolon 15), opposite the Corfu ferry quay, is handy for a quick meal. *Restaurant Martinis-Bakalis (☎ 24 357)* on the corner of Fevrouariou and Grigoriou Lambraki, serves reasonably priced, tasty food. The locals eat here, so you can be assured of good value. Plan on about 2500 dr for a meal at both places.

Getting There & Away

Bus From the bus station (☎ 22 309) there are buses to Ioannina (two hours, 1800 dr, nine daily), Parga (one hour, 1150 dr, five daily), Athens (eight hours, 8300 dr, three daily), Preveza (2½ hours, 2100 dr, two daily) and Thessaloniki (eight hours, 7800 dr, one daily).

Ferry There are ferries to Corfu Town every hour between 5 am and 10 pm (1½ hours, 1300 dr), and six a day to Lefkimmi (one hour, 750 dr) in southern Corfu. There are also three boats a week to Paxi (1½ hours, 1600 dr). Tickets are sold at booths opposite the quay.

Most of the ferries to/from Italy also stop at Corfu. There are also weekly passenger and car ferries to Corfu from Sagiada (45 minutes, 1100 dr), 20km north of Igoumenitsa.

See the introductory Getting There & Away chapter for information on ferries to Italy. For a comprehensive brochure of ferry options, go to Chris Travel (☎ 25 351, fax 25 350) at Ethnikis Antistasis 60. You can also book most ferry companies at Alfa Travel (☎ 22 797, fax 26 330) at Agion Apostolon 167 opposite the new port.

ASTAKOS Αστακός
☎ 0646

The small resort of Astakos, in Sterea Ellada (Central Greece), makes a handy stepping stone to the island of Ithaki, although it is also becoming popular as a holiday destination in itself.

Places to Stay & Eat
If you need to stay overnight, there's one hotel – the C class *Hotel Stratos* (☎ 0646-41 096) – and some domatia in summer. Try the *Dina Taverna* which has rooms from 8000 dr.

Getting There & Away
Bus There are two buses a day to Astakos from Terminal A in Athens (five hours, 5200 dr). KTEL buses also run to and from Agrinio and Vonitsa.

Ferry From June to September, there's a boat every day at 1 pm to Piso Aetos on Ithaki (three hours, 1300 dr).

PATRAS Πάτρα
☎ 061 • pop 153,300

Patras is Greece's third largest city and the principal port for ferries to the Ionian islands, as well as for international services to Italy. It's not particularly exciting and most travellers hang around only long enough for transport connections. There are great views of Zakynthos and Kefallonia from the Venetian **kastro**, which is reached by the steps at the top of Agiou Nikolaou.

Orientation
The city is easy to negotiate and is laid out on a grid stretching uphill from the port to the old *kastro* (castle). Most services of importance to travellers are along the waterfront, known as Othonos Amalias in the middle of town and Iroön Polytehniou to the north. The various shipping offices are to be found along here. The train station is in the middle of town on Othonos Amalias, and the main bus station is close by.

Information
Tourist Offices The EOT (☎ 620 353) is outside the international arrivals terminal at the port. In theory, it's open 8 am to 10 pm Monday to Friday; in practice, it's often closed. The most useful piece of information is an arrow pointing to the helpful tourist police (☎ 451 833), upstairs in the embarkation hall, who are open 7.30 am to 11 pm daily.

Money The National Bank of Greece on Plateia Trion Symahon has a 24-hour automatic exchange machine.

Post & Communications The post office, on the corner of Zaïmi and Mezonos, is open 7.30 am to 8 pm Monday to Friday and 7.30 am to 2 pm Saturday. The main OTE office, on the corner of Dimitriou Gounari and Kanakari, is open 24 hours. There is also an OTE office at the port, near the EOT office.

For Internet access, head inland to the Rocky Racoon Music Bar, Gerokostopoulou 56. It's open 9 am to 3 am daily.

Left Luggage You can leave bags at the left luggage offices at the port arrivals area (500 dr per item per day) or at the train station (1000 dr per item per day).

Emergency There's a first-aid centre (☎ 277 386) on the corner of 28 Octavriou and Agiou Dionysiou.

Places to Stay & Eat
Most travellers go to *Pension Nicos* (☎ 623 757), up from the waterfront on the corner

of Patreos and Agiou Andreou. It provides doubles with shared facilities for 6500 dr, and single/double rooms with bathroom for 4000/7000 dr.

The C class *Hotel Rannia (☎ 220 114, fax 220 537, Riga Fereou 53)*, facing Plateia Olgas, has comfortable and air-conditioned singles/doubles with TV for 10,000/15,000 dr – reduced to 8000/12,000 dr outside peak season. A step up from this is *Hotel Adonis (☎ 224 213, fax 226 971, Zaïmi 9)* behind the bus station. It charges 13,200/16,500 dr, including breakfast, and the rooms have good views out over the port.

Europa Centre (Othonos Amalias 10) is a convenient cafeteria-style place close to the international ferry dock. It has a range of taverna dishes as well as spaghetti (from 900 dr) and a choice of vegetarian meals (900 dr).

Locals prefer the nameless *restaurant* at Michalakopoulou 3, which specialises in traditional dishes like *entosthia arnisia* – translated as lamb bowels on the menu! Travellers will probably be happier with a large bowl of fish soup (1100 dr) or roast chicken with potatoes (700 dr).

Getting There & Away
Many people assume that the best way to get from Patras to Athens is by bus. The bus is faster, but is more expensive and drops you off a long way from the city centre at Terminal A on Kifissou. This can be a real hassle if you're arriving in Athens after midnight – when there are no connecting buses to the city centre, leaving newcomers at the mercy of the notorious Terminal A taxi drivers.

The train takes you quite close to the city centre, within easy walking distance of good accommodation.

Bus There are buses to Athens (three hours, 3500 dr) every 30 minutes, with the last at 9.45 pm.

There are two buses a day to Lefkada (3450 dr), leaving from the bus station on the corner of Faverou and Konstantino-poleos. Buses to Zakynthos (3½ hours, 2900 dr) and Kefallonia leave from the bus station

at the corner of Othonos Amalias and Gerokostopoulou. They travel via the port of Kyllini. Fares include the ferry ticket.

Train There are nine trains a day to Athens. Four are slow trains (4½ hours, 1580 dr) and five are express intercity trains (3½ hours, 2980 dr). The last intercity train leaves at 6 pm, the last slow train at 8 pm.

Ferry There are daily ferries to Kefallonia (four hours, 3200 dr), Ithaki (six hours, 3500 dr) and Corfu (10 hours, 5800 dr). Services to Italy are covered in the Getting There & Away chapter at the start of this book. Ticket agents line the waterfront.

Getting Around
Local buses leave from the bus stops on either side of Aratou. Car rental outlets include Europcar (☎ 621 360), Agiou Andreou 6; Hertz (☎ 220 990), Karolou 2; and Reliable Rent A Car (☎ 272 764), Othonos Amalias 44.

KYLLINI Κυλλίνη
☎ 0623
The tiny port of Kyllini (Ki-**lee**-ni), 78km south-west of Patras, warrants a mention only as the jumping-off point for ferries to Kefallonia and Zakynthos. Most people pass through Kyllini on buses from Patras that board the ferries. It's an unattractive port with few facilities and not an easy place to get to or from if you are without private transport. The only reason you'd want to end up there is if you have your own wheels and can escape fast south into the Peloponnese or north to Patras and another ferry connection.

Stretching south from Kyllini is a succession of excellent beaches.

Orientation & Information
The port police (☎ 92 211) are at the quay. The ticket office for the Zakynthos-Kyllini ferry (☎ 92 385) is also on the quay.

There are no official exchange facilities or banks in Kyllini, but the ferry ticket office on the quay can change money for you. The office is open from 7 am to 10 pm.

Places to Stay & Eat

Ionian Hotel (☎ 92 318) is to the right just past the beach as you exit the ferry quay. It has simple single/double rooms with bathroom for 9000/11,200 dr in low season and 11,200/14,000 dr in high season. Behind the hotel is *Matina's Pension (☎ 92 161)* which has double rooms for 6000 dr.

There isn't a great choice for food. *Sou Mou* taverna next to the Ionian Hotel and opposite the beach with the Hawaiian-style thatched umbrellas serves Greek staples. A better choice could be the family run *Mezedopleio* taverna, to the left of the ferry quay as you exit and one block back from the waterfront road. Just in front of it is a decent *bakery*.

Getting There & Away

Bus There are regular buses to Kyllini (1¼ hours, 1500 dr) from the Zakynthos bus station in Patras, as well as at least three buses daily from Pyrgos (50 minutes, 1050 dr).

There is no KTEL bus station in Killini. The nearest KTEL station is at Lechiana, 13km away. You can catch a taxi to Lechiana or possibly hitch a ride with someone coming off the ferry and heading that way.

Ferry There are up to five boats a day to Zakynthos (1½ hours, 1400 dr). Car transportation costs 7600 dr. There are also four boats a day to Poros (1¼ hours, 1620 dr).

Strintzis Lines (☎ 92 337, fax 92 461) runs ferries to Argostoli on Kefallonia (2¼ hours, 2800 dr) twice daily at 11 am and 7 pm, although in low season the evening ferry does not always run. Tickets cost 11,300 dr for a car. The ferry from Argostoli for Kyllini departs at 7.30 am and 3.30 pm. The ticket office is on the quay.

GYTHIO Γύθειο
☎ 0733   • pop 4900

Gythio, once the port of ancient Sparta, is an attractive fishing town at the head of the Lakonian Gulf.

The town is set around, and sprawls back from, a long narrow harbour. There are a number of good beaches in the vicinity, and more than enough *kafeneia* and tavernas to keep you occupied if you find yourself holed up here due to bad weather or bad connections.

It is the most convenient port of departure for the Ionian island of Kythira, and also has services to Kastelli-Kissamos on Crete.

Orientation

Most things of importance to travellers are along the seafront on Akti Vasileos Pavlou. The bus station is at the northern end, next to the small triangular park known as the Perivolaki. Vasileos Georgiou runs inland from here past the main square Plateia Panagiotou Venetzanaki, and becomes the road to Sparta.

The square at the southern end of Akti Vasileos Pavlou is Plateia Mavromihali, hub of the old quarter of Marathonisi. The ferry quay is opposite this square. Beyond it, the waterfront road becomes Kranais, which leads south to Areopoli. A causeway leads out to Marathonisi Islet at the southern edge of town.

Information

The EOT (☎/fax 24 484) is about 500m north of the waterfront at Vasileos Georgiou 20, open 11 am to 3 pm Monday to Friday.

The post office is on Ermou, in the newer part of the town two blocks north of the bus station, and the OTE office is between the two at the corner of Herakles and Kapsali.

The tourist police (☎ 22 271) share lodgings with the regular police (☎ 22 100) on the waterfront between the bus station and Plateia Mavromihali.

There are several banks in Plateia Panagiotou Venetzanaki, including the National Bank of Greece and Alphabank, both of which have an ATM.

Things to Do

According to mythology, the island of **Marathonisi** is ancient Cranae, where Paris (a prince of Troy) and Helen (the wife of Menelaus of Sparta) consummated the love affair that sparked the Trojan War. An 18th century **tower** at the centre of the island has been restored and converted into a **museum**.

Gythio's small but well preserved **ancient theatre** is next to an army camp on the northern edge of town. Most of ancient Gythio lies beneath the nearby Lakonian Gulf.

Places to Stay

You'll find plenty of domatia signs around town. *Kontogiannis Rooms to Rent (☎ 22 518)*, up the steps next to the police station on Akti Vasileos Pavlou, has spotless singles/doubles with bathroom for 7000/ 10,000 dr. *Leonidas Domatia (☎ 22 389)* also on the waterfront is another cheapie with single/double rooms for 8000/ 10,000 dr.

Next door, and slightly upmarket, is the *Hotel Aktaion (☎ 23 500, fax 22 294)* which is open all year. Rooms look out over the harbour and pleasant doubles cost 12,000 dr to 18,000 dr depending on the season.

Hotel Pantheon (☎ 22 289, fax 22 284) also on the waterfront, has air-conditioned singles/doubles with TV and telephone for 10,000/14,000 dr rising to 12,000/18,000 dr in high season.

Saga Pension (☎ 23 220, fax 24 370) on the seafront south of Plateia Mavromihali, charges 7000/10,000 dr for singles/doubles with bathroom.

Places to Eat

Take your pick of the waterfront fish tavernas with very similar menus. *Kozia* fish taverna displays the fresh catch of the day in a cabinet on the footpath and hangs its octopus on a string in front of the tables.

For something completely different, head inland to the tiny *General Store & Wine Bar (☎ 24 113, Vasileos Georgiou 67)*. You'll find an unusually varied and imaginative menu featuring dishes like orange and pumpkin soup (600 dr) and fillet of pork with black pepper and ouzo (2800 dr).

Self-caterers can stock up at *Kourtakis supermarket*, around the corner from the bus station on Heracles.

Getting There & Away

Bus There are five buses a day to Athens (4¼ hours, 4500 dr) via Sparta (one hour, 750 dr).

Ferry There are daily ferries to Kythira (two hours, 1600 dr) in summer, continuing twice a week to Antikythira and Kastelli-Kissamos on Crete (seven hours, 5100 dr). Note that ferries will not stop at Antikythira if the sea is rough. Tickets are sold at Golden Ferries (☎ 22 996, fax 22 410) opposite the tourist office on Vasileos Pavlou.

NEAPOLI Νεάπολη
☎ 0734 • pop 2500

Neapoli, close to the southern tip of the eastern prong of the Peloponnese, is the 'other' port serving Kythira – which is clearly visible to the south. Few travellers come this way, as the ferries from Gythio are much more convenient.

There are worse places to get stuck for the night than Neapoli – Patras or Piraeus for a start. It is an attractive little port. The waterfront is the centre of activity and a popular place for locals as well as visitors to hang out. There is even a decent beach where you can while away a few hours should you need to.

Orientation & Information

There are several banks along the waterfront which do foreign exchange. The Commercial Bank of Greece, directly opposite the ferry quay, and the National Bank of Greece, to the right of the ferry quay as you look out to sea, have ATMs.

Places to Stay & Eat

Neapoli is popular enough with the local holiday-makers to have three seafront *hotels* and several *domatia*. The most convenient place to stay is the *Akvali Hotel (☎/fax 22 287)* about 100m from the ferry quay. The staff are friendly and clean simple single/double rooms cost 6300/7600 dr rising to 8000/10,000 dr in high season.

A little farther along the road out of town (300m from the ferry quay, past the Akvali Hotel) is *Stathaki Domatia (☎ 22 038)* which has basic singles/doubles for 5000/ 7000 dr.

There are several *ouzeri* along the waterfront which set up barbecue grills on the pavement to entice passers-by to stop for an ouzo or a beer and a nibble of char-grilled octopus (around 650 dr). *Bananas* tavern is popular with the locals. It has the painted blue doors and is next to the National Bank of Greece.

Getting There & Away

Bus There are 11 buses a day from Athens to Sparta (3¼ hours, 3700 dr), and four buses a day from Sparta to Neapoli (three hours, 2550 dr).

Ferry There are three ferries a week from Neapoli to Agia Pelagia on Kythira (one hour, 1500 dr). Tickets are sold at Vatika Bay Travel (☎/fax 22 660), Agios Traidos 3, opposite the ferry quay. The office transfers to a car at the end of the ferry quay about 30 minutes before the boat departs. Passen-

gers can buy tickets just before they board, but in high season, or if you are travelling with a vehicle, it is essential to book and pay for the ticket in advance.

In July and August, there is sometimes a Sunday afternoon hydrofoil service to Kythira (20 minutes, 3000 dr), although it was not operating at the time of research. Minoan Flying Dolphin runs a (passenger only) hydrofoil service between Piraeus and Neapoli every Friday, Sunday and Monday in high season (four hours, 9900 dr). Tickets can be obtained from Captain D Alexandratis (☎ 22 940, fax 23 590), between the Commercial Bank of Greece and the National Bank of Greece. The agency also operates as a currency exchange and as a yacht and motor launch charter service. It's open 8 am to 2 pm and 5 to 9.30 pm daily.

Corfu Κέρκυρα

☎ 0661/0662/0663 • pop 107,592

Corfu is the second largest, greenest Ionian island and the best known. In Greek, the island is called Kerkyra (**ker**-kih-rah). Homer described it as a 'beautiful and rich land' and wrote of the 'well-watered gardens', and it was Odysseus' last stop on his journey home to Ithaca.

Shakespeare reputedly used it as a background for *The Tempest*. In the 20th century, the Durrell brothers, among others, have extolled its virtues.

With its beguiling landscape of vibrant wild flowers and slender cypress trees rising out of shimmering olive groves, Corfu is considered by many as Greece's most beautiful island.

With the highest rainfall, it's also the nation's major vegetable garden and produces scores of herbs. The island is covered with olive groves (60% of the trees on Corfu are olives), and figs, oranges and grapes grow in abundance.

Mt Pantokrator rises 906m in the northeast of the island. Its surrounding foothills and peaks are great places for off the beaten track walks.

Indeed Corfu is a walker's paradise, and heading inland on foot is by far the best way to get away from the crowds.

Corfu has the highest population of the Ionian islands and is the seat of the regional administration. Its economy is essentially driven by tourism.

Over one million tourists visit the island each year, the vast majority of them on cheap packages from Britain and northern Europe, looking for sun and fun in beach resorts on the western, northern and eastern coasts.

The beach resorts on the east coast to the south of Corfu Town were among the first to suffer from mass tourism in the 1970s, and are best avoided today.

Indiscriminate package tour operators have a lot to answer for on Corfu, and it is difficult, if not impossible, for the inde-

pendent traveller to visit places which have not been spoilt to a greater or lesser degree. But mass tourism is a self-perpetuating industry and avaricious locals, out to make a fast and easy tourist buck by hastily throwing up ubiquitous purpose-built *domatia* blocks or setting up low-quality restaurants and bars, must also be held accountable.

Despite being overrun, Corfu does have something for almost everyone. The island

CORFU

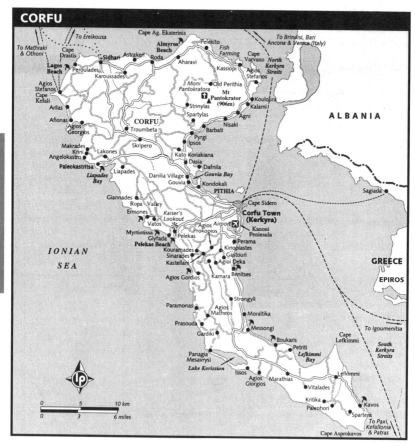

CORFU

capital, Corfu Town, is an elegant settlement full of interesting museums, beautiful Venetian architecture, good restaurants and cafes and decent shops.

Various ancient sites are dotted about the Kanoni Peninsula, situated 5km south of Corfu Town.

The West Coast is famous for its long sandy beaches, with watersports in abundance. Inland villages make a great detour for those with their own transport or energetic legs.

The northern coast has long beaches with shallow waters and is popular with families,

while the north-east of the island is perhaps the most unspoilt, with a narrow winding road skirting the base of Mt Pantokrator and even more winding roads leading down to pebbly coves and crystal clear waters ideal for swimming and snorkelling.

If nightlife is what you are after you'll find it in abundance in the tackier resorts such as Ipsos, Sidhari and the notorious lager lout haven of Kavos.

HISTORY

Archaeological evidence suggests that the island was inhabited from the Palaeolithic

Age (30,000-7000 BC). Excavations near Sidhari in the north of the island indicate a Neolithic settlement dating from 6000 BC. Bronze Age sites have also been discovered in the north-west.

The prehistoric peoples of Kerkyra seem to have developed an original culture similar to that of the Apulian people in southern Italy, which was quite distinct from the culture developing in southern and eastern Greece.

The first Greeks to arrive on Corfu (around 750 BC) were Eretrian emigrants. The Corinthians settled on the island around 735 BC, in the area where Corfu Town stands today, and gave the island its name, Kerkyra.

The Corinthian colony spread to the Kanoni Peninsula, south of present day Corfu Town.

Thanks to its favourable trading position, Kerkyra rapidly acquired wealth and began to compete with Corinth, founding its own colonies on the mainland nearby.

In order to gain its independence from Corinth, Kerkyra fought Corinth in a famous sea battle in 664 BC, although the Corinthians again imposed their rule from the end of the 7th century BC.

Kerkyra's revolt against Corinth and subsequent allegiance to the city-state of Athens sparked the Peloponnesian Wars, which raged from 431 to 404 BC.

Defeated, the island took a long time to recover, and was subjected to the tyrants of Syracuse in Sicily and the kings of Epiros and Macedonia, before becoming the first Greek territory to assume Roman protection in 229 BC. It remained under Roman rule until 395 AD, when it passed into the Byzantine Empire.

Kerkyra was but a distant outpost of the empire and the island was not well defended. As a result it came under repeated attack from the Vandals, Goths, Saracens, Normans and others.

From the 11th to the 14th century Corfu was ruled by Norman and Angevin kings. They were followed by the Venetians, who held the island for four centuries and protected it from Turkish occupation. Under the Venetians the arts and architecture flourished, and Italian was for some time the official language.

Venice fell to Napoleon in 1797. Two years later, under the Treaty of Campo Formio, Corfu and the other Ionian islands were allotted to France. In 1799 Russian forces wrested the islands from Napoleon, but by 1807 they were his again. By then, the all-powerful British couldn't resist meddling.

As a result, in 1815, after Napoleon's downfall, the Ionian islands became a British protectorate under the jurisdiction of a series of Lord High Commissioners based on Corfu.

British rule was oppressive but led to a great deal of civic construction, which included the neoclassical Palace of Saints Michael and George (see Things to See under Corfu Town later in this chapter). In 1862 Britain relinquished Corfu and the other islands to Greece.

In WWII the Italians invaded Corfu as part of Mussolini's plan to resurrect the mighty Roman Empire.

Italy surrendered to the Allies in September 1943 and, in revenge, the Germans launched a vicious aerial bombardment, destroying over a quarter of the buildings in Corfu Town. They also arrested some 5000 Corfiot Jews who were sent to Auschwitz.

GETTING THERE & AWAY
Air
Corfu has at least three flights to Athens every day (20,700 dr). There are flights to Thessaloniki on Monday, Thursday and Saturday (20,900 dr). The Olympic Airways office (☎ 38 694, fax 36 634) is at Polyla 11, Corfu Town.

Bus
KTEL buses go to Athens (11 hours, 8150 dr including ferry, twice daily) at 9 am and 6.30 pm, and one to Thessaloniki (8000 dr) at 7 am daily. Tickets must be bought in advance. The KTEL long distance bus station is on Avramiou, inland from the new port.

Ferry – Domestic

From Corfu, hourly ferries go to Igoumenitsa (1¼ hours, 1400 dr). Every Friday a ferry goes to Sagiada on the mainland (45 minutes, 1100 dr). Car ferries go to Paxi (four hours, 1900 dr) four times weekly, via Igoumenitsa. In summer, a fast hydrofoil leaves Corfu's new port for Paxi twice daily (one hour, 3500 dr), stopping on some trips at Igoumenitsa. Corfu's port police can be contacted on ☎ 32 655.

Ferry – International

Corfu is on the Patras-Igoumenitsa ferry route to Italy (Brindisi, Bari, Ancona, Trieste, Venice), though some ferries originate in Igoumenitsa. About six ferries daily go to Brindisi (9½ hours). At least one ferry daily goes to Bari and Ancona, and one goes to Venice daily (27 hours) in summer.

A fast daily catamaran service links Corfu with Brindisi from 1 July to 19 September with reduced services between April and June. The price of a one-way ticket is 27,000 dr. The Corfu agents are Italian Ferries.

Brindisi-bound ferries tend to leave Corfu's new port between 8.30 and 9.30 am.

Prices to Italy from Corfu are the same as those from Igoumenitsa on the mainland. Depending on the carrier, high season deck class fares from Corfu to Brindisi cost between 7000 dr and 18,000 dr. To Bari, fares cost from 12,500 dr to 15,800 dr. Fares to Venice cost from 16,600 dr to 21,800 dr and to Ancona from 9600 dr to 21,800 dr.

Agencies selling tickets are mostly on Xenofondos Stratigou. Shop around for the best deal. You can take one of the frequent international ferries to Patras (10 hours, 5800 dr), daily in summer.

Here are the main ferry offices:

Adriatica (☎ 38 089, fax 35 416) Ilios Holidays Ltd, Xenofondos Stratigou 46
ANEK Lines (☎ 24 503, fax 36 935, email booking@anek.cha.forthnet.gr) Mancan Travel, Eleftheriou Venizelou 38
Fragline (☎ 24 912, fax 37 967) Ahilleas Avramidis, Eleftheriou Venizelou 46
Hellenic Mediterranean (☎ 39 747, fax 32 047, email hml@otenet.gr) Eleftheriou Venizelou 46

Italian Ferries (☎ 36 439, fax 45 153) 3rd Parodos, Eleftheriou Venizelou 4
Minoan Lines (☎ 25 000, fax 46 555, email vergis@minoan.ker.forthnet.gr) Ethnikis Antistasis 58a
Strintzis Lines (☎ 25 232, fax 46 945, email sales@strintzis.gr or ferry-cf@otenet.gr) Ferry Travel, Ethnikis Antistasis 2
Ventouris Ferries (☎ 32 664, fax 36 935, email info@ventouris.gr) Mancan Travel, Eleftheriou Venizelou 38

GETTING AROUND
To/From the Airport

There is no bus service between Corfu Town and the airport. Bus No 3 from Plateia San Rocco in Corfu Town stops on the main road 500m from the airport.

Bus

Destinations of KTEL buses (green-and-cream) from Corfu Town's long distance bus station (☎ 30 627) are as follows:

destination	duration	frequency	via
Agios Gordios	40 mins	4 daily	Sinarades
Agios Stefano	1½ hours	5 daily	Sidhari
Aharavi	1¼ hours	4 daily	Roda
Glyfada	45 mins	6 daily	Vatos
Kavos	1½ hours	10 daily	Lefkimmi
Loutses	1¼ hours	4 daily	Kassiopi
Messonghi	45 mins	7 daily	Benitses
Paleokastritsa	45 mins	7 daily	Gouvia
Pyrgi	30 mins	9 daily	Ypsos

Fares range from 300 dr to 800 dr. Sunday and holiday services are reduced considerably, often by as much as 70%.

The numbers and destinations of local buses (dark blue) from the bus station at Plateia San Rocco, Corfu Town, are:

destination	bus no	duration	frequency	via
Agios Ioannis	11	30 mins	9 daily	Pelekas
Ahillion	10	20 mins	6 daily	Gastouri
Kanoni	2	20 mins	8 daily	
Kastellani	5	25 mins	14 daily	Kourmades
Kontokali	7	30 mins	hourly	Gouvia & Dasia
Perama	6	30 mins	12 daily	Benitses
Potamos	4	45 mins	12 daily	Evroupoli & Tembloni

The flat rate is 200 dr. Tickets can be bought on board or on Plateia San Rocco.

Car, Motorcycle & Bicycle

Reliable Rent a Car (☎ 21 870, fax 35 840), Donzelot 5, near Corfu Town's old port has small (Group A) cars from 14,000 dr per day or 80,000 dr per week. In the same street, Top Cars (☎ 35 237, ☎ 38 040, fax 35 237), Donzelot 25, has Group A cars (such as a Fiat Panda) from 11,000 dr per day, and larger Group B cars (Fiat Punto) from 13,000 dr per day.

Other car hire companies in Corfu Town include Autorent (☎ 44 623/24/25), Xenofondos Stratigou 34; Avis (☎ 24 042), Ethnikis Antistasis 42; Budget (☎ 22 062), Donzelot 5; and Europcar (☎ 46 931/32/33), Xenofondos Stratigou 32.

Easy Rider (☎ 43 026), Eleytheriou Venizeloy 50 (at new port), rents scooters and motorbikes. New scooters cost 5000 dr per day or 30,000 dr per week. Slightly older ones are a little cheaper at 4000 dr per day or 25,000 dr per week. A 125cc motorbike will cost you 7000 dr per day or 42,000 dr per week, a 250cc bike 9000 dr per day or 56,000 dr per week and a 600cc bike 12,500 dr per day (75,000 dr per week). The price includes helmets, locks and insurance. Payment is by cash or travellers cheques only, and in lieu of a deposit you leave your drivers' licence with them. This is the only moped/motorbike rental place on Corfu that has representatives in other parts of the island who will come to your rescue if the bike breaks down. They will also arrange free delivery of a bike (for three or more days rental) to other parts of the island between 9 am and 8 pm (earlier or later delivery incurs an additional charge of 2000 dr). There are other motorcycle hire outlets on Xenofondos Stratigou and Avramiou.

Mountain bikes can be hired in Corfu Town from Charitos Travel Agency (☎ 44 611/20, fax 36 825), Arseniou 35.

Taxi

You can pick taxis up at taxi ranks all over Corfu Town, and radio taxis can be called on ☎ 33 811. There are standard fixed price fares for tourists: from the airport to Corfu Town 2000 dr, from Corfu Town to Kanoni 2000 dr, from Corfu to Roda or Sidhari 8500 dr, from Corfu to Paleokastritsa 5500 dr, from Corfu to Benitses 4000 dr, and from Corfu to Kavos 9000 dr. Drivers rarely put their meters on, but might do so for a short trip within Corfu Town.

Corfu Town

☎ 0661 • pop 36,000

The island's capital is Corfu Town (Kerkyra), built on a promontory. It's a gracious medley of numerous occupying influences, which never included the Turks.

The Old Fortress on a twin peaked headland on the town's eastern side was started by the Byzantines in the 6th century AD and at one time housed the entire population. In subsequent centuries the town expanded to the west and south.

The Spianada (esplanade) is green, gardened and boasts Greece's oldest cricket ground, a legacy of the British. After a match, spectators may join players in drinking ginger beer made to an old Victorian recipe or, typically, tea or gin and tonic.

The Liston, a row of arcaded buildings flanking the north-western side of the Spianada, was built during the French occupation and modelled on Paris' Rue de Rivoli. The buildings function as upmarket cafes, lamplit by night. Georgian mansions and Byzantine churches complete the picture. The Venetian influence prevails, particularly in the enchanting old town, wedged between two fortresses. Narrow alleyways of 18th century shuttered tenements in muted ochres and pinks are more reminiscent of Venice or Naples than Greece. As Lawrence Durrell so eloquently put it, 'The architecture is Venetian; the houses above the old port are built up elegantly into slim tiers with narrow alleys and colonnades running between them; red, yellow, pink, umber – a jumble of pastel shades.'

Corfu Town was badly damaged by Nazi bombing during WWII. A major facelift for the EU summit in 1994 has returned it to its

CORFU TOWN

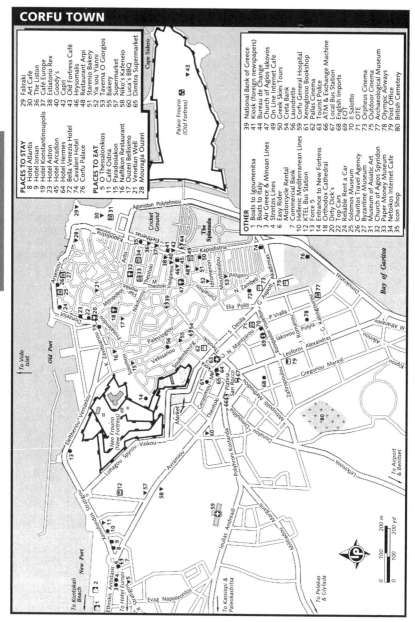

PLACES TO STAY
8 Hotel Atlantis
9 Hotel Ionian
19 Hotel Konstantinoupolis
23 Hotel Astron
45 Hotel Arcadion
64 Hotel Hermes
72 Bella Venezia Hotel
74 Cavalieri Hotel
76 Corfu Palace

PLACES TO EAT
5 O Thessalonikios
15 Café Ostria
15 Paradosiakon
16 Ninetis Restaurant
17 Ouzeri Bellisimo
21 Venetian Well
28 Mouragia Ouzeri
29 Faliraki
30 Art Café
36 The Liston
37 Café Europe
38 Estiatorio Rex
40 Goody's
42 Capri
43 Old Fortress Café
46 Hrysomalis
48 Restaurant Arpi
51 Starenio Bakery
52 Yia sou Yianni
53 Taverna O Giorgios
57 Bakery
57 Supermarket
58 Niko's Kafeneio
60 Luca's BBQ
65 Dimitra Supermarket

OTHER
1 Boats to Igoumenitsa
2 Boats to Italy
3 Air Greece & Minoan Lines
4 Strintzis Lines
6 Easy Rider
7 Motorcycle Rental
10 Commercial Bank
11 Hellenic Mediterranean Lines
12 KTEL Bus Station
13 Force 5
14 Entrance to New Fortress
18 Orthodox Cathedral
20 Dirty Dick's
22 Top Cars
24 Reliable Rent a Car
25 Solomos Museum
26 Charitos Travel Agency
27 Byzantine Museum
31 Museum of Asiatic Art
32 Church of Agios Spyridon
33 Paper Money Museum
34 Netoikos Internet Cafe
35 Icon Shop
39 National Bank of Greece
41 Kiosk (foreign newspapers)
44 Bureau de Change
47 Church of Agios Iakovos
49 On Line Internet Cafe
50 Greek Skies Tours
54 Creta Bank
56 Laundrette
59 Corfu General Hospital
61 Xenoglosso Bookshop
63 Pallas Cinema
66 Tourist Police
67 ATM & Exchange Machine
67 Local Bus Station
68 English Imports
69 EOT
70 Il Salotto
71 OTE
73 Orpheus Cinema
75 Outdoor Cinema
77 Archaeological Museum
78 Olympic Airways
79 Post Office
80 British Cemetery

former beauty, and it is undoubtedly one of the loveliest towns in Greece.

ORIENTATION
The town is separated into northern and southern sections. The old town is in the northern section between the Spianada and the New Fortress. The Palaio Frourio (Old Fortress) is east of the northern section and projects out to sea, cut off from the town by a moat. The Neo Frourio (New Fortress) is west. The Spianada separates the Old Fortress from the town. The southern section is the new town.

The old port is north of the old town. The new port is west. Between them is the hulking New Fortress. The long distance bus station is on Avramiou, inland from the new port. The local bus station is on Plateia San Rocco. Local buses serve the town and nearby villages.

INFORMATION
Tourist Offices
The EOT (☎ 37 520, fax 30 298) is situated on Rizospaston Voulefton. The tourist police (☎ 30 265) are at Samartzi 4, near Plateia Solomou.

Money
The National Bank of Greece is at the junction of Voulgareos and G Theotoki. It has a 24 hour cash exchange machine as does the Commercial Bank opposite the new port, and many others. There is a handy bureau de change booth located at the southern corner of the cricket ground. AmEx is represented by Greek Skies Tours (☎ 32 469) at Kapodistria 20a.

Post & Communications
The post office is on Leoforos Alexandras. It is open 7.30 am to 8 pm Monday to Friday, 7.30 am to 2 pm Saturday, and 9 am to 1.30 pm Sunday. The OTE phone office at Mantzarou 9 is open 6 am to midnight daily.

Email & Internet Access
There is an Internet cafe, Netoikos, at Kaloxairetou 14 between St Spyridon's church and the Liston. Internet access costs 500 dr for a minimum of 20 minutes, one

hour costs 1500 dr and a special five hour card is available for 6000 dr. It is open from 9 am to 1 am every day and drinks and snacks are also available.

Brand new is the On Line Internet cafe (☎ 46 226) at Kapodistria 28 opposite the Spianada. This hip and lively cafe is run by Anita, a friendly Dutch woman, and her partner Costas. Net access costs 1800 dr per hour (charged on a pro rata basis with a minimum of 15 minutes). It is open from 10 am to 2 am Monday to Saturday and from 6 pm to 2 am on Sunday, and also serves reasonably priced drinks (from coffee and tea to beer and spirits). There are also fax and printing facilities.

Internet Resources
The Ionian islands regional authorities have their own Web site at www.ionianislands.gr. The site has pages specific to Corfu, offering general historical and tourist information. Another useful Web site with dozens of links to other tourism-related sites is at www.Corfu1.com.

Bookshops
The Xenoglosso Bookshop, G Markora 45, stocks English-language books including novels and a few travel guides.

English Imports, in a side street off Methodiou, stocks English-language magazines and daily newspapers. Foreign newspapers and magazines can also be found at Kiosk, 11 Kapodistria, behind the Liston. The tiny shop has hundreds of titles and the friendly owner speaks English.

Laundry
There is a self-service laundrette in Velissariou St (the street with Cretabank at the end of it). The staff speak English and service washes are also available at no extra charge. Washes cost 1900 dr per load including soap and softener and drying is 1000 dr. It is open from 9.30 am to 3 pm on Monday and Wednesday, 9.30 am to 3 pm and 5.30 to 8 pm Tuesday, Thursday and Friday, 10 am to 3.30 pm on Saturday.

There is also a self-service laundrette at the new port (opposite the quay).

Left Luggage

There is a left-luggage service at the new port (500 dr per piece per day). It is open from 6 am to 11 pm daily.

Medical Services

The Corfu General Hospital (☎ 45 811) is on I Andreadi.

THINGS TO SEE
Palaio Frourio

One of Corfu Town's most dominant landmarks, the Palaio Frourio (Old Fortress) rises on a natural headland to the east of the old town. The earliest fortifications were built by the Byzantines, after Goth raiders destroyed the original Corinthian settlement of Corcyra on the Kanoni Peninsula in 550 AD. The surviving Corcyrans decided not to rebuild their ruined city but established themselves instead on the high headland with its natural defences. Materials from the ancient city were used in the construction of the new town.

From 1550 the Venetians extended the fortifications and dug a moat which was spanned by a retractable wooden bridge. Many of the buildings inside the fortress were built by the British for military use, including the church of St George which was designed to look like an ancient temple and dates from 1840.

There are sweeping views from the fortress south across the Bay of Garitsa to the Kanoni Peninsula and the Mon Repos estate and west to the old town, and an attractive bar/restaurant for refreshments. The fortress is open 8.30 am to 3 pm Tuesday to Sunday, although you can wander around the lower ramparts (and the restaurant) at any time. Entrance is 800 dr.

Neo Frourio

The promontory on which the Neo Frourio (New Fortress) stands was first fortified in the 12th century. The Venetians built the outer walls of the fortress between 1576 and 1588, although the buildings within – stairways, tunnels and vaulted chambers which children, in particular, love exploring – were constructed by the British. The citadel at the top was completed in 1843. The views from the top of the fortress over Corfu Town and the rest of the island are spectacular. There's also a bar at the top to refresh those worn out by the uphill climb. At the base of the fortress near the entrance is a children's playground. The New Fortress is open 9 am to 10 pm daily from 1 February until 31 October. It is closed during the winter months. Entrance is 400 dr and children under 11 are free. Walk up Solomou St from New Fortress Square (behind the old port) then follow the stone steps up to the entrance.

Campiello

Lying behind the seafront between the Old and New Fortresses is Corfu's old town, known as the Campiello. As the population living within the Old Fortress grew, houses were built in this area. Wandering through the medieval maze of narrow streets and pastel-coloured houses, with washing hanging out above your head, you could be forgiven for thinking you were in Venice. Traffic is nonexistent; the tiny lanes are paved with stone and connected by stone stairways and dotted with neighbourhood shops, *kafeneia* and artisan workshops.

The streets lying between the Campiello and the New Fortress to the west are all that remain of the old **Jewish quarter**, home to 5000 Jews from the 1600s until 1940. The community was decimated during WWII, with most of the Jews sent to Nazi death camps. Fewer than 100 of them survived.

The Liston & Spianada

The elegant arcade of the Liston and the Spianada (Esplanade) park opposite it are still the focus of life in Corfu Town. This is where Corfiots young and old – as well as tourists of all descriptions – come for their morning coffee or evening *volta* (stroll).

The Liston was built by the French during their administration of the island, and was designed to look like the Rue de Rivoli in Paris.

The northern half of the Spianada was used by the British during their protectorate as a cricket ground. Matches between the five local teams and visiting sides are still played there on summer afternoons. The **Maitland Rotunda** at the southern end of the Spianada was built to honour the first British high commissioner of the Ionian State, Sir Thomas Maitland. Nearby is a statue of Ioannis Kapodistrias, the Corfu-born first prime minister of independent Greece.

Palace of Saints Michael & George

Sitting like an English stately home at the northern end of the Spianada is the neoclassical Palace of Saints Michael and George, built between 1819 and 1824 under the spendthrift Sir Frederick Adam (whose statue stands in front of the palace) as the residence of the British Lord High Commissioners. The palace, built of Maltese marble, was later the summer residence of the Greek royal family. You can visit the state rooms.

Housed in the palace is the **Museum of Asiatic Art**, an impressive collection of 10,000 objects from Asia bequeathed to the nation by the Greek diplomats Grigoris Manos in 1926. Other collectors, including Nikolaos Hatzivasiliou, donated works to the collection. It includes Chinese and Japanese porcelain, bronzes, screens, sculptures, theatrical masks, armour, books and prints, as well as art works from Thailand, Korea and Tibet. The museum is open 8.30 am to 3 pm Tuesday to Sunday, although at the time of writing only part of the collection was on display, as much of the museum was being renovated. Admission is free.

Also housed in the Palace of St Michael and St George is the **Municipal Art Gallery** (entrance is from the courtyard behind the palace). Here work by late 19th and early 20th century Corfiot artists is on display together with some lovely late 16th and early 17th century altarpieces in the Byzantine style and an eclectic collection of work by contemporary local artists. The display continues on the main floor of the palace (entrance is to the right of the main palace doors) and admission is with the same ticket.

The highlights of the collection are the 19th century paintings, including some beautiful watercolours by Gallinas Angelos of seascapes and market scenes. George Samartzis' 1913 oil *Night in Corfu* shows that a busy evening at the Liston is no more crowded now than it was at the beginning of the 20th century. There are also some modern religious works of questionable quality which recall the kitsch of El Greco. The museum is open 9 am to 9 pm in summer and 10 am to 6 pm in winter. Admission is 500 dr.

Church of Agios Spyridon

The deep red dome of the church of Agios Spyridon is one of Corfu Town's most important landmarks. The simple exterior disguises an elaborate interior, complete with a white marble icon screen and dozens of icons and other paintings.

The church is a major point of pilgrimage for the faithful as it houses the mummified body of the island's miracle-working patron St Spyridon. His feet are clad in embroidered slippers which are replaced every year. The casket in which his remains lie is paraded on Palm Sunday, Easter Sunday, 11 August and the first Sunday in November.

The church, located on Agiou Spyridonos, was built in 1590. The ceiling paintings in elaborate gilt frames are copies of the originals by Panayiotis Doxaras, the leader of the Ionian School, and show scenes from St Spyridon's life.

Archaeological Museum

Corfu's Archaeological Museum is small but sweet. It was built between 1962 and 1965 to house the finds from both past and ongoing excavations on the island, particularly those south of the present town and on the Kanoni Peninsula.

The star exhibit is the *Gorgon Medusa* sculpture (on display in the Gorgo hall on the 1st floor), one of the best preserved pieces of Archaic sculpture in Greece. It was part of the west pediment of the 6th century Temple of Artemis at Corcyra (the ancient capital), a Doric temple which stood on the Kanoni Peninsula south of the town. The petrifying Medusa is depicted in the instant before she was beheaded by Perseus.

Corfu's Patron Saint

The story of St Spyridon – the island's patron saint, after whom so many of Corfu's children are named – is more a story of his life after death than before it.

Spyridon started his life as a humble shepherd in Cyprus. When his wife died, he entered a monastery, and through his immense faith rose to become the Bishop of Tremanti. At the time of his death at more than 90 years of age he was already regarded as a saint. After his burial a series of miracles occurred, including a spray of red roses that grew out of his tomb.

When Cyprus fell to the Saracens his remains were removed to Constantinople and buried there. When the Turks took Constantinople, a wealthy priest called Georgio Kalochairetis came to Spyridon's rescue. He hid the embalmed corpse of the saint in a sack of straw, together with the bodily remains of St Theodora Augusta who was stuffed into another sack, and slung the two over the back of his donkey. He took the relics to Corfu where they remained in the possession of his family, who charged the public to view them. In 1596 the bones were finally laid to rest in a silver reliquary and installed in the church built by Kalochairetis' descendants.

According to the Corfiots, St Spyridon has delivered them from evil on several occasions, and is responsible for having kept the island clear of famine, Turks and cholera. Corfiots gleefully recount that when the Turks were heading for Corfu it was Spyridon who repelled them by creating a great south-westerly squall. Another tale refers to the island's Roman Catholic occupiers trying to place an altar in the Greek Orthodox church; Spyridon expressed his displeasure by causing a lightning bolt to blow up a supply of munitions on the Old Fort.

St Spyridon gets an airing four times a year, on Palm Sunday, Easter Saturday, 11 August and the first Sunday in November, when the whole island converges on Corfu Town to view the relics as they are paraded around the streets accompanied by a great deal of pomp and circumstance.

This precipitated the birth of her sons, Chrysaor and Pegasus (the winged horse), who emerged from her headless body. Note the interesting circular marks carved into the lion's body, and the disturbing snakes that emerge from Medusa's hair.

Also impressive, in the south hall on the 1st floor, is the 7th century BC crouching lion, found close to the Menecrates Tomb. Archaeologists ascertained that it stood on top of the tomb. The work of a Corinthian sculptor, it is an example of Corinthian art at its peak. The lion has a fierce expression on its face and its crouching body is impressive in its expression and simplicity.

There is an extensive collection of coins (as well as maps indicating how widely the Corfiot coins were disseminated) and many other small archaeological finds, including delightful figurines in bronze and terracotta, small clay heads, household objects made out of bone, and medical instruments in bronze.

The museum (☎ 30 680) is south of the Spianada at Vraïla 5. It is fully accessible for disabled visitors in wheelchairs. Opening times are 8.45 am to 3 pm Tuesday to Saturday and 9.30 am to 2.30 pm Sunday. Admission is 800 dr.

Byzantine Museum

The Byzantine museum (☎ 38 313) in the Church of Our Lady of Antivouniotissa on Arseniou, has an outstanding collection of

MARTIN HARRIS

The *Gorgon Medusa* is one of the best preserved pieces of Archaic sculpture in Greece.

Byzantine and post-Byzantine icons dating from the 13th to the 17th centuries. There are around 100 icons on display, depicting individual saints and biblical scenes, including icons by Cretan painters Michael Damaskinos and Emanuel Tzanes. The interior layout of the church is also interesting, as the central nave has an ornately coffered and painted ceiling and is completely surrounded by an ambulatory. The museum is open 8.30 am to 2.30 pm Tuesday to Sunday. Admission is 500 dr.

Solomos Museum
The Zakynthos-born poet Dionysios Solomos lived in Corfu for 30 years and his former home is now a museum exhibiting memorabilia of his life and work. The museum, while a charming indication of how the poet's house must have appeared, will really be of interest to experts only – or at least to Greek speakers. There is no explanatory information and exhibits are labelled only in Greek. A more modern museum in Zakynthos Town has more to offer the casual visitor. Look for the sign at the western end of Arseniou. The museum is open 9.30 am to 2pm Monday to Friday (200 dr).

Paper Money Museum
Unique in Greece, the Paper Money Museum examines the history and production of bank notes. There is paper money from all over the world, and a display of Greek bank notes since independence. The museum is housed in the Ionian Bank building on Plateia Agiou Spyridona, behind the Liston. It is open 9 am to 1 pm Monday to Saturday. Admission is free.

British Cemetery
The well kept, tranquil British cemetery at the northern end of Kolokotroni has been a fitting resting place for British expats from the British occupation to the present day. Many fine trees and flowers, including wild orchids, grow here. George Psaila, the cemetery's resident gardener since 1944, was awarded an MBE in 1988 for conscientious service.

Other Churches
The **Orthodox Cathedral** near the old port in the heart of the old town is filled with icons. It is dedicated to St Theodora, whose body was brought to Corfu together with that of St Spyridon (see the boxed text 'Corfu's Patron Saint').

The Roman Catholic Church of **Agios Iakovos** was built in 1588 as a place of worship for the various Catholic occupiers of the island. The locals know it by the name of San Giacomo. The church was rebuilt in the early 18th century after being destroyed in a siege. It suffered again during a WWII bombardment which left it severely damaged, although its bell tower remained untouched. Today's parishioners are mostly Corfiots of Maltese descent.

ACTIVITIES
Sailing
Go yachting with a crew or bareboat in fabled waters. See under Yacht in the Getting Around chapter.

Walking
Walking enthusiasts should pick up a copy of *The Second Book of Corfu Walks* by Hilary Whitton Piapeti, at Xenoglosso (see Bookshops under Information earlier in this chapter), and take to the streets around Corfu Town or to the hills further afield. The book also contains mountain-bike tour details.

ORGANISED TOURS
Charitos Travel Agency (☎ 44 611, fax 36 825), Arseniou 35, offers coach, mountain-bike and walking tours. One full day coach tour (leaving at 10.30 am and returning at around 6 pm) covers the Ahillion Palace, Paleokastritsa and its monastery, swimming time, lunch and a drive through the northern part of the island. It costs 8900 dr.

Sarris Cruises offers day trips to Paxi and Antipaxi which include a stop at Parga on the mainland. Boats are well appointed with bars and sundecks and there is plenty of opportunity for swimming. Tickets (officially priced at around 9500 dr but often sold for less – try bargaining) can be bought from

CORFU

Varthis Travel (☎ 31 140, fax 31 334), Donzelot 5. You can also get tickets from the Sarris Cruises office at the new port. Boats depart from the old port at 9 am and return at 7.30 pm.

PLACES TO STAY – BUDGET

Most of Corfu Town's D class hotels have closed, resulting in a shortage of budget accommodation. There are no EOT-approved domatia but locals who unofficially let rooms often meet the boats – you may strike it lucky. Be wary of booking rooms for Greece in advance in Italy before arrival. A few unscrupulous agencies may suggest your preferred choice is closed or full – and reap a tidy commission from the places booked through them.

Hotel Europi (☎ 39 304), near the new harbour, is the town's only D class hotel. Small and modern, it has little to recommend it other than being near the new port and therefore convenient for those arriving by ferry. Singles/doubles cost 5500/6000 dr with shared bathroom and doubles with private bathroom are 7000 dr. A sign points to the hotel at the western end of Xenofondos Stratigou.

Hotel Hermes (☎ 39 268, fax 31 747, G Markora 14) is just off San Rocco, directly opposite one end of the daily fruit and vegetable market in an atmospheric if noisy location. It has basic but clean rooms and is popular with backpackers.

The only positive thing about *Hotel Ionian* (☎ 30 628, fax 44 690, Xenofondos Stratigou 46) at the new port is its position (for early arrivals or late departures by ferry). It is however the cheapest C class with rooms (most of them very noisy) for 8500/10,600 dr.

PLACES TO STAY – MID-RANGE

Hotel Arcadion (☎ 37 670, fax 45 087, Kapodistriou 44) has small, comfortable rooms for 13,000/17,000 dr, including breakfast. *Hotel Atlantis* (☎ 35 560, fax 46 480, email atlanker@mail.otenet.gr, Xenofondos Stratigou 48) is handy for the new port. All rooms are air-conditioned and range from 15,000/18,000 dr for singles/

doubles in low season to 18,000/21,600 dr in high season. It is directly opposite the new port and handy if you are arriving late or leaving early.

The refurbished C class *Hotel Konstantinopoulis* (☎ 48 716, fax 48 718, Zavitsianou 1), reincarnated from a shabby backpacker's favourite into a splendid Art Nouveau hostelry, has rates of 14,000 19,000 dr with breakfast. The multilingual staff are friendly and knowledgeable. Although there's no air-conditioning, its position makes this one of Corfu's best deals. Note that the hotel does not accept credit cards. Situated nearby, the B class *Hotel Astron* (☎ 39 505, 33 708, Donzelot 15) has a neoclassical ambience. Room rates are 19,500/ 28,000 dr.

The B class *Bella Venezia Hotel* (☎ 46 500, fax 20 708, email belvenht@hol.gr, Zambeli 4) is yet another neoclassical-style hotel. Rates are 15,400/18,500 dr.

PLACES TO STAY – TOP END

The A class *Cavalieri Hotel* (☎ 39 041, fax 39 283, Kapodistria 4) occupies a 300-year-old building and has an interior of classical elegance. Rates are 30,000/35,000 dr and family suites cost 40,000 dr.

Corfu Palace (☎ 39 485, fax 31 749, email cfupalace@hol.gr) on Dimokratias is the town centre's only deluxe hotel, the choice of Prince Rainier and the late Princess Grace. It has two bars, two restaurants and pools. Rates are a healthy 54,000/74,000 dr.

About 10 minutes drive north of Corfu Town is the wooded promontory of Kontakali. The five star A class *Kontokali Bay Hotel* (☎ 90 500, fax 91 901, email kontobay@compulink.gr) is a plush option for those that like their creature comforts. High season singles/doubles cost from 24,000/ 39,000 dr including an American buffet breakfast.

PLACES TO EAT – BUDGET

As it was not conquered by the Turks, Corfu maintains a distinctive cuisine influenced by other parts of Europe, including Russia.

There are several low-priced eating options close to the new port. Both the tiny

O Thessalonikios on Xenofondos Stratigou and *Luca's BBQ* on Avramiou serve low-priced, succulent spit-roast chicken.

There's a cluster of atmospheric restaurants at the southern end of the old town. *Taverna O Giorgios (Guilford 16)* serves reasonably priced *mezedes* and main courses at outdoor tables under a grapevine. The cosy *Yia sou Yianni (Idremenon 19)* has similar food and prices.

Nearby, *Restaurant Arpi (Giotopoulou 20)* is a classy little place with *pastitsada* for 1900 dr and *sofrito* for 1700 dr.

One of Corfu's oldest restaurants is *Hrysomalis (Nikiforou Theotoki 6)*, situated just behind the expensive Liston cafe strip. Lawrence and Gerald Durrell used to dine here. The food is cheap and tasty and the local rosé wine is superb.

Farther north, most eateries are touristy and downmarket, but there are exceptions. *Paradosiakon (Solomou 20)* serves delicious food and *Naftikon Restaurant (Nikiforou Theotoki 150)* has fair prices and Corfiot food. At *Ouzeri Bellisimo* also on Nikiforou Theotoki, a tasty mezedes plate costs 1900 dr.

Eating options at the new port aren't extensive but there are some reasonably priced cafes for light snacks and drinks. *Café Ostria* a few metres from the offices of Hellenic Mediterranean Lines ferries, has good coffee and you can pick up a tasty cheese or spinach pie.

If souvlaki and gyros don't satisfy your fast food cravings, head for *Goody's* in Voulgareos St near the corner of Kapodistriou. It's a Greek version of McDonald's and in addition to tasty and cheap burgers and fries, does good pasta and has an extensive salad bar. For a snack on the run, the *bakery* behind the Creta Bank in Velissariou sells arguably the best cheese and spinach pies in town, baked fresh at several times throughout the day.

PLACES TO EAT – MID-RANGE

Indulge in a little people-watching on the Liston. You will pay around 1250 dr for coffee and croissant at any of the cafes, and can sit either under the loggia or across the road in the totally open-air terraces which border the cricket ground.

Capri at the southern end of the Liston has delicious (if slightly pricey) ice coffee for 700 dr and a decent range of light meals and snacks such as omelettes and salads from about 850 dr to 1750 dr. Closer to the Liston's northern end is *Café Europe* which has a similar range of drinks and snacks at fractionally higher prices.

Just inland from the old port is the delightful *Venetian Well (☎ 44 761, Kremasti Square)*, whose tables take over an entire square in the centre of which is (funnily enough) a decorative Venetian well. The food is excellent. You'll pay 1900 dr for an appetiser and 2500 dr for a main course. Creative dishes include duck served with cumquats, and the swordfish kebabs are something else.

Mouragia Ouzeri (Arseniou 15) has a large range of mezedes. The small mixed fish plate (2250 dr) or the grilled beef patties *(soutzoukakia)* makes an enjoyable meal overlooking the sea.

Behind the Liston is another established eatery which has operated since 1932, *Estiatorio Rex (Kapodistria 66)*. Claiming to be the oldest restaurant in town, it is now a quietly modern, tasteful eating place, with main courses averaging around 2200 dr.

Faliraki (☎ 21 118) on the corner of Arseniou and Kapodistria is a refurbishment of a popular Victorian bathing spot. It's a great waterside spot for a meal in the shadow of the old Kastro. There are traditional Greek appetisers such as tzatziki and taramas (both 800 dr), main courses including mousaka 1700 dr and pastitsada for 2100 dr, and a good selection of fresh fish.

Old Fortress Café at the old fort is a pleasant and stylish spot to stop for a fresh fruit juice drink or a beer or wine. Light meals such as pasta and salads are also available. The 1000 dr appetiser plate has a bit of everything on it and although meant to be a snack to accompany your drink is really a meal in itself.

Art Café is in gardens behind the Palace of St Michael and St George and is peaceful and shady at all times of the day. An ice coffee is 550 dr.

CORFU

Self-Catering

The daily produce *market* is located just to the north of Plateia San Rocco. This is the place to head for fruit, vegetables and fish. The stalls are there from around 8 am to 2.30 pm every day (except Sunday).

Nearby, the *Dimitra supermarket* on G Markora next to the Hotel Hermes will supply you with the rest of your groceries. It is open 8 am to 3 pm Monday, Wednesday and Saturday and 8 am to 9 pm Tuesday, Thursday and Friday. There is also a large *supermarket* near the long distance bus station, about 200m from the new port on Avramiou.

ENTERTAINMENT

The English language monthly magazine *The Corfiot* has listings of concerts, exhibitions and traditional festivals taking place around the island. The more sedate at heart may enjoy horse and carriage rides around the old town – great for taking photos or making a quick home video memento.

Bars

Having fun in Corfu is comprised mainly of strolling around, sitting at the cafes on the Liston or being cool at the multitude of little bars and pubs that dot the old and new town. Young and old have their favourite spots and you can identify these venues at a glance.

Dirty Dick's is a popular lively watering hole at the old port on the corner of Zavitsianou and Donzelot. Drinks are cheap and the atmosphere is relaxed.

Perhaps the most entertaining spot to spend an idle hour or two is at one of the cafes bordering the cricket ground, watching cricket on a Sunday afternoon. Keep your eye on the ball, or it may land for a six in your beer.

Clubs & Pubs

Corfu's disco strip is 2km north-west of the new port. Here, high-tech palaces of hype jostle cheek by jowl for the tourist buck. The *Hippodrome* is the biggest and flashiest – it's even got a pool. *Apokalypsis* and *Coco Club* are garish and expensive and there's a pseudo *Hard Rock Café* to complete the

scene. Don't expect an evening at any of these clubs to be a cheap night out. Drinks cost around 1000 dr each and you usually pay around 3000 dr to get in.

There are no specifically gay clubs. *Mobile club* also on the disco strip is particularly gay-friendly although it does attract a mixed crowd. Most other discos can probably best be described as gay tolerant.

Cinema

If it's visual entertainment you want, Corfu Town has two indoor cinemas: the *Pallas* on G Theotoki and the *Orpheus* on Aspioti. A little farther south of the latter, there's an outdoor cinema that screens films intermittently during summer.

SPECTATOR SPORTS
Cricket

Corfu is the only place in Greece where cricket is played. Matches take place on Corfu's main cricket ground on a rather scruffy pitch abutting the Liston. The actual wicket is made of artificial turf and resounds, during the summer months, to the rather incongruous sound of leather balls on willow bats as white-clad players of the few Corfu cricket clubs attempt to score sixes by dropping the balls into the coffee cups of the spectators watching from the Liston (see boxed text 'Is it Cricket?').

AROUND CORFU TOWN
Vido

Visible from Corfu Town's northern seafront, the large wooded islet of Vido is a privately run bird sanctuary and a pleasant place for a picnic. Over the centuries it has been a strategic point in defending and attacking Corfu, and has served as a prison, a cemetery and an execution ground. A caïque plies back and forth to the island from the old port every hour.

Kanoni Peninsula

About 5km south of Corfu Town, dangling below the Bay of Garitsa, is the Kanoni Peninsula, the site of the ancient capital. It is easily reached by the blue city bus to Kanoni from San Rocco Square, but more

Is it Cricket?

Newcomers to Corfu's Liston promenade cafe scene may be puzzled by the sight of men dressed in white surrounding another man dressed in white attempting to hit a hard leather ball out of the rather scruffy park with a long willow bat. This is cricket – Greek-style. Travellers from the former British Empire will recognise and delight at this eccentric and quintessentially British game replete with its sixes, fours, LBWs and owzats!

The game was imported to Corfu by the British during their 49 year hegemony of the island from 1815 to 1864. It has remained firmly entrenched in Corfu ever since. The few teams around the island gather to battle it out on sunny Sundays. While the pitch has seen better days and the distance from the batting crease to the tables of the Liston cafes can seem alarmingly close, the game is played with unusual verve and enthusiasm. Corfu is the only place in Greece where cricket is played, but the Liston pitch is no longer unique as the game's popularity is growing.

MARTIN HARRIS

The basic aim, for those unfamiliar with the game, is to score 'runs' by hitting the ball as far as possible and then running to and fro between the wooden wickets before the ball is returned by the fielders. Batters are considered 'out' when the ball hits their wickets, when a fielder catches the ball, when the ball hits the leg when it could have hit the wicket, or when the fielder hits the wickets before the batter has returned to the crease after running.

It's a complex game and spectators enjoy its subtleties as well as its seemingly slow pace as much as the players do. Good cricket watching is always accompanied by copious amounts of beer, the occasional shouts of encouragement from the sidelines and the odd comment on the weather. It wouldn't be cricket any other way – even in Corfu.

energetic walkers could make a good day's hike out of a trip there.

Ancient ruins are scattered throughout the area, although little has been properly excavated and there is not a great deal to see. Just north of the peninsula proper on the corner of Marasli and Kiprou Sts, about 300m south of the archaeological museum, is the circular **Tomb of Menecrates** dating from the end of the 7th century BC. The so-called *Lion of Menecrates*, a highlight of the Archaeological Museum, was once positioned on top of the cenotaph.

Another important archaeological site is the 6th century BC **Temple of Artemis** where the magnificent Gorgon pediment (now housed in the Archaeological Museum) was discovered.

Remnants of the city walls, built in the 5th and 4th centuries BC survive in two locations. The excavated remains of a Roman villa and bathhouse as well as the ruins of the 5th century AD Christian **Basilica of Agia Kerkyra** can be seen on the road to Kanoni, opposite the Mon Repos villa gates, although the sites are not open to the public.

The **Church of Agios Iason and Agios Sosipater** is a gem of Byzantine architecture. It was built in the 10th or 11th century and is dedicated to the two disciples of St Paul, Jason and Sosipatros, who brought religion to Corfu in 70 AD. At the time of writing the inside was little more than a construction site and there appears to be no end in site to the renovations.

MARTIN HARRIS

The *Lion of Menecrates* was once positioned on top of the cenotaph of the circular Tomb of Menecrates, just north of the Kanoni Peninsula.

Just off the southern tip of Kanoni are two pretty islets. On one is the monastery of **Moni Vlahernas**, reached by a causeway. On the other, **Mouse Island** (Poutikonisi), there is a 13th century church. Caïques ply back and forth from the top of the Kanoni Peninsula.

Mon Repos Villa The neoclassical villa was built in 1831 by Sir Frederick Adam, the second high commissioner of the Ionian State, for his Corfiot wife. It was later used as a summer residence by the Greek royal family. Prince Philip, Duke of Edinburgh, was born in the villa in 1921. The residence has been restored to its former beauty but is empty inside and currently used only for the odd official reception.

The wooded parkland surrounding the villa is dotted with ancient ruins, including two Doric temples, one of which, the Kardaki temple, dates from about 500 BC. It is a lovely place to walk even in the height of summer as the paths are reasonably shady.

The Greek government repossessed the villa from ex-king Constantine in 1994 and handed it over to the local authorities. Work is currently being carried out to turn the estate into an archaeological park. The grounds can be visited (free admission) and the public will eventually be admitted to the villa as well. The grounds are open from 8 am to 8 pm daily.

North of Corfu Town

☎ 0661/0663

Most of the northern Corfu coast is package-tourist saturated, and mainly de-Greeked. The busy road heading north – which passes through Kondokali, Gouvia (where Corfu's marina is located), Dasia and Dafnila to Ipsos and Pyrgi – is lined with hotels, apartments, camp sites and restaurants, almost all of which have been built with an absolutely dazzling disregard for aesthetics. The beaches in this area are predominantly narrow strips of pebbles, and the calm seas make it ideal for watersports such as water-skiing and parasailing.

The independent traveller would do better to continue to the north-east corner of the island to the pretty resorts of Kalami, Kouloura and the larger Kassiopi, or along the north coast to the long sandy beaches of Almyros and Aharavi. Once you get to Roda and Sidhari the tacky tourist sprawl rears its ugly head again. To get away from it all head inland and uphill to the top of Mt Pantokrator and the mountain villages nearby, or head to the ghost town of Old Perithia.

GETTING THERE & AWAY

A KTEL long distance bus runs along the coast road between Corfu Town and Kassiopi stopping at, or at least not far from, all the resorts en route. Blue suburban buses also run from Plateia San Rocco as far as Dhassia and Ipsos. The resorts along the northern coast are served by regular KTEL buses from Corfu Town. These often travel via scenic inland routes.

DASIA TO IPSOS
☎ 0661

The wooded bays of **Dasia** (Δασιά) and its neighbour Dafnila have blended into one resort. It is the first place worth stopping at along the north-east coast. The beaches here are pebble and there are a variety of watersports available including parasailing and water-skiing.

The resort of **Ipsos** (Υψος), 2km north of Dasia and about 14km north of Corfu Town, will appeal only to those for whom a good holiday means crowded beaches by day and rowdy bars by night. The former fishing village is now a strip of clubs, tavernas and takeaway food joints that stretches 2km north and encompasses the neighbouring resort of Pyrgi which is even gaudier than Ipsos. The narrow stretch of beach is separated from the fun and entertainment by a very busy road. Umbrellas and sun lounges can be hired (500 dr each). You will probably not want to linger long in Ipsos if you are seeking solitude, although with a variety of camping grounds it could be a good budget choice.

Places to Stay & Eat
Dasia boasts Corfu's best camp site, *Dionysus Camping Village (☎ 91 417, fax 91 760)*, well signposted on the right between Dafnila and Dasia. It offers bungalows for 2250 dr per person as well as excellent facilities for campers, including a pool, shop and restaurant.

In the mid-range is *Dassia Beach Hotel (☎/fax 93 224)* set on the beachfront surrounded by olive trees. Double rooms with bathroom are 14,000 dr including breakfast. More upmarket is the A class *Elea Beach (☎ 93 490)* which has singles/doubles for 28,000/38,000 dr.

There are plenty of mediocre restaurants in the area, but for a good meal head to

Greco in Dafnila. Its blue-and-white decor is more reminiscent of the Cyclades than the Ionians, and it serves specialities such as home-made pies filled with chicken or zucchini. The owner and his daughter coach their guests in Greek dancing most nights.

In Ipsos all the accommodation in the ghastly main strip and much of it is block-booked by package holiday companies. At *Ipsos Travel (☎ 93 661)* you can also organise accommodation as well as boat hire. *Camping Corfu Ipsos (☎ 93 246, ☎ 93 579, fax 93 741)* about halfway along the strip charges 1200 dr per person, 700 dr per car, 800 dr for a tent, and 700 dr per day for electricity. The other camping grounds are *Ipsos Ideal (☎ 93 243)* and *Paradise Camping (☎ 93 557)* at Pyrgi. *Costas Beach Hotel (☎ 93 205)* has double rooms from 10,000 dr to 14,000 dr depending on the season.

The best place for a traditional Greek meal is *Asteria Taverna* at the southern end of the resort near the small marina.

BARBATI TO AGNI
☎ 0663

Once you venture beyond Pyrgi to the north-eastern coast, you enter some of Corfu's most privileged scenery. Heading around the winding coastal road you will first hit **Barbati** (Μπαρμπάτι), a long pebbly beach with umbrellas, watersports facilities, sun lounges, and all the shops and minimarkets you could need.

More appealing are the little fishing hamlets of Nisaki and Agni, reached down narrow winding lanes from the main road. **Nisaki** is little more than a small cove with a pebble beach, a couple of tavernas and some domatia. Trails lead farther around the headland to a series of small shingle coves. It is a popular place especially for snorkelling and swimming. You can also hire small boats with outboard motors to get to other coves nearby and there is a water-skiing school. Continuing north-east towards Kalami, pretty **Agni** (Αγνή) is regarded by some as the gourmet heart of Corfu. It comprises three excellent tavernas, a tiny pebbled cove and some yacht mooring jetties.

Places to Stay & Eat

Rooms are a bit thin on the ground in Barbati, however *Helga Holiday Services* (*☎/fax 91 547, email helga@otenet.gr*) can help for stays of a few days (or preferably a week) in studios and apartments from about 12,000 dr per person.

Up the hill above the beach and road is *Hotel Pantokrator* (*☎ 91 005, fax 91 004*), which caters predominantly to package tourists, although it might be worth trying if you have trouble elsewhere. In high season rooms cost 9000 dr per person on a halfboard basis, dropping to around 4000 dr in low season. Its *Olive Tree Restaurant* has a daily changing menu.

All accommodation in Nisaki is handled by the British-run *Falcon Travel* (*☎ 91 318, fax 91 070*), although a minimum three day stay is required.

There are several good places to eat at Nisaki, the best of which is the innovative *Olive Press* signposted from the road down to the beach. Virtually on the beach *Taverna Mitsos* and *Taverna Zeus* both serve good quality basic Greek fare.

The tiny cove of Agni offers three excellent tavernas: *Toula's*, which specialises in fish and is noted for its prawn pilaff, *Taverna Nikolas* which does genuine Corfiot cuisine, and the traditional Greek *Taverna Agni* which has been run by descendants of one family for 124 years.

KALAMI TO AGIOS STEFANOS
☎ 0663

Writers Lawrence and Gerald Durrell knew this area well and spent much of their creative years along this coastline which, in parts, is little more than a short boat hop to the Albanian coastline opposite.

Lawrence Durrell and his wife Nancy lived in Kalami (Καλάμι) just before the outbreak of WWII. Henry Miller, who was their guest, wrote that 'days in Kalami passed like a song'. They still do, although today's visitor has to contend with many more people sharing the uncomfortably pebbly beach than in the Durrells' days. Kalami is particularly popular with Italian tourists in July and August.

The large white building at the southern end of the bay, the White House, was the Durrells' home. It is perched right on the water's edge, as Durrell wrote 'set like a dice on a rock already venerable with the scars of wind and water', and must have been idyllic during the writer's time here. He wouldn't have had the disappointing view of the massive complex of pink holiday apartments that clings to the hillside opposite. (See boxed text 'The Brothers Durrell'.)

Just round the next headland north-east is the picturesque little harbour of Kouloura, where many daily excursion boats from farther north bring visitors. The Venetian occupiers left their mark on Kouloura with a 16th century villa and fortified tower and two 17th century patrician dwellings. There is a pleasant restaurant overlooking the harbour here. From both Kalami and Kouloura the houses and buildings of Butrint in neighbouring Albania can be seen quite clearly.

Even closer to Albania is the gorgeous – and pricey – resort of Agios Stefanos (Αγιος Στέφανος), a popular mooring spot for yachts. Yiannis Boats in the middle of the harbourfront rents small motorboats by the day or hour.

The KTEL bus to Kassiopi follows the coast road, and will drop you about 1km above Kalami and Kouloura. It's a longer – but very pleasant – hike down to Agios Stefanos from the coast road and back up again!

Places to Stay & Eat

Much of the accommodation in this area is in luxury villas handled by upmarket UK travel agencies, including Greek Islands Club (☎ 020-8232 9780), Greek Options (☎ 020-7233 5233), Simply Ionian (☎ 020-8995 9323/1121, email ionian@simply-travel.com) and CV Travel (☎ 0870-606 001, fax 020-7591 2802, email cv.travel@dial.pipex.com). See Organised Tours in the Getting There & Away chapter.

Accommodation dries up quickly in Kalami in high season and just turning up without a reservation is not advisable. *Sunshine Travel* (*☎/fax 91 170*) can help with advance bookings. It has apartments sleeping four people for 22,000 dr to 26,000 dr

The Brothers Durrell

The name Durrell is synonymous with Corfu, though it is perhaps surprising that of the two brothers, Lawrence (1912-90) and Gerald (1925-95), it is the naturalist Gerald rather than the poet and novelist Lawrence who has so inextricably linked the name of this famous duo with the island of Corfu and the little village of Kalami on Corfu's north-east coast. The brothers arrived on Corfu with their family in the early 1930s.

Gerald Durrell was born in India and gained considerable repute among conservationists for his role in breeding endangered animal species for eventual release in the wild. He founded the world famous Jersey Zoo in the Channel Islands. He was also a prolific author, producing more than 35 informative yet amusing books about animals. Durrell's love of animals started when living in Corfu in the 1930s. His best known books were *The Overloaded Ark* (1953), *Three Singles to Adventure* (1953), *My Family and other Animals* (1956), *A Zoo in my Luggage* (1960) and *Birds, Beasts and Relatives* (1969). Gerald Durrell continued to visit Corfu until his death in 1995, and was particularly outspoken about environmental damage to the island from chemical pesticides.

Brother Lawrence, also born in India, was the dedicated writer in the family. He was at once a novelist, poet, writer of topographical books, verse plays and farcical short stories. He is best known for the *Alexandria Quartet*, a series of four interconnected novels. His Greek trilogy included *Prospero's Cell* (1945) in which he describes his life in Corfu during 1937 and 1938, *Reflections on a Marine Venus* (1953) for which he spent two years in Rhodes in 1945-46 as press officer for the Allied government, and *Bitter Lemons* about Cyprus (1957) where he spent the 1952-56 years as a teacher and government official – latterly during the Cypriot insurgency. His observations of the villages and customs of Corfu so eloquently described in *Prospero's Cell* bear only a little resemblance to the tourist ravaged island of today. The title of the book came from the theory that Corfu was the setting for Prospero and Miranda's exile in *The Tempest* by William Shakespeare. Lawrence Durrell travelled widely and eventually settled in France.

Both brothers were well known around Corfu and some of the older restaurant owners near Corfu Town's Liston still remember their illustrious literary patrons. The White House, overlooking the sea at the village of Kalami, in which Lawrence Durrell and his wife Nancy lived and where Durrell wrote *Prospero's Cell*, is now a quaint fish restaurant. The upper floor has been converted into holiday apartments which can be rented by the week through CV Travel (☎ 0870-606 001, fax 020-7591 2802, email cv.travel@dial.pipex.com), 43 Cadogan Street, London SW3 2PR, UK.

MARTIN HARRIS

Poet and novelist Lawrence Durrell and wife Nancy lived in Kalami just prior to the outbreak of WWII.

CORFU

per day, and double studios for 18,000 dr to 20,000 dr.

One of the best deals is ***Villa Rita*** (☎ *91 030*). A lovely Greek couple run these spotless studios and apartments set among olive trees, all of which are well equipped and perfect for a longer self-catering stay (although the owners will rent them for a night or two if available). Each one has its own terrace or balcony. Smaller studios (for two people) cost 10,000 dr, larger four-person apartments cost 17,000 dr.

The *Villa Matella* (☎ 91 371, ☎ 91 073) restaurant also has a few double rooms/studios for 12,000/14,000 dr. It's set back from the beach on the road through the village and you'll have an excellent meal here. Tables are set in a pretty stone courtyard overflowing with flowers and the meals feature fresh ingredients from the owner's gardens in the mountains.

All the accommodation at Agios Stefanos is snapped up by the British blue-chip villa companies, so it is best visited on a day trip.

If you are a Durrell fan, you can have a nostalgic meal at the *White House* in Kalami. The restaurant slightly trades off its name and position, but a decent fish meal will cost you around 3600 dr.

Agios Stefanos has some nice restaurants and bars. *Damiano's*, a bar on the waterfront, serves wicked cocktails including the 'Corfu Special' of Bacardi, Grand Marnier, orange juice, lemon juice and grenadine. A few too many and you'll probably end up in the harbour. Other good places to eat include *Cochili Taverna* which does good home-style Greek cooking, and *Eucalyptus* on the north side of the bay beside a shingle beach which does excellent Greek and international food.

KASSIOPI Κασσιόπη
☎ 0663
The next major port of call is **Kassiopi** which might make a good base for exploration of the northern and north-eastern coasts. It is a sizable little resort village around a circular harbour, bordered at its western side by a headland.

Kassiopi was an important Hellenistic town and, strategically positioned in the path of foreign invaders, it has seen a lot of history. The Romans surrounded the settlement with walls and built a temple to Zeus. Cassius resided here and others that passed through included Cicero and the Emperor Nero. Emperor Tiberius also built a villa here. In time the temple was replaced by a Christian church, destroyed in the Turkish siege of 1537. The Venetians immediately built another church, **Our Lady of Kassiopi**.

The ruins of a Byzantine fortress sit atop the headland west of the harbour. It was captured by Robert Guiscard and his Norman troops during their quest for Constantinople. It was destroyed by the Venetians.

Orientation & Information
The main street, Kassiopitras, doglegs from the coast road down to the harbour, from where paths lead around the headland to various small coves. Halfway down, next to a small square with a well, is an Ionian Bank ATM. Kassiopi boasts some good – albeit touristy – shops selling locally made lace. You can take an excursion boat every day (1000 dr return) to the much nicer sandy beach at **Kalamki**. The beach, in a protected cove, is ideal for families, as it has a shallow shelf for about 50m. There are a couple of good tavernas.

Kassiopi Travel Service (☎ 81 388, fax 81 154) rents small motorboats, exchanges money and can help with accommodation. The Travel Corner (☎ 81 220, fax 81 108, email info@travcor.gr) exchanges money, has a metered phone and offers an email service. There are two offices in the village, one by the port and one by the central square. They also provide information on apartments and studios. Ionian Renta Bike near the central square rents mountain bikes.

Places to Stay & Eat
Elli Tsiliyianni (☎ 81 483) rents apartments for four people for 17,000 dr. They are located in the yellow and white building in the street behind the beach on the western edge of the resort. *Oasis Hotel* (☎ 81 210, fax 81 067, Kassiopitras St) 50m from the port, offers double rooms for 8000 dr. Its restaurant serves good Greek and international food and is a good place to watch the passing people parade. *Agathi* (☎ 81 315) who runs the lace shop of the same name in Kassiopitras St, rents apartments for four people for 14,000 dr and for five people (17,000 dr), although she usually gives generous discounts on these rates. She also has a villa (sleeping six) for 20,000 dr. Inquire at the shop.

Fulvia Travel (☎ 81 040, fax 81 042) can assist with accommodation (as well as car rental). Studios are available from 11,000 dr per night, and four-person apartments for 16,000 dr.

On the harbourfront, *Ben Limani* and *Wave* are popular hang-outs, while *Kostas* on the path up to the fortress is a lively place. *Castello* by the beach on the western side of the village has a good selection of fish. *Bucabilia Cafe* at the water's edge is a good place to stop for a caffe frappé, ice cream or milkshake.

MT PANTOKRATOR Παντοκράτωρ

From Pyrgi a road continues east around the base of Mt Pantokrator, at 906m the island's highest peak. Another road snakes north and inland over the western flank of the mountain to the north coast. A detour can be made to the picturesque village of **Strinylas**, a popular base for walkers in spring and autumn.

There are no official domatia in Strinylas, but you could ask about rooms at either of the two tavernas, *Oasis* and *Elm Tree Taverna*, which share the village's central square with a handful of free-range chickens and a small workshop selling olive wood products.

A newly surfaced road leads through stark terrain to the summit where there are stupendous views. The pretty monastery of **Moni Pantokratora** (those wearing shorts and skimpy tops will be loaned a shawl) is straddled by an enormous and incredibly ugly radio antenna. How it was allowed to be positioned there is anyone's guess. There is a small taverna which provides drinks and snacks.

Beyond Kassiopi is a turn-off for the fascinating, half-derelict and almost abandoned village of **Old Perithia** (no buses go there), high up on Mt Pantokrator. This and other inland villages were established by Byzantine people fleeing repeated pirate raids on their coastal settlements. Most of the buildings are derelict although there is a shady taverna that operates in summer. Around the village you can see the framework of terraced orchards and fields.

Abandoned villages can also be found at Old Sinies and at Rou on the western side of Mt Pantokrator. Old Perithia can also be reached by an unsealed road from Strinylas but should only be attempted by those with a four wheel drive vehicle. There are paths to the summit of Mt Pantokrator from Strinylas and Old Perithia. Only experienced walkers with good maps should attempt the trek.

ALMYROS Αλμυρός
☎ 0663

The northern coast road continues beyond Kassiopi but is rather dull and uninspiring after the arresting scenery of the east coast opposite Albania. If you blinked you'd miss Almyros Beach, which consists of a few houses and villas and the odd taverna. However one suspects that in true Corfiot fashion, it won't be long before it is swallowed up by neighbouring Aharavi.

The beach at Almyros is sensational and virtually deserted. The long stretch of golden sand is clean and the water shallow until a long way out – ideal for children. Bring your own umbrella if you want shade – at the time of writing there were no facilities on the beach, and only one tiny taverna and a small shop.

The House on the Hill (☎/fax 63 531) is a tastefully built complex of studios and larger apartments on the inland side of the main road, about 600m from the beach. Very nice studios (for two) go for 13,000/15,000 dr and apartments (for four) start at 25,000 dr. There's a pool and bar, and bikes can be rented.

Otherwise, the best option for a room is if you head towards Aharavi. *Taverna Avra (☎ 63 633, fax 0661-26 185)*, on the beach between Almyros and Aharavi, has studios from 13,000 dr and larger apartments from 16,000 dr (breakfast is not included). The owner, Spiros Koskinas, also has other rooms along this stretch of coast so is a good place to start. The taverna is one of the nicest on the northern coast and serves good Greek food. *Liberty's* taverna and domatia behind it is also a good place for a meal but the rooms tend to be block-booked.

CORFU

AHARAVI Αχαράβη
☎ 0663

The coast road continues to the resorts of **Aharavi** and **Roda** which will soon be indistinguishable (Roda is a few kilometres west of Aharavi). The beach at Aharavi – long and sandy – continues to Roda, but is nicer and slightly less crowded. It's particularly popular with families, as the water is shallow until a long way out. There are plenty of good tavernas and bars on the beach and umbrellas and sun lounges can be had for 500 dr a piece. An extensive range of watersports is also on offer.

There are ruins of a 5th century Doric temple dedicated to Apollo on the main road towards Roda.

Orientation & Information

The township of Aharavi is growing at an alarming rate. The first buildings weren't constructed until the early 1980s when farmers from Agios Pandelemon, a nearby hill town, sold off land for tourism development. Now those first buildings and a few pre-existing houses are referred to as the 'old town' and development in the late 1980s and 1990s has created the 'new town', a busy commercial centre on both sides of the main road. Fortunately the beachfront itself is still fairly pleasant, and lined with tavernas.

The atmosphere is good. As a 'new' resort most of the businesses are run by young, enthusiastic management and staff and competition keeps them all on their toes.

There's an Ionian Bank in the main street with an ATM for Visa and MasterCard. There are also offices of both Avis and Hertz car rentals, and the local company Eurohire. Tee Travel tourist office (☎ 64 108) will exchange money, organise car or bike hire, boat trips or boat hire and can also help with rooms or apartments in and around Aharavi. It is 100m from the main road (towards the beach) next door to the Akharavi Beach Hotel.

Places to Stay & Eat

The enormous B class *Akharavi Beach Hotel* (☎ 63 103, fax 63 461) takes up much

of the Aharavi littoral and is the main complex in the area. Its apartments and studios are usually block-booked but there are often rooms available for independent travellers. Doubles with breakfast cost 22,000 dr.

Up in the 'old town', the charming and tranquil *Dandolo* (☎ 63 557, fax 63 457), set among a garden filled with flowering shrubs and shady trees, accepts only independent travellers. Its apartments (all with kitchen and terrace) for two people cost 16,000 dr or 25,000/28,000 dr for three/four people.

Aharavi boasts one of Corfu's best restaurants, *Maistro* (☎ 63 020), which is on the beachfront. Corfiots come from Corfu Town (40km away) just to eat here, and it is no wonder – it offers authentic Corfiot cooking in a pleasant environment (right on the beach) with friendly staff. The menu includes starters (about 800 dr each) such as *saganaki* (Greek cheese with breadcrumbs and ham, fried in butter) and *tiganopsomo* (home-made bread with fried feta cheese).

Main courses include perennial favourites such as *stifado* (veal cooked in tomato, red wine and brandy with small whole onions), lamb *kleftiko* (oven-cooked with garlic, white wine, tzatziki, feta and mushrooms) and *giaurtlu* (beefburger with yoghurt and red pepper sauce served on pitta bread).

To get there turn off the main coast road 20m east of the roundabout, following signs to the Ionian Princess Hotel and follow the road down to the beach. An alternative route is to walk along the beach – you can't miss it.

The streets of the 'old town' are lined with bars and tavernas, many of which buzz until the early hours. The streets are closed to traffic at night to give the revelry a helping hand. The main road also has plenty of options.

RODA Ρόδα
☎ 0663

The coast road continues to the resort of **Roda**, which was once a nice fishing village that has now been swallowed by mass tourism and hasn't got a lot to recommend itself to the independent traveller.

Porto Spilia harbour, Meganisi

Traditional architecture, Lefkada Town

Street scene in the popular yacht port of Lefkada Town

House and bougainvillea, Kefallonia

House, Assos, Kefallonia

Northern Kefallonian port of Fiskardo

The town is arranged in the shape of an inverted triangle, with the seafront (which deceptively appears to be unspoilt) serving as the base and two main streets of the usual array of minimarkets and souvenir shops diverging from a point about 200m inland. The small fishing harbour at the eastern end of the main beach still functions and is quite picturesque.

British package tourism has left its mark here as well – most of the available accommodation is block-booked and it's not difficult to find your Caffrey's Bitter or eggs and chips.

The beach scene is not all that brilliant – the sand seems a bit muddy – and you would do better heading east to Aharavi or west to Sidhari.

There are various watersports on offer in front of the Roda Inn Hotel. Parasailing costs 12,000 dr for two people, and water-skiing 6000 dr. Boats can be hired from Sam's Motor Boats at the eastern end of the town (just beyond the harbour and the river mouth). HN Travel (☎ 64 252) at the beginning of the main drag as you come into the resort from the main road, can help with accommodation in rooms and apartments (as well as car hire, excursions and the like).

Places to Stay & Eat

Down on the seafront, the *Roda Inn Hotel* *(☎ 63 358, fax 63 974)* has pleasant singles/doubles with bathroom, terrace and sea view for 7000/10,000 dr. Hotel guests get a discount on umbrella and sun lounge hire (500 dr each) on the beach in front of the hotel.

Taverna Agra, in an old Venetian building overlooking the beach, serves simple taverna fare and good fresh fish. There's an alarming number of places that serve full English breakfasts and chips with everything. However, wander the rabbit warren of little streets between the two sides of the triangle and you'll probably do OK.

Entertainment

If you fancy some nocturnal activity, Roda's got plenty to offer including the *Mercedes* disco just beyond the turn-off

from the main coast road. Under construction at the time of writing, when it is completed by early 2000 it will be Corfu's biggest dance venue. Most bars/discos are on the road on the western side and buzz until the early hours.

AROUND RODA

To the west of Roda, off the Roda-Sidhari road, are several small settlements. Often located down steep and winding roads or tracks these are probably only suitable for those with their own transport.

Most of the limited accommodation around these beaches has been snapped up by northern European package tour operators, but there are a few places which offer rooms and several tavernas.

Agnos Beach is quiet and unspoilt. For rooms you could try *Villa Maria apartments* *(☎ 0663-31 322)*. The next settlement is **Astrakeri**, a delightful (as yet) unspoilt fishing village with a handful of rooms to rent. This is what Corfu's northern towns must all have been like about 20 years ago. Inquire about rooms at the minimarket/travel centre just before the beach. *Gregory's* overlooking the beach is an atmospheric spot for a meal. It's one of a few tavernas in the hamlet.

The small coves at **Agios Andreas** and **Yalos Beach** are also worth exploring. Each has a narrow strip of sand but their relative inaccessibility means that they don't get crowded. There are tavernas at both plus a handful of rooms.

SIDHARI Σιδάρι
☎ 0663

Sidhari is a busy resort town which is fast going the same way as nearby Roda and Benitses in the south. There's certainly no shortage of watering holes and tavernas plus a number of clubs and discos.

It is one of the few resorts which also has enough bars and tavernas open out of season to make a winter stay possible and even pleasant.

Independent travellers will probably only find themselves in Sidhari if they want to head out to the Diapondia Islands. The beach, while large and sandy, is certainly not the cleanest beach on the island, although its shallow waters are ideal for children. Naturalists will enjoy a walk south along a footpath by the River Tyflos, a habitat for terrapins, herons and egrets.

Orientation & Information

Following the road in from the major T-junction outside town you soon come to the busy centre of the resort. The beach is situated to the north-east and north of the main drag (the approach road curves to the left).

There's a branch of the Ionian Bank in the main street which also has a Visa and MasterCard-friendly ATM.

Vlasseros Travel, run by friendly entrepreneur Philip Vlasseros, is halfway along the main street and can help with accommodation, car or moped hire, excursions (including day trips to the Diapondia Islands, boat trips to Paxi, east coast cruises and Corfu Town shopping trips), horse riding and fishing trips. It also offers foreign currency exchange at bank rates.

You can get information online from www.corfuonline.gr.

Places to Stay & Eat

Much of the accommodation in Sidhari is block-booked by tour operators. Your best bet is probably to head for *Vlasseros Travel* (☎/fax 95 695), which will find whatever accommodation you need, from hotel rooms to studios, apartments and luxury villas. Prices start at 3000 dr per person.

Mike's Place (no phone, inquire at the Acropolis Bar next door) has double rooms with bathroom for 12,000 dr.

The *takeaway* next to Vlasseros Travel serves great chicken and pork gyros with a special fresh tomato sauce for 400 dr. Many of the locals eat at *Zorbas*, and the restaurant at the *Three Brothers Hotel* has good taverna fare as well as an international menu. Expect to pay 3000 dr to 4000 dr for a meal.

Popular bars, which also do food, are *Vlad*, *Kahlua* and *Caesar's*.

For self-caterers the *Berretta's* supermarket stocks essentials and you can get your fruit next door. At the intersection with the main road to Roda there's a large *supermarket* opposite the petrol station.

AROUND SIDHARI

Just to the west of Sidhari's main drag is the so-called **Canal D'Amour** rock formation, originally a sea arch that has long since collapsed, which attracts an inordinate number of visitors. Legend has it that if you swim through the arch, your romantic dreams will come true. The beaches on either side are small but inviting.

Peroulades, 3km west of Sidhari, is less developed and has a few tavernas. Halfway through the village just by the church there is a turn-off to the right to **Cape Drastis**. The asphalt road soon becomes a dirt track which ends about 1.5km later at a tiny cove flanked on both sides by wind-hewn cliffs. It is a great swimming spot, and even in the busiest season you'll only ever encounter a couple of other people there.

Continuing through Peroulades, following the signs for Sunset Beach, you come to **Lagos Beach**, also good for swimming. A proper path leads down to the small sandy beach from a cemented parking area above with several bars and tavernas.

AGIOS STEFANOS

Αγιος Στέφανος
☎ 0663

Farther around the coast **Agios Stefanos** is still quite pleasant out of high season. It has a long beach with rather muddy sand extending under the lee of high sand cliffs and is a good spot for windsurfing. Cars and camper vans can still drive right on to the beach.

Agios Stefanos claims to be the place where Odysseus was shipwrecked and where he came across the beautiful Princess Nausicaa and her maids. She provided him with clothes, food and drink. The river which separates the northern and southern ends of the village was where Odysseus bathed.

In summer the *Neachos* takes supplies to the Diapondia Islands. The boat is not an official means of public transport, but it will take passengers. It leaves from the harbour

(1.5km from the village centre, past the church). The one travel agent, San Stefano Travel, can help with accommodation and also organises boat trips including day excursions to Mathraki and Ereikousa (3800 dr and 4000 dr respectively plus a combined trip to both for 7000 dr) although these leave from Sidhari.

Places to Stay & Eat

Hotel Nafsika (☎ *51 051, fax 51 112*) is reasonably priced at 7000 dr a double including breakfast. Despite the presence of many package holiday-makers, owner Spiros Mouzakitis has tried to keep the place as Greek as possible. The hotel's *Nafsika* taverna sets the standard for food in Agios Stefanos, and has excellent mezedes including *spetsofye*, a fiery mix of traditional Greek sausage and peppers in a spicy tomato sauce. The waiters regularly get diners up for impromptu and informal Greek dancing.

San Stefanos Golden Beach Hotel (☎ *51 053/154*) by the bus stop has comfortable single/double rooms and studios for 7500/9000 dr.

Evanos above the northern end of the beach has decent taverna fare but is probably best just for a drink to watch the sunset over the Diapondia Islands. *Manthos Taverna* overlooking the beach has a charcoal grill every night and serves traditional Greek dishes. You'll pay around 1800 dr for a main course and 400 dr for mezedes.

Diapondia Islands
Τα Διαπόντια Νησιά

☎ 0663

Scattered like forgotten stepping stones to Puglia in Italy lie a cluster of little-known and even less visited satellite islands belonging administratively to Corfu.

Of the five islands only Ereikousa, Mathraki and Othoni are inhabited, though many of their original residents have long since departed for the lure of New York City and only return in the summer months to renew their ties.

Often isolated by tricky seas, the islands are worth the extra effort to visit them and serious island collectors should place them high on their agenda. Development is proceeding slowly and cautiously and all offer places to stay. Most people visit on day trips from Sidhari, though regular ferries do link the islands with both Agios Stefanos and Corfu Town.

GETTING THERE & AWAY

The most reliable link is the thrice-weekly service from Corfu Town (1500 dr to 1800 dr) with the *Alexandros II* which leaves shortly after dawn for the long haul round Corfu to bring supplies and the odd vehicle. From Agios Stefanos a small passenger boat, the *Neachos*, services Ereikousa and then Othoni and Mathraki alternatively at least twice weekly (1000 dr). It usually departs on Monday and Thursday at 10.30 am returning at 3 pm, but schedules vary without warning so check beforehand (☎ 094-999 771 or ☎ 0663-95 248).

The easiest solution may be to jump on a day excursion out of Sidhari harbour. Excursions are advertised widely around Sidhari's hotels and travel agencies. Vlasseros Travel (see under Sidhari earlier in this chapter) offers a variety of excursions in high season. Day trips to Ereikousa leave on Monday, Wednesday, Thursday, Saturday and Sunday at 9.30 am returning at 4.30 pm and cost 3000 dr. Trips to Mathraki leave on Monday, Wednesday and Saturday and cost 4000 dr (or 6500 dr including a barbecue lunch).

However, if you want to take the excursion boat to the islands and stay overnight, returning the next afternoon (or whenever), you'll have to pay for two excursion tickets, ie 6000 dr or 8000 dr return.

In winter, boats to islands are supposed to run once a week from Sidhari to the islands but it is probably more reliable to take it from Corfu Town or Agios Stefanos.

EREIKOUSA Ερείκουσα

Ereikousa (eh-**ree**-koo-sah) is perhaps the most visited and popular of the three inhabited islands and the closest of the three

CORFU

to Corfu Town and Sidhari. Touted as a desert island getaway, Ereikousa does in fact have some decent beaches and if you can only manage to visit one of the Diapondia Islands, then consider Ereikousa. Not surprisingly it attracts many visitors and can get busy in high season.

If you want to stay, contact the one hotel, *Ereikousa Hotel* (☎ *71 555)* for room availability. For eating you have *Anemomylos Taverna* (☎ *71 647)*. It also has a few domatia.

MATHRAKI Μαθράκι

Wild and wooded Mathraki is the least developed of the inhabited trio, but offers solitude, some fine walking, at least three seasonal tavernas and some domatia to stay at. There is a very long beach – which is also home to the loggerhead turtle, so discretion is necessary when beachcombing – a small scattered settlement inland and a tiny harbour with a cardphone. Excursion boats will inevitably drop you off at Piadini Beach, which is a 30 minute walk east along a rough dirt track to the harbour.

Taverna o Yiannis (☎ *72 108)* on Piadini beach will be open if you have come by excursion boat. By the harbour is the modern *Port Center Restaurant* owned by Spyridoula Kassimi and her husband and up in the village is the *kafeneio*/restaurant/store *Taverna o Geis* run by Spyros and his wife.

Accommodation is provided by the *domatia* of Christos Argyris (☎ *71 652)* who has doubles for 6000 dr with breakfast, or newer *apartments* (☎ *71 700)* run by Anastasios Kassimis.

OTHONI Οθονοί

The largest of the group is also the farthest out. Othoni (o-tho-**nee**) is popular with Italian yachties. The interior is wooded and the 35 minute walk up to the inland village of **Horio** is worth the effort for the views. Beach bums will find little comfort in the island's two pebbly beaches near the port.

Gourmets will find one decent Italian restaurant, *La Locanda dei Sogni* (☎ *71 640)*, which also has rooms, but other eat-

ing options include *New York* and *Mikros*. Rooms can also be found courtesy of the owner of New York; ring ☎ 71 581 for availability.

South of Corfu Town

☎ 0661/0662

Beyond the Kanoni Peninsula, the coast road continues south. Other than the Ahillion Palace there isn't much of great interest, and if you were going to give one part of the island a miss this would be it. Due to its proximity to the airport, it was the first part of the island to benefit financially but suffer in all other ways from mass tourism in the 1960s and 70s. Many of the package tour operators have moved on to other areas on the western and northern coasts and resorts such as Benitses are more agreeable now than they would have been a decade ago, but there's not much here to hold the independent traveller for long.

GETTING THERE & AWAY

Blue suburban buses depart regularly for the Ahillion Palace from Plateia San Rocco. There are seven KTEL long distance buses daily to Messonghi which also stop in Benitses, and 10 buses daily to Kavos via Lefkimmi.

AHILLION PALACE

Το Αχίλλειον

One of Corfu's prime attractions, the Ahillion Palace is located near the hillside village of Gastouri. It was built in the 1890s as a summer palace for 'Sissi', Austria's Empress Elizabeth (King Otho of Greece was her uncle). She dedicated the villa to Achilles and the beautifully landscaped garden is guarded by kitsch statues of her other mythological heroes.

The palace is an astonishing farrago of excessive elements of styles fashionable in the late 19th century. In *The Colossus of Maroussi*, Henry Miller described it as 'the worst piece of gimcrackery I have ever laid eyes on.' On view are an ornately decorated entrance hall, Sissi's private chapel and reception rooms filled with photographs and documents relating to the palace's two famous owners.

Sissi was assassinated by an Italian anarchist in 1898, and the palace was bought in 1908 by Kaiser Wilhelm II. The building was eventually taken over by the Greek state but lay unused until it was converted into a casino in 1963. The palace (☎ 0661-56 245) is open 9 am to 4 pm daily. Admission is 1000 dr.

BENITSES Μπενίτσες
☎ 0661

The resort of Benitses used to be the playground of holiday hooligans, but in recent times has made strenuous efforts to get its act together. Still, the excesses of too much package tourism in the past have taken the sheen off the little fishing village, but the narrow winding streets of the old village still maintain an air of authenticity.

The town has spread out along the coast road to either side of the small harbour. The beaches are not much to write home about – two narrow strips of beach which are at the same time both pebbly and sandy. Beach umbrellas and chairs can be hired for the day (500 dr for a chair, 500 dr for an umbrella). The water is clean and doesn't get too deep too quickly so it's popular with families.

If the beach scene is not to your liking, head inland for a splendid 30 minute walk along an almost tropical-looking valley to the scene of old waterworks, built during the time of the British protectorate. It used to supply water for the whole island but now the product gets guzzled up by Benitses alone.

Alternatively hire bikes from one of the ubiquitous bike hire outlets (virtually every second shop on the main drag) and head up or down the coast. Beware that the road is narrow and the passing traffic moves fast.

Benitses is home to the **Corfu Shell Museum** (☎ 72 227, ☎ 42 900) which reputedly contains the best private shell collection in Europe. Shells, coral, fossils, sharks' teeth, sea horses and stuffed fish are among other objects gathered from the deep. It is located at the northern end of the town and is clearly signposted. It is open 10 am to 8 pm daily. Entrance is 500 dr.

Places to Stay
There is no shortage of accommodation in Benitses. Most places are located on the main street. A good place to start looking would be **Vento Travel** (☎ 71 096, fax 72 453) which has lists of rooms, studios and apartments available from 8000 dr (single) and from 9500 dr for a double. These are starting prices and haggling seems to be positively encouraged.

Filothea Studios (no phone) at the southern end of town has two-person studios for 11,200 dr. **Corfu Maris Hotel** (☎ 72 035) opposite is run by a Greek-Northern Irish couple. All rooms have a sea view and the hotel has its own beach equipped with sunbeds and umbrellas. It offers singles/doubles for 15,000/17,000 dr which includes breakfast.

Just south of the fishing harbour is the enormous **Hotel Potomaki** (☎ 71 140, fax 72 451). Fairly basic singles/doubles/triples cost 10,400/15,800/19,800 dr and include breakfast. All rooms have bathroom and balconies, most with a sea view. The hotel, which has seen better days, has its own swimming pool and periodically has Greek dancing in the entrance courtyard.

Hotel Loutrouvia (☎ 72 258, fax 72 152) nearby has doubles/triples for 12,000/17,000 dr. Its central position means that it can be noisy into the early hours thanks to the bars and discos on the street below.

Just north of Benitses and up a steep hill is the huge **Hotel San Stefano** (☎ 71 117, fax 71 124, email sanstefano@hol.gr). Well equipped with all the package holidaymaker wants, including air-conditioning, the biggest saltwater swimming pool in Corfu and a kid's club, it could well be the independent traveller's biggest nightmare. Singles/doubles cost 25,000/33,000 dr including breakfast, and a studio for two costs 30,000 dr.

CORFU

Places to Eat

Tavernas, restaurants and fast-food outlets have almost swallowed up the original village of Benitses. Cruise the strip until you see a place that appeals. As far as Greek specialities go, you can't really go past *Marabou* opposite the fishing harbour, which offers mezedes for 3200 dr or fish mezedes for 3500 dr. Greek specialities include *crassato*, fillet of pork cooked in white wine. It also does pizza (1200 dr to 1500 dr) and pasta dishes (1200 dr to 1950 dr) and has special children's menus.

For a quick fill-up, head for *The Magic Corner* which does doner kebab and gyros from 800 dr – you pick your ingredients – or, *The Kebab House* just off the main road (take the road inland towards the old village from the Cava Supermarket) which fancies itself as the best of its kind in Benitses.

If you've had enough Greek food, you have a couple of choices. *Avra* on the beach (under the Vento Travel offices) does authentic Neapolitan cooking (the chef, the basil and the wine have all been imported from Naples). You'll pay around 4000 dr for a meal. Up towards the old village is the curious *Flower Garden*, possibly the only restaurant extant anywhere in the world that combines Greek and Chinese cooking. The Chinese fixed menu (three courses) costs 7000 dr for two people.

Entertainment

The road is lined with bars, tavernas and discos including a karaoke bar, *The Cutty Sark* (a disco-bar which also offers traditional Greek grub for hungry partiers), discos with names like *42nd Street Bar*, *Show Bar* (which plays a noisy mixture of 80s disco tunes) and *The G-spot* (you shouldn't have any problems finding it).

MORAÏTIKA & MESSONGHI

Μωραΐτικα & Μεσογγή
☎ 0661

Heading farther south from Corfu Town you will next hit Moraïtika and Messonghi, originally two separate resorts which have now merged into one and are a little quieter than Benitses. The beach scene, while not

ideal, is certainly better than its neighbour farther north.

Activities

Nautilus Diving (☎ 76 684, ☎ 094-741133) has been running BSAC and CMAS scuba courses at Moraïtika for 14 years. Dives take place off both the eastern and western coasts. Courses range from a one day introduction to diving, to a four day beginner's course and ocean diver courses of a week or more.

Places to Stay

Hotel Sea Bird (☎ 75 400, fax 76 152), down on the beachfront, has doubles for 14,000 dr. Follow the signs at the intersection where the main road splits for Messonghi/Lefkimmi. *Christina Hotel and Restaurant (☎ 75 294, fax 75 616)* right on the beach is a friendly family-run affair. Rooms cost from around 16,000 dr per person.

Hotel Roulis (☎ 75 311, fax 75 353) is a pretty pink building about 30m from the Christina. Single/double rooms can be had for 6000/9000 dr.

Messonghi Beach (☎ 76 684, fax 75 334, email geogroup@otenet.gr) is a huge complex with 2500 beds that is almost totally filled with package tourists. Although it's an independent traveller's nightmare, it is well equipped, has its own beach with various water activities (including scuba diving) and is good for families. Single/double rooms including breakfast cost 15,600/23,200 dr.

Apollo Palace Hotel (☎ 75 433, ☎ 75 600, fax 75 602, email apollopl@mail.hot .gr) is pleasant enough but has 'package tour' written all over it. It's expensive in high season too – 25,000 dr per person with breakfast and dinner included.

Places to Eat

The Three Brothers, *Taverna Meandros* and *Zaks Taverna*, all basic Greek tavernas, are all on the road where Moraïtika and Messonghi merge, near the Messonghi Beach Hotel.

Hotel Roulis has a nice restaurant with a vine and morning-glory covered courtyard.

The restaurant serves Corfiot and Greek food. A meal will cost you around 2500 dr to 3000 dr.

Just outside Messonghi, off the road to Boukaris, is a fork to Spilio, perched up on the hillside, where there are a couple of atmospheric tavernas with great views including *75 Steps Taverna* and *Café Bar Bella Vista Spiros*.

BOUKARIS TO KAVOS
☎ 0662

The winding coastal road between Messonghi and Boukaris is decidedly more appealing than the previous stretch and is dotted with a few tavernas and small pebbly beaches. It's a quiet spot and virtually the only place on this part of Corfu where you can get away from the crowds. Your own transport – car, moped or mountain bike – will be a distinct advantage to explore this part of the island.

The *Vlachopoulos family (☎ 51 791 or ☎ 51 260, fax 51 792)* has accommodation options in **Boukaris** (Μπούκαρης) wrapped up. One part of the family runs rooms, studios and larger apartments, while the other owns the two hotels in the resort. Apartments for two/three people cost 9000/14,000 dr. If you turn up out of season, call ☎ 52 240. They will probably be able to find you a room.

Boukaris Beach Restaurant (also run by the Vlachopoulos family) is the best choice for food, and does great fish. If you choose lobster you can select which victim you want from the seawater tank in the courtyard. A seafood meal will set you back about 4000 dr.

Beyond Boukaris an unsealed road heads along the coast to **Petriti**, or you can travel inland and then towards the coast on asphalt. Petriti is a sleepy fishing village and a popular place for yachts to tie up although there's no beach to speak of. Accommodation possibilities are not extensive. *Pension Egrypos (☎ 51 949)* has double rooms for 10,000 dr and about 2km inland the *Regina (☎ 52 132, fax 52 135)*, very popular with German tourists, has singles/doubles for 10,000/14,000 dr including breakfast.

Inland, **Lefkimmi** is primarily an agricultural village, seemingly untouched by tourism, where the older women often wear traditional Greek costume and sometimes use donkeys for transport. *Maria Magdalena (☎ 22 386)* has rooms to rent (9000 dr a double). It's in the middle of the old town, uphill from the canal area, near the turn-off to Molos. Ferries run from Lefkimmi's port to Igoumenitsa on the mainland. There are six departures daily in high season, and the journey takes an hour.

Virtually at the southern tip of the island is **Kavos** (Κάβος), a latter day ladsville which is best avoided at all costs. There is an acceptable beach but that's about the only positive thing you can say about the place. It is here most of the British lager louts seem to have been banished and where the inevitable mayhem they cause can be isolated from the rest of the island. Don't go anywhere near it.

The West Coast

Corfu's best beaches are on the dramatic West Coast. Development on this coast is not yet as bad as in the south and on parts of the northern coast – thanks mainly to the mountainous and hilly terrain – but the telltale signs are already apparent.

Paleokastritsa in the north is one of the most popular destinations, however you'll be battling for a place on the beach in high season. Farther south there's the hill town of Pelekas and the backpacker haven of Agios Gordis. Nature lovers and windsurfers should head for Lake Korission and Issos beach respectively.

GETTING THERE & AWAY
The West Coast resorts are well served by KTEL buses from Corfu Town, although hopping up or down the coast may prove difficult as the resorts are not linked by public transport.

There are seven buses daily from Corfu Town to Paleokastritsa, six buses daily to Glyfada via Vatos and four daily to Agios Gordios via Sinarades.

ARILAS Αρίλλας
☎ 0663

The most northerly resort on the West Coast, Arilas has received a lot of bad press but is really rather a nice place and not yet too overrun by commercialism. The road into the village winds down the hillside, coming to an end at a very narrow strip of golden sand which is also pebbly in parts. The bay has an attractive backdrop of forested hills.

The bougainvillea covered *Pension Margarita (☎ 51 460)* about 200m from the beach on the road to Pagi has fruit trees in its driveway and a garden filled with flowers. Single/double rooms cost 4000/6000 dr which includes breakfast. *Villa Mon Amour (☎ 51 106)* on the same approach road, is equally pretty and a little closer to the beach. It has rooms for similar prices.

At the centre of the resort, the purpose-built *Hotel Akti Arillas (☎ 51 201, fax 51 221, email aktiaril@otenet.gr)* is good value at 8000 dr per person including breakfast and dinner. *Hotel Marvellous (☎ 51 120, fax 51 490)* about 300m from the beach has double rooms for 13,000 dr. *Arillas Travel (☎ 51 280, fax 51 381)* can also help you find a room or apartment.

There are several eating spots. *Illusions* cafe opposite the Hotel Akti Arillas reportedly does the best breakfast in town.

AGIOS GEORGIOS Αγιος Γεώργιος
☎ 0663

A haven for watersports enthusiasts, Agios Georgios features a 3km stretch of golden sand framed by Cape Arilas in the north and Cape Falakron to the south – but not much else. The village has developed in response to the beach traffic. Chairs and umbrellas can be rented all the way along the beach.

Head north-west from Agios Georgios, up to nearby **Afionas** village, for magnificent views out towards the Diapondia Islands and the Gravia islets closer to shore. The latter are reputedly the petrified remains of Odysseus' ships. The village boasts traces of Neolithic remains and it is thought to be a possible location of King Alcinous' castle about which Homer wrote

in *The Odyssey*. There is a good walk out to the lighthouse at Cape Arilas, which offers excellent views to the north and south.

Activities
The Diving Fun Club (☎ 097-246921) does scuba diving on Agios Georgios. Sailing enthusiasts should head to the northern end of the beach. Windsurfers can be rented for 3500 dr an hour, lasers from 4000 dr per hour, and catamarans for 8000 dr an hour.

Sun Fun Club at the southern end of the beach also organises watersports, including parasailing (13,000 dr for two people, 10,000 dr for one), motorboat hire (from 15,000 dr to 20,000 dr per day) and water-skiing as well as the ubiquitous big banana and ringos rides. It also organises evening fishing trips and tours to Paleokastritsa.

Places to Stay & Eat
The massive *Hotel Alkyon Beach* occupies the southern end of the beach but won't be much use to the independent traveller as all its rooms are block-booked. *Corfu Star Hotel (☎ 96 210)* on the beach has doubles for 15,000 dr including breakfast. *Spiros Village (☎ 96 029)* at the northern end of the beach, *Angelo's Rooms* (behind the Golden Moon taverna) and *Theo's (☎ 96 482)*, a big yellow building on the approach road into the resort, all have reasonably priced rooms.

In Afionas, the *Three Brothers* taverna has a magnificent view towards the Diapondia Islands and the Gravia islets. Even if the view wasn't any good – it is unbeatable – it would be worth coming here for the home-made baklava which is delicious, syrupy but not too cloyingly sweet.

PALEOKASTRITSA
Παλαιοκαστρίτσα
☎ 0663

The West Coast's largest resort, Paleokastritsa lies 26km west of Corfu Town. Built around sandy and pebbled coves with a green mountain backdrop, it's incredibly beautiful. Once paradisal, it's been the victim of rampant development. While the water here looks enticing, it is generally considerably colder than at other parts of the island.

Orientation

There are several beaches to choose from at Paleokastritsa, and plenty of opportunities to head off to more secluded coves. The main beach – to the left of the causeway – gets totally overcrowded in summer. This is where the various taxi boats and excursion boats leave from. To the west, past the Astakos Taverna, is a small cove with pebbly sand and a few rocks. Beyond the eastern headland of Agios Nikolaos is a small bay and harbour, Alipa Port, which has a lot of boating activity.

Moni Theotokou monastery perches on the rocky promontory beyond the causeway above the shimmering turquoise sea.

Information

Beach chairs and umbrellas can be hired on all the beaches for 500 dr a piece.

The Boatmen's Association of Paleokastritsa is an informal grouping of taxi and excursion boats that operates off the pontoon on the main beach at the resort. Trips are organised to various grottoes in the area, including Blue Eye, San Nicholas Cave and Nausicaa Cave. Prices seem to be fairly flexible, depending on the number of people in the boat, but roughly cost 2500 dr. The taxi boat to the nearby beaches of Limni, Kastelli or Rovigna won't depart until there are enough people in it, and costs around 3000 dr per person.

There are several car rental agencies. George Michalas (☎ 41 485, ☎ 42 017, fax 41 643) operates out of two locations, one on the approach road into the resort just after the Lakones turn-off, and one down at Alipa Port ('George at the Port'). Small cars (eg Fiat Panda) cost from 24,000 dr for three days and 51,000 dr for a week. A convertible Suzuki jeep costs from 47,000 dr for three days and 101,000 dr for seven days. He also has bicycles for 1500 dr to 2000 dr per day and mopeds for 2000 dr to 7000 dr.

At Alipa port, Yiannis Spiros (☎ 41 096, ☎ 41 313) rents motorboats by the hour,

day or week. A boat from 10 am to 4 pm will set you back 18,000 dr plus fuel (you pay for what you consume at a rather pricey 350 dr/litre). Boat rental for three hours is 12,000 dr (plus fuel). Weekly rentals get good discounts.

Moni Theotokou Μονή Θεοτόκου

The monastery was founded in the 13th century but the present building dates from the 18th century. The pretty church has a lovely iconostasis, topped with a series of 12 icons of the 12 apostles. The *Last Judgment* above the doorway is notable. Don't be surprised if the priest guarding the church is asleep while on duty.

The whitewashed monastery walls and banana-coloured church are drowning in bougainvillea – shocking pink, snow white and the brightest magenta hues. The picturesque bell tower of the church must be one of the most photographed sights in Corfu. A small museum contains icons. It is open 7 am to 1 pm and 3 to 8 pm daily. Admission is free, but a donation is expected. Women wearing shorts and skimpy tops will be asked to don a gathered cotton skirt and a shawl (in a rather attractive array of printed fabrics) while they are visiting the monastery.

Activities

The Korfu Diving Centre (☎ 41 604) at the easternmost beach (follow signs to the right of the road that leads up to the monastery, past Astakos Taverna) is German-run. It organises diving courses from beginners to advanced and organise boat trips to numerous sites off Paleokastritsa including reefs, arches, canyons and caves. Introductory dives cost around 10,000 dr.

Places to Stay

Paleokastritsa Camping (☎ 41 204, fax 41 104) is on the main approach road to the resort, shortly after the signposted turn-off to the village of Lakones. It's a reasonably well organised camp site, with a restaurant and minimarket on site, but is a fair way back from the beach scene. The bus will drop you at the entrance. Paleokastritsa also has many hotels, studios and domatia. *Vatos Camping* (☎ *0661-94 505*) near the village of Vatos is a quiet retreat but handier if you have some kind of transport of your own.

Bouganville Studios (☎ *41 328*, ☎ *41 460*) is one of the first places you see as you come into the resort (up a steep drive on the right hand side of the road before the Hotel Paleokastritsa) and is run by George Bakiras who also has other accommodation possibilities, including the *Green House* (with doubles for 7000 dr).

Christina (☎ *41 273*) has single/double studios set in a pretty, shady garden for 6000/10,000 dr. Down by the main beaches, *Astakos* (☎/fax *41 359*), run by the Ziniatis brothers, has single/double rooms with bathroom and fridge for 7000/8000 dr.

The unofficial *Tourist Office* (☎ *41 886*) on the approach road to the resort, can organise studios for 12,000 dr for two people. It also has other studios and apartments from 11,000 dr and C class hotel rooms from 16,000 dr per person. *Michalas General Tourist Office* (☎ *41 113*, fax *41 298*) even farther away from the centre can also help with rooms.

Places to Eat

In Paleokastritsa there is a fairly wide choice but little difference in quality between the eating places. *La Grotta*, down a long flight of steps off to the left of the main approach road to Paleokastritsa is an enchanting taverna. It is particularly atmospheric at night sitting by the water and watching the fireflies.

Astakos Taverna in the centre of town between the main beach and the most northerly beach (clearly signposted), is a good choice and popular with families. It features very fresh seafood and Greek dishes such as stuffed tomatoes. *Corner Grill* also serves up Greek and tourist favourites.

For an upmarket meal, the best choice is *Alipa* restaurant (☎ *41 614*, ☎ *41 214*) at Alipa port. It keeps live sea bream and lobster in cages down on the beach – you can choose your dinner and they'll cook it for you. Expect to spend about 7500 dr for a slap-up meal.

AROUND PALEOKASTRITSA

From Paleokastritsa a path ascends to the unspoilt village of **Lakones**, 5km inland. Walk back along the approach road and you will come to a signposted footpath on the left. Climb the steps, at the fork go right, and at the asphalt road turn left. After 40m take the narrow path on the right which leads to Lakones.

High up overlooking Paleokastritsa and just beyond the village of Lakones is *Golden Fox Apartments* (☎/fax *0663-41 381*) with studios costing 13,000 dr. The swimming pool here must have the best view in the whole of Greece. The pool is open to the public and is free. You could do worse than spend a few hours here. *Golden Fox Taverna* has terraces on three levels with magnificent views down over the coast. The menu has excellent charcoal-grilled fresh fish, steaks and other meats and a full range of Corfiot dishes.

The aptly named *Bella Vista* farther along the road looks nothing special but the views are equally breathtaking. Reputedly the Kaiser, Tito and Nasser all dined here. It is a good place to stop for a coffee or snack.

There are superb views along the 6km road west to **Makrades** and **Krini**. The restaurants along the way extol the views from their terraces.

Angelokastro Αγγελόκαστρο

From Krini you can explore the ruins of the 13th century Byzantine fortress of Angelokastro where the inhabitants of Paleokastritsa took refuge from attackers. The fortress played a key role in the defence of the island for centuries, as it had a clear view of the West Coast and any potential invaders. During the Turkish sieges of 1537, 1571 and 1716, several thousand islanders took refuge within it.

A long distance bus goes twice daily to Krini from Corfu Town.

ERMONES Ερμονες
☎ 0661

The first major settlement south of Paleokastritsa is Ermones, one of the busiest resorts on Corfu, and with the added advantage for golfers of being only a stone's throw from Corfu Golf Course, the largest in Europe. According to some classical scholars, Ermones was where Odysseus was washed ashore.

Activities

The Corfu Golf Club (☎ 94 221, ☎/fax 94 220,) in Ropa Valley is 1km from Ermones Beach. The 18 hole course was designed by Donald Harradine and is considered to have the best greens in the Mediterranean. The resident pro, Jonathan Hunt from the UK, has been there for nine years.

Green fees cost 16,000 dr for the first day then go down a sliding scale to 8000 dr for the fourth day, 6000 dr for a seventh day and free on the eighth day. Clubs can be hired for 2750 dr, locker hire costs 700 dr per day, lessons are 8000 dr for a half-hour and the driving range costs 1000 dr for 50 balls. Golf buggies are also available for hire (9500 dr).

The course is open year-round although the clubhouse, bar and other facilities shut from October to April.

Also at the Golf Club are the Ropa Valley horse riding stables. General hacks cost 8000 dr for two hours. Lessons are also available. Contact Julie Haywood at the Golf Club.

Places to Stay & Eat

If you are looking for a place to stay, take the left fork of the road at a little bridge as you come into Ermones and follow the road towards sea. About 50m along the road and up a steep driveway on the left is *Georgio's Domatia* (☎ 94 950), a good choice for the budget conscious. Studios for two/three people cost 9000/11,000 dr. If they are full, try *Pension Katerina* next door which has rooms for similar prices.

Farther along on the right is *Hotel Elena* (☎ 94 131/33, fax 94 633) which has comfortable rooms with bathroom and balconies overlooking the sea for 18,000 dr a double including breakfast and dinner. There is also a large swimming pool and children's playground. The hotel caters mainly to German package tourists but the management welcomes independent travellers. Its restaurant serves usual taverna fare.

PELEKAS Πέλεκας
☎ 0661

Hill-top Pelekas is renowned for its spectacular sunsets. It's as busy as the coast, but with young independent travellers, rather than package tourists. Pelekas is close to the sandy beaches of Glyfada, Pelekas and Myrtiotissa. There is a free bus (every hour or two – shops, bars and restaurants display the timetable) from Pelekas to the first two beaches.

Don't miss the superb panoramic views over Corfu from the Kaiser's Lookout high up above Pelekas village. From the lookout there is a 360° view of the whole island. On a clear day you can see across to Corfu Town and the Greek mainland beyond. The walk uphill from Pelekas was the favourite stroll of both Empress Elizabeth of Austria and Kaiser Wilhelm II of Germany. Just follow the main road upwards to the end. It is certainly worth climbing the hill for the view, especially at sunset (when the world and his dog comes up here) and having a drink on the terrace of the Levant Hotel.

Places to Stay

At Pelekas, the family-run *Alexandros Pension* (☎ 94 215, fax 94 833) on the road signposted 'sunset' has pleasant doubles from 6000 dr to 10,000 dr depending on the season.

A bit farther along the same road, *Rooms to Let Thomas* (☎ 94 491, fax 94 190) has clean, comfortable singles/doubles with private bathroom for 9000/11,000 dr, as well as doubles with shared bathroom for 6000 dr.

Back near the central square, the bougainvillea-smothered *Pension Tellis & Brigitte* (☎ 94 326) has pleasant doubles for 6500 dr with bathroom.

The stylish and neoclassical *Levant Hotel* (☎ 94 230, fax 94 115), higher up on the Pelekas road, was once a private house which has been converted into a hotel. It is one of the most elegant hotels on the island, with charming, helpful staff and a restaurant

CORFU

terrace with views to die for. Magnificent singles/doubles go for 18,000/25,000 dr. The nearby church dates from 1500 and is worth a look for some lovely icons.

Pelekas Country Club (☎ *52 239, fax 52 919, email reservations@country-club.gr)* is an A class luxurious resort inland from the sea but still within easy striking distance of the beaches at Glyfada, Pelekas and Myrtiotissa (see Around Pelekas later in this chapter). It's actually an 18th century mansion surrounded by 60 hectares of grounds including olive groves. The outbuildings have been converted into luxury studios and apartments and are furnished with antiques. A studio for two costs 53,000 dr, while apartments for four start at 80,000 dr and go for as much as 110,000 dr per night. All prices include brunch. There is a tennis court and large swimming pool. Central heating means that it is open throughout the year. Booking is essential.

Places to Eat

At the intersection of the roads to Pelekas Beach, Kaiser's Lookout (labelled 'sunset') and Corfu Town is *Jimmy's*, a popular hang-out with enthusiastic and friendly multilingual staff. Its specialities are Corfiot dishes such as sofrito, pastitsada and *bourdeto*. It is also an excellent choice for vegetarians, with vegetarian moussaka and vegetarian rice on the menu. And at night the atmosphere is lively.

Next door the *Alexandros* taverna is always full which must be a good sign. Opposite, *Antonis Restaurant* is a little more upmarket, with an excellent choice of mezedes and basic Greek dishes. Down the road near the centre of the village, *Vasiles* does good souvlaki.

Heading up towards Kaiser's Lookout, about 300m from the top, is *Vavel*, the red building on the bend. Only open at night, it's a popular bar and hang-out for locals.

AROUND PELEKAS
Myrtiotissa Μυρτιώτισσα
☎ 0661
Myrtiotissa is Corfu's unofficial nudist beach. It is reached by a predominantly dirt

track signposted off the Pelekas-Corfu Town road halfway between Ermones and Glyfada. If you take the free bus from Pelekas to Glyfada and get off at the minimarket before the bus starts its descent to Glyfada, you'll have to walk about another 2km.

The road down to the beach is wide enough to squeeze a car – but take it at your peril. The numerous potholes could cause havoc and if there are already cars parked on the road you might find yourself reversing up a really steep gradient. It's probably better to park where the 'parking' sign is and walk for 10 minutes down to the beach. The return hike uphill will take you about 15 minutes.

The beach is a pretty cove with golden sand and crystal clear water sheltered by huge cliffs. There are umbrellas and sunbeds to rent for the day (500 dr each). The nudists and freelance campers (there's a pipe of fresh water that reaches the beach) tend to gather at the beach's southern end. You'll often find an artist entertaining the naturists by doing full body painting there.

Places to Stay & Eat It's probably only a matter of time before Myrtiotissa goes the way of other nearby beaches and the approach road is fully asphalted allowing rampant development, but at the time of writing at least there was only one makeshift bar/taverna at the northern end of the beach.

Five minutes uphill from the beach is *Mirtiotisa* (☎ *94 113)*, a restaurant serving the usual fare which also has single/double rooms for 5000/8000 dr. The garden also doubles as an unofficial car park. You'll be relieved of 300 dr if you want to be a little closer to the beach and avoid some of the return hike.

Glyfada Γλυφάδα
☎ 0661
Very much a family beach, the golden sands and crystal clear waters of Glyfada would be even more inviting if it wasn't so overrun with people. Boardwalks are laid down over the sand which gets very hot underfoot. Umbrellas and sunbeds can be hired for 500 dr each.

If you are in a car, you'll find parking difficult. Your best bet is probably to pay the 500 dr for the whole day in the main car park by the beach.

Activities Glyfada Water Sports (☎ 54 504, ☎ 0944-803580) has parasailing for 10,000 dr (two people) or 7000 dr (for one), jet-skis (10,000 dr for 15 minutes), water-skiing (5000 dr for six minutes or 5000 dr for beginners until they get up on skis), pedalos for 2000 dr/hour, canoes for 1000 dr/hour and motorboat hire for 6000 dr/hour for up to six adults and two children.

Places to Stay & Eat Most accommodation in the resort is block-booked by tour operators, although if you are willing to fork out 52,000 dr for a double the *Louis Grand* (☎ 94 140, fax 94 146) will probably squeeze you in.

A better bet is *Villa Iris* (☎ 94 340, ☎ 94 380) next to the car park. You can also make inquiries in the minimarket nearby (owner Costas Carridis runs both businesses). Studios (for two or three people) cost 15,000 dr and apartments that sleep up to five people cost 24,000 dr. There's also a 10 to 15% discount for stays over a week.

Another option is *Menigos* resort (☎ 94 943, fax 94 933, email xeniark@ker.forth net.gr) which has small apartments for two (or four) people from 15,000 dr to 31,000 dr and larger apartments which sleep four or six from 19,500 dr to 40,500 dr. It also has its own minimarket, restaurant, bar and pool.

Back on the Ermones-Pelekas road but only 1.5km from Glyfada, is *Villa Georgia* (☎ 94 617, ☎ 25 489), which has studios sleeping two/three for 14,000/20,000 dr. It also has larger apartments.

Aloha, bang in the centre of Glyfada beach, is a beach bar and restaurant which serves drinks, snacks and taverna meals with fresh fish and seafood every day. It also has parties every evening from around 5pm.

Pelekas Beach Παραλία Πέλεκας
☎ 0661

Until quite recently, Pelekas Beach was a backpackers' haven and considered one of Corfu's best beaches, reasonably free of mass tourism. Unfortunately, with the opening in 1999 of the Pelekas Beach Hotel, the flavour of the resort has changed irreversibly, and Pelekas Beach is on its way down. The beach itself is beautiful, with a long stretch of golden sand and numerous rocky coves. The new hotel is an ugly development with a funicular railway running halfway down the cliff.

All sorts of watersports can be enjoyed on the beach, run by Watersports Thomas. These include parasailing (single 8000 dr, double 10,000 dr), water-skiing is 5000 dr, ringos 3000 dr and the big banana is 3000 dr (the last two are towed by a speedboat). You can also rent a motorboat (8000 dr for one hour, 14,000 dr for two hours).

Places to Stay & Eat If package tourism is your cup of tea then head for *Pelekas Beach Hotel* (☎ 52 233, fax 52 234), where singles/doubles with breakfast cost 10,000/ 16,200 dr. You'll also have use of the swimming pool and tennis court.

Otherwise try *Maria's Place* at the southern end of the beach, where basic rooms cost 5000 dr per person. This authentic taverna has friendly service and great food. On the menu are Maria's famous tzatziki (she puts carrot in it as well and it has to be the best on Corfu if not in all of Greece), homemade wine and fish caught fresh daily by Maria's husband Costas. Beware that, although delicious, a grilled snapper might cost you 5000 dr.

Vrachos beyond Maria's and higher up the hill is fast becoming the backpacker's favourite. A great meal will cost you about 2000 dr per head, and there are also a few rooms to rent.

AGIOS GORDIOS Αγιος Γόρδιος
☎ 0661

Agios Gordios is a popular backpacker hang-out 8km south of Glyfada. The beach is reasonably pretty, but the village is rather overdeveloped with the usual conglomeration of shops, souvenir stalls, eateries and domatia. It is also home to the infamous Pink Palace. Overall it's a laid-back kind of

CORFU

place and will appeal to travellers interested primarily in the 'beach and bar' scene. The beach is long and sandy, and umbrellas and sun lounges can be hired for the day.

At **Sinarades**, 4km from Agios Gordios, the **Folk Museum of Central Corfu** occupies a 19th century house. It is open 9.30 am to 3 pm Tuesday to Sunday. Admission is around 300 dr.

There are three long distance buses daily from Corfu Town to Agios Gordios, via Sinarades.

Orientation & Information

The road from Sinarades winds steeply down the hill, ending at the beach. Almost all the action is on this road and smaller roads off it.

Karoukas Travel (☎ 53 909, fax 53 887, email karoukas@otenet.gr) is a general tourist agency that offers a variety of services including rental cars, charter flights to northern Europe and Internet access (1000 dr for 30 minutes). It can also help with accommodation in Agios Gordios, in other places in Corfu and on all the other Greek islands – useful for island-hoppers. Double rooms start at 11,000 dr and studios for two from 14,000 dr.

Activities

Available watersports include parasailing, pedalos (2300 dr/hour), canoes (1300 dr/hour) and water-skiing (4000 dr/hour). Inquire at the booth on the beach.

The Calypso Diving Centre (☎ 53 101, fax 53 369) on the beach, offers PADI, CMAS and ANIS scuba courses. Courses start weekly in high season. The diving is tailored to suit the experience of the divers with opportunities for deep dives, scenic dives for photographers and viewing varied marine life. The centre also organises a variety of excursions for divers up to Paleokastritsa and south to Paxi.

Places to Stay & Eat

Dandidis on the beach has double rooms for 15,000 dr including breakfast. It serves all the usual taverna fare (you'll pay around 3000 dr for a meal). *Pink Palace (☎ 53 103)* at Agios Gordios is a brash backpacker hostel designed for the under 25s who want fun and sun without the hassles of having to look for it. You'll pay between 5000 dr and 10,000 dr per person for average accommodation – and that includes breakfast and dinner.

Those over 25 may prefer some peace and quiet at *Mires House (☎ 53 378)*, just back from the long sandy beach where nicely furnished doubles cost 8000 dr and studios are 10,000 dr.

Romantic (☎ 53 273) is a large restaurant on several levels. There's a great *souvlaki bar* just up from the beach which serves excellent marinated chicken souvlakis and gyros – popular with backpackers recovering from a hard day's sunworshipping. *Alex in the Garden* opposite is also a good bet. It has styled itself as a family place with family cooking and family prices, but does typical taverna fare.

LAKE KORISSION

Λίμνη Κορισσιών

The main road south continues to **Agios Mattheos**, a pleasant village overlooked by a pine-clad mountain. It's a one hour walk to the summit.

Freshwater **Lake Korission**, a little farther south, is a habitat for wading birds including the greenshank, avocet, curlew and black winged stilt. The artificial lagoon of 607 hectares was created by the Venetians, who built a short reinforced channel from the sea and flooded existing marshlands. If you visit in late summer you will enjoy the sight of the dunes covered in white sea daffodils. Over 120 bird species have been recorded in the lake. Over winter, many migrants including the mallard, shelduck and teal make the lake their home. Inland, to the east and north-east are low lying hills, quite a different landscape from the more mountainous north.

ISSOS & AGIOS GIORGIOS Ισσος

& Αγιος Γεώργιος
☎ 0662
The long stretch of inviting sand and dunes between the lake and sea continues to Issos.

This is one of the least spoilt stretches of Corfu's coast, but it's back to rampant development at Agios Giorgios.

Part of the James Bond film, *For Your Eyes Only*, was filmed in the dunes behind **Issos**, one of the best beaches in the entire archipelago. The wide sandy bay is the best spot for windsurfing on Corfu with its cross-shore winds. The beach is a nesting ground for loggerhead turtles so care should be taken, and you should not go near the beach at night.

From May until early October, British Graham Taylor rents boards and runs a windsurfing school on the beach. School boards for beginners cost 3500 dr/hour, and fun boards can be rented for 4500 dr/hour. Lessons cost 2000 dr/hour plus board hire. He also rents sunbeds and umbrellas (500 dr each) and canoes (2000 dr/hour).

The nearest facilities for food and accommodation are at overdeveloped and not particularly appealing **Agios Giorgios**, although most accommodation there is block-booked by package groups. ***Blue Sea Hotel*** (☎ *51 172, fax 51 624*) has double rooms for 9000 dr, while the more upmarket ***Golden Sands Hotel*** (☎ *51 225, fax 51 140*) has rooms for 17,000 dr a double including breakfast. Both hotels have basic tavernas.

There are several ***souvlaki bars*** on the main street which do very tasty gyros. ***Panorama*** taverna, also on the main street, does salads, omelettes, grilled meats and Greek dishes, plus the ubiquitous full English breakfast – if sausage, bacon and eggs are what you want.

There are two branches of ***Star Travel & Tourism*** (☎*/fax 51 631,* ☎ *52 800, email star-tvl@otenet.gr*) at either end of the main street. Both can help with finding rooms, studios and apartments (from 4400 dr per person) as well as other tourist services such as day trips and ferry tickets.

CORFU

Paxi & Antipaxi Παξοί & Αντίπαξοι

Paxi (pahx-**ee**), 10km long and 4km wide, is the smallest main Ionian island separated from Corfu's southernmost tip by 11km of water.

Also known by its anglicised name of Paxos, the island has a captivating landscape of dense, centuries-old olive groves, snaking dry stone walls, derelict farmhouses and abandoned stone olive presses. The olive trees have amazingly twisted, gnarled and hollowed trunks, which give them the look of sinister, ancient monsters. Walking through the olive groves at dusk is quite eerie.

The small island of Antipaxi, with just over a handful of inhabitants, lies 2km south of Paxi and is famous for its wine.

Paxi

☎ 0662   • pop 2200

Paxi has escaped the mass tourism of Corfu and caters for small, discriminating tour companies.

However exclusivity comes at a price and Paxi is the most expensive island in the Ionians, mainly due to the fact that everything has to be imported. Accommodation is not as plentiful as on the other islands and absolutely impossible to find in July and August. Make sure you book ahead if you are coming in high season.

Many of today's tourists are return visitors. People come here because they have fallen in love with Paxi's inimitable cosy feel, or have heard about its friendly islanders and its captivating scenery.

There are only three coastal settlements – Gaïos, Longos and Lakka – and a few inland villages. The whole island is walkable, though good roads do cover the length of the island. Paxi's gentle east coast has small pebble beaches, while the west coast has awesome vistas of precipitous cliffs, punctuated by several grottoes only accessible by boat.

HIGHLIGHTS

- Rent a dinghy and discover deserted coves and spectacular caves
- Sip a fresh melon and vodka mega-cocktail at Taxidi in Longos
- Walk to Trypitos and marvel at the views of Antipaxi
- See over 100 species of sea creatures at the Lakka aquarium
- Enjoy octopus in tomato sauce at Afthendiko in Gaïos

PAXI

IONIAN
SEA

ANTIPAXI

Paxi is an absolute must for any serious island-hopper and is worth the extra effort needed to get there.

HISTORY

According to mythology, Paxi was cut off from the mainland by a single blow from Poseidon's trident. The sea god is said to have dragged the piece of land south to create an idyllic island retreat for himself and his mistress. The trident is the symbol of the island.

In the 3rd century BC Paxi was the scene of a great sea battle between Kerkyra (ancient

PAXI & ANTIPAXI

Corfu) and the Illyrians. Kerkyra was assisted at first – and unsuccessfully – by Greeks from the mainland and later by a Roman fleet, and subsequently became part of the Roman Empire.

In 31 BC, before their defeat by the Roman emperor Octavian in the Battle of Actium, Antony and Cleopatra are thought to have dined on Paxi.

The first settlers on the island were shepherds from mainland Greece who arrived in the 6th century AD. Archaeological evidence from this period includes a ruined chapel near Ozias in the south of the island. Together with the northern Ionian region and the nearby mainland, Paxi soon became part of the Byzantine Empire.

From the late 14th century, Venetian settlers transformed the island into one giant olive grove.

The Paxiots were encouraged to plant as many olives as possible and received a healthy payment for every tree planted. Paxi olive oil is widely regarded as among Greece's best. The hilly terrain meant that many of the olive groves had to be terraced, and the characteristic gnarled trees contained by drystone walling are still visible

in many parts of the island today (see boxed text 'Paxiot Produce').

The Venetian influence can also be seen in Gaïos harbour, in the buildings in Gaïos and other parts of the island, and in the remains of cisterns.

Under British protection, Paxi received the basis of its road network and more giant cisterns. As on Corfu, educational and governmental systems were also put into place. During WWII, German troops were stationed on the island, and it is said that German bombers stationed on Corfu used Paxi as target practice.

Shipping magnate Aristotle Onassis was a fan of Paxi and donated funds to build the main road that runs from Gaïos to Lakka.

GETTING THERE & AWAY
Bus
There is a direct bus service to Athens (eight hours, 8150 dr) three times weekly. Tickets are available at Bouas Tours (☎ 32 401). Buses from Athens to Paxi depart from the Hotel Marina (☎ 01-522 9109), Voulgari 13 in Athens, at midnight.

Ferry – Domestic
At least one regular passenger ferry, the *Pegasus*, connects Paxi and Corfu daily in summer (1½ hours, 3300 dr). Twice weekly the *Pegasus* also calls in at Lakka on the north coast.

Other larger car ferries also run throughout the year from Corfu via Igoumenitsa on the mainland. The service is daily in summer but reduces to three times a week in winter and the journey takes several hours. At the time of research, the car ferry left Gaïos daily at 7.30 am, arriving in Corfu at 12.15 pm, and departed from Corfu at 1 pm, arriving in Paxi at 5.15 pm. Passenger tickets cost 2000 dr one way, and cars cost 12,000 dr one way.

Daily excursion boats also come from Corfu and Parga on the mainland. Ferries dock at Gaïos' new port 1km east of the central square, though the *Pegasus* departs from the Gaïos waterfront. Excursion boats dock by the central square and along the quay towards the new port.

PAXI & ANTIPAXI

Paxiot Produce

The olive has been part of life in the eastern Mediterranean since the beginnings of civilisation. Olive cultivation can be traced back about 6000 years. It was the farmers of the Levant (modern Syria and Lebanon) who first spotted the potential of the wild European olive (Olea europaea) – a sparse, thorny tree which was common in the region. These farmers began the process of selection that led to the more compact, thornless, oil-rich varieties that now dominate the Mediterranean.

Whereas most westerners think of olive oil as being just a cooking oil, to the people of the ancient Mediterranean civilisations it was very much more. It was almost inseparable from civilised life itself. As well as being an important foodstuff, it was burned in lamps to provide light, it could be used as a lubricant and it was blended with essences to produce fragrant oils.

The olive oil produced on Paxi is regarded as among Greece's best, and based on quality and price can give Italy's best oils a run for their money.

Paxi's economy and fortune were changed irrevocably under Venetian occupation when islanders were encouraged to plant olives on any spare piece of land. Trees cover around 80% of the island. It is estimated that there are between 250,000 and 500,000 of them, and it is said that even today, every family on Paxi owns at least 500 trees.

Olive oil production is the second largest money earner after tourism, and indeed it works well for those islanders who run a taverna or domatia in the summer as the olives are harvested and the trees tended in the winter months. Traditionally the olives were collected by hand as they fell from the trees. Today large nets are placed at the base of the trees to catch the fallen fruit. The stone presses of yesteryear have now been retired and high tech mechanical presses in Gaïos, Lakka and Fontana produce all the island's oil.

Olive trees also cover part of Antipaxi, but the island is noted more for its vineyards and the red and white wines it produces. Although not of an exportable quality, the locals swear that it is an excellent drop, and it is served in many tavernas on Paxi.

Tickets for Corfu and Igoumenitsa can be obtained from Zefi Travel (☎ 32 114, fax 32 253) on the waterfront. *Pegasus* tickets can be obtained from Gaïos Travel (☎ 32 033, fax 32 175). Paxi's port police can be contacted on ☎ 31 222.

Ferry – International

In July and August a ferry goes two or three times weekly from Paxi to Brindisi in Italy, via Igoumenitsa and Corfu. Ticket prices are the same as from Corfu. A catamaran service to Brindisi via Corfu also runs from 8 July to 5 September, making the trip in 5¼ hours. A one-way ticket costs 33,000 dr.

Tickets can be obtained from Paxos Magic Holidays in Gaïos (see Orientation & Information under Gaïos later in this chapter).

Hydrofoil

The Petrakis company introduced its *Santa II* hydrofoil in 1999 which runs between Corfu, Igoumenitsa and Paxi. At the time of research it was running a service from Paxi to Corfu twice daily at 8.30 am (express service Paxi-Corfu, 55 minutes) and 4.10 pm (via Igoumenitsa, 80 minutes). The same hydrofoil runs from Corfu to Paxi twice daily at 6.45 am (via Igoumenitsa, 80 minutes) and 3 pm (express service Corfu-Paxi, 55 minutes). On Sunday all journeys go via Igoumenitsa, with departures from Corfu for Paxi at 8.30 am and 4 pm, and from Paxi for Corfu at 10.30 am and 5.45 pm. Tickets cost 3500 dr one way.

For detailed information call ☎ 0662-32 401 or ☎ 32 249 (in Paxi), or ☎ 0661-38 690 or ☎ 25 155 (in Corfu), or ☎ 0665-22 001 or ☎ 28 745 (in Igoumenitsa).

GETTING AROUND

Even though cars can be brought onto Paxi, many visitors usually arrive without their own transport and rely on the local transport options of bus, motorcycle or moped, taxi and – best of all – motorised dinghies.

Bus
Even if you have your own transport a trip on Paxi's local bus is an experience not to be missed. Everyone uses it – from backpackers to the local residents to well heeled tourists patronising Paxi's upmarket villas. It travels at a snail's pace between Gaïos, Longos and Lakka and you can flag it down at any point in between.

In summer, the first bus departs from Lakka at 9.15 am, stopping in Longos at 9.25 am and arriving in Gaïos at 9.40 am. Other buses leave Lakka at 11 am, noon, 2.15 pm, 4.30 pm, 6.15 pm, 9 pm and 11.30 pm (although not all of them stop in Longos). From Gaïos to Lakka, the bus departs at 10.15 am, 11.30 am, and 1.30, 5.30, 8 and 10.30 pm. Tickets are purchased on the bus, and cost 300 dr one way from Gaïos to Lakka. For detailed information call ☎ 32 401, fax 32 610.

A bus also departs from Gaïos' bus stop for the new port twice daily, 30 minutes before the departure of the *Santa II* hydrofoil to Corfu. The same bus brings arriving passengers back to Gaïos. There seems to be no charge for this service.

Car & Motorcycle
Car rental on Paxi is ridiculously expensive – mainly because there aren't that many cars available. Inquire at any of the travel agencies listed in the Gaïos and Lakka sections later in this chapter.

Rent a Scooter Vassilis (☎ 32 598) next to the bus stop has the biggest range of scooters and mopeds on the island. Scooters are available for 5000/6000/7000 dr per day depending on power and condition. Be warned – you get what you pay for and some of these vehicles appear to be well past their use-by date.

Motorcycles can also be hired from Makris Motorcycles (☎ 32 031), on Gaïos' waterfront.

At Lakka, try Andreas bikes which has scooters for 5000 dr to 7000 dr per day or Scootermania which has bikes for similar prices. Discounts are usually offered for rentals of three days or more.

Taxi
There are plenty of taxis on the island and they do a brisk business in high season. Taxis normally meet hydrofoils and ferries. Set rates apply – the journey from Gaïos to Lakka costs 2500 dr.

Boat
The best way to explore Paxi – other than on foot – is with a small dinghy equipped with an outboard motor. These can be rented from Gaïos, Longos and Lakka, and cost around 5000 dr to 10,000 dr per day depending on the season. Petrol costs extra, and is worked out according to what you consume. For safety reasons, there are strict rules as to where you can and cannot take these boats, and you will be fined by the port police if you go beyond the prescribed boundaries. You should be given a map when you rent the boat. The west coast in particular is strictly out of bounds to small boats. The protected and often deserted coves of the east coast are perfect mooring points.

GAÏOS Γάιος
Gaïos, on a wide, east coast bay, is the island's capital. It's a delightfully attractive place with crumbling 19th century red-tiled pink, cream and whitewashed buildings. Agios Nikolaos Islet, topped with ruins of a 15th century Venetian fortress, almost fills its harbour. Moni Panagias Islet, named after its monastery, lies at the entrance to the bay. On 15 August, a lively festival ends with dancing in Gaïos' central square.

Orientation & Information
The main square abuts the central waterfront. The main street of Panagioti Kanga runs inland from here to another square where you'll find the bus stop. The post office is just beyond here and the OTE is next door.

There is no tourist office, but the staff at Paxos Magic Holidays (☎ 32 269, fax 32 122, email paxoshld@hol.gr) on Panagioti Kanga are very helpful.

PAXI & ANTIPAXI

Walking Paxi

Paxi lends itself to walking. The main Gaïos-Lakka road is a good starting point, passing through various hamlets along the route. It's not difficult to get off the beaten track by wandering into an olive grove or following an unsealed road, and unless you've got a seriously bad sense of direction it is unlikely that you will get lost. However, if you want to do a few walks, pick up a copy of *The Bleasdale Walking Map of Paxos*, an illustrated map with notes on various footpaths around the island. The walks are clearly marked on the map, and the accompanying booklet provides exact directions.

The Paxos Cultural Association – basically a group of local residents with interests in wildlife and walking – organises walks on the west coast, either daily or every few days in spring and autumn. These cost 4000 dr per person including a picnic of cheese and wine, or 2000 dr for the walk. For information contact ☎ 31 326, fax 31 723 or call in at Spiros Anemoyannis's bar Taxidi in Longos (see Places to Stay & Eat under Longos in this chapter).

The Thomas Arvanitakis Travel Agency (☎ 32 007, fax 32 460) in the main square in Gaïos opposite the church, can also be of help, and offers a range of services and activities including currency exchange, car hire, boat hire and excursion tickets.

Both agencies also sell the *Bleasdale Walking Map of Paxos* (3000 dr), which comes with an explanatory booklet. The Road Editions *Corfu and Paxi* map is currently the best map available for the island.

The port police are located at the northern end of the waterfront heading towards the new port. There is a branch of the National Bank of Greece (with ATM) just off the main square, which also has a currency exchange. The other banks in town do not operate a foreign exchange service.

Things to See & Do

The excellent **Cultural Museum of Paxi** on the waterfront has a well displayed eclectic collection. Make sure not to miss the mind-boggling stirrups hanging from a four-poster bed – a 19th century sex aid. The museum is open 7 to 10.30 pm daily (sometimes it is also open 11 am to 1.30 pm). Admission is 500 dr.

If you want to pick up some good local olive oil straight from the barrel and at bargain prices, head for the unnamed and unsignposted warehouse on the waterfront road to the new port (before the port police building). It is run by Michel Lekkas and

his family, who have been producing oil on Paxi for many years. For 1000 dr you can get a 500ml bottle, or you can buy 6L of oil for 2000 dr.

The best way to get to know Paxi is to walk the island along its many pathways lined with dry stone walls through the countless olive groves that blanket the island. See the boxed text 'Walking Paxi'.

Paxos Magic Holidays also organises horseback picnic rides (13,900 dr) and an island discovery cruise (5400 dr). A popular tour is the History and Traditions Evening which includes a visit to a working olive oil press, feta cheese making, cooking and finally a traditional Greek meal with music and dancing (8500 dr, all inclusive). Any travel agent on the island can sell you tickets for this tour.

Places to Stay

Accommodation tends to mostly consist of prebooked studios and apartments, though you can always find somewhere private to stay. The large *San Giorgio Rooms to Rent* (☎ 32 223) above the waterfront, 150m north of the central square, has well kept doubles for 6000 dr, studios for 8000 dr and apartments for 14,000 dr.

Up the hill opposite the bus stop are a few *domatia*. *Magda's Domatia* (☎ 32 573) has a few clean and basic doubles/triples for 6000/8000 dr. Next door up the hill is *Spiro's Domatia* (☎ 31 172). His somewhat better serviced rooms go for around 8000 dr a double.

The best value rooms in Gaïos are run by the delightful *Thekli Zenebisis (☎/fax 32 313)*, just south of the port and set slightly back from the road. Her immaculate and well equipped two-person studios with balcony cost 8000 dr to 17,000 dr depending on the season. Air-conditioning costs an extra 2000 dr per day. The rooms have great views and are cleaned every day.

The B class *Paxos Beach (☎ 31 211, fax 31 166)* is a bungalow complex, overlooking the sea, 1.5km south-east of Gaïos. The tastefully furnished doubles cost 35,000 dr (half-board) in high season. The complex has a tennis court, beach, bar and restaurant.

Places to Eat

Gaïos has a glut of generally good eating places. Cheap, popular and quick is *George's Corner* on the main square. Go there for his great gyros or chicken. Off the south side of the square is *Taverna Andreas*. This cosy little eatery is the best place for fresh fish and home cooking. Close by is the homy *Kirki*, offering among other tasty fare a chicken dish done in mustard sauce. Kirki is open all year round. *Spiro's*, diagonally opposite the National Bank of Greece, is a pretty yellow building with green shutters. Friendly service and tasty grilled meats and Greek favourites such as stuffed eggplant are the drawcards.

A great evening's eating can be had at the tastefully furbished *Afthendiko* at the inland end of Gaïos. This tavern does superb home-cooked dishes – try octopus in tomato sauce or rooster with *pastitsada*. Both dishes are around 2000 dr.

If you fancy a walk, head uphill along the signposted Vellianitatika road and look for the rather laid-back but still popular *O Kakaletzos (☎ 32 129)*, diagonally opposite the Paxos Club, just west of Gaïos. It serves a wide range of ready-cooked dishes and grilled food.

The best coffee in Gaïos can be had at the aptly named *Cafe Espresso Bar* just west of the central square (heading towards the bus stop). The bar is attractive with exposed beams and there are a handful of tables outside. In addition to coffee any way you want it (Italian, French or Greek style) it does excellent sandwiches (600 dr to 700 dr) and tasty pastries and pies.

Self-catering supplies can be picked up at the *Paxos Market & Delicatessen* on the central square. There's a surprisingly good selection of fruit and vegetables, cured meats, cheese, yoghurt and wine.

Entertainment

Like Corfu, night-time entertainment on Paxi mainly consists of sitting around in bars and tavernas until the early hours. However, there are a couple of discos which cater specifically for high season tourists but remain closed the rest of the year. *Tango* opposite the bus stop at the inland end of Gaïos is especially popular with young Italians who descend on Paxi in July and August. *Phoenix* above the new port attracts a more mixed crowd.

Around Gaïos

The islet of **Mongonisi**, 5km south of Gaïos, is a pleasant hour's walk from the port and is joined to the southern tip of Paxi by a short causeway. There is a small sand beach, a taverna and a camp site. There are various rocky coves good for swimming and sunbathing along the road from Gaïos to Paxi.

LONGOS Λόγγος

A fishing village-cum-resort, Longos is 5km north of Gaïos, and has several beaches nearby. It's much smaller than Gaïos and has a more intimate feel. The village consists of little more than a cramped square and a winding waterfront with a couple of roads leading in and out. It's a great base if you want a quieter stay on Paxi.

The pretty little harbour is full of fishing boats, many of them with names such as *Ozzie* and *Sydney* – testimony to emigrants who have returned to Paxi. Of the 120 or so inhabitants, there are five fishers left, and much of the fish is now brought in from Corfu. Longos attracts yachties although fewer than at Gaïos or Lakka.

PAXI & ANTIPAXI

Orientation & Information

Longos is tiny and picturesque, with most buildings clustered around the east-facing harbour, at the north end of which is a disused factory. There is no bank, although local travel agencies can deal with currency exchange transactions.

Places to Stay & Eat

Most of the accommodation is monopolised by tour companies, including *Planos Holidays* (☎ 31 744) based in Lakka, and for high season you will definitely need to book ahead. The office of *Glyfada Beach Villas* on the waterfront might be worth a try. Otherwise your best bet is *Babis Dendias* (☎/fax 31 597) who rents four-person studios for between 22,000 dr and 28,000 dr. Inquire at his *pantopoleio* (general store), 20m beyond the bus stop.

For eating, try *Nassos* on the waterfront, which has Greek ready-cooked dishes, an extensive (if slightly pricey) choice of fish and an unusually good and well explained wine list. Other recommended tavernas include *Kagarantzas*, which has a changing daily menu featuring Greek favourites and imaginative variations of them, or *Taverna o Gios*. Coffees and cold drinks can be taken at *Ores* music cafe and wine bar in between the two. Right at the end of the harbour in a whitewashed building with green roof and shutters and two seafront terraces is *Taxidi*, a cocktail bar run by friendly and well travelled Spiros Anemoyannis. Even if you don't fancy one of his intoxicating fresh melon and vodka mega-cocktails, it's worth calling in for some local advice. He usually knows of several individuals who have private rooms to rent.

The best bread on the island can be found at the ramshackle *Loukas Bakery*, up a little alley off the square.

INLAND & THE WEST COAST

You don't have to make a special trip to appreciate Paxi's inland villages as you will no doubt pass through them either on the local bus or with your own transport if you are travelling from Gaïos to Longos or Lakka. Venetian-style architecture and a few pretty churches are the main items of interest in **Bogdanatika** and **Magazia**, villages which still retain a nontouristy feel.

Magazia has a traditional *kafeneio* (next to the church) serving excellent Greek coffee, and there are two decent places to eat – *Lilas* grill room which is mainly frequented by locals looking for a good souvlaki or roast meat, and a slightly more expensive *fish taverna*.

Both Bogdanatika and Magazia are good starting points for exploration (on foot) of Paxi's rugged west coast. The best views, and the best place to view its wildlife – dolphins, seabirds and turtles – can only be had from the water. The caves along Paxi's west coast are the best in the Ionians and big enough to enter in a small boat. The 'around-the-island' cruises in small fishing caïques offer the best chance to check the caves, and leave (weather permitting) from each of the three main ports. Inquire at any travel agency for details.

The beach at **Agrilas** on the west coast, west of Bogdanatika, is one of the few easily accessible on foot. A wide track leads off from the church of the Pantokratoras (with triple-arched bell tower) in the hamlet of Makratika. The clearly defined path heads off through an olive grove. You'll pass a group of buildings including a circular building with a domed top, possibly a converted windmill. The path forks after the buildings. Take the right fork and continue, keeping the olive grove on your left and the rock ledges on your right. The path narrows but is still discernible. It leads down to a small pebble beach.

You can walk to **Trypitos**, a high cliff from where there are stunning views of Antipaxi. From Gaïos, walk westwards along the Makratika road and turn right uphill at Villa Billy's, marked with a small sign on the wall. Stay on the main track and just before it ends turn left onto a narrow path which leads to Trypitos.

LAKKA Λάκκα

This is another pretty harbour and feels more like Gaïos. It lies at the end of a deep, narrow bay on the north coast and is another popular yachtie call. It's an ideal alternative base to Gaïos since you can also take the twice-weekly ferry to Corfu from here. Lakka has a couple of decent beaches, Vigla and Mesorahi, around either side of the bay's headland, and some great walks.

Orientation & Information

Most of the action and activity in Lakka focuses on the waterfront where the main tourist agencies, shops and restaurants are located. There are also some good tavernas and kafeneia clustered around the atmospheric village square, set slightly back from the harbour.

The two main travel agencies in Lakka are Routsis Holidays (☎ 31 807, fax 31 161) and Planos Holidays (☎ 31 744), both of which can organise accommodation, excursions to Antipaxi and boat hire (from 5000 dr to 10,000 dr per day depending on season, plus petrol). There are daily trips on a caïque to Antipaxi (3000 dr) taking in the west coast cliffs and caves.

Kids will love the Lakka aquarium (☎ 31 389) at the back of the village near the bus stop. Run by the knowledgeable and enthusiastic Vassila family, the aquarium boasts over 100 species of sea creatures including octopuses and sea horses. It's pot luck as to what you'll see in the tanks – at the beginning of each season the Vassila children gather the creatures using nets, then put them all back into the sea for winter. The aquarium is open 10 am to 2 pm and 7 to 10.30 pm daily. Tickets cost 1000 dr (600 dr for children).

Places to Stay

If you would like to stay, contact *Routsis Holidays (☎ 31 807, fax 31 161)* situated on the waterfront. The helpful owners are the agents for many rooms in and around Lakka – but beware that they fill up early. *Planos Holidays (☎ 31 744, 31 821),* also on the waterfront, might have something available. However its properties, many of which are let through a British parent company, tend to be more upmarket and are priced at the higher end of the scale.

Places to Eat

Lakka also has a glut of good and tasteful tavernas, though *Souris* on the square and *Stasinos* in a little side street off the square are worth looking at first.

La Rosa di Paxos on the eastern side of the waterfront is probably the prettiest restaurant in the Ionians. Tables spill over two terraces and are surrounded by (some might say drowning in) flowering plants. The international menu gives a nod to Greek cuisine but there's also an Italian influence with lots of grilled vegetables in local olive oil and fresh fish displayed in a fridge on the waterside.

La Piazza on the main square is extremely popular with Greeks as well as foreigners. It has a basic taverna menu and a permanent grill for meats, but vegetarians have plenty of options with stuffed vegetables and ready-made dishes and some delicious *mezes. Diogenis* opposite serves basic Greek fare and is always full.

On the central harbourfront, places for a drink include the stylish and popular *Akis,* and *Fanis* which has comfy wicker chairs, doubles as a home for a gaggle of local geese and serves sublime fresh peach juice. The best coffee can be had from *Spiros* kafeneio on the main square just near the bus stop.

The *Sweet Gallery* bakery just off the waterfront serves delicious pastries, best eaten warm out of the oven early in the morning. Try stopping at just one ham and cheese or spinach pie.

Antipaxi

☎ 0662

Diminutive Antipaxi is covered with grapevines from which excellent wine is produced (see boxed text 'Paxiot Produce'). Caïques and tourist boats run daily out of Gaïos and usually pull in at a couple of beaches and at the small port of Agrapidia. Vrika Beach at the north-eastern tip is sandy and gently sloping.

A coastal path links Vrika Beach with Voutoumi Beach, farther south round a couple of headlands. Voutoumi Beach is very pretty, but is made up of large pebbles. A *taverna* high up on the bluff serves hungry bathers.

If you don't fancy just beach bumming, take a walk up to the little scattered settlement of Vigla, stopping to admire the many little vineyards along the way and dotted throughout the village.

The west coast of Antipaxi is hard to get to and has no beaches of note.

GETTING THERE & AWAY

The cheapest way to get to Antipaxi is via the morning boat run by Antipaxos Lines from Gaïos that leaves at 10 am and returns from Vrika Beach at 5 pm. The cost is 1300 dr return. Fishing caïques also make the trip.

In high season there are nine high speed express boats which leave Gaïos between 10 am and 2.30 pm. The return boats leave Vrika at 2.30, 5 and 6 pm. Tickets cost 1500 dr return and can be bought from the kiosk on the quay. Note that if the wind blows up boats will not leave.

PLACES TO STAY & EAT

There are several houses (rather than villas) on Antipaxi which can be rented (with prior booking). It's best to contact *Thomas Arvanitakis Travel Agency* (☎ *32 007, fax 32 460*) in the main square in Gaïos opposite the church. Although there is no official camp site, camping is tolerated at Voutoumi beach.

At Vrika, two restaurants, *Spiro's Taverna* and *Vrika Taverna*, serve the often busy tourist trade. There are also two tavernas at Agrapidias.

If you are planning to stay, be sure to bring enough provisions with you as the tavernas close after the last day-trippers leave.

Lefkada & its Satellites

Lefkada is the fourth largest island in the Ionian group. Theoretically it is not an island at all, but is joined to the mainland by a narrow isthmus, through which the occupying Corinthians dug a canal in the 8th century BC. The 25m-wide canal is spanned from the mainland by a causeway.

Lefkada is mountainous with two peaks over 1000m. It is also fertile, well watered by underground streams, with cotton fields, acres of dense olive groves, vineyards, fir and pine forests. The name refers to the ancient Greek word for 'white', and alludes to the island's dazzling white cliffs and barren mountains.

Lefkada's beauty is also in its people, who display intense pride in their island and a respect for the past. Many of the older women wear traditional costume. Despite the growing tourist presence, Lefkada is the least Anglophone of the northern Ionians.

Lefkada has 10 satellite islets: Meganisi, Kalamos, Kastos, Madouri, Skorpidi, Skorpios, Sparti, Thilia, Petalou and Kythros. Several of these are privately owned and cannot be visited. However, there are several excursion boats from Nydri, south of Lefkada Town, which do tours of various islets, and hiring a motorised dinghy will give you the freedom to get close to even those islands that are officially off limits.

HIGHLIGHTS

- Swim in the phosphorescent turquoise waters off Lefkada's west coast
- Take a day cruise to the satellite islets of Madouri, Sparti, Skorpidi and Skorpios
- Launch yourself into a windsurfing paradise at Vasiliki
- Head inland to Karya and shop for lace and embroidery
- Visit the lush and beautiful islet of Kastos

Lefkada Λευκάδα

☎ 0645 • pop 21,100

Once a very poor island, Lefkada's traditional agriculture-based economy is changing. Until 10 years ago olive oil and wine production made up 50% of the economy, with fishing making up 20%. Now most islanders tend to work in the tourism industry during summer and return to their agricultural or pescatorial tasks in winter.

An International Festival of Literature & Art, involving performers from diverse cultural backgrounds, takes place in summer with events held each week from late June to late August.

Lefkada Town is a popular anchorage for yachties, but most of the island's visitors are package tourists based along the east coast. The more accessible eastern coastal beaches are pebbled, while most on the west are white sand. Indeed the difficult-to-get-to west coast beaches are among the best in the Ionians, with water that can fairly be described as a phosphorescent shade of turquoise.

HISTORY

Dorpfeld's excavations revealed archaeological evidence from the Neolithic period

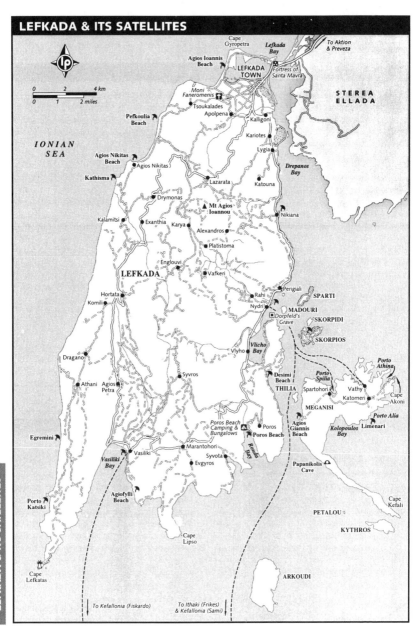

LEFKADA & ITS SATELLITES

(8000 BC). Traces of Mycenaean civilisation during the Copper Age have also been unearthed.

The Corinthians conquered Lefkada in the 7th century and established a colony near the site of present day Lefkada Town. During the Pelopennesian War, as loyal allies of Corinth, the Lefkadians sided with the Spartans.

From 338 BC the island, like the rest of Greece, was under the control of Macedonia. Lefkadian soldiers took part in Alexander the Great's expedition against the Persians. In 198 BC Lefkada became part of the Roman Empire. The island flourished under the Romans, who orchestrated the construction of bridges, walls and arcades. However the foundation of a new Roman colony at Nikopolis on the mainland (near present day Aktion) in 31 BC drained away Lefkada's wealth and population, and left the island at the mercy of pirates and the elements of nature.

The historical record of Lefkada is subsequently very thin. From the 5th century AD, Lefkada's fate resembled that of the other Ionian islands under the Byzantine Empire. In the early 13th century, with Corfu and Paxi, the island fell under control of the Byzantine Despotate of Epiros. In 1293 it was claimed by Count Orsini, who subsequently ruled Kefallonia and Zakynthos. Orsini built the Agia Mavra fortress for protection from pirates. From 1331 Lefkada was under the domination of oppressive Frankish knights. The Venetian De Tocci family took control in 1362 and remained in power until 1479. During this time the island enjoyed financial development and religious liberties, all of which came to an end with the Turkish conquest in 1479. The Turks destroyed the island, slaughtering thousands of inhabitants and selling others for slavery. Monasteries were turned into mosques while the remaining population lived in poverty.

The return to Venetian rule in 1684 brought some relief. At this time Lefkada Town was developed.

With the fall of Venice, there was a short interlude of French and then Russian control. In 1799 Ali Pasha, the tyrant of Epiros, tried to get his hands on Lefkada, which had been promised to him in negotiations with the British. Protecting their own interests, and assisted by the then Russian foreign secretary and future first president of Greece, Ioannis Kapodistrias, who recognised how disastrous the move would be, the British reneged on the agreement.

Lefkada became part of the independent Septinsular Republic. Together with other islands it passed into British protection, during which major structural works (including the first anti-seismic buildings) were carried out.

In 1864 AD, together with the other six Ionian islands, Lefkada became part of unified Greece.

GETTING THERE & AWAY
Air
Lefkada has no airport but Aktion airport, near Preveza on the mainland, is a 30 minute bus journey away. It has four flights weekly to Athens (13,900 dr). Lefkada's Olympic Airways office (☎ 22 881) is at Dorpfeld 1; Preveza's (☎ 0682-28 343) is at Spiliadou 5.

Bus
From Lefkada Town's KTEL bus station (☎ 22 364) there are buses to Athens (5½ hours, 6200 dr, four daily), Patras (three hours, 2900 dr, two weekly) and Aktion airport (30 minutes, 360 dr, five daily).

Ferry
From Vasiliki, at least two ferries daily go to Fiskardo (1½ hours, 940 dr) on Kefallonia and Frikes (2½ hours, 940 dr) on Ithaki in high season. In summer one ferry leaves daily from Nydri for Frikes on Ithaki and then Fiskardo.

You can contact Lefkada's port police on ☎ 22 322.

GETTING AROUND
Bus
From Lefkada Town, frequent buses go to Nydri and Vlyho (up to 18 daily), Poros (four daily) and Vasiliki (10 daily). There

are regular buses to Karya (seven daily), Agios Nikitas (six daily), Kalamitsi (four daily), Kathisma (10 daily) and Athani (four daily).

Other villages are served by one or two buses daily. Tickets cost from 200 dr to 400 dr depending on distance.

Car & Motorcycle

Cars can be hired in Lefkada Town from EuroHire Car Rental (☎ 21 458, fax 0661-23 685), Golemi 5 (by the harbour).

It has competitive rates for small cars (Group A) such as a Fiat Panda for 17,800 dr per day, 36,400 dr for three days and 80,600 dr for a week with unlimited kilometres. A larger Fiat Punto costs 24,600 dr per day, 50,700 dr for three days and 112,000 dr per week.

Rent a motorbike from Motorcycle Rental Santas (☎ 23 947), on Aristoteli Valaoriti in Lefkada Town. At the top of Ioannou Mela, turn right.

LEFKADA TOWN
☎ 0645 • pop 6800

Lefkada Town, the island's capital and primarily a yacht port, is built on a promontory at the south-east corner of a salty lagoon called the fish pond which is, appropriately, used as a fish hatchery. The town was devastated by earthquakes in 1867 and 1948. After 1948, many houses were rebuilt in a unique style constructed in the hope they would withstand future earthquakes. The buildings have wooden frames, with the lower floors panelled in wood and the upper floors lined with painted sheet metal or corrugated iron that is strangely attractive. The belfries of churches are made of metal girders – another earthquake precaution. Damage from the 1953 earthquake was minimal, but the town suffered severely during an earthquake in 1971.

One of Lefkada Town's claims to fame is that the first brass band in Greece was established here in 1850.

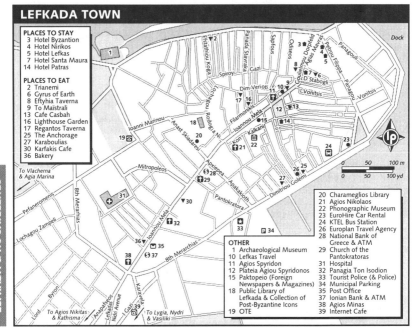

LEFKADA TOWN

PLACES TO STAY
3 Hotel Byzantion
4 Hotel Nirikos
5 Hotel Lefkas
7 Hotel Santa Maura
14 Hotel Patras

PLACES TO EAT
2 Trianemi
6 Gyrus of Earth
8 Eftyhia Taverna
9 To Maïstrali
13 Cafe Casbah
16 Lighthouse Garden
17 Regantos Taverna
25 The Anchorage
27 Karaboulias
30 Karfakis Cafe
36 Bakery

OTHER
1 Archaeological Museum
10 Lefkas Travel
11 Agios Spyridon
12 Plateia Agiou Spyridonos
15 Paktopeio (Foreign Newspapers & Magazines)
18 Public Library of Lefkada & Collection of Post-Byzantine Icons
19 OTE
20 Charameglios Library
21 Agios Nikolaos
22 Phonographic Museum
23 EuroHire Car Rental
24 KTEL Bus Station
26 Europlan Travel Agency
28 National Bank of Greece & ATM
29 Church of the Pantokratoras
31 Hospital
32 Panagia Ton Isodion
33 Tourist Police (& Police)
34 Municipal Parking
35 Post Office
37 Ionian Bank & ATM
38 Agios Minas
39 Internet Cafe

LEFKADA & ITS SATELLITES

Orientation

The bus station is on the eastern waterfront. The town's animated main thoroughfare, Dorpfeld, starts just south of the causeway at the Hotel Nirikos. This street is named after 19th century archaeologist Wilhelm Dorpfeld, who is held in high esteem for postulating that Lefkada, not Ithaki, was the home of Odysseus. Dorpfeld leads to Plateia Agiou Spyridonos, the main square where locals enjoy *soumadia* (an almond drink), during the evening *volta* (stroll). After the square the thoroughfare's name changes to Ioannou Mela. It is lined with interesting shops and several *kafeneia*.

Information

There is no tourist office on Lefkada. The tourist police (☎ 26 450) are in the same building as the regular police on Dimitriou Golemi, but they are not very helpful.

The National Bank of Greece and the Ionian Bank (both with ATMs) and the post office are on the east side of Ioannou Mela. The OTE phone office is on Zambelou.

You can get onto the Net at the Internet Cafe (☎ 21 507, email intercaf@lefkada .hellasnet.gr), Ioannou Gazi 5, which is a five minute walk south (inland) from the bus station.

The staff at Lefkas Travel (☎ 22 430, fax 23 566), Dorpfeld 50, are friendly and helpful and can assist you with car hire and accommodation all over the island. Europlan (☎ 25 398, fax 25 193, email europlan@ lefkada.hellasnet.gr) on the eastern waterfront can also help with accommodation, car hire and other travel details.

Paktopeio on Iaonnou Mela near the central square sells foreign newspapers and magazines.

Things to See

Churches Lefkada Town boasts several 18th century churches which were opulently decorated by leading artists of the Ionian school.

Their simple architecture – it was believed that single-aisled rectangular buildings would withstand earthquakes – belies the often extravagant interior decoration.

Most of the churches are privately owned by families and have unconventional opening hours. Don't be surprised if you find them closed. The best time to visit is probably just prior to or following the morning or evening services.

Agios Spyridon is situated on Plateia Agiou Spyridonos and features an intricately carved wooden iconostasis. The church of **Panagia Ton Isodion** (also referred to as the church of the Theotokou) has ceiling friezes by Lefkada artist Spiridon Gazis after Raphael and is the only church on Lefkada with a stone belfry. **Agios Minas**, at the southern end of Ioannou Mela, has a superb carved gilt iconostasis and ceiling paintings by Nikolaos Doxaras (the son of Panagiotis Doxaras, the founder of the Ionian school). The church of **Agios Nikolaos** has an ornate carved wooden screen and interesting ceiling paintings.

Archaeological Museum The Lefkada Archaeological Museum has moved into a brand new building on the corner of Sikelianou and Svoronou. The small collection of artefacts found on the island is well displayed and labelled. One of the earliest objects, dating from the late 6th century BC, is a delicate terracotta figurine of nymphs dancing around a flute player. Other figurines date from the Archaic and Hellenistic periods.

Highlights of the museum are a bronze mirror from the early classical period, a superb terracotta sculpture of Leda and the Swan, stone funerary urns from the Hellenistic period and a full tomb authentically arranged, with skeleton and the deceased's burial objects.

The museum (☎ 21 635) is open 7.30 am to 2.30 pm Monday to Friday and 8 am to 1.30 pm on Saturday and Sunday. Admission was free at the time of writing but an entrance charge was planned.

Collection of Post-Byzantine Icons Works by icon painters from the Ionian school are housed in a late 19th century building off Ioannou Mela (the Public Library of Lefkada is located on the first floor). The icons – including work by Pana-giotis Doxaras – come from churches and monasteries in Lefkada and from private collections. The museum also contains Russian icons, religious books, and other artefacts, including a series of sacred vestments presented to the Bishop of Lefkada by Catherine the Great in 1769. It is open 8.30 am to 1.30 pm Tuesday to Saturday and also 6 to 8.15 pm on Tuesday and Thursday evenings (if it appears to be closed, ask at the library upstairs). Admission is free.

Charameglios Library Anyone interested in the history of Lefkada should head to this documentation centre on Lefkadian studies in Plateia Marka (off Skiadaresis). It has hundreds of books about Lefkada, mainly in Greek but also in some foreign languages. The collection includes prints, articles and maps as well as work by native artists and writers of Lefkada. It's open in the mornings from Monday to Saturday. The art gallery on the ground floor of the library has temporary exhibitions by local artists in spring and early summer.

Phonographic Museum More a curio shop than a museum, Lefkada's phono-graphic museum (☎ 21 088) at Kalkani 10 has a collection of venerable gramophones and memorabilia and sells tapes of old Greek songs – including traditional Lefkada *kantades* – for 1000 dr. It's signposted from Ioannou Mela. Admission is free, although you'll be 'encouraged' to buy a cassette.

Other Things to See
The 14th century Venetian **Fortress of Santa Mavra** is on the mainland. It was first established by the crusaders but the remains mainly date from the Venetian and Turkish occupations of the island.

Moni Faneromenis, 3km west of town, was founded in 1634, destroyed by fire in 1886 and rebuilt. Inhabited by a few monks and nuns, the monastery's church can be visited. The views of the lagoon and town are worth the ascent.

West of the lagoon, past windmills, is **Agios Ioannis Beach** where, at sunset,

clouds are neon-lit islands in the sky. The nearest beaches to town are at the northern side of the lagoon, about a 2km walk away.

Places to Stay
The nearest camp site to Lefkada Town is **Kariotes Beach Camping** (☎ 71 103), on the east coast, 5km away. **Episkopos Camping** (☎ 23 043) is 3km farther south.

The D class **Hotel Byzantion** (☎ 21 315, *Dorpfeld 4*) has clean, well kept doubles/triples for 5500/8800 dr. The C class **Hotel Santa Maura** (☎ 21 308, fax 26 253) nearby has quite pleasant singles/doubles for 9000/14,000 dr.

At the comfortable B class **Hotel Nirikos** (☎ 24 132, fax 23 756) on the corner of the waterfront and Dorpfeld, rooms cost 14,000 dr (half-board) for singles and doubles alike. Close by, facing the port, the palatial B class **Hotel Lefkas** (☎ 23 916, fax 24 579, *Panagou 2*) has rates of 17,000/26,000 dr with breakfast. Overlooking Plateia Agiou Spyridonos is the very old-fashioned and slightly run-down **Hotel Patras** (☎ 22 359), open only in July and August. Doubles go for 12,000 dr and triples for 14,000 dr. The owners speak only Greek.

Places to Eat
The **Karaboulias Restaurant** on the eastern waterfront offers traditional fare with flair. The intimate **Eftyhia Taverna** (*Stambogli 2*) has hearty, inexpensive food. **Regantos Taverna** (*Vergioti 17*), off Dorpfeld near the central square, is another atmospheric little place with good food. A meal of stuffed eggplant, Greek salad and wine costs around 2200 dr.

To Maïstrali on Dorpfeld near Plateia Agiou Spyridonos is another good eatery in the heart of town. Look out for the green and yellow decor. **Cafe Casbah** on Plateia Agiou Spyridonos does great breakfasts and coffee and is a good place to chill out for an hour or two. **Lighthouse Garden** (*Filarmonikis*) is a traditional Greek taverna with a delightful vine-covered courtyard and is popular with locals.

The western side of the waterfront is lined with groovy new bars and eateries frequented by hip Lefkadians. *Trianemi*, which does excellent Greek dishes, is well worth trying.

For takeaway, you can't beat the gyros and souvlaki from *Gyrus of Earth*. Past the central square on Ioannou Mela, *Karfakis Cafe* does excellent coffee and is a great place to sit and watch the world go by.

Self-caterers have a good choice of *fruit and vegetable shops* along Ioannou Mela, and the quality of the produce is better than anywhere else in the Ionians (outside of Corfu Town). There's a *bakery* opposite the Ionian Bank on Ioannou Mela which sells great pies, biscuits, breads and the local speciality, *lemonopita*, a cake made of almond flour, lemon, sugar and honey and topped with sesame seeds. There's a *supermarket* just outside the town on the road to Nydri.

EAST COAST

The accessible east coast of Lefkada hosts the majority of the island's tourism industry and in parts resembles Corfu's eastern coastline. Just south of Lefkada Town are the resorts of **Lygia**, **Nikiana** and **Perigiali** which have barely acceptable beaches and good views across to the mainland.

Hotel Aliki (☎ 0645-71 602, ☎ 72 070, fax 72 071) in Nikiana is relatively new and tastefully furnished. Double studios go for 15,000 dr in low season and up to 25,000 dr in high season, with air-conditioning costing an extra 2000 dr per night. The hotel is open year-round and has a swimming pool. A narrow goat track leads down to a rocky cove where you can swim, but there's no beach.

Nydri Νυδρί

Not so long ago, Nydri, situated 16km south of Lefkada Town, was a sleepy fishing village but it fell hook, line and sinker to the lure of the tourist trade.

Now it's a very busy, commercialised town, and the departure point for innumerable day cruises that take in the satellite islets of Madouri, Sparti, Skorpidi and Skorpios (see Lefkada's Satellites later in this chapter).

Orientation & Information Nydri consists of a not unattractive harbour lined with yachts and pleasure cruisers on the water side and tavernas and bars on the land side. The seafront is called Akti Aristoteli Onasi, after shipping magnate Aristotle Onassis.

Most of the bars and tavernas also have entrances onto the busy main street – lined on both sides with minimarkets, travel agencies, car hire companies and tacky souvenir shops plus the odd tasteful boutique – which can best be described as an eyesore. There are two ATMs – both good for Visa, MasterCard, Maestro and Cirrus cards – at the northern end of the main 'strip'.

Various travel agents, all located in the main street, can help with accommodation, car and moped hire and boat hire, as well as selling tickets for cruises to the satellite islands. Try Samba Tours (☎ 92 658, fax 92 659) or Kosmas Frangoulis (☎ 92 577, fax 92 164).

Avis Rent a Car (☎ 92 136, fax 92 440) rents bikes (1000 dr/day) and mopeds (3000 dr to 6000 dr per day depending on size). Cars cost 11,000 dr to 45,000 dr per day (cheaper by the week).

Things to See & Do The beach isn't up to much but there are a few sunbeds and umbrellas that can be hired and lots of watersports (head to the northern end of town beyond the quay where the ferries and cruise boats moor). A better beach (also with watersports) and popular with boating parties is Dessimi Beach on the Geni Peninsula, about 5km south of Nydri.

Windsurfing, water-skiing, parasailing and sailing (bareboating with licence or crewed yachts) out of Nydri can be organised by Nikos Thermes' Sport Boat Charter (☎ 92 431), Perigiali (1.5km north of Nydri). Englishman Andy Fenna runs the island's only PADI School of Diving (☎ 92 286) from Nydri.

You can't leave Nydri without having gone on one of the many available **boat cruises**. Tickets are sold at any of the travel agents in Nydri's main strip – they all sell the same cruises for the same prices. You should book a day or two ahead, especially

LEFKADA & ITS SATELLITES

in the high season. Examples of excursions offered include: Kefallonia, Ithaca, Meganisi and Skorpios, 9 am to 7 pm daily, 5000 dr; Meganisi and Skorpios, 10 am to 4.30 pm, 2500 dr; Meganisi, Marathia (on the Greek mainland) and Skorpios on an old war ship (which includes lunch, drinks, snacks, use of mask, snorkel, and beach umbrellas), 9 am to 5 pm daily, 9000 dr; Parga, Paxi, Antipaxi, 8 am to 8 pm Sunday only, 8000 dr.

If you would rather explore the islets independently, boats can be hired from Trident Travel Agency (☎/fax 92 037) situated on the main street. Small boats with outboard motors cost around 10,000 dr a day (excluding fuel) and sailing dinghies are 8000 dr. The agency also has motorcycle and car hire and a room-finding service. Kosmas Frangoulis (☎ 92 577, fax 92 164) rents motorboats for 12,000 dr to 15,000 dr plus fuel. Avis Rent a Car (☎ 92 136, fax 92 440) rents dinghies with outboards (12,000 dr per day plus fuel).

The quiet village of **Vlyho** is 3km south of Nydri. Beyond here, a road leads to a peninsula where Wilhelm Dorpfeld is buried. Just west of the Nydra-Vlyho road are the Bronze Age ruins which he excavated, leading him to believe Lefkada was Homer's Ithaca.

West of Nydri, past the hamlets of Rahi and Dimosari, a signposted track leads to a **waterfall** (you'll see a smaller one and a more spectacular larger one). It's just over 3.5km from Nydri – an easy 40 minute walk and a good place for a picnic.

Places to Stay There are two very good camping grounds – *Santa Maria Camping* (☎ 95 007) and *Desimi Beach Camping* (☎ 95 223) on Desimi Beach (signposted after Vlyho) on the Geni Peninsula.

There are a large number of rooms and studios in Nydri though a fair few get block-booked by package companies.

Armeno Beach Hotel (☎ 92 112, fax 92 018) at the quieter northern end of Nydri, has some wonderful rooms overlooking the beach and the island of Skorpios. Doubles go for 18,000 dr in high season and 10,000

dr in low season. In a small side street opposite the Avis car rental office, is the friendly, family-run *Gorgona Hotel* (☎ 92 197, fax 95 634) set in a shady, flower-filled garden. Simple, spotlessly clean doubles go for 6000 dr to 10,000 dr depending on the season.

If you are having problems finding a room, head a few hundred metres out of town in either direction where you will see 'rooms to let' or '*domatia*' signs. *Kosmas Frangoulis Tourist Office* (☎ 92 577, fax 92 164) can also help. He works as an agent for many individuals in and around Nydri and can find you a room or studio for 10,000 dr to 15,000 dr depending on size and season. He also deals with upmarket houses and apartments.

Just south of Nydri, on the Geni Peninsula, is *Australis Apartments* (☎ 95 521) run by a friendly Greek-Australian. Basic but clean and spacious studios with balcony go for 5000 dr in low season, rising to 13,000 dr in high season.

Places to Eat You can take your pick of any of the countless seafront tavernas, but they are pretty touristy and serve more or less the same Greek and international dishes (as well as English breakfasts) at more or less the same price. None are exceptional although *Apollo* is recommended by some locals.

A better dining experience will be had if you head a few kilometres out of town. Nydri is famous in Lefkada for having excellent quality meat, as butchers in the area sometimes rear and often slaughter their own animals.

At Perigiali, 1km north of Nydri, is *Mangano* (☎ 93 188) one of the best restaurants in the area and much better value for money than the tourist oriented harbourfront joints. The moussaka is mouthwatering and you can dine on the beach. The restaurant is close to Armeno Beach Hotel. *Keramidaki*, also on the main road at Perigiali, is recommended for fish and grills.

On the Geni Peninsula, *Elena* is a popular restaurant specialising in fish that the

The Mellisani Cave near Sami, Kefallonia

The monastery of St Gerasimos, Kefallonia

The cave of St Gerasimos, Kefallonia

An upmarket Greek speciality – sun-dried octopus, Gythio (Peloponnese)

Traditional architecture, Kioni, Ithaki

A wide range of ceramics on display at a market stall, Zakynthos Town

The crystalline aquamarine waters of Zakynthos' west coast

Catch of the day, Zakynthos Town

SALLY WEBB

Kapsali through a stone fence at the kastro at Hora, Kythira

SALLY WEBB

Hora from its kastro, Kythira

owners catch fresh every day. In the same area, on the road leading to Desimi Beach is *Bella Vista* taverna which has spectacular views over the lagoon to Nydri.

Kharaviatika Taverna in the hamlet of the same name, 2km up a winding road inland from the main Nydri-Vlyho road is famous for its grilled meats and is extremely popular with Greeks. The barbecued lamb chops are sublime.

Poros Πόρος

Poros is a little village overlooking Rouda Bay, which makes a great alternative base to the often raucous Nydri. The beach, **Mikros Gialos**, is good and there are boats for hire.

There is a camp site – *Poros Beach Camping & Bungalows (☎ 95 452)* – and the cosy, cool domatia of *Yiannoula (☎ 95 507)* at the eastern end of the bay. A double with kitchen will cost you 9000 dr. *Rouda Bay Apartments and Suites (☎ 95 634, fax 92 268)* run by Christina Manolitsi, has attractive and spacious studios and apartments from 8000 dr to 20,000 dr (depending on the size and the season).

For meals, try the nearby *Zolithros* or *Molos*, both quaint and friendly tavernas.

Vasiliki Βασιλική

Purported to be *the* best windsurfing location in Europe, Vasiliki is a once pretty, now grungy, fishing village with a disappointing pebble beach. It attracts a sizable crowd each season and you can hop over to Kefallonia from here if you are heading south.

There are no banks but several tourism agencies also function as a foreign exchange including Samba Tours (☎ 31 520, fax 31 522), also the official agents for ferry tickets to Kefallonia, and Star Travel (☎ 31 833, fax 31 834, email startrvl@lefkada.hellas net.gr). Star Travel organises day cruises to Skorpios, Kefallonia and Ithaki. It also offers Internet access for 1500 dr per hour.

Things to See & Do You can rent surfboards from Club Vas (☎ 31 588) and instruction for all levels is available. It's crowded in summer so prepare to commute. Wild Wind (☎/fax 31 610) rents out cata-

marans and offers instruction. You can take a cruise (☎ 93 116) on a *felucca*, an old-fashioned sailing boat, for between 10,000 dr and 12,000 dr, including food and drink.

Nonwindsurfers will find the beach a bit of a disappointment. Caïques take visitors from Vasiliki to swim at the best sand beaches on the west coast, which include Porto Katsiki, Egremini and Kathisma. A boat will also take you to the unspoilt **Agiofylli Beach**, south-east of Vasiliki Bay.

Places to Stay & Eat The best bet for accommodation is to drop in to *Samba Tours (☎ 92 658, fax 92 659)* and see what's available. Rooms go for between 8000 dr and 11,000 dr in season. Studios cost from 15,000 dr to 20,000 dr. *Star Travel* can also help with accommodation and has rooms from 5000 dr a night in low season rising to around 19,000 dr (for an apartment) in high season.

Pension Holidays (☎ 31 011, fax 31 522) beyond the ferry quay has pleasant double rooms with TV, fridge and air-conditioning for 9000 dr to 13,000 dr and studios for 10,000 dr to 12,000 dr depending on the season. *Leodidis Christos (☎ 31 221)* runs the minimarket opposite the ferry quay and has rooms from 7000 dr.

On the road parallel to but set back from the beach are two other options. *Billy's House (☎ 31 418)* has double rooms for 10,000 dr and *Pension Angela (☎ 31 129, fax 31 285)* has studios for a little more.

The waterfront restaurants are all pretty similar but there's a bit of a grungy rundown air about them. You could try *To Steki ton Piraton*, set back from the waterfront on the main street. *Alexandros*, on the west end of the waterfront, offers a wide range of Chinese dishes if you hanker after something other than Greek food. *Stelios Tavern* right on the waterfront opposite the ferry quay is a good place for those who like garlic with everything – from mushrooms to beans to bread. It also has all the regular Greek staples.

Entertainment In Vasiliki you don't have to look hard for nightlife. There are plenty of bars around the harbour with lengthy beer lists. Cruise the quayside until you find what you are looking for. **Center Club** is a popular dance venue in a small arcade halfway along the main shopping street which leads off from the harbour. **Zeus Bar** near the ferry quay has happy hour from 7 to 9 pm every night. **Remezzo Bar** on the beach is a disco/bar and is open until the early hours.

INLAND VILLAGES

Lefkada is not all coastline. The interior comes as a pleasant surprise to those who make the effort to see it. The winding road through the uplands in the mountain south of Lefkada Town passes through several traditional farming villages.

Karya Καρυά

The large village of Karya is the centre of Lefkada's lace and embroidery industry, and shops selling lace, embroidery and hand-woven goods line the main street. The sceptical traveller might recognise many pieces of lace that most likely hail from Chinese sweat shops, but there is some stunning local lace among them. Although you'll probably find few bargains, the handiwork can only be admired.

The descendants of one of the village's greatest lacemakers and embroiderers, Maria Koutsochero, run a charming **museum** (open 9 am to 8 pm, admission 500 dr). Her work was famous not only on Lefkada but throughout the rest of Greece and abroad. The museum – actually the family's original house – is a fascinating insight into village peasant life, as well as demonstrating the craftswoman's enormous skill.

There are seven buses operating daily from Lefkada Town to Karya.

Places to Stay & Eat Karya's one hotel, formerly a great base for walkers, was the **Kyria Village Hotel** (☎ 51 030). It is now open only in August, when it's generally too hot to walk anywhere. Your best bet for rooms is to head to **Pierros** (☎ 41 760), a snack bar in the central square, and ask its

British owner, Brenda Sherry, to point you in the right direction. While you're there have one of Brenda's toasted sandwiches (she's famous for them) and a cup of real Tetley's tea if you're missing it.

Other options for eating out, or just hanging out, are all on – or just off – the central square. **O Rousos** taverna is recommended.

Around Karya

For those with their own transport, a little exploration is fun. Above Karya a road heads uphill towards **Mt Agios Ioannou**, offering great views. The road ends in a military installation to which entry is prohibited. **Englouvi**, about 10km along a winding road south of Karya is the highest village on the island and is famous not only for lace production but also for its excellent lentils. There's plenty of local activity at **Alexandros**, even though it's crumbling to bits. Nearby the 17th century monastery of Agios Georgios at Kolivata has a church with frescoes (not always open).

WEST COAST

Beach lovers should skip the east coast and head straight for the west. The sea in this part of the island is the best in the Ionian – an incredible pale turquoise blue that is almost iridescent – and most beaches feature pale golden or white sand. The road that leads south offers varied scenery, and is often shared by locals on donkeys. You will also find numerous stalls set up along the roadside with islanders selling delicious honey, wine and olive oil.

There are six buses daily from Lefkada Town to Agios Nikitas and Kathisma. Two of these continue to Kalamitsi. There are two buses daily from Lefkada Town to Athani.

Agios Nikitas Αγιος Νικήτας

Agios Nikitas is hardly Lefkada's best kept secret, but it is the island's most tasteful resort. The village nestles amid olive groves and the architecture is a sympathetic blend of pastel-coloured weatherboard buildings erring on the side of twee. There is a surprisingly good choice of places to stay and eat for such a small resort, but it's a good idea to book ahead in high season, as it is very popular with German and Scandinavian tourists.

There's not much of a beach to speak of at Agios Nikitas. Most sun worshippers head to beautiful **Mylos Beach** just around the headland, which is inaccessible by road – you have to take a taxi boat from the Agios Nikitas beach or do a mountain goat scramble over the headland. Remember to take your own umbrella and drinks as there are no facilities.

Places to Stay *Hotel Agias Nikitas (☎ 97 460, fax 97 462)* is a tasteful complex of whitewashed buildings with wooden balconies on the coastal road into the village. Three tastefully decorated buildings are set around a central courtyard and surrounded by olive groves. Double rooms with fridge, air-conditioning and balcony – including breakfast – cost 15,000 dr in low season and 22,000 dr in high season. Suites sleeping up to four people with TV and air-conditioning cost 25,000 dr to 35,000 dr. There are also apartments (sleeping four) with cooking facilities which go for 18,000 dr to 24,000 dr depending on the season.

Next door, *Nikos Smeros (☎ 97 006, fax 97 469)* has studios for 7000 dr to 15,000 dr depending on the season. He also has another house in the village with rooms only for 6000 dr to 13,000 dr.

In the same street a few metres farther on and down a narrow path is the *Olive Tree Hotel (☎ 97 453)* set, as its name suggests, among olive trees. It has its own path leading down into the village proper and is very peaceful with plenty of terrace areas on which guests can relax. Simple but pleasant studios with balcony cost 8,000 dr to 16,000 dr depending on the season. Breakfast is an extra 2000 dr.

In the heart of the village itself (great for proximity to bars and restaurants but not so good as far as late night noise is concerned) is the attractive *Hotel Nefeli (☎ 97 400, fax 97 402)*. The owners don't speak much English but are very friendly. Double rooms including breakfast go for 14,000 dr to

21,000 dr depending on the season. Opposite, the larger *Odyssey (☎ 97 351, fax 97 421, email filippas@otenet.gr)* has more of a large hotel feel but provides pleasant air-conditioned double rooms and studios from 19,000 dr to 24,000 dr. There is a very nice rooftop pool and bar with great views over the village and the sea.

Places to Eat Although Agios Nikitas is a little more expensive on the dining front than other places, the food is noticeably better. One of the nicest places to eat in the village is the *Poseidon* taverna, run by a Greek-Swiss woman and her family. The meat (pork, lamb or chicken) on the grill and the fish soup are all excellent and there's an extensive choice for vegetarians. Expect to pay about 3000 dr to 4000 dr per head for a full meal.

Sweet-tooths should head to *Elena* for wonderful cakes and sweets.

Kathisma Beach Παραλία Κάθισμα

The next beach round from Agios Nikitas is a 2km stretch of sand and sea. This beachcomber's paradise is showing signs of development, with several new apartment blocks on a once-deserted beach. It is popular with freelance campers even though camping is officially prohibited.

Theocharis Brothers (☎/fax 97 335) run a huge taverna at the northern end of the beach with several spanking new studios attached. Double rooms with cooking facilities go for 14,000 dr in low season rising to 24,000 dr in high season. Triples cost from 17,000 dr to 28,000 dr. The slightly older *Sunset (☎ 24 142)* has studios for similar prices.

Nestled in the hills above Kathisma beach is **Kalamitsi**, with incredible views over the west coast. *Panoramic Restaurant (☎ 99 369)* on the road from Kathisma into the village is a great place to stop for a meal or a drink. It also has rooms starting at 6000 dr and rising to 12,000 dr in high season.

In the village proper, rooms are available at similar prices at the *Blue and White House (☎ 99 413, ☎ 99 448)* set in a shady garden. Follow the signs through the centre of the village.

Human Sacrifices & the Lesbians' Leap

According to the ancient writers, Cape Lefkatas was the site of human sacrifices as part of the annual celebrations to honour the god Apollo, who took care of sailors. A convict was chosen as an expiatory victim and thrown off the edge of the promontory into the sea. Feathers or sometimes live birds were attached to the convict's body to ease his fall. If the victim survived, his life was spared.

Such cult practices existed from 1200 BC until Roman times. The human sacrifice was thought to purify the island of its sins. Leaping from the cliff was also thought to relieve the torment of unrequited love. Legend has it that Aphrodite was the first to throw herself over the edge out of love for Adonis. More famously, mythology holds that the proto-lesbian poet Sappho threw herself off the cliff out of unrequited love for a man. Byron wrote of Cape Lefkatas as a 'lover's refuge, and the lesbian's grave'.

The fact is, there is not a shred of evidence to say that Sappho ever set foot on Lefkada at all, and her place in the island's history has come about from historical reinterpretation of her poetry. Some claim that her male love interest was an invention by historians who found her homosexuality hard to deal with.

Sappho is renowned chiefly for her poems that speak out in favour of lesbian relationships, though her range of lyric poetry extends beyond works of an erotic nature. She was born in 630 BC in the town of Eresos on the western side of the island of Lesvos. Little is known about her private life other than that she was married, had a daughter and was exiled to Sicily in about 600 BC. Only fragments remain of her nine books of poems, the most famous of which are the marriage songs. Among her works were hymns, mythological poems and personal love songs. Most of these seem to have been addressed to a close inner-circle of female companions. Sappho uses sensuous images of nature to create her own special brand of erotic lyric poetry. It is a simple yet melodious style, later copied by the Roman poet Catullus. Lesvos is today visited by many lesbians paying homage to Sappho.

Athani to Cape Lefkatas

Athani (Αθάνι) has set itself up as a regional centre for people heading farther south. In reality there's not much to the place – basically a few tavernas, two of which offer accommodation. The long, sandy beach at **Gialos** is reached by a long winding road from Athani.

Alekos Taverna (☎ 33 484) has basic, clean rooms for 5000 dr to 9000 dr depending on the season. The similarly priced *Panorama (☎ 33 291)* has a cocktail bar and rooms with magnificent views. The *Lefkatas* taverna on the road out of Athani has simple Greek fare and good views.

The road south of Athani passes through a barren landscape. Roads lead down to the beaches of **Egremini** (after 4km) and Porto Katsiki (after another 5km), both with pale golden sand and phosphorescent turquoise water. The cliffs behind the beaches offer some shade, and umbrellas and sun lounges can be rented at Porto Katsiki. Despite requiring an effort to get to, these beaches are often full of day-trippers from Vasiliki.

You'd have to be really interested in mythology or shadeless hiking to leg it all the way down to **Cape Lefkatas** (Ακρωτήρι Λευκάτας), Lefkada's southern tip, 14km south of Athani. On the promontory's west side, the sheer white cliffs drop 60m into the Ionian Sea below. A sanctuary of Apollo once stood at Cape Lefkatas, the remains of which were excavated by Dorpfeld; a modern stone lighthouse now stands on site. According to legend, the goddess Aphrodite and the poet Sappho both threw themselves over the edge of Cape Lefkatas out of unrequited love (see boxed text 'Human Sacrifices & the Lesbians' Leap).

Lefkada's Satellites

The closest of Lefkada's 10 satellite islets to Nydri is Madouri, where the Greek poet Aristotelis Valaoritis (1824-79) spent his last 10 years (see under Literature in the Facts about the Ionians chapter). His pretty house, still owned by his descendants, can be seen from the water, but boats are prohibited from landing on the island.

It's not officially possible to land on the Onassis island of Skorpios, where Aristotle, sister Artemis and children Alexander and Christina Onassis are buried in a cemetery visible from the sea. However excursion boats and small dinghies can usually drop anchor off a sandy beach on the north side of the island.

MEGANISI Μεγανήσι
☎ 0645   • pop 1250
Meganisi has the largest population of Lefkada's three inhabited satellite islets, but like many small Greek islands it has suffered depopulation. It's easily visited on a day trip.

It's a tranquil islet with a lovely, verdant landscape and deep bays of turquoise water, fringed by pebbled beaches. It's visited primarily by yachties and is untouched by package tour operators. It has three settlements: the capital of Spartohori, the port of Vathy and the village of Katomeri.

Getting There & Away
There are about four ferries daily between Nydri and Meganisi. They usually call in first at Porto Spilia and then into Vathy before heading back to Nydri. In the past there have been services from Meganisi to Kefallonia and Ithaki; check to see if they are running again.

A minibus meets boats at both ports and takes passengers to Spartohori and Katomeri.

There are numerous day trips to Lefkada's satellite islets on excursion boats from Nydri (see Things to See & Do under Nydri earlier in this chapter). The cruises vary in price depending on the route and what is involved. The basic Meganisi and Skorpios tour costs around 3000 dr, or 7000 dr if a barbecue and unlimited drinks are included.

The Onassis Family & Skorpios

The most famous of all shipping magnates is undoubtedly the Turkish-born Greek Aristotle Socrates Onassis, who was born in Smyrna (now İzmir) in 1906, the son of a tobacco merchant. At the age of 16 his family fled from Turkish hostility to Athens. The following year he arrived in Buenos Aires with a total of $60 and worked as a telephone operator by night while building up his own tobacco business during the day.

At the age of 25 he was already a millionaire and the following year he began what became the world's largest independent shipping line, investing in six Canadian freighters in the midst of a serious recession and putting them into service as the market recovered. Onassis was one of the pioneers of supertankers in the 1950s, and he was awarded the contract to operate the Greek national airline, Olympic Airways, which started in 1957.

Onassis purchased the island of Skorpios in the 1960s. At 62 he married President John F Kennedy's widow, Jacqueline. The wedding took place on Skorpios. He died in 1975 and is buried together with his sister Artemis and children Alexander and Christina Onassis, on the island.

The Onassis fortunes, including Skorpios, are now held in trust for Christina Onassis' teenage daughter Athina Onassis Roussel, who spends virtually no time at all on the island – or indeed in Greece itself. The directors of the Onassis foundation in Athens are increasingly concerned about Athina's shunning of her Greek heritage and it is said that she barely speaks Greek at all, preferring her father's native French.

The beautifully manicured gardens and several villas on Skorpios are maintained by workers from Nydri, and there is round the clock armed security to deter curious trespassers.

Spartohori Σπαρτοχώρι

Spartohori, with narrow, winding lanes and pretty, flower-bedecked houses, perches on a plateau above Porto Spilia.

Boats dock at Porto Spilia. No-one lives here, but there are several tavernas. A road ascends steeply to Spartohori or you can walk the 1km there up steps. To reach Spartohori's main street and central square turn right at Tropicana Pizzeria. The island's only post office is at Vathy.

One of the island's best beaches is **Agios Giannis**, a long stretch of small pebbles, 3km south-west of Spartohori.

Other good beaches are on the island's tapering southern tail. In summer, the owner of Taverna Lakis takes visitors there in his boat.

Places to Stay & Eat There's no official camp sites, but wild camping is tolerated.

The owner of *Chicken Billy's Psistaria (☎ 51 442)* has some low-priced *domatia*. Beyond the central square, just before the main street curves left, turn right, and Chicken Billy's is on the right. It serves delectably tender, low-priced chicken. In its heyday, it was visited by Christina Onassis – her photograph is on the wall to prove it.

Kostas rooms (☎ 51 372) are clean and well kept and there's a communal kitchen. Doubles/triples are 6000/8000 dr. Take the street signposted to Agios Giannis and the rooms are on the right. The immaculate *Studios For Rent Argyri (☎ 51 502, fax 24 911)* has double/triple studios for 10,000/12,000 dr. Inquire at Oasi Bar, opposite Chicken Billy's.

Tropicana Pizzeria has pizzas for 1200 dr and stunning views of Skorpios.

Taverna Lakis offers tasty Greek fare and features Greek evenings. When things really get going, Mamma Lakis, who is no spring chicken, dances with a table on her head.

Down on Agios Giannis Beach, *Paradiso* restaurant operates in season.

Vathy Βαθύ

This is the island's second port. The post office is on the waterfront near the quay. Far-

ther round there's a children's playground. Beyond here, the road climbs to Katomeri, 700m away.

There are no EOT-approved domatia in Vathy or Katomeri, but locals let rooms unofficially – ask around. For dining try *Taverna Porto Vathy*, a small fish tavern right next to the ferry quay, or *Rose Garden*, a rose-covered restaurant-cum-cafe on the little square.

There are several beaches near **Katomeri**. At secluded Porto Elia beach, *Porto Elia Rooms (☎ 51 341)*, owned by the English-speaking Fotis Katopodis, are lovely studios costing 12,000 dr.

Well signposted *Hotel Meganisi (☎ 51 240)* has spotless, modern singles/doubles for 9000/13,000 dr with bathroom. Its restaurant serves tasty traditional dishes.

Restaurant Niagas at Porto Athina Beach serves well prepared, freshly caught fish.

KALAMOS Κάλαμος
☎ 0646 • pop 400

The beautiful, mountainous and wooded **Kalamos** is the second largest of Lefkada's satellite islets. Dense pine forests go right down to the sea. It has two settlements, the port of Kalamos, on the south-east coast, where most of the inhabitants live, and the north coast village of Episkopi, 8km away. Most of the houses in Episkopi are derelict and only 20 inhabitants remain. Kefali, 8km south-west of Kalamos, was abandoned after the 1953 earthquake, but its church is well kept.

A few adventurous yachties sail into Kalamos port, but it is extremely unusual for any other type of tourist to turn up.

Kalamos Village is built on a steep hillside. Its narrow lanes wind between well kept little houses with pretty gardens. There's a post office in the village and a cardphone on the waterfront.

The beautiful pebbled **Agra Pedia Beach** is a short walk away; locals will direct you.

There is only one place to stay, *Dionysis Lezentinos Rooms (☎ 91 238)*, just back from the waterfront in Kalamos. Basic but clean doubles/triples are 5500/6500 dr. A reservation is essential in July and August.

There are several restaurants on the waterfront. **Restaurant O Zefyros** is owned by a friendly couple. The food is delicious and reasonably priced.

Infrequent ferries serve Kalamos from Lefkada. A caïque leaves Mytikas on the mainland every morning around 11 am to take supplies to Kalamos. Excursion boats go from Vathy (on Ithaki) to Kalamos (and Kastos) three times a week in summer.

KASTOS Κάστος
The islet of Kastos is now home to only a few fishing and farming families. Originally the island was covered with vines which produced a good wine; there are now not enough people to tend them. The islet is lush and extremely beautiful. Its protected coves are popular with yachties. Tourism consists of one taverna. As yet there is nowhere to stay, so bring your sleeping bag. This may be the undiscovered paradise that you've been looking for.

You can get to Kastos by caïque from Mytikas on the mainland but there is no regular boat. Excursion boats go from Vathy on Ithaki to Kalamos and Kastos three times a week in summer.

Ithaki Ιθάκη

☎ 0674 • pop 3100

Ithaki (ancient Ithaca) was Odysseus' long-lost home, the island where the stoical Penelope sat patiently, weaving a shroud for her father-in-law. She told her suitors, who believed Odysseus was dead, that she would choose one of them once she had completed the shroud. Cunningly, she unravelled it every night in order to keep her suitors at bay, as she awaited Odysseus' return. Ithaki is separated from Kefallonia by a strait, only 2 to 4km wide. The unspoilt island has a harsh, precipitous east coast and a soft, green west coast. The interior is a mountainous and rocky region with pockets of pine forest, stands of cypresses, olive groves and vineyards. The islanders have traditionally been involved in sea trading, fishing and the cultivation of vines, raisins and olives.

The island has been described as three drowned mountains. Mt Roussano rises 520m at the northern end of the island, Mt Niritas soars 784m at its centre and Mt Stefano rises to 648m in the south. The capital Vathy, is about 20km south of the northern settlements, and the southern half of the island is connected to the northern by a high narrow isthmus. Looking north from Vathy, you could be forgiven for thinking that the two parts are not connected at all. There are nine settlements on the island, the oldest of which are Anogi, Perachori and Exogi.

Because of its general lack of good beaches, and virtually no flat land for developers to get their greedy hands on, Ithaki doesn't attract large crowds. It's a great place to spend a quiet holiday, perhaps walking or just relaxing. Accommodation options are not extensive, so book ahead if possible.

HISTORY

Archaeological remains found in northern Ithaki date from 4000 BC. The first inhabitants lived in the north of the island but by

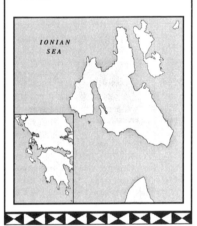

1500 BC settlements had also been established in the south.

During the Mycenaean period (c1200 BC) ancient Ithaca was the capital of a kingdom which encompassed Kefallonia, Zakynthos, Lefkada and part of the nearby mainland. According to Homer this was Odysseus' kingdom, and the composition of *The Odyssey* is thought to have occurred around this date (prior to 1000 BC).

The Dorians conquered Ithaki in 1000 BC, and the kingdom lost its power and political importance. This was not regained

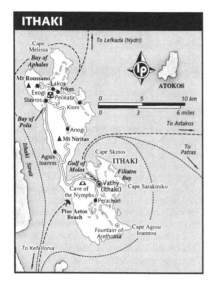

ITHAKI

under subsequent occupation by the Corinthians and later the Romans.

Under the Byzantines, Ithaki's fate resembled that of neighbouring Kefallonia, but it was attacked more often by pirates and other raiders. In 1185 the Normans landed on the island and in 1204 the Venetians took control.

After a violent Turkish raid in 1479, the island was abandoned. When the Venetians reclaimed it in 1500, they had to offer mainland Greeks and Venetians tax and property

Ithaki's Windmills

Stone windmills were once a feature of Ithaki, and their ruins are dotted around the landscape. Built in the 18th and 19th centuries, the windmills were placed on high ground to take advantage of strong currents. The wind powered millstones which ground the wheat, and the roof had the ability to turn to whatever direction the wind was blowing from. Donkey paths connected the windmills to the nearest settlement. Some of these cylindrical towers have been renovated, whitewashed and turned into houses.

incentives to settle there. The Venetians built a fortified harbour at Vathy and in the following two centuries the population expanded from a few hundred to 12,000 in the 1790s.

When Venice fell to Napoleon, Ithaki and the other islands passed into French hands. French domination was followed by a Turkish-Russian alliance. In 1800 Ithaki became part of the autonomous Septinsular Republic, and in 1815 became part of the British protectorate.

Union with Greece in 1864 sparked a great migration from Ithaki, with many islanders emigrating to Romania, Australia and South Africa. This diaspora continued in the 20th century.

Ithaki was devastated during the 1953 earthquakes and almost every house on the island was reduced to rubble. Amazingly, only one person was killed during the quakes – an old woman who was riding a donkey and was hit by falling rocks. The donkey survived.

In the bitter aftermath of the earthquakes, many Ithacans left their island and headed for Australia, the bulk of them to Melbourne. They were given two years to pay off the loans for the boat tickets. Many emigrants lived most of their lives abroad, sending money home to their families and returning only every five years or so, or to retire.

GETTING THERE & AWAY

Ithaki is served by three ports: Frikes, Vathy and Piso Aetos. The telephone number of Ithaki's port police is ☎ 32 909. The following ferries are in high season. Off season they are less frequent.

From Ithaki there are daily ferries to Patras (3½ hours, 3200 dr, two daily) and to Astakos on the mainland (three hours, 1300 dr, one daily).

From Piso Aetos, there are regular ferries to Vasiliki on Lefkada via Fiskardo on Kefallonia (two hours, 940 dr, two daily), and to Sami on Kefallonia (40 minutes, 480 dr, four daily). From Frikes, there is a ferry to Nydri on Lefkada (1¼ hours, 940 dr, one daily) and to Fiskardo on Kefallonia (one

ITHAKI

hour, 480 dr, one daily). From Vathy there are regular ferries to Sami on Kefallonia (two hours, 1300 dr, one daily).

GETTING AROUND
The island's one bus runs two or three times daily to Kioni (via Stavros and Frikes) from Vathy (550 dr).

VATHY Βαθύ
• pop 1800
Vathy (also known as Ithaki Town) is small with a few twisting streets, a central square, nice cafes and restaurants, and a few tourist shops, grocers and hardware stores. Old mansions rise up from the seafront.

Orientation & Information
The ferry quay is on the west side of the bay. To reach the central square of Plateia Efstathiou Drakouli, turn left and follow the waterfront. The main thoroughfare, Kallinikou, is parallel to, and one block inland from, the waterfront.

There is no tourist office on Ithaki. The tourist police (☎ 32 205) are on Evmeou, which runs south from the middle of the waterfront.

The National Bank of Greece is just south-west of the central square. It has an ATM. The post office is situated on the central square and the OTE is farther east along the waterfront.

Dela Tours (☎ 32 104, fax 33 031, email delas@otennet.gr), run by friendly Stavros Dellaportas, is on Vathy's main square. You can buy tickets for the ferry to Kefallonia, Lefkada or Astakos here.

Polyctor Tours (☎ 33 120, fax 33 130) also on the main square is a shipping agent, tour operator and agent for Olympic Airways.

Boat excursions leave from Vathy harbour, and include a round Ithaki trip, a day trip to Lefkada and excursions to Kalamos and Kastos.

Things to See
The town's **archaeological museum** is on Kallinikou. Most of the objects on display were unearthed during Schlieman's excavations at the ancient city of Aetos (above pre-

sent day Piso Aetos). Exhibits include clay pots and plates painted in the Corinthian geometric pattern, bronze figurines, terracotta figurines dating from the 7th to 5th centuries BC, ivory and amber jewellery and other semi precious stones. There is also a collection of bronze coins found at Aetos dating from the 4th and 3rd centuries BC. The coins feature the head of Odysseus wearing his conical traveller's hat. Finds from more recent excavations (1994-99), including Roman oil lamps, are also on show. The museum is open 8.30 am to 3 pm Tuesday to Sunday. Entrance is free.

The **Folklore and Nautical Museum** is housed in an old electrical power generating station behind the Agricultural Bank. Ithaki was the first place in Greece to have electricity, thanks to the generosity of George Drakoulis, a wealthy Ithacan shipowner. The museum contains old costumes including children's clothes, lace trimmed linens, musical instruments, tools, cooking utensils, some nautical uniforms, furniture and ephemera relating to Ithaki, including some fascinating old photographs and prints of Vathy before the earthquakes. It is open 10 am to 4 pm and 7 to 10 pm Monday to Saturday in summer and 8 am to 2.30 pm Monday to Friday in winter. The admission charge is 250 dr.

About 2km above Vathy is the village of **Perahori** which dates from the Venetian occupation of Ithaki. Most of the island's wine – white *thiako* and red *mavrodaphne* – comes from this area, and soap, olive oil and almonds are still produced here. Farther uphill is the abandoned village of Paliochora the first settlement and original administrative capital of southern Ithaki which features some ruined medieval houses and churches in which traces of frescoes can still be seen.

A music and theatre festival is held in Vathy in summer.

Places to Stay
The nearest campsites are at *Dexa Bay* (☎ 32 855) and at *Filiatro Beach* (☎ 33 243).

In Vathy, *Andriana Kouloupi Domatia* (☎ 32 387), just south of the quay, has quite agreeable single/double rooms for 5000/ 6600 dr with shared bathroom, as well as doubles/triples with private bathroom for 8000/10,000 dr. At *Vasiliki Vlasopoulou Domatia (☎ 32 119)* pleasant doubles with bathroom cost 8000 dr. Turn left from the quay and right at the town hall, take the steps ahead, and you will see the *domatia* sign.

Just off the eastern waterfront, *Dimitrios Maroudas Rooms & Apartments (☎/fax 32 751)*, signposted 180m beyond the OTE, provides clean doubles/triples for 7000/ 10,000 dr and four-person apartments for 14,000 dr.

Hotel Odysseus (☎ 32 381, fax 32 587) on the western waterfront has quite pleasant doubles for 9000 dr.

The B class *Hotel Mentor (☎ 32 433, fax 32 293)* near the OTE has a bar, restaurant and roof garden. The attractive single/double rooms cost 12,500/ 17,000 dr.

Vathy's newest accommodation is at *Captain Yiannis Hotel (☎ 33 311, fax 32 049)*, a hotel complex on the opposite side of the harbour from the ferry dock. Double rooms with bathroom and including breakfast cost 12,000 dr to 15,000 dr depending on the season. There also are apartments sleeping up to four people which cost from 20,000 dr to 25,000 dr.

Places to Eat

Taverna Trehantiri, a long-established place west of the central square, serves quality traditional Greek dishes. *O Nikos*, one block back from the square, does great fish dishes which you can wash down with fine Ithacan wine. The classy *Sirens Yacht Club Restaurant & Bar*, nearby, has old photos of Vathy on its walls. The imaginative menu includes shrimps with lemon and mushroom sauce. *Restaurant Kantouni*, on the waterfront, excels in reasonably priced fish dishes.

Young locals meet at the stylish *Drakoulis Cafe* in a waterfront mansion, which was the home of George Drakoulis. It has a fishpond – filled from the sea – in the front garden.

Gregory's Taverna on the far side of the bay is a good spot for a meal and some swimming, although the beach is narrow.

Try the sweet, gooey *rovani*, the local speciality made with rice, honey and cloves, at one of the waterfront's *zaharoplasteia*.

ODYSSEUS SITES

Ithaki has a few sites associated with Homer's *Odyssey*. Though none is impressive, you may enjoy (or endure) the scenic walks to them. The most renowned is the **Fountain of Arethousa**, where Odysseus' swineherd, Eumaeus, brought his pigs to drink and where Odysseus, on his return to Ithaca, went to meet him disguised as a beggar after receiving directions from the goddess Athena. Lesser mortals have to deal with inadequate signposting. The walk takes 1½ to two hours. Take plenty of water as the spring shrinks in summer.

A shorter trek is to the **Cave of the Nymphs**, where Odysseus concealed the splendid gifts of gold, copper and fine fabrics that the Phaeacians had given him. The cave is signposted from the town. Below the cave is **Dexa Bay** (where there is decent swimming), thought to be ancient Phorkys where the Phaeacians disembarked and laid the sleeping Odysseus on the sand.

The location of Odysseus' palace has been much disputed and archaeologists have been unable to find conclusive evidence. Schliemann erroneously believed it was just off the Vathy-Piso Aetos road whereas present day archaeologists speculate it was on Pelikata hill near Stavros.

ANOGI Ανωγή

Fourteen kilometres north of Vathy, Anogi was the old capital. You can approach it from two directions. From the south, it is a steep ascent up the road to Mt Niritas past **Moni Katharon** and its lighthouse, believed to be built on the site of an ancient temple to Athena.

The monastery and its church can be visited and the views from the lighthouse are amazing.

Approached from the north via Stavros, it is a more winding route through fertile agricultural land and vineyards. Both routes offer spectacular scenery and views – and

Homer, *The Odyssey* & the Ionians

To the average traveller in Greece, it is mainland sites such as Mt Olympus and Ancient Delphi that are most closely and immediately connected with Greek mythology. The Ionian islands, virtually bereft of major archaeological sites, come a fair way down the list. However, they do lay claim to be the setting for one of the greatest Greek stories ever told – Homer's *The Odyssey*.

The identity of Homer still perplexes classical scholars, none of whom can determine exactly who he was, where he lived or when he composed his poems. The most popular consensus among classicists is that his long narrative poems, *The Iliad* and *The Odyssey*, which deal with the Trojan War and its aftermath, were composed around 750-700 BC. Many classicists question Homer's single authorship of the two surviving epics, and maintain that they were in fact the work of several individuals over a period of centuries.

Whatever the compositional history of the poems, they were set down in writing (which the Greeks had learnt from the Phoenicians) within a few decades of their composition. Over time, as they were told and retold, the narratives gained much extraneous material. However, scholars agree that in their basic character and outline the epics are predominantly the original compositions. *The Odyssey* is the story of Odysseus' homecoming from the Trojan War. It is most likely a combination of myth and legend with actual historical and geographical detail.

Ithaki (Ithaca) has long been the symbolic image for the end of a long journey. For mythical hero Odysseus, Ithaki was the home he left to fight in the Trojan Wars. According to the often wild tales recounted in *The Iliad*, though more specifically in *The Odyssey*, it took the wily Odysseus 10 long years to return home to Ithaki from Troy on the Asia Minor coast. Unlike Achilles, the protagonist of *The Iliad*, Odysseus (whom the Romans knew as Ulysses) was not famous for his great strength or bravery, but for his ability to deceive and trick. It was Odysseus' idea to take Troy by offering its citizens a large wooden horse secretly filled – as the Trojans found out to their detriment – with Greek soldiers.

The pantheon of gods frowned on Odysseus and his homecoming was delayed for 10 years, most of which he spent on an island with the beautiful sea nymph Calypso. *The Odyssey* recounts that Odysseus is offered a choice: either to live on the island with Calypso and become immortal like the gods, or to return to his kingdom of Ithaca, to rejoin his faithful wife Penelope and son Telemachus and live a mortal existence. He chooses the latter, and much of the rest of the work is an examination of immortality and the nature of mortal life, as well as the obstacles faced by the protagonist in his quest for Ithaca.

Tossed by tempestuous seas, attacked by sea monsters, delayed by a cunning siren yet helped on his way by friendly Phaeacians, Odysseus finally made landfall on Ithaki. Here, disguised as a beggar, he teamed up with Telemachus and his old swineherd Eumaeus, and slayed a castleful of conniving suitors who had been eating him out of home and fortune while trying unsuccessfully to woo the ever patient Penelope, Odysseus' long suffering wife who had waited many years for him to return.

Odysseus as a mythical man is everyone's hero, a preclassical Robin Hood or John Wayne, both villain and king bundled into one well marketed package. Classical Greek writers presented him sometimes as an unscrupulous politician, and sometimes as a wise and honourable statesman. Philosophers usually admired his intelligence and wisdom. Whether he actually existed or not is almost irrelevant since the universal human qualities that he embodied are those that most of us, whether we want to or not, admire and aspire to.

you're guaranteed to run into herds of goats. Anogi is easily reached by car but would be an energetic day's outing for fit hikers.

Anogi's restored 12th century church of **Agia Panagia** has beautiful Byzantine frescoes. Ask in the *kafeneio* on the square for Gerasimos who has the key.

Homer, *The Odyssey* & the Ionians

Throughout the 24 books of the narrative, Odysseus' voyage with his warriors from Troy to his kingdom of Ithaca is closely interwoven with the voyage of his son Telemachus, whose quest to find his father coincides with his own metaphorical voyage into manhood.

While the various Ionian islands argue among themselves for the siting of *The Odyssey*, some classical scholars suggest that much of the action did not take place in Greece at all, but in places as far afield as Gozo, the Straits of Messina between Italy and Sicily, the Aeolian islands off Sicily's northern coast and even Tunisia.

Classicists and archaeologists in the 19th century concluded that Homer's Ithaca was modern Ithaki, his Sami was Sami on Kefallonia, and his Zakynthos was today's Zakynthos, which sounded credible. But in the early 20th century German archaeologist Wilhelm Dorpfeld put a spanner in the works by claiming that Lefkada was ancient Ithaca, modern Ithaki was ancient Sami and Kefallonia was ancient Doulichion. From 1901 to 1914 Dorpfeld searched all over Lefkada for ruins which could claim to be Odysseus' palace. Although he did not find the palace, he did unearth a settlement dating from around 1900 to 1600 BC just outside Nidri. Dorpfeld's theories have now fallen from favour with everyone except the people of Lefkada, who named a street in Lefkada Town in his honour. They cling firmly to Dorpfeld's Homeric claims – after all, the validation of such a connection would undoubtedly bring big tourist rewards.

A modern attempt to reconstruct Odysseus' epic voyage supports the Ionians' claim that his kingdom was indeed in Ithaki and its neighbouring islands. In *The Ulysses Voyage: Sea Search for the Odyssey*, explorer Tim Severin recounts how in 1985 he and a group of classical scholars and sailors carried out a reconstruction of Odysseus' journey, using a full-scale model of the type of ship available to Mycenaean civilisation. They pieced together Odysseus' adventures by matching descriptions of the landscape with the islands and sea around them and by navigating according to the astronavigational details described by Homer.

Like many classicists before him, Severin proposed several places on the island of Ithaki as important Odysseus sites, including Dexia Bay as the site of the Cave of the Nymphs, Pelikata being the location of Odysseus' palace, and Arethousa, south of Vathy, as the location of the spring where the swineherd Eumaeus, a loyal servant of Odysseus, brought his pigs to drink. These sites have become firmly entrenched in Ithaki's tourist history. Moreover, Severin suggested that King Alcinous' castle was located in modern day Paleokastritsa on Corfu's western coast, and that Ermones, on the same coast a little farther south, was where Odysseus was washed ashore. Other Odysseus locations were identified on Paxi and Lefkada.

Homeric scholarship received an injection of interest in late 1999 with the publication of *Homer's Secret Iliad* by a couple of retired British scholars, Florence and Kenneth Wood, who spent decades examining Homer's epics.

They suggested that *The Iliad* was not a mythological narrative at all, but was in fact a guide to the constellations, a memory aid for the movement of stars, constellations and planets visible from the Aegean and Ionian seas. Their contentious thesis is bound to be provocative, but will be the most significant new development in Homeric scholarship for many years. The authors are now working on *The Odyssey*, which they claim is all about calculating time. Perhaps Odysseus never really made that voyage at all.

STAVROS Σταυρός

The village of Stavros, 17km north-west of Vathy, nestles on a shelf of land above the Bay of Polis. Like many of the villages in the north of the island, it developed with the end of piracy during the 19th century, when residents of the isolated capital Anogi (to the south-east) moved down to a more accessible settlement, closer to the sea and with a better water supply.

Although there is a paucity of archaeological evidence to support the scholars' claims, a close reading of *The Odyssey* and examination of the topography of the island gives credence to the theory that Odysseus' palace was located near Stavros. Homer wrote that the palace overlooked three bays; from the hills above Stavros you can see clearly the bays of Polis, Aphales and Frikes. Further support for the placement came from the discovery of a Bronze Age settlement on the summit of Pelikata hill, just north of Stavros.

Stavros has a small, interesting **archaeological museum** (☎ 31 305) which houses a rare collection of artefacts found across the island, and dating from 3000 to 300 BC. Although the exhibits are labelled only in Greek, the museum's enthusiastic keeper, Mrs Couvaras, who speaks fluent English, is extremely knowledgeable and is happy to provide information about the artefacts and their excavation. On display are vases, cutlery and tools from the prehistoric and pre-Mycenaean periods, and Mycenaean wine goblets and perfume droppers. There are also ceramic plates and vases from the Corinthian period (including a plate decorated with a cockerel, said to represent both Odysseus and fertility), a collection of small clay vessels (used to catch the tears of the grieving) dating from 700 BC and terracotta figurines, including a delicate sculpture of an embracing couple dating from 500 BC. The museum is open 9.30 am to 2 pm Tuesday to Sunday. In winter the hours tend to be a bit irregular; call in advance to make sure it's open. Admission is free.

From Stavros it's 1km downhill to the **Bay of Polis**, which has a stony beach and a pier. It is believed to be the site of an ancient city which was swallowed by the sea during an earthquake. It is the main fishing port for all of Ithaki and northern Kefallonia.

Places to Stay
Villa St Ilias (☎ 31 751) situated near the museum has lovely rooms with bathroom for 12,500 dr.

Ithaca House Apartments (☎ 31 396, 0945-215220), just outside the centre of Stavros on the road to Frikes, has pleasant rooms for 8000 dr to 12,000 dr depending on the season and apartments sleeping four people for 18,000 dr to 22,000 dr.

Around Stavros
The hamlet of **Exogi** (meaning 'beyond the earth'), perched on the mountainside above Stavros, is one of the three oldest settlements on the island (continue along the road past the archaeological museum, following the signs to Exogi). At the end of the 19th century Exogi had 1000 inhabitants; today there are only a handful of people living there. The road leading up to the settlement is lined with ruined and abandoned houses – victims of the 1953 earthquakes.

The path uphill out of the village diverges. The right fork leads you towards the summit of Mt Roussano where you can enjoy magnificent views of Kefallonia, Lefkada, Arkoudi, Meganisi, Kythros, Kalamos and the mainland. The crumbling remains of two windmills can also be seen, as can the ruined church of Agios Andreas and next to it three rather strange pyramids, built in 1933 by a local pyramid enthusiast who had himself buried under one and his mother under another. The left fork of the road out of Exogi leads to the abandoned monastery of Pernarakia and the ruins of the settlement of Agia Kyriaki.

FRIKES Φρίκες
This charming fishing village with windswept cliffs is 1.5km north-east of Stavros. Founded in the 17th century by families from Exogi, it was a bustling port for over 200 years, handling much of the olive oil and lentil trade between Ithaki, the mainland and the other Ionian islands. In 1953 the population of Frikes was almost 300. Today there are only about 20 permanent residents.

At the back of the village, on the right before the intersection to Stavros, is the village's olive press, which replaced the donkey drawn presses that each village used up until the mid-1980s.

Kiki Travel Agency (☎ 31 726, fax 31 387), owned by helpful Angeliki Digaletou, has a range of services including moped hire, boat hire, currency exchange, ferry tickets and excursions.

Polyctor Tours branch (☎ 31 771) sells long distance ferry tickets and is an agent for Olympic Airways.

Places to Stay & Eat

Kiki Domatia *(☎ 31 726)* has tastefully furnished, spotless doubles for 12,000 dr with bathroom. **Raftopoulos Rooms** *(☎ 31 733)*, 1km away in a quiet rural setting, has clean doubles/triples for 8000/9500 dr. Inquire about these at Restaurant Ulysses. The well kept, C class **Hotel Nostos** *(☎ 31 644,* ☎ *31 716)*, in lovely verdant countryside behind the village, has spacious, modern singles/doubles for 13,000/17,000 dr and friendly, helpful owners.

Symposium Restaurant, owned by two friendly sisters, serves imaginative fare including local dishes from their grandmother's recipes. **Restaurant Ulysses** on the waterfront does fresh fish and lobster which you choose from a large tank.

KIONI Κιόνι

Four kilometres south-east of Frikes, Kioni is perhaps one of Ithaki's better kept secrets. Kioni was settled in the early 19th century by islanders from Anogi after the threat of pirate attacks had subsided. It is a small village draped around a verdant hillside spilling down to a picturesque little harbour where yachties congregate. There are tavernas and a couple of bars, though it's not the best place to swim. Instead, seek out the little bays between Kioni and Frikes.

Places to Stay & Eat

Kioni's cheapest accommodation is the immaculate **Maroudas Apartments** *(☎ 31 691, fax 31 753)*, opposite the doctor's surgery. Double/triple studios are 12,000/16,000 dr. Farther back up the hill, the well maintained and beautifully furnished **Captain's Apartments** *(☎ 31 481, fax 31 090)* run by the Delaportas family, have spacious double studios with TV and phone for 12,000 dr and four-person apartments for 20,000 dr.

Cafe Mentor is a good place for light meals, snacks, pies and very indulgent ice creams. **Restaurant Avra** is a basic taverna but usually busy and popular. Locals hang out at the **kafeneio** (with a permanent corrugated iron sunshade) situated close to the breakwater.

Galatis does fresh fish and (expensive) lobster and hogs most of the waterfront. **Café Spavento** set back from the waterfront opposite the minimarket is good for fresh juices, caffe frappé and hanging out.

Kefallonia Κεφαλλονιά

☎ 0671/0674 • pop 32,500

Kefallonia, the largest of the Ionian islands, has rugged, towering mountains. The highest, Mt Enos (1520m), is the Mediterranean's only mountain with a unique fir forest species, *abies cephalonica*. While not as tropical as Corfu, Kefallonia has many species of wild flowers, including orchids and, when you approach it by sea on a windy summer's day, the scents of thyme, oregano, bay leaves and flowers will reach you before you land.

Kefallonia receives package tourists, but not on the same scale as Corfu and Zakynthos. The island has received unprecedented publicity in recent times thanks to the novel *Captain Corelli's Mandolin* by Louis de Bernières which is set in Kefallonia (see boxed text 'The Cult of Captain Corelli').

Kefallonia boasts a diverse array of wildlife. The nature reserve on Mt Enos (or Ainos) on Kefallonia is home to a handful of wild horses, known as the Enos mountain horses. It is also a nesting ground for loggerhead turtles, which lay their eggs on southern beaches in June. Turtle numbers ashore have remained stable, unlike on Zakynthos. See boxed text 'At Loggerheads in the Ionians' in the Zakynthos chapter.

Europe's rarest mammal, the Mediterranean monk seal, was once very common in the Ionian Sea, but is now on the brink of extinction. The precious few monk seals left can sometimes be seen on the north-west coasts of Kefallonia and Ithaki.

Kefallonia's capital is Argostoli but the main port is Sami. As the island is so big and mountainous, travelling between towns is time consuming.

In summer there are art exhibitions in the major towns. From mid-July until the end of August Kefallonia hosts a cultural festival with concerts in various villages around the island.

HISTORY

Argostoli's archaeological museum contains fossils and tools from settlements dating

HIGHLIGHTS

- Titillate your taste buds with a Kefallonian meat pie
- Drive through hill-top hamlets on the Lixourian Peninsula for great views across the Argostoli Gulf
- Gaze upon the superb gold-plated icon screen at the church of Theotokos in Domata
- Hike to your heart's content through Mt Enos National Park
- Visit the delightful village of Assos and spectacular Myrtos Beach

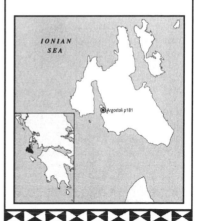

back to 50,000 BC. In the 14th century BC Mycenaean culture was brought to the island from the Peloponnese by the Achaeans, who established an important colony at Krani near present day Argostoli. The tombs at Krani are said to be the best examples of Mycenaean tombs in Greece.

From the Bronze Age onwards Kefallonia was separated into four autonomous city-states, all allies of Corinth. The most powerful was Samos (or Sami) – probably where Odysseus sailed from for the Trojan

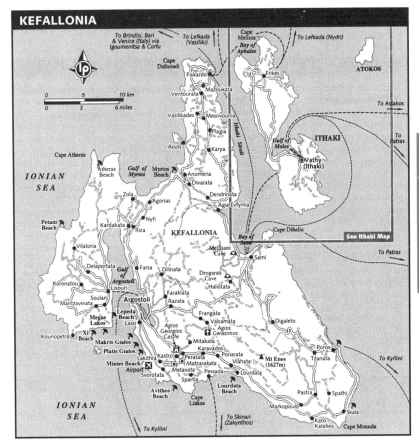

KEFALLONIA

War. Archaeological evidence remains from all four city-states.

During the Peloponnesian War the autonomous states were conquered by Athens. In the subsequent period the island shifted its allegiance between Athens and Sparta.

Kefallonia's strategic position attracted attention from the world powers and pirates alike. When Rome turned its attention to the island in 189 BC, three of the city-states acquiesced; Sami held off and was besieged and then annihilated by Roman forces.

Under the Byzantines, Kefallonia prospered, although its geographical position meant that it was on the receiving end of repeated attacks from Spanish and Sicilian pirates. In the 9th century, the Byzantines created the administrative division or *thema* of the Ionian islands of which Kefallonia was made the seat.

The island resisted the attacks of the Saracens, the Venetians, and the Genoans but wasn't so successful with the Normans. In 1085, under Robert Guiscard, they attacked the Ionian islands. Guiscard took control of the entire island but died within a few weeks of landing at Kefallonia's most northern port – Fiskardo – which is named after him.

The Cult of Captain Corelli

You haven't read *Captain Corelli's Mandolin* yet? Don't worry, copies are easy to get hold of in Kefallonia as they are on sale at virtually every shop on the island, and most beach bums will have a well-thumbed copy.

English writer Louis de Bernières has become almost a cult figure following the success of the novel – his fourth – which tells the emotional story of a young Italian army officer sent to the island of Kefallonia during WWII. The book has even been credited with a slight increase in tourism on Kefallonia. The beaches of Avithos and Spartia, backed by precipitous cliffs, are probably the settings for some of the scenes in the book.

At the time of research, there was a buzz around Kefallonia about a film based on the book. A huge Hollywood production was due to start in early 2000, directed by Roger Michel of *Notting Hill* fame. The film, starring Nicholas Cage as Captain Corelli (his mandolin has yet to be cast) will be shot near Sami in Kefallonia. The islands of Ithaki and Corfu will also be used as locations for their historic buildings, none of which were left standing on Kefallonia after the devastating 1953 earthquakes.

It was on a package holiday to Kefallonia that the author, a former soldier, received his inspiration for the story. Instead of relaxing on the beach he spent his holiday learning about the island's history.

Despite record sales of the book, it seems not everyone loved it. De Bernières has been accused of distorting history and crude anti-communism by Britain's low-circulation post-communist daily newspaper *Morning Star*. In July 1999, De Bernières was involved in a war of words with the *Morning Star*, after being branded as an apologist for the excesses of the right wing in mid-20th century Greece, and seeking to portray the Greek dictator Metaxas and the Italian fascists in a sympathetic light. What most riled the *Morning Star* reviewer was the author's representation of the Greek communists as 'dehumanised sadists'. De Bernières considered the negative notice as complete vindication, and branded communism as 'the biggest failure and disappointment since the non-return of Christ'.

Tourist agencies have yet to introduce a 'Captain Corelli's Mandolin' theme tour of Kefallonia, but with the interest that the novel has generated, tour operators on the island think it won't be long.

When Constantinople fell to the Crusaders, Kefallonia fell to the Venetians. Together with Zakynthos and Ithaki, the island was part of the County Palatine of Kefallonia, administered by the powerful Orsini family.

The Turks captured Kefallonia in 1483 and remained in power until 1500, when, after a bloody siege, the Venetians gained control. Over the next 300 years the island's society and commerce were closely modelled on those of Venice, and Kefallonia enjoyed significant economic and cultural development.

A short period of French and then Russian dominance from 1797 came to an end when the British took over in a bloodless invasion. British dominance brought turmoil

– fuelled by ideas of the French Revolution, the islanders often rebelled against the authorities, and Kefallonia was the focus for resentment of the British in the Ionian archipelago in general. In 1848 there were violent clashes in Argostoli, and protesters were imprisoned, exiled and their property confiscated. In 1849, after a rebellion at Skala, 21 nationalist leaders were executed. The unrest came to an end only when Britain ceded Kefallonia and the other Ionian islands to Greece in 1864.

During WWII Kefallonia was seized by the Italians but they failed to gain any real control. In fact the occupation was relatively peaceful; many Kefallonians had Italian blood and some still spoke the language. The problems arose in September 1943,

A Captain's Tale

Of the 5000 Italian soldiers on Kefallonia in September 1943, only 34 survived the German massacre. One of them allegedly swam to Ithaki where he was sheltered by the local Greeks until he escaped. Until recently he was a captain on one of the Brindisi-Patras ferries, and every time he passed Ithaki he gave a long toot on the ship's horn to salute his Greek friends.

when Mussolini fell from power and the Italian government surrendered to the Allies. Overnight, the Italians became enemies with their former ally Germany.

In the confusion of administrative control that followed, the occupying Italian forces received contradictory commands; a message from Rome instructed them to repel the Germans, while a few days later a message from Athens, which was under German control, told them to surrender. The Italian commander on Kefallonia hesitated; there were more Italian troops than Germans on the island, although he had no air power, and the Allies were advancing in the Aegean. The Germans subsequently launched a vicious aerial bombing campaign on Kefallonia and Corfu. Hopelessly overpowered, more than 5000 Italian officers and troops surrendered to their former allies. The Germans – apparently acting on direct orders from Hitler himself – promptly massacred them in villages in the foothills of Mt Enos and then burnt the

bodies to hide the evidence. These Italians are known by the Greeks as the Kefallonia martyrs. The atrocity is poetically retold by Louis de Bernières in *Captain Corelli's Mandolin*.

Kefallonia has always suffered from seismic activity. In 1863, Edward Lear wrote of experiencing 43 small tremors. The island was literally shaken to pieces during the 1953 earthquakes. Every town – with the exception of Fiskardo – was demolished. One inhabitant of Argostoli – which was totally flattened – recorded that the ground undulated like a 1m swell on the sea.

GETTING THERE & AWAY

Air
There is at least one flight daily from Kefallonia to Athens (17,900 dr). The Olympic Airways office (☎ 0671-28 808) in Argostoli is at R Vergoti 1.

Bus
Four daily return buses leave Athens' A terminal for Argostoli (eight hours via ferry to Poros, 7500 dr).

Ferry
The island of Kefallonia has six ports – the telephone numbers of the port police are in brackets: Sami (☎ 0674-22 031), Argostoli (☎ 0671-22 224), Poros (☎ 0674-72 460), Lixouri (☎ 0671-94 100), Pessada, and Fiskardo (☎ 0674-41 400).

Domestic There is a direct ferry to Corfu once a week in summer. Otherwise services are via Patras.

Domestic Ferry Routes

from	to	time	fare	frequency
Fiskardo	Lefkada (Vasiliki)	1½ hours	940 dr	2 daily
Fiskardo	Ithaki (Frikes)	1 hour	480 dr	1 daily
Fiskardo	Lefkada (Nidri)	2 hours	1335 dr	1 daily
Sami	Ithaki (Piso Aetos)	40 minutes	480 dr	4 daily
Sami	Ithaki (Vathy)	1½ hours	1300 dr	1 daily
Sami	Corfu	4½ hours	5200 dr	1 weekly
Sami	Patras	2½ hours	3200 dr	2 daily

KEFALLONIA

Four Islands Ferries runs services between Kefallonia (Fiskardo and Sami) and Ithaki, Lefkada and Astakos (on the mainland). In high season it is essential to book especially if you are travelling with a car. You can reserve a place on the boat by phoning ahead, then you just have to pay for and collect the ticket about 20 to 30 minutes before the boat departs. Information and tickets can be obtained from the following: in Fiskardo from Nautilis Travel (☎ 0674-41 440); in Sami contact Valetas Travel (☎ 0674-22 456, fax 22 818) or Sami Travel (☎ 0674-23 050). A list of high season services follows:

There are also services from Argostoli to Kyllini on the mainland (2½ hours, 2310 dr, two daily), from Poros to Kyllini (1½ hours, 1620 dr, four daily) and from Pessada to Skinari on Zakynthos (two hours, 1025 dr, two daily).

International A weekly ferry leaves Sami for Brindisi in Italy, via Igoumenitsa and Corfu. There are daily services via Patras. In high season two or three ferries weekly leave Sami for Ancona and Venice, via Igoumenitsa and Corfu.

Tickets can be obtained in Argostoli from either Vasilatos Shipping (☎ 0671-22 618, fax 24 992) on Metaxa 54, or Romanos Travel (☎ 0671-23 541, fax 25 451) at Antoni Tristi 48.

In Sami tickets can be purchased from Valetas Travel (☎ 0674-22 456, fax 22 818) or Sami Travel (☎ 0674-23 050).

GETTING AROUND
To/From the Airport
The airport is 9km south of Argostoli. There is no airport bus. A taxi costs 2000 dr.

Bus
From Argostoli's bus station (☎ 0671-22 276) frequent buses go to Platys Gialos and Sami (500 dr), three daily to Poros (850 dr), via Peratata, Vlahata and Markopoulo, two daily to Skala (800 dr) and two daily to Fiskardo (850 dr). But in the off season, only one return service daily connects Fiskardo (1000 dr) with Argostoli.

Car & Motorcycle
Care are available for hire from Ainos Travel (☎ 0671-22 333, fax 24 608), G Vergoti 14, and motorcycles from Sunbird Motor Rent (☎ 0671-23 723), on the waterfront in Argostoli. Vehicle hire is recommended during the off season because of the infrequency of buses.

Car hire Hertz (☎ 0674-24 438) has two offices in Argostoli, the main one on Main Road, Lassi, and a smaller agency at G Vergoti 18 just off the central square. A Group A car (such as a Fiat Cinquecento) costs 21,400 dr per day, 53,000 dr for three days and 100,000 dr per week. A slightly larger car with air-conditioning costs 120,000 dr per week.

The Avis representative is CBR Travel (☎ 0671-22 770, fax 24 552, email cbr@ compulink.gr) at the southern end of the central square. It has Group A cars for 14,000 dr per day or 80,000 dr for a week. For scooter rentals head for Go Easy on a Scooter (☎ 0671-28 090) at G Vergoti 44.

Boat
Frequent ferries run every half-hour between Lixouri and Argostoli from 7.30 am to 12.30 am daily (30 minutes, 350 dr). Tickets are sold on board.

ARGOSTOLI Αργοστόλι
☎ 0671 • pop 7300
Argostoli, unlike Zakynthos Town, was not restored to its former Venetian splendour after the 1953 earthquake. It's a modern, lively port set on a peninsula. Its harbour is divided from Koutavos lagoon by a British-built causeway connecting it with the rest of Kefallonia. There is a colourful produce market on the waterfront on most mornings.

Orientation
The modern and (for once) very user-friendly KTEL bus station is on the southern waterfront near the causeway. The EOT and the main ferry quay are at the waterfront's northern end. Ferries to the Lixouri Peninsula depart from a quay just north of the main dock.

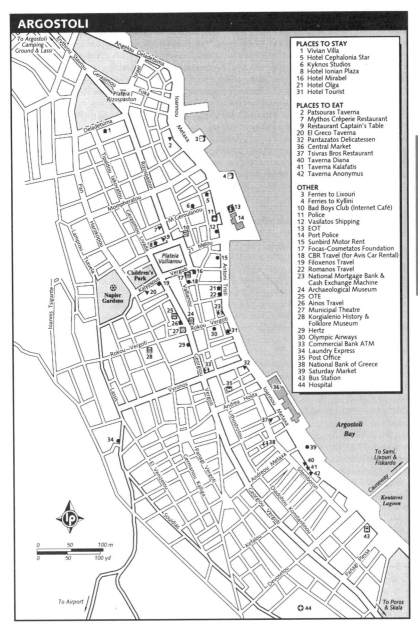

ARGOSTOLI

PLACES TO STAY
1 Vivian Villa
5 Hotel Cephalonia Star
6 Kyknos Studios
8 Hotel Ionian Plaza
16 Hotel Mirabel
21 Hotel Olga
31 Hotel Tourist

PLACES TO EAT
2 Patsouras Taverna
7 Mythos Crêperie Restaurant
9 Restaurant Captain's Table
20 El Greco Taverna
32 Pantazatos Delicatessen
36 Central Market
37 Tsivras Bros Restaurant
40 Taverna Diana
41 Taverna Kalafatis
42 Taverna Anonymus

OTHER
3 Ferries to Lixouri
4 Ferries to Kyllini
10 Bad Boys Club (Internet Café)
11 Police
12 Vasilatos Shipping
13 EOT
14 Port Police
15 Sunbird Motor Rent
17 Focas-Cosmetatos Foundation
18 CBR Travel (for Avis Car Rental)
19 Filoxenos Travel
22 Romanos Travel
23 National Mortgage Bank &
   Cash Exchange Machine
24 Archaeological Museum
25 OTE
26 Ainos Travel
27 Municipal Theatre
28 Korgialenio History &
   Folklore Museum
29 Hertz
30 Olympic Airways
33 Commercial Bank ATM
34 Laundry Express
35 Post Office
38 National Bank of Greece
39 Saturday Market
43 Bus Station
44 Hospital

The centre of Argostoli's activity is Plateia Vallianou and surrounding streets and the waterfront (Antoni Tristi, which becomes Ioannou Metaxa).

Information

Tourist Offices The EOT (☎ 22 248) is open 8 am to 2.30 pm daily in summer and also 4 to 9 pm in July and August. Out of season it is open 7.30 am to 2.30 pm Monday to Saturday.

Money The National Bank of Greece is one block back from the southern end of the waterfront. The National Mortgage Bank on the waterfront has a 24 hour cash exchange machine.

There is also a Commercial Bank ATM on the corner of Vyronos and G Vergoti.

Post & Communications The post office is on Diad Konstantinou and the OTE phone office is on G Vergoti. Plateia Vallianou is the huge palm-treed central square up from the waterfront off 21 Maïou.

There's an Internet cafe of sorts, Bad Boys Club (or BB's) in Plateia Vallianou, which specialises in *very* loud music. The cost of Internet access is 1700 dr per hour but at the time of research there was only one terminal.

Travel Agencies Ainos Travel (☎ 22 333, fax 24 608, email ainos1@compulink.gr), G Vergoti 14, can help with most travel services which includes accommodation, air tickets, ferry tickets, and currency exchange. Filoxenos Travel (☎ 26 577, fax 28 114), G Vergoti 2, offers similar services.

Olympic Airways (☎ 28 808) has an office on R Vergoti. It can also be contacted at the airport (☎ 41 511).

Laundry Laundry Express is a self-service coin laundry at Lassi 46B, a steep uphill walk from the central square. It is open 9 am to 10 pm daily.

Things to See

The **archaeological museum** (☎ 28 300) on R Vergoti has a small collection of island relics including Mycenaean finds from tombs. The museum is much smaller than those in Corfu or Zakynthos Town, but has an interesting array of exhibits including pottery, jewellery, glassware, architectural artefacts and funerary objects. Opening times are 8.30 am to 3 pm Tuesday to Sunday. Admission is 500 dr.

The **Korgialenio History and Folklore Museum** (☎ 28 835), farther up R Vergoti, has a collection of traditional costumes, furniture and tools, items which belonged to British occupiers, and photographs of pre- and post-earthquake Argostoli. The museum is open from 9 am to 2 pm Monday to Saturday. Admission is 500 dr.

Focas-Cosmetatos Foundation (☎ 26 595), Vallianou 1, is a former private mansion which was destroyed and then sympathetically rebuilt after the earthquake. It is now a small museum with an eclectic collection of 18th and 19th century lithographs, which includes some topographical scenes by Edward Lear, as well as coins and banknotes. It is open 9 am to 1 pm and 6.30 to 9 pm Monday to Saturday. Admission is 500 dr.

Argostoli's new **municipal theatre** on G Vergoti was inaugurated by the late Melina Mercouri. There's an art gallery on the ground floor.

Organised Tours

KTEL organises a variety of tours: a full day island tour including Drogarati Cave, Melissani Lake and Fiskardo (5000 dr); a half-day 'Treasures of Kefallonia' tour including the monastery of St Gerasimos, the Robola wine factory, the Byzantine museum at St Andreas and Kourkoumelata village (3500 dr); Ithaki (8000 dr); Zakynthos (8500 dr); and a day trip to Olympia (10,500 dr).

Each of these tours can be booked at the KTEL bus station (☎ 22 276, fax 23 364) on Antoni Tristi. Pick up the handy island bus timetable and tour brochure while you're there. Travel agencies also take bookings for these tours.

The Pub Old House (☎ 23 956) can organise cruises on its glass bottom boat which departs from Argostoli. This tour is sold by travel agents around the island.

Places to Stay

The pleasant *Argostoli Camping (☎ 23 487)* is on the coast, 2km north of town.

One of the nicest places is *Vivian Villa (☎ 23 396, fax 28 670, Deladetsima 9)*. The friendly owners offer beautiful, spotless double/triple rooms for 10,000/12,000 dr with bathroom. Studios cost 13,000/15,800 dr and a large, well equipped apartment costs 21,000 dr. Another pleasant option is *Kyknos Studios (☎ 23 398, M Geroulanou 4)*, where doubles are 12,500 dr.

There are C class hotels along the waterfront. *Hotel Cephalonia Star (☎ 23 181, fax 23 180, Ioannou Metaxa 60)* has comfortable and air-conditioned singles/doubles for 12,000/17,000 dr. At *Hotel Tourist (☎/fax 22 510, Antoni Tristi 109)* rates are 13,000/20,000 dr and the beautifully refurbished *Hotel Olga (☎ 24 981, fax 24 985)* on Antoni Tristi charges 14,400/ 21,050 dr.

Argostoli's finest hotel is the marble-decorated *Hotel Ionian Plaza (☎ 25 581, fax 25 585)* on Plateia Vallianou. Comfortable air-conditioned suites cost 11,900/ 16,400 dr.

Hotel Mirabel in the south-eastern corner of the central square has pleasant singles/ doubles with bathroom (breakfast included) for 15,200/19,000 dr in high season. Rooms facing onto the square can be noisy at night.

Places to Eat

The waterfront's neighbouring restaurants *Taverna Diana*, *Taverna Kalafatis* and *Taverna Anonymus* are all commendable, and the Kalafatis – around since 1945 – stays open all year. Kefallonia has a distinctive cuisine, represented by meat pies and *skordalia* (garlic dip) which accompanies fish. Greeks find these dishes at *Patsouras Taverna (Ioannou Metaxa 40)* opposite the ferry quay. Ask for the island's famed Robola wine, which is expensive but wonderful and comes from grapes grown in stony, mountainous soil.

El Greco Taverna (Kalypsous Vergoti 3), opposite the children's park, is also popular

with locals. Well prepared cod with skordalia is 1700 dr. The old-fashioned *Tsivras Bros Restaurant (☎ 24 259)*, just off the waterfront, serves filling goat broth for 1000 dr and many dishes under 1000 dr.

Off the central square, *Captain's Table (Rizospaston 3)* is one of Argostoli's top restaurants and the place to go for a splurge – don't expect much change out of 9000 dr for a meal. Despite the fact that the place prides itself on its fish and seafood, choosing either can inflate the bill considerably. A better choice is the lamb *kleftiko*, small pieces of lamb cooked with fetta cheese and tomato sauce in a silver foil parcel. Vegetarians will also be happy with an extensive choice of dishes including *briam*, a zucchini and potato bake, and olive oil and garlic laced mashed potatoes, which shouldn't be missed.

Nearby, *Mythos Crêperie Restaurant* has a similarly priced selection of crepes and Mexican and Chinese dishes.

Pick up self-catering supplies from *Pantazatos Delicatessen (37 Antoni Tristi)* opposite the *Central Market* where you can get all the fresh fruit and vegetables that you need.

AROUND ARGOSTOLI

If you're staying in Argostoli but looking for sandy beaches, chances are you'll end up at one of the beaches on the west coast of the **Lassi Peninsula**, 5km south of Argostoli – **Makris Gialos**, **Platis Gialos** and the popular **Minies** (whose detraction is the fact that it's only a few hundred metres from the noisy airport runway). At Minies you can see the ruins of a small 6th century BC Doric temple.

Lassi has dozens of hotels, almost all of which are block-booked by mainly British tour operators, and you'll do better for accommodation in Argostoli.

There are frequent buses between Argostoli and Lassi.

LIXOURIAN PENINSULA

Χερσόνησος Ληξούρι
☎ 0671

The landscape of the peninsula west of Argostoli is almost like a moonscape – mainly arid with patches of fertile land. This area can really only be appreciated if you have your own wheels as there's only one bus service operating on the peninsula itself – from Lixouri to Xi. Your own transport will allow you to penetrate the interior, passing through tiny hill-top hamlets drowning in bougainvillea, and enjoy some great views across the Argostoli Gulf.

A car ferry leaves the quay at Argostoli (just north of the port police) every half-hour on the half-hour for Lixouri. Tickets cost 350 dr per person and 1000 dr for a car (one way).

Places to Stay

It's not the most interesting area of the island and easily visited on a day trip from Argostoli. Should you want to stay, however, there are several options – but mostly in the higher price range.

Summery (☎ *91 771, fax 91 062)* is 300m from the harbour on the Lixouri seafront. Despite its name, it's open year-round (but sometimes block-booked by British tour operators) and high season singles/doubles cost 11,200/16,200 dr including breakfast. Taxi transfers are provided from the airport if you stay a week or more.

Farther along the road towards Soulari, the *Ionian Sea* (☎ *92 280, fax 93 280)* is a lovely B class hotel set back about 200m from the sea in shady, flower-filled gardens. Singles/doubles including breakfast cost 15,000/18,000 dr in high season.

For rooms/studios your best bet is to head to *Taverna Apolafsi* (☎ *91 691)* on the road south of Lixouri heading for Lipedha beach. It's about a 20 minute walk or five minute drive. *Petdikis Travel* (☎ *91 097)* on the ferry quay can also help with accommodation in studios and apartments.

South of Lixouri

Heading south through the villages of both **Soulari** and **Mantzavinata**, the scenery bears the scars of the 1953 earthquakes. The first decent sandy beach is at Xi. A daily bus goes from Lixouri to Xi at 9.30, 11.30 am and 3 pm, returning to Lixouri at 9.45 and 11.45 am and 3.15 pm.

MARTIN HARRIS

Parasailing is a popular watersports pursuit at Xi Beach.

The sand at **Xi Beach** is a deep golden colour. Umbrellas and sun lounges can be rented and watersports enthusiasts can do water-skiing, parasailing or have a ride on a big banana. There is a huge beachside taverna and a small bar providing drinks and light refreshments.

The only accommodation option here is *Cephalonia Palace Hotel* (☎ *91 111, fax 92 638)*, which appears almost like an oasis in the desert. It is a self-contained complex with pool, bars and restaurants. All its well appointed rooms have a balcony and sea view. Single/double rooms with breakfast and dinner included cost a hefty 18,400/27,850 dr in low season rising to 25,000/34,100 dr in high season.

Passing back through Mantzavinata a road leads down to **Cape Akrotiri** at the southern tip of the peninsula. There are two good beaches, at **Kounopetra** (which also has a tiny harbour) and **Agios Nickolaos**, which rarely get crowded.

There are no tavernas on either beach and no shade either – you'll have to bring your own umbrella.

West Coast

Heading inland from Lixouri you see more of the mooncrater landscape, with the occasional patch of fertile land, peppered with small sleepy villages and a seemingly disproportionate number of churches.

The best beach on the island is **Petani**, about 14km north-west of Lixouri. It's a spectacular cove with sparkling turquoise water and a long beach of fine pebbles. The approach road down to the beach has a series of hair-raising hairpin bends but is a spectacular drive.

At present there are only two *tavernas* serving a good range of fish, grills and salads and one private house, but the shells of buildings going up on the hill behind the beach may mean that there will be accommodation possibilities soon.

Umbrellas and sun lounges can be hired (2000 dr per day for an umbrella and two chairs). Signs state that camping is prohibited although it doesn't always put off determined travellers in camper vans.

LIVATHO Λείβαθο
☎ 0671

The region to the south and south-east of Argostoli is known as the Livatho. There is a distinct suburban feel to this area and the distance between settlements is small. It has always been the island's most highly populated and prosperous region, where merchants and sea captains built their mansions. There are regular buses from Argostoli to Kourkoumelata but it is best explored with your own transport. Accommodation in this area is limited – you'd do better to stay in Argostoli or at Lourdas beach.

Lakithra is the regional centre and is made up of large villas, communal squares and broad streets. In the 1930s, archaeologists discovered four late Mycenaean tombs and ancient grain silos carved out of the rock. Lakithra has also been claimed as the site of Odysseus' palace.

At nearby **Domata**, the church of Theotokos or Panagia (the Virgin Mary) has a superb gold-plated icon screen (12,000 gold sovereigns were melted down for the gilt) dating from the 19th century. The coffin of the martyred Patriarch of Constantinople, Gregory V, is also in the church. He was hanged by the Turks on 10 April 1821, and his body was recovered from the Bosphorus by a Kefallonian mariner. His remains were buried in Odessa, but the coffin ended up in Domata. Gregory's feast day is celebrated every year on 10 April.

The church in **Kaligata** boasts a fine icon screen dating from the early 19th century. The village, home of the Kalligas winery which produces some of Kefallonia's best wines, sits high above the small sandy coves of **Ligia** and **Avithos**. These beaches, backed by precipitous cliffs, are probably the settings for some of the scenes in *Captain Corelli's Mandolin*. They look out towards the tiny islet of Dionisi and its chapel dedicated to the Panagia of Vlahernon.

Kourkoumelata has all the elements of a pleasant middle class suburb, and is designed to look like a Swiss town. The villas are painted in pastel colours with manicured gardens. Funds for much of the building (or post-earthquake reconstruction) were donated by the shipping tycoon George Vergotis. Lord Byron stayed at **Metaxata** for a short time in 1823 before he went to Missolonghi to help train Greek freedom fighters where he died. Important Mycenaean graves were discovered at **Matzarakata** by a team of Greek and Dutch archaeologists. The contents remain in Argostoli's archaeological museum.

Kastro, above the village of **Peratata**, 9km south-east of Argostoli, was the island's capital from the Middle Ages until 1757. Ruined houses stand beneath the 13th century castle of **Agios Georgios**, which affords magnificent views.

The fortress covers an area of 16,000 sq metres and the outer walls have a perimeter of 600m. It is one of the best preserved structures of its kind in the Ionian islands, even though it was extensively damaged during an earthquake in the 17th century. It is open 8.30 am to 7 pm Tuesday to Saturday and 8.30 am to 3 pm on Sunday. Admission is 500 dr. The monastery of Agios Andreas in Peratata contains Byzantine icons.

Pessada on the coast is notable only as the departure point for ferries to Zakynthos (Skinari) twice daily in summer (7.45 am and 6 pm). The journey takes two hours. There are no facilities at the 'port' other than a small snack bar and no public transport, but taxis dropping people off usually pick up passengers (jump off early in order to grab one – or hook up with a fellow passenger with a car and get a lift to another town on the island).

Sunrise Inn (☎ *69 586, fax 69 621, email sunriseinn@otenet.gr)*, in the village of Koundourata, next to Pessada, is a convenient place to stay if you are catching an early morning ferry to Zakynthos but otherwise quite out of the way. Quite pleasant single/double rooms including breakfast cost from 10,000/16,000 dr rising up to 21,000/32,000 dr in high season.

The small sandy coves at **Agios Thoma** offer great swimming (a flat shelf of rock makes a natural diving board) and there are a couple of decent *tavernas* on the beach. There's a small church perched above the beach, and several paths leading to quieter coves a short walk away.

LOURDATA Λουρδάτα
☎ 0671

The villages of Vlahata on the principle Argostoli-Poros road and Lourdata (or Lourdas) down the hillside on the coast have merged into one. Lourdata gets its name from the English lords who spent time here in the 19th century.

The beach is long and sandy, equipped with sun lounges and umbrellas (2000 dr for an umbrella and two chairs), and watersports enthusiasts have a good choice of activities. Horse riding is also available.

There is a WWF nature trail from Lourdata – a scenic 2½ hour circular walk passing thickets, orchards and olive groves with flowers and birds, and returning along the coast. The trail passes the ruins of the Monastery of the Virgin of Sissia founded in the early 13th century and named after St Francis of Assisi as he returned to Italy from Egypt. A free trail guide is available from the EOT in Argostoli.

Places to Stay & Eat

Lourdata and Vlahata offer several accommodation options. At the *Ramones Studios* (☎ *31 032)* Dionisia Kamilatos and her family offer double rooms for 11,000 dr and studios with kitchenette (sleeping up to four people) for 16,000 dr. Nearby, *Adonis* studios has rooms and studios for similar prices and, unusually for *domatia* owners, accepts credit cards.

The superb two to four-person apartments of *Ionian Star* (☎ *31 419, fax 31 019)* make a great base for this part of the island. Prices range between 17,000 dr and 25,000 dr in high season.

There are several decent tavernas in and around the village. *La Mer* on the road from Vlahata down into the village proper has great views, while *Dionysis* closer to the village centre is recommended. The latter has good Greek fare at decent prices.

MT ENOS & AROUND Ορος Αίνος
☎ 0671

Mt Enos (Ainos) is the highest mountain in the Ionians, rising to 1627m. The Mt Enos National Park was founded in 1962 to protect the forest of Kefallonian firs *(abies cephalonica)* which are particular to the area. It also encompasses nearby Mt Roudi. There is a network of forest paths for walkers and hikers, but little else in the way of facilities. Mt Enos National Park is home to a handful of wild horses, known as the Enos mountain horses. They are the descendants of a group of tamed horses let loose in the 1920s and 1930s. Birds of prey, such as falcons and eagles, are common.

There are roads leading up to the reserve from Matzarakata; another approach is from the Sami-Argostoli road, past the village of Frangata.

Beware, though, that the roads give way to unsealed tracks which a normal car won't handle. A four wheel drive – or two legs – is best.

The remains of Kefallonia's patron saint, Gerasimos, lie in a silver reliquary at the monastery of **Agios Gerasimos** near the hamlet of Valsamata. Pilgrims come from all over Greece to visit the site.

Just behind the monastery is the Robola Producer's Cooperative (☎ 0671-86 301, fax 86 481). It produces three very good white wines – San Gerassimo, made from the first press of the grapes, Robola and Enos – and is open for free tastings every day. The grapes are cultivated in seven villages in the foothills of Mt Enos, and the wine is made by five female winemakers.

KATO KATELIOS Κάτω Κατελειός
☎ 0671

Kato Katelios is an odd little place, not quite a thriving resort but no longer the small farming and fishing community that it once was. It's a good alternative to Lourdata if that village is full. There are signs of development in the valley, with a few new apartment blocks and there's an extensive selection of tavernas and bars on the seafront for such a small place.

The beach at Kato Katelios is a mixture of golden sand and large, uncomfortable-to-lie-on pebbles and stones, but there are a few umbrellas and sunbeds for hire and it's great for swimming.

The next cove to the east is **Kaminia Beach** (below the village of Ratzakli), a 2km stretch of golden sand, and shallow, gently shelving water.

It is Kefallonia's main nesting ground for the loggerhead turtle.

A nonprofit environmental organisation, the Katelios Group for the Research and Protection of Marine and Terrestrial Life, runs the Kefalonian Marine Turtle Project (☎ 81 009, fax 81 058) based at Kato Katelios. The group, headed by Caterina Xenopoulou, organises an environmental festival each year at the beginning of August. Volunteers are needed to monitor and protect the turtles' nests during the breeding season, and for the other projects with which the group is involved, such as promotion of sustainable tourism and development and a sustainable waste management project involving the production of organic compost from seaweed.

Markopoulo, nestled in a natural balcony on the hills above Kato Katelios, is thought to be where the Italian explorer Marco Polo

hailed from. Kefallonia was under Venetian control at the time of his birth (c1254), so it is just possible. The village is the site of an extraordinary event on 15 August (the Feast of the Assumption), when its church becomes infested with harmless snakes with crosses on their heads. The snakes are said to bring good luck. The church stands on the site of a former convent. Legend has it that when the convent's nuns were attacked by pirates, they prayed to be transformed into snakes so that they wouldn't be imprisoned. The snakes reappear every year, and villagers collect them and release them near the icon of the Panagia Fidon (Virgin of the Snakes). Sceptics claim that the church is merely on the snakes' natural migratory path or that village priests are involved in some illicit snake breeding.

Places to Stay & Eat

Your best bet for apartments or rooms is through *Venus travel* (☎ 81 650) in the little road parallel to (and one block back from) the seafront. It handles accommodation as well as acting as a foreign exchange and car hire agency.

Hotel Odyssea (☎ 81 614) is confusingly named as it isn't a hotel at all but rather a block of very nice, spacious apartments one block back from the seafront at the western end of the main drag. The apartments cost 18,000 dr in high season (less out of season) but tend to get snapped up very quickly, especially in July and August.

There are several *tavernas* to choose from along the beachfront.

SKALA Σκάλα
☎ 0671

Skala, on the south-eastern tip of Kefallonia, is larger than Lourdata and Kato Katelios, and has a long sand and pebble beach backed by a pine wood. The beach is equipped with umbrellas and sun lounges, and there are plenty of watersports at its southern end. If you want to get away from the crowds, then head to the northern end. The water is shallow till a fair way out making it ideal for children but also for the loggerhead turtles which nest on the beach.

Unfortunately tourism seems to have won out over ecology in this instance.

A Roman villa, thought to have belonged to a noble family, was discovered here in 1957. It features colourful and well preserved mosaic floors and inscriptions dating from the 2nd century AD. The ruins are open daily (admission is free).

Information

There are several tourist agencies in the main street of Skala, all of which can help you with accommodation, car hire and also excursions.

Skalina Tours (☎ 83 175 or ☎ 83 275) is probably the best option if you're stuck for accommodation. CBR Travel (☎ 83 451) is the Avis Car Rental agency in Skala but can also point you in the right direction for accommodation. Next door, Rent a Bike (☎ 26 286, ☎ 83 144), has mopeds and motorbikes for hire.

Etam Travel Service (☎ 83 101) has reasonably priced car rental (from 36,000 dr for three days for a small car) and a long list of excursions, including a day trip to Ithaki on Wednesday (10,000 dr) and a day cruise to Zakynthos (10,000).

Places to Stay

Golden Coast Studios (☎ 83 115) are only available in low season (block-booked the rest of the time). You'll pay 7000 dr to 10,000 dr for a studio for two.

Star Light Hotel (☎ 83 226, fax 83 435) in a quiet location at the back of the resort (follow signs from the church) has doubles with balcony for 15,000 dr in low season but rising to 25,000 dr in July and August. A third bed in the room costs 30% more. Around the corner, for the more budget conscious, are two good domatia.

Elena (☎ 83 118) has pleasant double rooms with fridge from 10,000 dr to 16,000 dr depending on the season. The owner is very friendly but does not speak English. In the same building, but on the first and second floors, is *Villa Caretta Caretta* (☎ 83 573), run by Franka Wright Nodarou. Her spotless, if somewhat overdecorated, rooms are similarly priced (12,000 dr to 13,000 dr

a double), but are probably only available at the beginning and end of the season.

Panorama Hotel (☎ 83 287, fax 83 585) above the pharmacy on the square is run by the friendly Dino Zapadis. Quite comfortable double/triple rooms with fridge and air-conditioning cost 18,000/20,000 dr including breakfast in high season but drop to about 14,000/16,000 dr off season.

Down on the seafront the attractive *Tara Beach Hotel* (☎ 83 250, fax 83 344) has double rooms/bungalows (with fridge but no cooking facilities) for 18,000 dr including breakfast. Prices drop in low season and although it is often used by tour operators, there are always a few spare rooms.

Places to Eat

On the seafront road, *Lucky House* beach bar-cum-taverna, serves burgers and pizza as well as a few Greek staples. It also does takeaway.

Café Pines Too (right on the beach) is popular at all times of the day and night, from breakfast to post-dinner cocktail hour.

At the end of the main street by the square, *The Pines* does more upmarket Greek and international food, but is also a good place to call in for breakfast or a coffee. Opposite, *La Luna* does delicious pizza. *To Arhontiko* in a side street off the main street of Skala, beyond the church and the children's playground, does Kefallonian specialities and is a good family restaurant.

POROS Πόρος
☎ 0674

The 14km coastal drive from Skala to the next town, Poros, is spectacular. About halfway along, you pass the small church of Agios Georgios, next to which are the ruins of an ancient temple.

Around Cape Kapri the beaches become narrow pebbly coves, and there are bizarre mushroom-like rock formations offshore.

Poros itself is overdeveloped and not very attractive, with a rather scruffy, pebbly beach. It stretches along and inland from the seafront, divided into three sections – the port, central seafront and northern seafront. In the commercial centre of town there's an ugly concrete embankment which serves as a promenade. Watersports are available at the northern part of the beach.

There's a branch of the Ionian Bank with an ATM in the main street. The post office is at the inland end of the main street. A doctor's surgery (☎ 72 552) is next to the post office.

Poros Travel (☎ 72 284, fax 72 069) in the main street can help with accommodation and rental cars.

The monastery of **Theotokou Atrou** (the Virgin Mary of Atros), up a winding mountain road about 3km north-west of Poros (500m above sea level) affords spectacular views.

Places to Stay
Poros Bay Hotel (☎ 72 595, fax 72 594) perched above the harbour on the Skala road has singles/doubles for 11,500/16,000 dr.

Pantelis restaurant/bar on the seafront has basic double/triple rooms (all with fridge and balcony) from 5000 dr to 8000 dr depending on season and apartments sleeping four for 10,000 dr to 16,000 dr.

Villa Metaxa (☎ 72 220, fax 0671-26 303) is run by a friendly Dutch woman. Basic double rooms with use of a communal kitchen cost 6000 dr to 8000 dr depending on season.

La Piazza Taverna (☎ 73 019) has several very basic rooms. It's in a good central position but can be noisy. No-frills doubles including breakfast cost 6500 dr to 9500 dr depending on season. The taverna underneath does decent grills and Greek dishes.

Anemos apartments and studios (☎ 72 924, fax 72 277) are a step upmarket with comfortable and clean rooms/studios for 10,000/12,000 dr.

Places to Eat
There are plenty of tavernas to choose from – many specialising in fish. They tend to be located near the central waterfront or at the northern end of the beach. *Flisvos* restaurant is appealing.

Ippocampus, on the central waterfront, is a popular bar for refreshments of the liquid variety. *Taverna Sunset* on the Skala road

at Cape Pronos is a great place to head for views and sunsets as well as Greek fare.

SAMI Σάμη
☎ 0674 • pop 1000
Sami, 25km from Argostoli and the main port of Kefallonia, was also devastated by the 1953 earthquake. Now with undistinguished buildings, its setting is pretty, nestled in a bay, flanked by steep hills. Classical Greek and Roman ruins have been found here. It's worth an overnight stay to visit the nearby caves. A post office, OTE and bank are in town. Buses for Argostoli meet ferries.

Orientation & Information
Sami is Kefallonia's main port and everything in the town is focussed on the long L-shaped seafront and harbour.

The crossroads at the centre of the seafront (opposite the quay where the ferries dock) is called the Plateia Kyprou. A grid of streets heads back inland, and much of the available accommodation plus supermarkets and other shops are located here rather than on the waterfront.

There is a Visa and MasterCard-friendly ATM on the seafront just north of Plateia Kyprou, and a Strintzis Lines office. There are also several tourist agencies on the seafront which deal with car and scooter hire, accommodation and foreign exchange, including Karavomilos Hire (☎ 22 034) by the crossroads.

Places to Stay
Campers should head west from the harbour for about a kilometre to the well equipped *Karavomilos Beach Camping (☎ 22 480, fax 22 932)*. Turn right from the quay and follow the coast.

Many domatia owners meet the boats. *Kyma Hotel (☎ 22 064)* on Plateia Kyprou has probably the best position for ferry arrivals but it is rather run down with fairly basic single/double rooms for 6000/10,000 dr. The *Ionion Hotel (☎ 22 035)* is more modern and more upmarket, with comfortable double rooms for 9000 dr.

The *Melissani (☎ 22 064)*, set in its own grounds at the northern end of town, with its own pool and tennis courts, is one of the better options. Staff are friendly and comfortable doubles cost 10,000 dr. Follow the signs from the quay side.

Kastro Hotel (☎ 22 656) might also be worth trying and is conveniently placed on the seafront near the ferries.

If you're stuck, head north and slightly inland from the central crossroads where various houses display 'rooms to let' placards. *Calypso Apartments (☎ 22 933)* in the suburb of Karavomilos, farther around the bay from Sami, could also be worth trying. Studios for two people cost 10,000 dr and four-person apartments cost 15,000 dr. Make inquiries at the pottery workshop.

Places to Eat

Almost all the places to eat in Sami are clustered along the harbour. *Calypso Bar* in the main street towards the northern end of the waterfront has friendly staff and is a good place for a coffee (500 dr) or a late breakfast (omelettes for 1200 dr). *Eugene*, virtually next door, has more or less the same fare at similar prices.

Adonis Restaurant does well out of its central position on the quay. So does *Faros*, which boasts that it is Sami's oldest restaurant (as no building is more than about 40 years old this doesn't appear to be such a great claim to fame). Menus at both places include the usual array of Greek dishes with a few international ones thrown in. One of the better places – and very popular with the locals – is *Delfinia* which does fish and meat on the grill and has a wider than normal choice of vegetarian Greek dishes.

AROUND SAMI
Mellisani & Drogarati Caves

The **Mellisani Cave** is a subterranean seawater lake. When the sun is overhead its rays shine through an opening in the cave ceiling, lighting the water's many shades of blue. The cave is 2.5km from Sami. To get there walk along the Argostoli road and turn right at the signpost for Agia Evfymia. There is a sign pointing left to the cave beyond the seaside village of Karavomilos. Admission is 1200 dr.

The large **Drogarati Cave** has impressive stalactites. It's signposted from the Argostoli road, 4km from Sami. Both caves are open all day and charge 1000 dr.

AGIA EVFYMIA Αγία Ευφημία
☎ 0674

This picturesque fishing village with its pebbled beach is 10km north of Sami. It is another popular yachting stop, as there are water and fuel supplies on the pier and hot showers available. All the action of the village centres on the harbour. The road skirting the harbour is known as the Boulevard. It is not a great spot for beaches, although the swimming is good, and those with their own transport can explore secluded coves between the town and Sami. There are one or two hotels and some domatia for travellers wishing to stay.

In high season there are two buses daily to Sami and to Fiskardo. There are ferry connections between Vathi and Piso Aetos on Ithaki.

Small boats can be hired for 12,000 dr a day from John Vrettos at the Hotel Boulevard Pyllaros. For rental cars, you should head to Gerolimatos Rentacar (☎ 61 036, fax 61 516).

Places to Stay

John Vrettos, who runs *Hotel Boulevard Pyllaros (☎ 61 800, fax 61 801)* seems to have Agia Evfymia's (limited) accommodation scene pretty well wrapped up. The spacious and extremely comfortable double rooms in his hotel have air-conditioning, balconies and include breakfast. Those with sea view cost 22,000 dr in high season, those without go for 20,000 dr. Suites (sleeping up to four people) cost 30,000 dr. He also has an ever increasing range of studios and apartments for up to four people for 24,000 dr. Guests have the use of two tennis courts and get a 20% discount on prices for boat hire.

Past the harbour, above a small beach called Paradise – which does not really live up to its name – is the modern *Hotel Gonotas (☎ 61 500, fax 61 464)*. Much of the decor looks like it could be the sets from an opera production, with fake plaster columns and Godfather-like baroque fountains, but it could be useful, especially if everything else is full. Doubles cost 10,000 dr to 20,000 dr depending on season, and triple rooms are available.

Just beyond the Gonotas is the ***Dendrinos*** taverna which has a couple of studios available to let.

Places to Eat

There are several tavernas. ***Spiros Restaurant*** (☎ *61 739*) on the south waterfront has great food; aim for the roast suckling pig on Saturday night. Phone ahead to book your plate.

Levante restaurant, part of the Hotel Pyllaros, serves reasonable food but it's the position you go there for. They set up tables on a pier that projects into the sea so you eat almost totally surrounded by water.

Dendrinos taverna above Paradise beach is probably the most popular spot for a meal.

FISKARDO Φισκάρδο
☎ **0674** • **pop 300**

Fiskardo, 50km north of Argostoli, was the only village not devastated by the 1953 earthquake. Framed by cypress-mantled hills, and with fine Venetian buildings, it's a delightful place, but could almost be described as twee. In fact, the pastel-coloured buildings around the central port make the town look as if someone has tried to turn it into a paint producer's colour chart.

As Kefallonia's only proper marina with electricity and water supply, and plenty of docking space, it is extremely popular with yachties. It can get very crowded in high season.

A Roman cemetery and Mycenaean pottery have been found here.

Activities

Fiskardo's Diving Centre (☎ 41 181, fax 41 032, email fnec@compulink.gr) is run out of the Nautical and Environmental Club. The PADI centre runs courses at all levels, from Open Water Certificate to Assistant Instructor. Courses cost around 100,000 dr for a minimum of one week. A Discover

Scuba Diving short lesson and introductory dive costs 12,500 dr.

The Nautical and Environmental Club (☎ 41 181, fax 41 032, email fnec@compulink.gr) is a nonprofit making organisation active in a variety of environmental areas, from studying terrestrial and marine flora and fauna and assisting the Kefalonian Marine Turtle Project (see under Kato Katelios earlier in this chapter) to locating, clearing and mapping old island footpaths and cleaning up local beaches. The group is also involved with the underwater exploration of two shipwrecks in the sea near Fiskardo. Volunteers (especially those on European Voluntary Services grants) spend six to 12 months working with the Nautical and Environmental Club.

You can charter a yacht at Filoxenia (☎ 41 410, fax 41 319). All regular safety requirements and conditions apply. A four berth boat costs from 55,000 dr per day, a six berth 80,000 dr, and there's a minimum one-week charter. A skipper costs 30,000 dr extra per day.

Filoxenia also organises fishing trips (65,000 dr to 70,000 dr for four people including drinks and snacks) two or three times a week.

Small boats with outboard motors can be hired by the day (10,000 dr to 15,000 dr depending on their size). Go to the Haagen Dasz ice-cream shop on the quay (☎ 41 179). It is open from 9 am to 9 pm every day.

Four Islands Ferries can organise day cruises from Fiskardo to Ithaki and to Lefkada, Meganisi and Skorpios. Both tours cost 6000 dr per person (3000 dr for children). Get your tickets from Nautilus Travel (☎ 41 440, fax 41 470) near the ferry dock.

Places to Stay

Upmarket British travel companies such as Simply Ionian and Greek Islands Club have snatched up some of the best properties in and around Fiskardo. You're unlikely to find accommodation during the high season. At others times it's OK, but prices are high.

Regina's (☎ *41 125*) at the back of the village is probably the best value for basic rooms. Double rooms without bathroom

KEFALLONIA

cost 6000 dr, and ensuite rooms go for 10,000 dr in high season. New studios are 12,000/ 15,000 dr.

John Palikisianos Rooms (☎ 41 304), opposite, has rates of 7000/8500 dr. To get to these from the bus stop, cross the car park, turn left at the church, turn left again, and look for the signs.

The *Philoxenia Traditional Settlement* (☎ 41 410, fax 41 319) occupies a lovely 19th century house near the square. Room rates are 20,700/22,000 dr. Luxury apartments and villas sleeping four to six people are also available and start at a hefty 50,000 dr a night. The proprietor can also organise yacht charters.

Athina's Dream (☎ 41 317, fax 41 345) is Fiskardo's prettiest apartment complex, an attractive group of pastel-coloured buildings with royal blue shutters covered in flowering creepers. It is situated just above the small pebbly beach opposite the lighthouse on the Fiskardo headland. Beautifully decorated and well equipped apartments with balcony and sea view sleeping two/four people cost 25,000/30,000 dr in high season with good off season discounts.

Nearby, *Kiki Apartments* (☎ 41 208, fax 41 278) has pleasant studios sleeping two or three people for 17,000 dr. Another 100m or so farther on, *Stella Apartments* (☎ 41 211, fax 41 262) is a large complex of studios and apartments which cost from 12,000 dr to 19,000 dr (two people) or 28,000 dr to 38,000 dr (four people) depending on the season.

The rooms at *Tselenti Domatia* (☎ 41 204), just back from and west of the central square, are tastefully furnished, but are a pricey 15,000/18,000 dr. Farther around the waterfront, *Fiskardo Centre* (☎ 41 495) above the Mokilla Bar has immaculate self-contained units and great sea views. Rates are 15,000 dr to 25,000 dr depending on the season.

If rooms are hard to come by, head out of the village in either direction. On the road for Assos and Argostoli there are several places offering rooms or apartments. In the other direction, about 1.5km out of the village, past a small pretty cove and a white-washed taverna, there's *Apartments Loula Antipas* (☎ 51 808). Immaculately kept and spotlessly clean apartments sleeping two/ four cost 15,000 dr to 21,000 dr/24,000 dr to 28,000 dr respectively depending on the season. Another 500m or so will bring you to the stylish *Agnantia Apartments* (☎/fax 51 801) which has tastefully decorated apartments at similar prices.

Places to Eat

The Captain's Cabin restaurant on the seafront is perennially popular with sailors who have fallen off their yachts. The menu is a limited version of the standard Greek/ international one. Farther along the quay *Tassia* (the restaurant with purple chairs) serves good fresh fish and seafood and is recommended for a decent green salad – something of a rarity in Greece.

Café Tselenti in a renovated old Venetian building set slightly back from the quayside is a nice place for a quiet drink.

Gaïta traditional grill house on the west harbourfront and *Lagoudera* just back from the harbourfront are both worth seeking out for a good traditional Kefallonian meal.

Nightlife in Fiskardo revolves around the port and its bars and shops. Should you feel the urge to boogie the night away however, then head for *Kastro Club* (☎ 41 010) an outdoor bar and disco about 250m out of town on the road to Argostoli.

Getting There & Away

The bus (there are connections with Sami and Argostoli) will drop you off on the road which bypasses Fiskardo.

Walk across the car park, then descend the steps to the left of the church and continue ahead to Fiskardo's central square and waterfront.

You can get to Fiskardo by ferry from Lefkada and Ithaki.

ASSOS Ασσος
☎ 0674

Assos village is a gem of whitewashed and pastel houses, straddling the isthmus of a peninsula upon which stands a Venetian fortress. Assos was damaged in the 1953

Fishing nets and church, Kapsali, Kythira

SALLY WEBB

Grilled octopus, Neapoli (Peloponnese)

SALLY WEBB

A beachside restaurant in the picturesque village of Kapsali, Kythira

SALLY WEBB

Watching the world go by, Potamos, Kythira

The ghost town of Kato Hora, Mylopotamos

Church near Hora, Kythira

Sunday market, Potamos, Kythira

earthquake but sensitively restored with the help of a donation from the city of Paris.

There's an outstanding white sandy beach at **Myrtos**, 3km south of Assos. If you explore by boat, you'll find nearby hidden coves between tall limestone cliffs.

The spectacular turquoise waters and pale pebbly cove of Myrtos beach could almost justify the long hike down to it from Divarata. Those with their own transport can drive right down to the beach which has a taverna. It is best as a day trip as accommodation is nonexistent.

Places to Stay

Assos is tiny and it's almost impossible to find accommodation, especially in high season, as several upmarket British tour operators have snapped up most places.

Linardos Studios (☎ *51 563*), the large beige and white building on the right as you reach the village just before the car park, has studios from 18,000 dr in high season. Low season prices are about 3000 dr cheaper. If you want to book in advance or contact the owners before early June, call their Athens number, ☎/fax 01-652 2594.

Another possibility is *Kanakis Apartments* (☎/fax 51 631) about 50m uphill on the opposite side of the road. Spotless apartments go for 20,000 dr to 24,000 dr (for two people) or 32,000 dr to 38,000 dr (four to five people). There is a small swimming pool and a nice sundeck with a truly breathtaking view. The owner can provide breakfast and (perhaps) some meals at an additional cost. Directly opposite, the *Drokkos family* (☎ 51 532) rents rooms in its house but note that telephone reservations are not accepted – just turn up and try your luck. Doubles with shared bathroom go for 8000 dr.

Zakynthos Ζάκυνθος

☎ 0695 • pop 32,560

The island of Zakynthos (**zahk**-in-thos) has inspired many superlatives. The Venetians called it Fiore di Levante (Flower of the Orient). The mountains of Zakynthos enclose the central fertile plain like a bowl holding something precious. The poet Dionysios Solomos wrote that 'Zakynthos could make one forget the Elysian Fields'. Indeed, it is an island of exceptional natural beauty and outstanding beaches.

Until the earthquake destroyed much of the Venetian architecture, the island must have appeared to be almost a cameo left behind by Venice.

Unfortunately, the earthquake wasn't the end of the damage to the island. Zakynthos' coastline has been the victim of the most unacceptable manifestations of package tourism. The lack of general budget accommodation and a rapacious attitude to tourism on the part of islanders make Zakynthos the least attractive of the Ionian islands as a destination for independent travellers. Even worse, tourism is endangering both the loggerhead turtle and the Mediterranean monk seal.

HISTORY

Zakynthos was first settled during the Mesolithic period (12,000-3000 BC) by Achaeans from the northern Peloponnese. The Zantiots fought alongside Odysseus during the Trojan War and later won their independence from Ithaca.

Zakynthos was allied with Athens during the Peloponnesian War (431-404 BC), but the island was subsequently conquered by the Spartans, and later overrun by Alexander the Great. Under the Romans, Zakynthos had relative autonomy.

Legend has it that Christianity came to the island in 34 AD with Mary Magdalene, who was en route to Rome. A church in the hilltop village of Maries is dedicated to her.

Zakynthos was part of the Byzantine Empire from the 2nd to 12th centuries AD, dur-

HIGHLIGHTS

- View the impressive collection of ecclesiastical art housed in the Neo-Byzantine Museum in Zakynthos Town

- Try water-skiing, jet-skiing, paraflying or windsurfing at Alikes

- Join up for a scuba diving course at Makris Gialos Beach

- Be spellbound by the views from the west coast village of Kambi

- Rent a motorised dinghy at Vromi Bay and visit Shipwreck Beach

Map showing IONIAN SEA and Zakynthos Town p198

ing which time it was plundered by pirates and Vandals.

In 1182, the island was captured by the Norman-Sicilian pirate Margatone. In 1185 Zakynthos along with Kefallonia and Ithaki broke away from the Byzantine empire and formed the semi-autonomous 'County Palatine of Kefallonia'. This mini-kingdom was ruled by a succession of regional aristocrats, the first of whom was Matteo Orsini, installed by the Normans. Years of skirmishes followed, with Rome, Venice, Naples and Ioannina in Epiros all asserting their control.

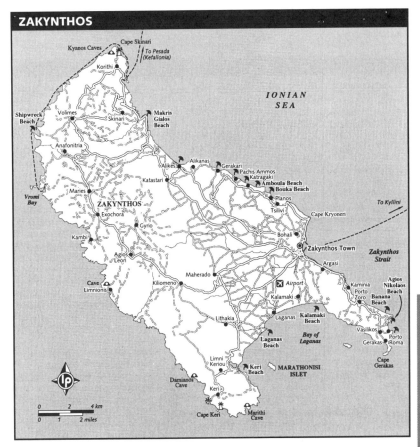

ZAKYNTHOS

The Turks took Zakynthos in a bloody battle in 1479, during which many Zantiots lost their lives. Turkish control lasted only briefly, and in 1483 the Venetians took the island back, subsequently presenting the sultan with a goodwill 'gift' of 500 gold ducats and an annual payment.

The Venetian occupation enriched the culture of Zakynthos and organised the island's government. The Venetians enlarged the harbour at Zakynthos Town and established trade links with Constantinople and northern Europe. Silk, cotton, licorice and beeswax were exported as well as the island's famous currants which were recognised as the best in the world.

But the nobles oppressed the ordinary people. As in Corfu, the Venetians introduced their *Libro d'Oro* (Golden Book), a social register of the favoured nobility. The Zantiot nobles flourished and amassed huge fortunes while the rest of the islanders suffered in poverty. In an uprising in 1628, the 'Rebellion of the Popolari', island merchants together with the local guilds seized control of the island for four years, although they were eventually beaten by the Venetians. Much blood was shed.

When the French republicans occupied the island and unseated the Venetians in 1797, the Zantiots welcomed them with relief. The nobles were totally corrupt and the government weak. The *Libro d'Oro* was publicly incinerated in Plateia Agiou Markou. There was mayhem across the island, and the former nobles appealed to the Russian Tsar to restore order.

A Russian-Turkish alliance besieged the island for several months in 1798, forcing the French and rebellious islanders to surrender. In 1800, the independent Septinsular Republic was established, but it was ruled by a Venetian-Zantiot noble, Count Giorgio Mocenigo, who re-established the aristocracy in 1801.

This provoked a renewed, but unsuccessful, populist rebellion.

The French briefly took control again in 1807 but by 1809 the British had taken the island. They modernised the administration, and invested in major public works. Zakynthos remained a British protectorate until the archipelago was given back to Greece in 1864.

During WWII, the island was occupied by Italian and then German forces. Zakynthos Town and villages all over the island were destroyed in the earthquakes of 1953, although many of the buildings have been reconstructed.

Pavlos' List

A monument in Plateia Solomou in Zakynthos Town commemorates a former mayor of the town, Pavlos Karreris.

In WWII, when the island was under the German occupation, the Nazis ordered the mayor to prepare a list of the names of all Zantiot Jews. When he did eventually hand over a list, there were only two names on it – his own and that of the Greek Orthodox Archbishop of Zakynthos. Karreris told the Germans that they would have to take himself and the Archbishop before he would allow them to touch any of his citizens, thus saving the lives of many Zantiot Jews.

GETTING THERE & AWAY
Air

There is one daily flight from Zakynthos to Athens (17,400 dr). The Olympic Airways office (☎ 28 611) in Zakynthos Town is at Alexandrou Roma 16. You can call the airport on ☎ 28 322.

Bus

There are five or more buses daily from Zakynthos Town to Patras (3½ hours, 2860 dr). The same bus continues on to Athens (seven hours, 6310 dr). Ticket price includes the ferry fare.

Ferry

Depending on the season, between three and seven ferries operate daily from Zakynthos Town to Kyllini, in the Peloponnese (1½ hours, 1400 dr). Tickets can be obtained from Zakynthos Shipping Cooperative (☎ 41 500, fax 48 301) at Lombardou 40. The tourist-weary staff there set new standards in unhelpfulness. If you are travelling with a car (tickets cost 7600 dr), you should buy your ticket the day before you intend to travel (in high season this is particularly important).

From Skinari the F/B *Ionion Pelagos* shuttles across to Pessada on Kefalonia from May to October (two hours, 1025 dr). There is inexplicably no bus from Pessada to anywhere else on Kefalonia. Check with the port police (☎ 42 417) for the times of the Skinari-Pessada ferries, though in general there are two departures daily from Skinari at 9.15 am and 7 pm.

GETTING AROUND
To/From the Airport

There is no shuttle service between Zakynthos Town and the airport, 6km to the southwest. A taxi costs 1400 dr.

Bus

Frequent buses go from Zakynthos Town's modern bus station (☎ 22 255) to Alikes (320 dr), Tsilivi (230 dr), Argasi (230 dr) and Laganas (230 dr). Bus services to other villages are poor (one or two daily). Check the current schedule at the bus station.

Car & Motorcycle

Avis (☎ 27 512, fax 26 330) has an office at 21st May 2, just by Plateia Agiou Markou.

Ionian Rentals (☎ 48 946) is in Makri street. It has mopeds from 5000 dr per day. Cars cost from 13,000 dr per day with discounts for rentals over two or three days. It also has offices in Laganas (☎ 51 797, fax 53 105), Argassi (☎ 41 121), Tsilivi (☎ 44 801) and Alikanas (☎ 83 983).

Another reliable motorcycle and car hire outlet is Moto Stakis, at Dimokratias 3.

ZAKYNTHOS TOWN

• pop 10,250

Zakynthos Town is the capital and port of the island. The town was devastated by the 1953 earthquake but was reconstructed with its former layout preserved in wide arcaded streets, imposing squares and gracious neoclassical public buildings. It is hardly cosy, given its strung-out feel, but it is a reasonable place for an overnight stop and in comparison to many of the overtouristed parts of the island there is at least a semblance of Greekness left in the town.

If you don't have your own wheels, Zakynthos Town could be a good central base for your whole stay.

Orientation

Central Plateia Solomou is on the waterfront of Lombardou, opposite the ferry quay. Another large square, Plateia Agiou Markou, is nearby. The bus station is on Filita, one block back from the waterfront and south of the quay. The main thoroughfare is Alexandrou Roma, parallel to the waterfront and several blocks inland.

Information

Tourist Offices Zakynthos Town has no tourist office. The very helpful tourist police (☎ 27 367) are at Lombardou 62 and are open from around 7 am to 10 pm. They have a map of the island which is impossible to use for navigational purposes.

Money The National Bank of Greece is just west of Plateia Solomou, while directly opposite is a Commercial Bank with an ATM. The Alpha Credit Bank in Alexandrou Roma has an ATM.

There is an exchange booth in Plateia Agiou Markou.

Post & Communications The post office is at Tertseti 27, one block west of Alexandrou Roma. The OTE phone office is situated on Plateia Solomou. It also has a currency exchange.

The Töpis Internet Cafe (☎ 26 650) is at Filita 34, near the bus station. It is open 9 am to 5 pm daily. Internet access costs 1500 dr an hour.

Travel Agencies Olympic Airways (☎ 28 611, fax 44 433) is at Alexandrou Roma 16.

Friendly Tours (☎ 48 030, fax 23 769), Foskolou 5, lives up to its name. The helpful staff can assist you with accommodation (even for only a few days) in Zakynthos Town and around the island, as well as car rentals, excursions and currency exchange.

Spring Tours (☎ 48 004, fax 26 315), Lombardou 50, handles accommodation, air tickets, ferry tickets to Italy, car rental and yacht charters. It has offices all over the island.

Medical Services The Zakynthos hospital (☎ 22 514) is west of town.

Things to See

Plateia Solomou Plateia Solomou is named after Dionysios Solomos, a statue of whom stands in the large square. The Statue of Liberty in the square near the waterfront commemorates Greek Independence won in 1821. It was erected in the 1960s. Skulls, bones and weapons lie at the base of the main figure, symbolically representing all the Greeks who died for their country during the War of Independence.

The 16th century **Church of Agios Nikolaos**, on Plateia Solomou, was built in Italian Renaissance style. Originally it stood on an islet off the coast of Zakynthos – a lantern placed on the church's bell tower meant that it doubled as a lighthouse – although the land behind has since been reclaimed. Partially

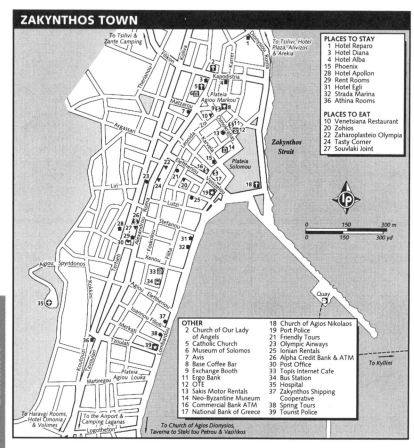

ZAKYNTHOS TOWN

To Tsilivi &
Zante Camping

To Tsilivi, Hotel
Plaza, Alivizos
& Arekia

Filikon
Koliva
Karreri
Dionysiou Roma

Therianou
Kapodistria
Plateia
Agiou Markou

Matzarou
Zoi
Tsikaliotou
Filita

Argassari
Koriita
Kanela

Liri
Eleftheriou
Venizelou

Lutzi

Roma
Alexandrou
Foskolou
Stefanou

Xenou
Filita

Agiou
Spyridonos
Tertseti
Kolliri

Agiou Eleftheriou

Ioannou Filioti

Merkati
Tzoulati
Lombardou

Koutouzi
Tavoulari
Plateia
Agiou Louka
Martinegou

To Haravgi Rooms,
Hotel Omonia
& Volimes

To the Airport &
Camping Laganas
Logotheton

Zakynthos
Strait

Zakynthos
Strait

Quay

To Kyllini

To Church of Agios Dionysios,
Taverna to Steki tou Petrou & Vasilikos

0   150   300 m
0   150   300 yd

PLACES TO STAY
1 Hotel Reparo
3 Hotel Diana
4 Hotel Alba
15 Phoenix
28 Hotel Apollon
29 Rent Rooms
31 Hotel Egli
32 Strada Marina
36 Athina Rooms

PLACES TO EAT
10 Venetsiana Restaurant
20 Zohios
22 Zaharoplasteio Olympia
24 Tasty Corner
27 Souvlaki Joint

OTHER
2 Church of Our Lady
   of Angels
5 Catholic Church
6 Museum of Solomos
7 Avis
8 Base Coffee Bar
9 Exchange Booth
11 Ergo Bank
12 OTE
13 Sakis Motor Rentals
14 Neo-Byzantine Museum
16 Commercial Bank ATM
17 National Bank of Greece

18 Church of Agios Nikolaos
19 Port Police
21 Friendly Tours
23 Olympic Airways
25 Ionian Rentals
26 Alpha Credit Bank & ATM
30 Post Office
33 Topis Internet Cafe
34 Bus Station
35 Hospital
37 Zakynthos Shipping
   Cooperative
38 Spring Tours
39 Tourist Police

ZAKYNTHOS

destroyed in the earthquake, it has been carefully reconstructed.

Zakynthos Museum Also known as the
Neo-Byzantine Museum, the Zakynthos
museum, on Plateia Solomou, houses an
impressive collection of ecclesiastical art
which was rescued from churches razed in
the 1953 earthquake.

Photographs on display show exactly
how devastated the island was after the
quake, and document the locals' efforts to
salvage their artistic patrimony. A scale
model of Zakynthos Town before the earth-

quake illustrates how sympathetically the
reconstruction was done.

Of particular interest and located in the
ground floor rooms, are two large icon
screens with superb icons, tooled silver
bible covers, chalices, crucifixes and many
other icons dating from the 15th to the 17th
centuries.

The first floor galleries contain frescoes
from the Agios Andreas monastery, which
was built in the late 16th century and decorated by anonymous artists in the 17th century. The frescoes – representing the life of
Christ and of the saints – were moved to the

museum after the 1953 earthquake and have been extensively restored.

There are works by 16th century Cretan artist Michael Damaskinos, the most famous painter of his day, and by other artists from Crete who fled to Zakynthos to avoid the Turkish occupation of their homeland.

Works by artists of the Ionian School – including its leading exponent Panagiotis Doxaras and his son Nikolaos – are also on display. Ceiling paintings, known as *ouranies*, formed a major part of Nikolaos' ouvre and there is an example originally from the church of the Phaneromeni.

The museum also contains work by two Zantiot painters, Nikolaos Koutzouzis and Nikolaos Kantounis, who assimilated the iconography and style of the Italian mannerists and baroque artists, and are believed to be the starting point for modern Greek painting.

The museum (☎ 42 714) is open 8 am to 2.30 pm Tuesday to Sunday, and admission is 800 dr.

Museum of Solomos The Museum of Solomos, on Plateia Agiou Markou, is dedicated to Dionysios Solomos (1798-1857), who was born on Zakynthos. His work Hymn to Liberty became the stirring Greek national anthem. Solomos is regarded as the father of modern Greek poetry, because he was the first to use Demotic Greek rather than Katharevousa.

This museum – which is much better than its sibling in Corfu and more user-friendly for the non-Greek speaker – is home to a varied collection of memorabilia associated with his life. There also are displays pertaining to the poets Andreas Kalvos (1792-1869) and Ugo Foskolo (1778-1827), who were also born on Zakynthos. The opening times are 9 am to 2 pm daily and entrance is 800 dr.

Church of Agios Dionysios At the southern end of town, the Church of Agios Dionysios is named after the island's patron saint and contains the saint's relics in a silver coffer. This is paraded around the streets during the festivals held in his honour on 24

August and 17 December. The church has notable frescoes.

Maritime Museum The Zakynthos Maritime Museum (☎ 28 249) is the only one of its kind in the Ionians and contains objects and ephemera relating to Greek naval history. It is located about 1km out of town (take Dionysiou Roma and then turn left following the signs to Bochali). It's an uphill trek. The museum is open 9 am to 2 pm and 6 to 9 pm daily.

The Kastro The ruined Venetian fortress to the north of Zakynthos Town is about the only historic site on the island, although little of the original structure remains. It's worth the 45 minute hike up to it (take Dionysiou Roma and then turn left following the signs to Bochali) for the magnificent views. It is open 8 am to 8 pm daily; admission is 500 dr. While you're up there wander around the pretty jasmine and bougainvillea-covered lanes of Bochali. It's a good place to stop for a meal.

Organised Tours
The KTEL has a 'round Zakynthos Island' tour which costs 3000 dr. Inquire at the bus station. There are many round-island boat tours operating from the northern end of the waterfront, but boat tours which visit Laganas and the blue cave should be avoided as they disturb the loggerhead turtles and monk seals.

Places to Stay
Budget The clean *Rent Rooms* (☎ 26 012, Alexandrou Roma 40) charge 6000/8000 dr for singles/doubles. Enter from Spyrou Gouskou. *Athina Rooms* (☎ 45 194, Tzoulati 29) are simply furnished and cost 5000/10,000 dr.

Walk south along Alexandrou Roma, at the fork head right along Agiou Lazarou and Xanthopoulou is 250m along on the left. The pleasant *Haravgi Rooms (☎ 23 629, Xanthopoulou 4)* has doubles/triples with bathroom for 9000/10,000 dr. Opposite, *Hotel Omonia (☎ 22 113, Xanthopoulou 7)* has rates of 10,000/12,500 dr. The small

ZAKYNTHOS

Hotel Apollon (☎ 42 838, Tertseti 30) with its unsmiling owner will do as an alternative resort. Its single/double rooms are 9000/13,000 dr.

The rather run-down *Hotel Egli (☎ 28 317, Loutzi 1)* has a great position on the seafront opposite the ferry quay, but other than that has little to recommend it. Very basic doubles cost 7000 dr to 10,000 dr depending on the season.

Mid-Range The C class *Phoenix (☎ 23 514, Plateia Solomou 2)* is situated close to the ferry quay, with standard rooms for 10,000/15,000 dr.

Farther back and just off Plateia Agiou Markou is the B class *Hotel Alba (☎ 26 641, fax 26 642, Ziva 38)*, which is good value with rates of 11,000/12,000 dr for small but adequate rooms.

Hotel Reparo (☎ 23 578, fax 45 617) at the corner of the waterfront Dionysiou Roma and D Voultsou streets (about 300m past Plateia Solomou) is a pleasant hotel which claims to offer superior class at B class prices. Most of the rooms have balconies overlooking the sea. Singles/doubles in low season go for 10,000/14,000 dr rising to 20,000/26,000 dr in high season.

A little farther along (heading out of town) is *Hotel Plaza (☎ 45 733, fax 45 059, 2 Kolokotroni)* facing the seafront. It has pleasant single/double rooms for 8000/10,000 dr in low season and 14,000/16,000 dr in high season.

In the centre of town, just off Plateia Agiou Markou is the smart *Hotel Diana (☎ 28 547, fax 45 047)*. Its well appointed single/double rooms cost from 10,000/14,000 dr to 15,000/20,000 dr depending on the season. It takes all credit cards but is only open from April to October.

One of Zakynthos' largest hotels is the *Strada Marina (☎ 42 761, fax 28 733)* well positioned on the seafront opposite the quay (just south of Plateia Solomou). It is open all year and has friendly and helpful multilingual staff. Comfortable singles/doubles with TV, phone and air-conditioning cost 9000/12,000 dr (low season) and 14,000/19,000 dr (high season).

Places to Eat

The centre of town is not the best place to go in search of a decent, reasonably priced meal. The restaurants and cafes in Plateia Agiou Markou serve acceptable food but are a little on the pricey side, while most of the waterfront tavernas and restaurants within spitting distance of the quay cater to day-trippers and serve poor quality, overpriced meals. You'd do better to pick up a cheese or spinach pie.

There are several 'fast food' type places that do them on Alexandrou Roma such as *Tasty Corner*. Also on Alexandrou Roma is a good *souvlaki joint* which is always full of locals and has great gyros and souvlaki. If you want a good meal at an acceptable price be prepared to head out of town in either direction.

One good family-run taverna of the no-frills variety is *Zohios (Psarron 9)*, between Alexandrou Roma and the waterfront. The choice is limited and depends on what the owner has whipped up that day but it is tasty home cooking. You'll pay about 2000 dr to 3000 dr for a meal with wine.

About 600m north of Plateia Solomou, heading along the waterfront, are two excellent tavernas, both very popular with the locals and not at all touristy.

Alivizos (Dionysiou Roma) does excellent fish and meat on the grill and also has an extensive menu of the regular Greek dishes – moussaka and *pastitsio* of course – but also signature dishes such as roast pork stuffed with bacon and cheese. Vegetarians will also be happy. A full meal with wine will cost about 6000 dr.

But better than the food is the nightly music session – by a group of three or four men, plus the restaurant's owner and any customer who wants to join in – of beautifully lyrical *kantades*, accompanied by a guitar and mandolin. You could get drunk on the music alone, but there's excellent house wine to help.

A few paces away is *Arekia (Dionysiou Roma)*. There is no menu – the owner tells you what she has made that day and you choose. The decor is low key; Zantiots come for the food as much as the setting and tables spill out onto the road. Her stuffed eggplants are particularly tasty. There is live music – kantades and the *arekia* of the restaurant's name – most nights.

Heading farther out of town, up in Bochali near the Venetian *kastro* (take Dionysiou Roma north, turn left at Plaza Hotel following signs to Bochali and then first left after the Maritime Museum) is the very good *House of Latas*. The setting is truly wonderful, with tables spread out under a bougainvillea-covered pergola and fabulous views over Zakynthos Town to Mt Skopos. The menu includes a good selection of *mezedes* and Greek cooked dishes but the to-order grilled meats and fish are the speciality.

Cafes featuring *mandolato*, a local nougat sweet, are on Alexandrou Roma. The traditional *Zaharoplasteio Olympia* has sheep's milk yogurt and rice pudding. *Venetsiana Restaurant (Plateia Agiou Markou 8)* is the best restaurant on the central square, with excellent pizzas.

The untouristy *Taverna To Steki tou Petrou*, 150m south of Agios Dionysios on Lombardou, serves delicious, reasonably priced food and is far enough out to dissuade the tourist throngs.

Entertainment

Base coffee bar, just off Plateia Agiou Markou, is a good place for a cocktail, evening drink or light snack. It is particularly popular with young Zantiots as a night-time hangout in the winter months, and there is often a DJ playing very loud, up-to-the-minute music.

TSILIVI, PLANOS & AMBOULA BEACH Τσιλιβή, Πλάνος & Παραλία Αμπούλα

The first major resort north of Zakynthos Town is **Tsilivi**, 5km north. It is virtually indistinguishable from the nearby settlements of Planos and Bouka Beach. North-west of Cape Gaidaros is a succession of small coves and associated settlements: **Amboula Beach**, **Katragaki**, **Pachis Ammos** and **Drosia**.

The beach at Tsilivi and Planos is nothing to write home about and is crowded even in the low season. You can hire umbrellas and sun lounges (they line the beach four or sometimes five deep), and every imaginable water sport is available – from water-skiing to parasailing to pedalos. Not surprisingly it's popular with families. Off the main thoroughfares, olive trees lead down to the coast. This must have been very pretty before the developers moved in.

Dionisos Tours (☎ 83 156, ☎ 41 237) handles accommodation in Tsilivi, Planos, Alikes and Alikanas (with offices in all places). It also has a long list of tours and excursions, although some of them should be avoided as they disturb the marine life, including the monk seals on the west coast and the loggerhead turtles in the south.

If you need a getaway, then head for Theo Rentals in Planos opposite the Hotel Mediterranee. Mopeds can be had for 2500 dr to 5000 dr per day and mountain bikes cost 1500 dr per day.

Scuba diving in this area can be done from **Amboula Beach** through Dive & Divers (☎ 63 527, ☎ 0977-889460). Italian scuba instructor Mario Giovanni Innesto runs PADI and CMAS courses (100,000 dr for a week) and Discover Diving introductory days for 8500 dr.

Places to Stay

Zante Camping (☎ 61 710) above Bouka Beach (2km north-west of Tsilivi), is a very popular camp site.

In Tsilivi, the *Planos Beach Apartments (☎ 44 463)* is a not especially attractive, rather overdecorated, complex around a noisy bar, but it is in the centre of things (read noisy). Studios go for 10,000 dr to 15,000 dr. Much better are the tasteful *Trentanove (☎ 28 427)* apartments and studios next to the gift shop of the same name. Studios sleeping two/three people cost 8000/9000 dr in low season, rising to 14,000/15,000 dr. The family-run *Pansion Rania (☎ 44 506)*, just off the main road opposite the petrol station, has simple, clean studios for 8000 dr to 15,000 dr depending on the season.

In Planos, *Hotel Mediterranee* (☎ 26 100, fax 45 464) on the main road, has pricey doubles (including breakfast) for 15,000 dr to 25,000 dr depending on the season.

About 2.5km along the coast road northwest of Planos is *Paradise Beach Camping* (☎ 61 888) above Amboula Beach. It is a pleasant, shady place, 100m from the sea. Park your van or pitch your tent under the olive trees.

If you are looking for luxury, *Plagos Beach Hotel and Bungalows* (☎ 62 800, fax 62 900), also at Amboula Beach, is a plush, upmarket complex with its own large pool, gardens, bar and restaurant. Prices are compatible with the luxury rating – single/ double rooms range from 32,000/49,000 dr to 38,000/55,000 dr, including both breakfast and dinner.

A little farther north and both cheaper and quieter is the attractive *Tsamis-Zante Hotel and Bungalows* (☎ 62 962, fax 61 659) set just back from the beach at Pachi Ammos (5km from Tsilivi). The whitewashed buildings are covered in brightly coloured bougainvillea and other creepers. In low season, double rooms go for 17,000 dr, rising to 25,000 dr.

Places to Eat

Food isn't a high point of this part of the coast, as a lot of people choose to self-cater.

In Tsilivi, there's a bit of an international flavour with two Asian-influenced restaurants – *Tai Pan* which does Chinese food and *Passeng to Asia* which creates Chinese and Indian food – and another joint called *Chicken Texas*. They are all grouped together on the road leading down to the beach.

Korali, heading towards Planos, has decent salads and Greek dishes with daily specials. There are a variety of cocktail/music bars (to head for or avoid, depending on your taste), including one, on the main road, which boasts 'laser karaoke' with over 2000 songs for the whole family. Don't say you weren't warned.

At Bouka Beach, above the tiny harbour, is the *Abracatabra Beach Bar* which offers

its patrons free use of its pool, sun lounges and umbrellas as well as the full taverna menu. Opposite *The Olde Vineyard Taverna* has traditional Greek dishes and salads under a shady vine-covered pergola.

At Amboula Beach, there are a couple of tavernas but the best food can be had at *Le Maschere*, where an Italian family produces genuine Italian grub and excellent pizzas from a wood-fired oven.

ALIKANAS & ALIKES Αλικανάς & Αλυκές

Beyond Gerakari off the main road heading north from Zakynthos Town is the village of **Alikanas**, surrounded by olive groves which run all the way down to the sea.

A little farther west is **Alikes** (although the two settlements have merged). Why anyone would want to build a resort in an area backed by salt pans and with a rather paltry narrow beach is questionable, but that's what has happened at Alikes. The end result is less than lovely, but it could make a good base to explore the surrounding countryside and inland villages if you have your own car, moped or mountain bike.

The usual range of watersports is available on the beach, including water-skiing, jet-skiing and parasailing. The windsurfing is particularly good.

Several of the round-the-island boat trips which depart from Zakynthos Town also pick up at Alikes. Any of the travel agents lining the main road in Alikes can sell you tickets.

Places to Stay

Many of the apartment complexes in both Alikanas and Alikes are block-booked by British package tour operators, although it might be worth inquiring if there are vacancies in low season.

In Alikanas, the rather soulless *Valais Hotel* (☎ 83 223, fax 83 748) is right on the beach and has pleasant singles/doubles from 9600/12,000 dr in low season. High season prices jump to 15,400/22,000 dr. The family-run *Panorama* (☎ 83 589) at the eastern end of the beach overlooking olive groves has a comforting and run-down guesthouse sort of appearance. Its double studios go for 5000 dr to 14,000 dr depending on the season. Next door, the *Gousetis family* (☎ *83 931*) offers well equipped self-contained apartments for two or four people for 20,000 dr to 25,000 dr.

At the western end of the beach are two *domatia* which offer great value in low season: *Blue Shadows* (☎ *83 849*) and, directly behind it, *Marino Kostas* (☎ *83 357*). Both offer well equipped and spotlessly clean apartments sleeping four from 15,000 dr; Blue Shadows also has studios for two from 8000 dr.

The best value hotel in Alikes is *Ionian Star* (☎ *83 416, fax 83 173*) run by the friendly Goussetis family. It fronts onto the beach and has a very pleasant vine-covered bar/taverna area. Single/double rooms in low season cost 7100/9200 dr and 13,700/16,200 in high season.

Hotel Montreal (☎ *83 241, fax 83 342*) farther along the waterfront at the northern end of the beach (near the salt pans) has doubles on a B&B basis from 14,500 dr.

Places to Eat

In Alikanas, down by the beach, is *Redskins* bar and taverna which boasts draught beer in iced glasses. Also on the beach, *Shoestring Taverna* attracts the beach-goers. Some other popular places to eat tend to be back at the junction of the main road and the road leading down to the beach.

Taverna Alkionis allows you to dine surrounded by fake Ionic columns, while its neighbour *Dionysis* is a popular and lively taverna.

Golden Dolphin in Alikes at the northern end of the beach prides itself as *the* fish taverna. For something completely different, *Taj Mahal*, on the main road down to the beach, does Indian and Chinese food.

Entertainment

If it's cocktail bars and music that you're after head to the crossroads at Alikanas, summer home to a number of places, including *Flame*, *Heaven* and *Iguana Bar*, which start up as the sun goes down and buzz until the early hours.

NORTH TO AGIOS NIKOLAOS

The road north from Alikes is lined with a few buildings that survived or partially survived the earthquakes, giving a vague idea of what the original island architecture would have looked like.

The north-eastern coast is harsh and has high cliffs with sheer and dramatic drops to the sea. The road snakes around offering good views but limited beach access. This is not the most picturesque part of the island, with windswept moors and stone quarries. You'll probably only pass through it if you are catching the ferry to Kefallonia. Diving sites in the north of the island are among the best in the Mediterranean, as there are many underwater caverns and caves to explore.

Above **Makris Gialos Beach** there's a rather exposed, shadeless camping ground, *Red Dolphin Camping*, with a taverna. There's little going for the place other than a diving school run by a qualified Austrian instructor, Hubert Schaffer (☎ 0932-772145). He hires out equipment, takes people on dives and runs PADI courses from May until October. A single accompanied dive costs 7500 dr including tank, weights and boat trip (five dives 36,000 dr and 10 dives 68,000 dr). PADI Open Water Diver courses cost 114,000 dr (including log book, certificate and all equipment) and Advanced Open Water Diver courses (with own equipment) cost 75,000 dr. A Discover Scuba Diving one-day course and dive costs 14,000 dr. Schaffer also rents full diving equipment to experienced divers and will help divers find alternative accommodation in apartments and studios in Alikes.

The road continues north to the small port of Agios Nikolaos and the hamlet of Skinari (where the ferry from Kefallonia docks). There are a couple of tavernas and some places which rent rooms, including *Panorama* (☎ *31 160*).

VASILIKOS PENINSULA

Χερσόνησος Βασιλικού
Argasi, 4km south of Zakynthos Town, is the first settlement you come to if heading

ZAKYNTHOS

down the Vasilikos Peninsula. It doesn't boast an especially nice beach, which is narrow and, because it's the closest beach to town, very crowded.

You are unlikely to want to stop here, unless you happen to have a cheap package, although it is known, together with Laganas, as the nightlife centre of the island. In summer various discos and live music venues spring up along the main road both north-west and south-east of Argasi: *Byblos*, *Mykonos Town* and *Thamous* are very popular places to groove.

Continuing down the coastal road, the first decent place to stop is **Kaminia**. The sandy cove of **Porto Zoro** also offers good sun and sea worshipping possibilities, and there are tavernas and accommodation at both places.

Virtually at the tip of the east coast, **Banana Beach** is a more pleasant place to hang out with a long (albeit narrow) strip of golden sand. There are lots of watersports, umbrellas and sun lounges.

Agios Nikolaos at the very end of the peninsula has great (turtle-free) watersports facilities and a few domatia and studios, and is where the more discerning Greek youth comes to hang out in the summer.

The coastline then heads due south to **Mavratzis Beach** which is ghastly and best

Up Mt Skopos

At 491m, Mt Skopos ('look-out') is not the highest mountain on the island, but it is one of the more accessible and affords great views of Zakynthos and across to the Peloponnese.

There's a clearly marked path from Argasi (signposted off the first hairpin bend south of Argasi). The hike up to the summit takes the best part of a day. On the way, you'll walk past the ruins of the 11th century church of Agios Nikolaos Megalomatis and, depending on the season, you'll pass banks of wildflowers and various species of indigenous orchid.

At the summit, the small whitewashed church of Panagia Skopiotissa is worth a look. Its interior is decorated with frescoes, has a mosaic floor and a carved stone iconostasis.

avoided, unless Disneyland is to your liking. It is dominated by the mock fortress of the Zante Palace Hotel, which is complete with portcullis in the gateway and multiple waterslides.

Beyond Mavratzis is the more pleasant beach of **Porto Roma** although the narrow strip of sand does get crowded.

On the other side of the peninsula, facing Laganas Bay, is Zakynthos' best beach, the long and sandy **Gerakas**. This is one of the main turtle nesting beaches (see boxed text 'At Loggerheads in the Ionians') and access to the beach is strictly forbidden between dusk and dawn during the breeding season.

Places to Stay

On the road down to Kaminia beach, *Villa Contessa* (☎ 35 161) provides spotless, well equipped studios (sleeping up to three) for 10,000 dr to 18,000 dr (depending on the season). Just below is *Villa Levante* (☎ 45 098, ☎ 35 475) which has studios for similar prices.

The very smart *Matilda Hotel* (☎ 35 376, fax 35 429) on the road between Kaminia Beach and Porto Zoro, has upmarket accommodation at upmarket prices. Rooms have balconies, air-conditioning and all mod cons. Doubles (including bed, breakfast and dinner) go for 25,500 dr to 38,000 dr depending on the season.

Porto Zoro (☎ 35 304, fax 35 087) has a monopoly on accommodation in Porto Zoro – it's the only place you can stay. It offers double/triple rooms for 10,000/12,000 dr rising to 14,000/17,000 dr in high season. There is a taverna but other than that there's just the waves and sand to entertain you.

At Porto Roma, *Dimitra Vitsou* (☎ 35 374) has very pleasant apartments (sleeping up to four people) to rent for 10,000 dr to 20,000 dr. Inquire at the minimarket. *Sailing Café Bar* (☎ 35 274) rents rooms for 8000 dr to 12,000 dr, and also has a couple of four person apartments for 18,000 dr to 30,000 dr depending on the season. *Villa Kapris* (☎ 35 331, fax 41 180) has studios for 7000 dr.

The only accommodation at Gerakas Beach, at the tip of the peninsula, is *Liuba*

ZAKYNTHOS

Bungalows (☎ 35 313) set in a field a few minutes walk back from the beach. Simple accommodation for two people costs 10,000 dr to 16,000 dr depending on the season. Bungalows for four people cost 25,000 dr to 35,000 dr.

Places to Eat

You haven't got much choice at Porto Roma where there is a single *taverna* on the seafront, and up on the road the *Mikri Platia Taverna* which has great views over the cape and the white cliffs. Similarly at Porto Zoro there is only one taverna.

BAY OF LAGANAS Κόλπος Λαγανά

Loggerhead turtles come ashore to lay their eggs on the golden sand beaches of the huge Bay of Laganas, on Zakynthos' south coast (a mere 5km south of Zakynthos Town). What could have remained an ecological paradise has become the exact opposite.

Laganas is a highly developed, tacky resort and is a truly dreadful place to spend a holiday unless you like lager and loud discos and would rather be in the UK than Greece. Avoid it like the plague, or at least drop by to see how Mammon and mass tourism have met in the most abominable set of circumstances.

The lack of regard for the loggerhead turtles' most important nesting site in Greece just makes you want to cry. Environmentalists are doing their best to preserve the area – legislation has been put in place to protect the newly declared National Marine Park of Zakynthos which divides the bay into three areas with strict boating, mooring and fishing restrictions – but it is a case of too little, too late. Speedboats, jet-skis and buoys still bob about in the sea off Laganas.

KALAMAKI Καλαμάκι

Kalamaki, 3km east of Laganas, is almost acceptable as a port of call for the independent traveller. It's as close as you would want to be to the ghastly mass commercialism of Laganas.

The beach is not especially wide, with slightly dirty, almost muddy looking, sand but you can't see much of it anyway with all the sunbeds and umbrellas lined up three and sometimes four deep.

The road from Kalamaki to Laganas is lined with new and ugly buildings housing restaurants, hotels and shops, indicating that the Laganas disease is still spreading. If you need to escape (highly likely), Hermes Car and Bike Rental (☎ 23 284) is about 150m along the road from Kalamaki.

Places to Stay & Eat

Camping Laganas (☎ 22 292) at Laganas Bay is well equipped and has plenty of natural shade.

Crystal Beach Hotel (☎ 42 788, fax 42 917) is one of the better hotels in Kalamaki and has an advantageous position right on the beach. Most rooms have a sea view, and there are some nice touches such as fresh flowers in the bedrooms, however it is like most other places – a purpose-built hotel. Single/double rooms in low season go for 15,300/17,300 dr and in high season for 17,300/30,600 dr.

Klelia (☎ 27 056, fax 41 288) has doubles from 12,500 dr to 20,500 dr depending on the season.

About 100m along the road from Kalamaki to Laganas is *Elena Apartments (☎ 49 003, ☎ 23 905)* near the minimarket of the same name. It has good value double studios for 7000 dr to 8000 dr.

Chives Restaurant on Kalamaki's main street is a swanky place. The menu has the usual Greek and international fare.

Also in Kalamaki, *Taverna Paris* has a nice setting. The extensive menu goes on for pages and includes a range of vegetarian options and children's meals. If your tastebuds need stimulating, head for the *Hong Kong* Chinese restaurant halfway down the main street.

KERI Κερί

Beyond Laganas, the road to **Keri Beach** is extremely pretty and lined with vineyards and olive groves. There is a small harbour where fishing boats moor and excursion boats depart, and a narrow pebble beach. It is much more pleasant, and quieter, than Laganas or Kalamaki. The village of **Keri,**

ZAKYNTHOS

At Loggerheads in the Ionians

Sea turtles have lived in the world's oceans for over 100 million years. Today they are facing extinction due to overfishing, destruction of their habitats and pollution. Of the seven species of sea turtle found in the world's oceans, only two breed in the Mediterranean: the loggerhead turtle (Caretta caretta), found in the Ionians, and the green turtle (Chelonia mydas). The loggerhead turtle nesting beaches are on Zakynthos, Kefallonia, Crete and the Peloponnese.

Female turtles take at least 10 and sometimes 50 years before reaching sexual maturity. They usually return to the beach where they hatched. During the nesting season (June to August) the female turtles swim ashore and then heave themselves up the beach to find a nesting site. They dig holes, around 25cm to 40cm deep, and lay small round eggs. An average nest would have 100 to 120 eggs. Once the nest is safely covered with warm sand the female turtle returns to the water.

Turtles will lay between three and six times during the breeding season and the eggs take about two months to hatch. After her final nesting for the season, the female turtle may not return to nest again for several years.

The baby turtles dig their way out at night and head instinctively for the water. Sometimes the hatchlings emerge during the day. If you see one, do not touch it or go anywhere near it. Do not pick it up to help it to the sea. It is essential to their survival that the hatchlings make their own way to the water. Of the hatchlings that make it into the sea, only one in 1000 will reach adulthood. The loss of a single adult female and her numerous progeny is disastrous for marine turtle populations in the Mediterranean.

The main nesting grounds for loggerhead turtles in the Ionian islands are on Zakynthos (Laganas Bay) and Kefallonia (Kaminia and Skala). Loggerhead turtles also nest in Kotychi and the Bay of Kiparissia (north-west and west coast of the Peloponnese respectively), Koroni and the Bay of Lakonikos (in the southern Peloponnese) and at Chania, Rethymnon and the Bay of Messara on Crete. The Laganas Bay area of Zakynthos is the most important nesting site in Greece, as it contains roughly half the nests in the whole of the country. In 1997 about 2000 nests were recorded and protected on Greek beaches, of which 1026 nests were on Zakynthos. In the same year about 150,000 hatchlings made it safely to the sea.

The impact of ill-planned tourist development and large industrial construction pushes turtles away from the beaches they have been frequenting for thousands of years. Even the humble beachside taverna – with its associated noise and light – is a major obstacle to turtle breeding.

This is where the work of the Athens based **Sea Turtle Protection Society** (STPS) and its volunteers, based near the nesting beaches, comes in. The STPS is seeking to 'promote a sustainable tourism that respects the environment and at the same time fully protects the nesting beaches.' The organisation aims to conserve and protect the remaining Mediterranean sea turtle populations through research programs, education, political liaison, publicity and fund raising. Of these activities, probably the most important are education – of those involved with the local tourism industry

about 5km inland in the hills, is quite untouristy. Walk or drive up to the lighthouse at **Cape Keri** for breathtaking views.

Keri Tourist Center – a glorified minimarket/souvenir shop – also rents motorboats and does bookings for excursions around the island, including to the nearby **Marathonisi Islet**. These should be avoided as the turtles also nest there.

Motorised dinghies can be hired from Blue Caves Motorboats (☎ 0931-966911, ☎ 0977-990131), operating from under an umbrella at the northern end of Keri beach. A dinghy for four hours costs 7000 dr (plus petrol).

Diving Center Turtle Beach (☎/fax 48 768) can offer dives but not diving courses. A single dive (including all equipment and boat trip) costs 9000 dr. If you buy six dives

At Loggerheads in the Ionians

and of beachgoers – and political liaison. All too often in Greece, the environment has been totally disregarded in the greedy race for more of the tourism dollar and it seems only national legislation will stop things going even further downhill.

Laganas Bay on Zakynthos is now an overdeveloped, ugly resort, with all variety of watersports and beach tavernas – everything in fact which works towards the nonsurvival of the turtles. The Greek government recently declared the area a National Marine Park and strict regulations are now in force regarding boating, mooring, fishing and watersports. At the ghastly resort of Laganas itself much of the damage has already been done, but other beaches in the area, such as Gerakas, are now completely off limits between dusk and dawn during the breeding season, and all boating and fishing is banned. The **Zakynthos branch of the STPS** is based at Gerakas where there is a public information centre (☎ 0695-28 658), which accepts volunteers for all its monitoring and research programs.

In Kefallonia, the **Kefalonian Marine Turtle Project**, part of the STPS, is part of the Katelios Group for the Research and Protection of Marine and Terrestrial Life (☎ 0671-81 009, fax 81 058). It is run by Caterina Xenopoulou out of the Environmental and Cultural Centre in Kato Katelios. The centre accepts volunteers for its activities, which includes marking and monitoring the nesting sites, and giving talks to local tourism industry workers and holiday-makers. The centre is set up like a mini-museum with a wealth of material and displays. They realise that it is impossible to reverse the tourism development but that it is possible to encourage sustainable ecologically and environmentally friendly tourism in the future.

Volunteers are needed, especially at the beginning of the breeding season in June and early July, to observe and monitor nests. Thanks to the efforts of the Kefalonian Marine Turtle Project, 1999 saw a noticeable increase in the number of nests.

What can you do to help? Keep away from the nesting beaches from dusk till dawn. Carelessly positioned sun umbrellas and sun lounges (which should be kept below the high water line), digging, driving mopeds or cars can easily disturb and destroy a nest. Take all litter away from the beach with you and flatten any sandcastles built or holes dug. Even the smallest piece of rubbish or pile of sand can hinder a hatchling's progress to the sea.

For further information about ongoing projects contact the Sea Turtle Protection Society of Greece (☎/fax 01-384 4146, email stps@compulink.gr), Solomou 35, 106 82 Athens. There is a good Web site at www.compulink.gr/stps.

SARAH JOLLY

ZAKYNTHOS

they are 8150 dr each and 11 dives are 7250 dr each. Dives including only weights, air-tank and the boat ride cost 6300 dr each. The Diving Center can also help with accommodation in the area.

Places to Stay & Eat

If you're travelling on the road from Laganas to Keri, you'll pass the very attractive and peaceful *Tartaruga Camping* (☎ 51 967), which has a wonderful setting amid terraced olive groves and vineyards.

At Keri Beach, the *Stefos family* (☎ 48 781) has good value apartments and studios from 5000 dr to 13,000 dr depending on the size and the season. They are located behind the *Tzanetos Taverna*, one of several tavernas on the seafront. It has a full taverna menu as does the *Keri* taverna which has friendly if somewhat pushy staff.

Rock Cafe is good for drinks and light snacks. Inland from the beach *La Bruschetta* serves authentic Italian food. Just beyond the hill-top village of Keri, the *Lighthouse* taverna has snapped up one of the best positions on the peninsula and is an atmospheric place to stop.

INLAND & THE WEST COAST

You can escape from the tourist hype by visiting inland farming villages. These are very difficult to get to without your own wheels, however there are a few around-Zakynthos bus tours which visit some of the villages (2000 dr).

Set in lush arable uplands, the village of **Maherado** is 10km west of Zakynthos Town. Terraced olive groves and orchards surround the village. Some impressive architecture survived the earthquake, including the 14th century church of Agia Mavra with a free standing bell tower. The church has a carved wooden iconostasis and a superb icon of the Madonna, framed in an ornate silver sculptured casing and bejewelled with gold necklaces and pendants.

Kiliomeno, 6km west of Maherado, is an attractive village with some houses that survived the earthquake. The village was originally known as Agios Nikolaos after its church, which has a decorated bell tower.

From **Agios Leon**, 4km farther on, a brand new road leads down to **Limnionis**, where a single taverna serves swimmers who plunge off the rocks below into a deep azure-green sea.

Exochora is a charming hamlet, almost totally untouched by tourism, with attractive old buildings and a central village kafeneio. From Exochora, 4km of winding

road leads to **Kambi**, overlooking sheer 300m-high cliffs on the west coast. There are a couple of hill-top *tavernas*, both of which are great places to watch the sunset, although prepare to share them with bussed-in tour groups in high season. The food is average but the view so sensational that you won't even notice. There's a small shop selling handicrafts, olive oil and honey.

The drive north from here to **Maries** and **Anafonitria** is through splendid hilly country. Maries has a church dedicated to Mary Magdalene who is said to have passed through the village on her way to Rome.

The famous **Shipwreck Beach** (Navagio), whose photos grace virtually every tourist brochure about Zakynthos, is at the northwestern tip of the island. It truly is a splendid beach with crystalline, aquamarine waters. However, unless you have your own boat, it can only be visited by excursion boat, best undertaken from the little harbour of **Vromi Bay** which in turn is reachable by a decently powered motorbike or scooter from Anafonitria. Small motorised dinghies can be rented at Vromi Bay. Take a picnic since there are no beach facilities.

Prepare for an onslaught of commercialism at **Volimes**, the largest of the island's hill villages, in the far north-west. Handicraft stalls selling fine embroidery and lacework and an awful lot of rubbish (turtle bathmats anyone?) are dotted throughout the village. KTEL buses go from Zakynthos Town to Volimes twice a day.

Make an effort to visit the little village of **Gyrio** in the centre of the island (there are roads from Agios Leon on the west coast drive and Kalithea off the eastern coast road) where there is a cosy *taverna* with live arekia music on weekends. It is patronised mainly by Greeks in the know.

Kythira & Antikythira

Κύθηρα & Αντικύθηραφ

The island of Kythira (**kee**-thih-rah) represents to many Greeks the Holy Grail of island-hopping. The 'Road to Kythira', a well known 1973 song by Dimitris Mitropanos, epitomises what for most people is the end of the line that is never reached. Indeed Kythira can be a hard place to get to – mentally, if not physically – since you have to make that special effort just to get there.

Approximately 30km long and 18km wide, Kythira is situated off the Laconian Peninsula of the Peloponnese between the often turbulent Ionian and Aegean seas. It is a curiously barren island in parts, with misty moors, winding lanes backed by low stone walls and hidden valleys that rent the dreamy landscape. More than 40 villages are scattered evenly across the island, and ghosts are said to roam the inland villages. Kythira was part of the British Ionian Protectorate for many years, evidenced by the sprinkling of arched stone bridges around the island.

The tiny island of Antikythira, 38km south-east of Kythira, is the most remote island in the Ionian group. It is a rocky island rising sheer from the sea, with few trees. It also is a valued notch in the belt of the independent traveller.

Kythira

☎ 0735   • pop 3100

Kythira is the least 'Ionian' of the Ionian island group. Physically separated from its nearest neighbour Zakynthos by a long stretch of sea, it is administered from Piraeus and mostly resembles the Cyclades in appearance and architecture.

Kythira has never depended on tourism for its wellbeing. Instead it has relied on the remittances of and visits from its expats, most of whom have made new homes in 'Big Kythira' – Australia.

HIGHLIGHTS

- Stroll to the water nymph waterfall at alluring Mylopotamos
- Gaze upon Minoan artefacts at Hora's Archaeological Museum
- Swim in the safe, sheltered aquamarine waters at Kapsali
- Buy the best honey in Greece from Prathrio Melioy in Aroniadika
- Visit Antikythira, the most remote island in the Ionian group

IONIAN SEA

KYTHIRA

ANTIKYTHIRA

Until recently, Kythira was little visited by foreign tourists because of uncertain shipping schedules and local indifference to tourism. The EOT has begun encouraging tourists to visit Kythira but it's still unspoilt. Its attractions are its relatively undeveloped and excellent beaches, its enduring feel as a special island and the fact that it is 'the end of the line'.

Accommodation can be very hard to find from mid-July to the end of August, so prebooking is absolutely essential. Budget

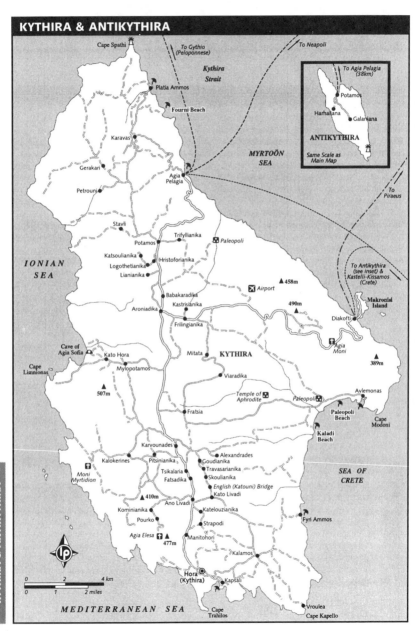

KYTHIRA & ANTIKYTHIRA

Cape Spathi
To Gythio (Peloponnese)
To Neapoli
Kythira Strait
Platia Ammos
Fourni Beach

To Agia Pelagia (38km)
Potamos
Harhaliana
Galaniana
ANTIKYTHIRA
Same Scale as Main Map

Karavas
MYRTOÖN SEA

Gerakari
Agia Pelagia
To Piraeus

Petrouni

Stavli
To Antikythira (see inset) & Kastelli-Kissamos (Crete)

IONIAN SEA

Potamos
Trifyllianika
Paleopoli
Katsoulianika
Hristoforianika
Logothetianika
Lianianika
Airport
458m
490m
Makronisi Island
Babakaradika
Kastrisianika
Aroniadika
Diakofti
Frilingianika
Cave of Agia Sofia
Kato Hora
Mitata
KYTHIRA
Agia Moni
Cape Limnionas
Mylopotamos
389m
507m
Viaradika
Temple of Aphrodite
Paleopoli
Avlemonas
Fratsia
Paleopoli Beach
Cape Modoni
Kaladi Beach

Karvounades
Alexandrades
Kalokerines
Pitsinianika
Goudianika
SEA OF CRETE
Tsikalaria
Travasarianika
Moni Myrtidion
Fatsadika
Skoulianika
English (Katouni) Bridge
Kato Livadi
410m
Ano Livadi
Katelouzianika
Kominianika
Pourko
Strapodi
Fyri Ammos
Agia Elesa
477m
Manitohori
Kalamos
Hora (Kythira)
Kapsali
0   2   4 km
0   1   2 miles
Vroulea
MEDITERRANEAN SEA
Cape Trahilos
Cape Kapello

accommodation is thin on the ground, but prices can be up to 50% lower out of season, which is the best time to visit anyway. The Web site www.kythera.com has information on accommodation, local events and places to visit.

Kythira's main port is Agia Pelagia, though hydrofoils depart from and arrive at the custom-built port of Diakofti. If the seas are high, the ferry boats from Neapolis to Agia Pelagia will sometimes dock at Diakofti instead.

Because public transport on Kythira ranges from abysmal to nonexistent, bringing your own wheels or renting them locally is advisable.

HISTORY

Excavations in the south of Kythira near Avelmonas indicate the presence of a Minoan trading post (c2000-1450 BC). In the 9th and 8th centuries BC, the Phoenicians inhabited the island, which was reputed to be rich in murex sea shells from which they extracted their famous reddish purple dye. The Mycenaeans were also present on Kythira.

During the Peloponnesian War Kythira was an ally of Sparta, but due to its strategic position the island was also occupied many times by Athens. With the decline of both powers, Kythira also fell into decline, although it continued to be inhabited during the Hellenistic and Roman periods. Between the 2nd and 6th centuries AD Kythira went through a period of desolation; it had few inhabitants, mainly hermits and monks.

By the 10th century the island had become all but abandoned due to the ferocity of the Saracens occupying neighbouring Crete. The island's fortunes started to turn when Crete was reconquered by the Byzantines. Inhabitants from the Peloponnese moved to Kythira, and the island was administered by the Evdaimonoyiannides family from Monemvassia. The family based itself at Paliochora, and was reputedly involved in piracy.

In 1204 the Venetians took Kythira. The island was ruled by the Venetian noble Marco Venieri, who claimed that he was descended from Aphrodite (whose Roman name is Venus). Venieri became the Marquis of Kythira in 1207. Deciding that Crete offered him more opportunities, Venieri left the island in the hands of its former rulers, the Evdaimonoyiannides family.

During the 15th and 16th centuries, many of the Byzantine churches on the island were built.

In 1530 the administrators of Crete, Venieri's descendants, revolted against Venice. To reassert their control, the Venetians reclaimed all their rights to Kythira, setting up an oppressive feudal administration. The peasants were not allowed to leave the island, and were forced to farm inaccessible and unsuitable plots of land.

The island was attacked by Barbarossa in 1537, who was heading back to Algeria after his unsuccessful siege of Corfu. Barbarossa razed to the ground the Byzantine capital of the island, Paliochora, on the north-eastern coast. He also destroyed the fortresses of Mylopotamos and Kapsali and took 7000 captives.

After the fall of Crete to the Turks in 1669, Kythira became a refuge for Greeks from the Peloponnese and Crete.

Venice held Kythira until 1797, apart from a brief period (1715-18) when the Turks gained the upper hand, and exercised a significant influence on its language, culture and architecture. After 1797 Kythira's fortunes followed that of the other islands. The French established a democratic regime, burned the gentry's records and gave hope to the population for justice and freedom. It lasted only a year, by which time a Russian-Turkish alliance threw out the French.

In 1800, under the Treaty of Constantinople, Kythira became part of the Septinsular Republic. However the treaty maintained privileges for the nobles, resulting in a rebellion of the peasants and middle classes in July 1800.

In the absence of any military force, they occupied the *kastro* at Hora and slaughtered some of the island gentry. In 1802 military force was re-established on the island, and the leaders of the rebellion were arrested and executed.

The French again occupied Kythira under the Treaty of Tilsit in 1807. The British stepped in in 1809, instigating many public works projects, which included the Katouni Bridge. The island became a refuge for many fighters and intellectuals during the War of Independence.

In 1864, Kythira, together with the other Ionian islands was ceded to Greece. However its path has diverged from that of the other islands, and politically it now belongs to Attica, and is administered from Piraeus.

GETTING THERE & AWAY
Air
There are flights to Athens (45 minutes, 14,400 dr) every day except Thursday. The Olympic Airways office (☎ 33 362) is on the central square in Potamos. Book also at Kythira Travel (☎ 31 390) in Hora. The airport is 10km east of Potamos.

Ferry
The modern car ferry F/B *Maria* of Golden Ferries sails from Agia Pelagia to Gythio in the Peloponnese twice daily during summer (two hours, 1600 dr), with twice-weekly connections to Antikythira (2000 dr, two hours) and Kasteli in Crete (4000 dr, 4½ hours). Schedules and times are often subject to delays so check at Agia Pelagia's Megalo-konomou Shipping Agency (☎ 33 490, fax 33 890). In Gythio, contact the Praktopeio Agency (☎ 0733-22 410, ☎ 22 996).

The older *Nisos Kythira* run by BOIAI Lines shuttles between Agia Pelagia and Neapoli (one hour, 1500 dr). A newer ship is planned and may be in operation by the time you read this. Tickets are sold at the quay before departure, or at the BOIAI office (Sirene Agency, ☎ 33 280) at the top of the main square in Potamos. In Neapoli, tickets and bookings are handled by Toula Dermati (☎ 0734-22 660) at the Vatika Bay Shipping Agency around the corner from the commercial bank.

With both of the above boats, if you are travelling with a car, especially in high season, you should book your passage a day or two before you want to travel as the number of car places is limited.

Note that if the seas are rough the boats are sometimes cancelled, or they can be diverted to the Kythirian port of Diakofti instead of Agia Pelagia.

The port police (☎ 33 280) are at Agia Pelagia on the waterfront.

Hydrofoil
In summer, there are five hydrofoils weekly from Diakofti on Kythira to Piraeus (five hours, 10,300 dr) via Monemvasia, Spetses and Hydra. Tickets can be bought from Kythira Travel in Hora, or Megalokonomou Shipping Agency in Agia Pelagia.

GETTING AROUND
Bus
Kythira's bus service is designed to ferry schoolchildren to and from school. Outside of term times it is nonexistent. During school terms a couple of services link Agia Pelagia with Kapsali twice daily – before school in the morning and in the early afternoon when school is out.

There is no airport bus. Not surprisingly, Kythira has many taxis and a taxi from Agia Pelagia to Kapsali will cost around 4000 dr. Hitching is fairly easy.

Car & Motorcycle
Panagiotis Defterevos at Moto Rent (☎ 31 600, mobile ☎ 094-263757, fax 31 789) situated on Kapsali's waterfront, rents cars, jeeps, mopeds and motorcycles. He also has offices (open summer only) in Hora (☎ 31 004), Tsikilaria (☎ 31 551) and Agia Pelagia (☎ 33 194). If you order a car in advance he will bring it to the port or airport to meet you. Cars cost from 10,000 dr to 25,000 dr per day depending on the size. Mopeds up to 80cc costs 3000 dr to 4500 dr per day. Motorbikes (100cc to 500cc) cost 5000 dr to 17,000 dr per day. Discounts are given for rentals of several days or a week.

Easy Rider (☎ 33 486) rents motorbikes at Agia Pelagia.

AGIA PELAGIA Αγία Πελαγία
• pop 280
Kythira's northern port of Agia Pelagia is a simple, friendly waterfront village ideal for

relaxing, swimming and finding peace of
mind. Lia at the Megalokonomou Shipping
Agency, opposite the quay, happily assists
newcomers.

Mixed sand and pebble beaches are to either side of the quay. The best place to swim
is to the north of the village, where the road
to the Hotel Romantica meets the sea.

Places to Stay – Budget
Prebooking in high season is almost essential in Agia Pelagia. At the top of the quay
is a room-finding office (no telephone),
which operates in high season.

One of the friendliest and most pleasant
places to stay is the *domatia* of *Georgos
Kambouris* (☎ 33 480). His wife, Maria,
maintains spotless, airy doubles/triples for
12,000/14,000 dr. The building is just in
front of Hotel Romantica. Opposite the
quay above the Faros Taverna, *Alexandra
Megalopoulou's Rooms* (☎ 33 282) are
tidy, simply furnished and with bathroom
cost 12,500 dr a double.

The welcoming D class *Hotel Kytheria*
(☎ 33 321, ☎ 33 825), owned by helpful
Angelo from Australia, has very comfortable, tidy singles/doubles with bathroom for
13,000/17,000 dr. Considerable discounts
to the above prices apply out of high season.

Places to Stay – Mid-Range &
Top End
Filoxenia Apartments (☎ 33 100, fax 33
610) each have a bedroom, lounge and
kitchen. However, the interior layout is a little claustrophobic. An attached pool makes
up for this. Rates for doubles/quads are
22,000/26,000 dr. Two-bedroom units for
four/six people are 26,000 dr. Turn left then
right from the quay.

The stunning *Hotel Romantica* (☎ 33
834, fax 33 915) provides sparkling self-
contained apartments for four (32,000 dr)
and double air-conditioned studios with TV
and phone for 25,000 dr. There is also a
swimming pool. Turn right from the quay
and look for the sign after 600m.

Another good place is *Venardos Hotel*
(☎ 34 205, fax 33 850, email venardos@
mail.otenet.gr), where airy singles/doubles

are 18,000/22,000 dr. Australians get a special welcome and the hotel is open all year.

The C class *Pelagia Aphrodite Hotel*
(☎ 33 926, fax 34 242, email pelagia@
citenet.gr) is the large whitewashed building about 800m from the village (turn left
out of the ferry quay and follow the signs).
It is open year-round and has extremely
comfortable singles/doubles for 13,000/
15,000 dr rising to 18,000/22,000 dr in high
season. Triple rooms cost from 17,000 dr to
27,000 dr.

Kythira's sole A class hotel, *Hotel
Marou* (☎ 33 466, fax 33 497), with the island's only tennis court, a bar, snack bar and
laundry, is above the north-west end of the
village. Doubles are between 18,000 and
24,000 dr.

Places to Eat
The blue and white *Faros Taverna* close to
the quay serves good, economical Greek
staples. To the far right, *Ouzeri Mous-
takias*, next to the minimarket, offers food
ranging from *mezedes* to seafood. *Kaleris*,
in between the two, is a tasteful little eatery
with old photographs and painted wooden
signs on the wall. The speciality is roast
wild goat.

For breakfast *Sempreviva Patisserie*
close by serves wickedly delicious Greek
cakes and jugs of freshly brewed coffee.

Bar life revolves around *En Plo*, *Oionos*
and *Mouragio*, all neat little bars slotted in
between the eateries.

POTAMOS Ποταμός
• pop 680
Potamos, 10km from Agia Pelagia, is the island's commercial hub. On Sunday it attracts almost every islander to market.

The National Bank of Greece is on the
central square. The post office and police
are south of the central square, and the OTE
is 150m north.

The only domatia are those of *Panayiotis
Alevizopoulos* (☎ 33 245). His neat doubles
are 13,000 dr. The one hotel is *Hotel
Porfyra* (☎ 33 329), where self-contained
units surround an internal courtyard and
doubles/triples are 11,500/14,000 dr.

Taverna Panaretos (☎ *34 290*) on the central square provides well prepared international and Greek dishes.

MYLOPOTAMOS Μυλοπόταμος
• pop 90

Mylopotamos is an alluring, verdant village 6km south-west of Potamos. Its central square is flanked by a much-photographed church and *kafeneio*. Stroll to the **Neraïda** (water nymph) waterfall. From the square, continue along the road and take the right fork. After 100m, a path on the right leads to the waterfall. It's magical, with luxuriant greenery and mature, shady trees.

To reach the abandoned **kastro** of Mylopotamos, take the left fork after the church and follow the sign for Kato Hora (lower village). The road leads to the centre of Kato Hora, from where a portal with the insignia of St Mark leads into the spooky kastro, with derelict houses and well preserved little churches (locked).

The **Cave of Agia Sofia** was first explored by the famous speleologists Ioannis and Anna Patrohilos, who also discovered the Diros Cave in the Peloponnese. In the 12th century, the cave was converted into a chapel and dedicated to Agia Sophia. Legend says she visited the cave with her daughters Pistis, Elpis and Haris (Faith, Hope and Charity).

The cave is reached by a precipitous 2km road or a steep path from Mylopotamos. Irregular opening times are pinned on a signpost to the cave beyond Mylopotamos' square. Admission is 500 dr and includes a guided tour.

HORA Χώρα
• pop 550

Hora (or Kythira), the pretty capital, with white, blue-shuttered houses, perches on a long, slender ridge 2km uphill from Kapsali.

The central square, planted with hibiscus, bougainvillea and palms, is Plateia Dimitriou Staï. The main street runs south of it. The post office is on the left, at its southern end. For the OTE, climb the steps by the side of Kythira Travel on the central square.

The National Bank of Greece is on the central square. Next to it is the Agricultural Bank which sports an ATM. The police station (☎ 31 206) is near the kastro.

Hora has no tourist office or tourist police but English-speaking Panayiotis Defterevos offers information to tourists at his Moto Rent office (☎ 31 600) on Kapsali's waterfront (see Getting Around earlier in this chapter).

Things to See
Kastro Hora's Venetian kastro is at the southern end of town. If you walk to its southern extremity, passing the Church of Panagia, you will come to a sheer cliff. From here there is a stunning view of Kapsali and on a good day of Antikythira.

Archaeological Museum The archaeological museum is situated north of the central square. The core of the collection was donated by a local high school teacher.

On display are Minoan artefacts, dating from the 7th to 5th centuries BC, found in the area of Paliopoli. These include amphoras, alabaster sculptures and ceramics. There's a beautiful carved marble lion dating from c550 BC when Kythira was under Spartan control. In 1660 the Venetians placed the lion at the entrance to Hora's kastro. In 1941, when the island was under German occupation, the lion disappeared, only to resurface at an auction in Berlin, where it was recognised by a Kytherian. It was brought back to Kythira in 1960.

There are also coins dating from pre-Christian, Byzantine, Venetian and Ionian State periods, and gravestones of British soldiers and their infants who died on the island in the 19th century.

The museum is open 8.45 am to 3 pm Tuesday to Saturday and 8.30 am to 2.30 pm Sunday. Admission is free.

Places to Stay
Hora's cheapest accommodation is *Georgiou Psi Rooms* (☎ *31 070*), where doubles are 8000 dr with shared bathroom. Walk south along the main street and look for the sign on the left.

Castello Rooms (☎/fax 31 069) are spacious, and have kitchens, bathrooms and terraces with breathtaking views. Rates are 9000 dr a double. There's a sign at the southern end of the main street. *Papadonicos Rooms* (☎ 31 129), a bit farther south, has pleasant double studios for 9000 dr.

Belvedere Apartments (☎/fax 31 761), just beyond the turn-off for Kapsali, features attractive apartments for 12,000 dr. It has terrific views of Kapsali.

The B class *Hotel Margarita* (☎ 31 711, fax 31 325) on the main street is a renovated 19th century mansion. Rates are 15,200/19,300 dr for singles/doubles with breakfast for air-conditioned rooms with both TV and telephone.

Places to Eat

There are not a lot of restaurant choices in Hora, but 100m south of the square is *Zorba's Taverna* (Spyridonos Staï 34) which offers tasty grilled food. On the square itself, *La Frianderie* on Plateia Staï is a hip place serving savoury and sweet crepes and snacks. Also on the square, there's *Vengera Cafe*, which serves evening snacks throughout summer.

KAPSALI Καψάλι
• pop 70

Kapsali is a picturesque village located down a winding road from Hora. It looks particularly captivating from Hora's castle, with its twin sandy bays and curving waterfront. Restaurants and cafes line the beach, and safe sheltered swimming in aquamarine waters is Kapsali's trademark.

Not surprisingly, it's a very popular place so accommodation can be scarce unless you book well beforehand. It can also get pretty crowded so if you like your beach in solitude look elsewhere.

Offshore you can see the stark rock island known as the **Avgo** (Egg) rearing above the water.

It is here that Kytherians claim Aphrodite sprang from the sea.

Canoes, pedal boats, surfboards and waterskis can all be hired from Panagiotis Defterevos at Moto Rent, on the waterfront.

The Birth of Venus

Mythology suggests that it is in Kythira that Aphrodite (Venus) was born. She is supposed to have risen from the sea where the god Zeus had thrown his father Cronos's sex organ after castrating him. The goddess of love then re-emerged near Paphos in Cyprus, so both islands haggle over her birthplace.

Worship of Aphrodite was probably introduced by the Phoenicians. The first temple dedicated to her was on Kythira. According to some ancient writers, the name Kythira comes from the verb which means 'I hide erotic love'.

Kapsali's port police (☎ 31 222) are next door.

Places to Stay

Kythira's camp site, *Camping Kapsali* (☎ 31 580), is pine-shaded and open in summer only. The site is 400m from Kapsali's quay and signposted from the inland road to Hora.

Irene Megaloudi's Rooms (☎ 31 340) has clean doubles/triples with bathroom for 10,000/12,000 dr. At *Poulmendis Rooms* (☎ 31 451) clean, pleasant rooms with bathroom cost 12,000/15,000 dr. Both are on the waterfront.

More expensive are the *Rigas Apartments* (☎ 31 365, fax 31 265). The accommodation – in a cluster of white terraced buildings set back from the waterfront – ranges from beautifully furnished double studios for 22,000 dr to two-bedroom maisonettes for 38,000 dr. The owners, Apostolis and Maria Rigas, welcome each new guest like a long lost friend and are full of helpful advice.

Kapsali's smartest hotel is *Raikos* (☎ 31 629, fax 31 801) perched up on the hill between Hora and Kapsali. Double/triple rooms go for 24,000/33,000 dr rising to 29,000/39,000 dr in the high season.

Places to Eat

There are three restaurants on the seafront road of Kytherias Afroditis.

The first, heading towards Hora, is *Artena*, noticeable for its striking blue chairs and tables. In operation since 1935, it has a wide range of ready-made and to-order fish dishes at mid-range prices.

Venetsianiko farther along serves a wide range of Greek dishes, pasta and fish, and the lively *Ydragogio* at the far end by the rocks specialises in fish and mezedes.

Cengo at the western end of the beach is a good place for a drink or coffee – or just a game of backgammon.

AROUND KYTHIRA

If you have transport, a tour round the island is rewarding. The monasteries of **Agia Moni** and **Agia Elesa** are mountain refuges with superb views. **Moni Myrtidion** is a beautiful monastery surrounded by trees.

From Hora, drive north-east to the picturesque village of **Avlemonas** via **Paleopoli** with its wide, pebbled beach. It was here that archaeologists spent years searching for evidence of a temple at Aphrodite's birthplace.

Beachcombers should seek out **Kaladi Beach**, near Paleopoli. It is reached by a rough track and then steep steps down to the beach itself. Another good beach is **Fyri Ammos**, closer to Hora.

Just north of the village of Kato Livadi make a detour to see the remarkable and seemingly out of place British-made **Katouni Bridge**, a legacy of Kythira's time as part of the British protectorate in the 19th century. One island story has it that the bridge was built on the orders of the British Governor at the time, John McPhail, so that he could cross the valley to see his lover.

In **Kato Livadi**, you will find Kythira's Byzantine Museum, housed in the post-Byzantine church of the Analipsi (Ascension). The collection includes paintings and frescoes from abandoned churches on the island. There are also fragments of early Christian floor mosaics from the ruined church of Agios Ioannis at Potamos. The museum (☎ 31 731) is open from Tuesday to Saturday.

Also in Kato Livadi, the Roussos Ceramics factory produces and sells hand-painted ceramics with traditional Kytherian designs. Just follow the road from Ano Livadi to Kalamos; the factory is signposted on the right after about 1km.

While heading out across the island, stop in at *Estiatorion Pierros (☎ 31 014)* in **Ano Livadi**. Here you will find no-nonsense traditional Greek staples in a great little roadside establishment. *Karydies Taverna (☎ 33 664)* in **Logothetianika**, near Potamos, attracts a good crowd to its weekend music evenings. Bookings are recommended.

When the mist is up and sweeping across the island stop by the little *Ouzeri-Kafeneio Grigoraki (☎ 33 971)* on the main road in **Aroniadika** and partake of an ouzo and mezedes. It can get quite spooky in this little village around which ghosts are reported to roam on dark and windy winter's evenings. Also in Aroniadika (at the crossroads with the roads heading north) is Prathrio Melioy (☎ 34 370), the honey producers' cooperative, where you can buy what is reputedly the best honey in Greece.

In the far north of the island the village of **Karavas** is verdant and very attractive and close to both Agia Pelagia and the reasonable beach at **Platia Ammos**.

Kytherian Honey

Arguably the best in Greece, Kytherian honey is sweet and potent. Apiarists on the island keep their bees in the area between Agia Moni, Mitata and Paliopoli, close to vast expanses of wild thyme and other herbs. It is the exposure to these herbs, and the traditional way it is made, that makes Kytherian honey so special.

A bee needs to visit around 250 flowers to collect a full load of 0.03g of pollen. A full day's work provides the hive with 0.4g of pollen and a bee has to work for over 10 days to produce 1g of honey.

The Kytherian Honey Cooperative was established in 1996, with the aim of maintaining the distinctive quality of Kytherian honey and supporting local apiarists so that they can continue to produce organic thyme honey in the traditional way.

Antikythira

☎ 0735 • pop 70

In antiquity Antikythira was called Aiglia. Archaeologists have unearthed artefacts from the 4th century BC, including coins that were minted there.

The wreck of a 1st century BC Roman ship was discovered by sponge divers near the island in 1900. It contained a number of valuable bronze and marble statues which are now on display in the National Museum in Athens. Also found on the ship was what is commonly believed to be the world's first astronomical computer, the Antikythira Mechanism.

Antikythira was captured by the Venetians in 1207. The Venetians fortified the island by constructing a small fort at Palaiokastro, but their presence over the years was inconsistent.

For a long time the island, strategically positioned on the trade route to the Aegean, was a perfect lair for pirates.

The present inhabitants are mainly descendants of Cretan colonists who settled there from 1792.

During the British Protectorate the island was used as a place of exile for distinguished residents of the Ionian islands.

Antikythira has only one major settlement, **Potamos** (there are several other mini-hamlets), one doctor (☎ 33 213), one police officer (☎ 33 767), one teacher (with five pupils), one metered telephone and a monastery. It has no post office or bank. The only accommodation for tourists is 10 basic *rooms* in two purpose-built blocks, open in summer only. Potamos has a *kafeneio* and *taverna*. It is not popular with

The Antikythira Mechanism

The Antikythira Mechanism, now housed in the National Archaeology Museum in Athens, is possibly the world's oldest computer. According to an inscription on the device, it was made on Rhodes in 82 BC. It was retrieved in 1900 from the wreck of a ship believed to have gone down while transporting the mechanism to Rome.

The astronomical computer had bronze dials inscribed with the days of the month and the signs of the zodiac. Various pointers indicated the phases of the moon and the position of the planets at any given time, and it was operated by a clockwork mechanism involving bronze cog wheels connected to a large four-spoke wheel and a driving gear and shaft. A moveable ring allowed for leap year adjustments.

The timekeeping mechanism on the 'computer' was stopped when the ship went down – so archaeologists have been able to precisely date the shipwreck to 5 May 59 BC. It demonstrates the advanced level of scientific knowledge that the Greeks had reached.

yachties as the only harbour is unsafe if the weather is unsettled – as it often is.

GETTING THERE & AWAY

The F/B *Maria* calls at least twice weekly in the early hours on the way to Crete, returning the same day to Kythira and Gythio. If the sea is choppy, the ferry does not stop, so this is not an island for tourists on a tight schedule. Check conditions in Piraeus if you intend to come direct, or with Megalokonomou Shipping Agency in Kythira's Agia Pelagia.

Language

The Greek language is probably the oldest European language, with an oral tradition of 4000 years and a written tradition of approximately 3000 years. Its evolution over the four millennia was characterised by its strength during the golden age of Athens and the Democracy (mid-5th century BC); its use as a lingua franca throughout the Middle Eastern world, spread by Alexander the Great and his successors as far as India during the Hellenistic period (330 BC to 100 AD); its adaptation as the language of the new religion, Christianity; its use as the official language of the Eastern Roman Empire; and its eventual proclamation as the language of the Byzantine Empire (380-1453).

Greek maintained its status and prestige during the rise of the European Renaissance and was employed as the linguistic perspective for all contemporary sciences and terminologies during the period of Enlightenment. Today, Greek constitutes a large part of the vocabulary of any Indo-European language, and much of the lexicon of any scientific repertoire.

The modern Greek language is a southern Greek dialect which is now used by most Greek speakers both in Greece and abroad. It is the result of an intralinguistic influence and synthesis of the ancient vocabulary combined with words from Greek regional dialects, namely Cretan, Cypriot and Macedonian.

Those wishing to delve a little deeper into the language should get a copy of Lonely Planet's *Greek phrasebook*.

Pronunciation

All Greek words of two or more syllables have an acute accent which indicates where the stress falls. For instance, άγαλμα (statue) is pronounced *aghalma*, and αγάπη (love) is pronounced *aghapi*. In the following transliterations, bold lettering indicates where stress falls. Note also that **dh** is pronounced as 'th' in 'then'; **gh** is a softer, slightly guttural version of 'g'.

Greetings & Civilities

Hello.	
*ya**sas***	Γειά σας.
*ya**su*** (informal)	Γειά σου.
Goodbye.	
*an**dio***	Αντίο.
Good morning.	
*kali**mera***	Καλημέρα.
Good afternoon.	
*he**re**te*	Χαίρετε.
Good evening.	
*kalis**pera***	Καλησπέρα.
Good night.	
*kali**nihta***	Καληνύχτα.
Please.	
*paraka**lo***	Παρακαλώ.
Thank you.	
*efharis**to***	Ευχαριστώ.
Yes.	
ne	Ναι.
No.	
ohi	Οχι.
Sorry. (excuse me, forgive me)	
*sigh**nomi***	Συγγνώμη.
How are you?	
*ti **kanete***?	Τι κάνετε;
*ti **kanis***? (informal)	Τι κάνεις;
I'm well, thanks.	
*kala efharis**to***	Καλά ευχαριστώ.

Essentials

Do you speak English?	
milate anglika?	Μιλάτε Αγγλικά;
I understand.	
*kata**laveno***	Καταλαβαίνω.
I don't understand.	
*dhen kata**laveno***	Δεν καταλαβαίνω.
Where is ...?	
pou ine ...?	Πού είναι ...;
How much?	
*po**so kani***?	Πόσο κάνει;
When?	
pote?	Πότε;

The Greek Alphabet & Pronunciation

Greek	Pronunciation Guide		Example		
Α α	a	as in 'father'	αγάπη	*agha*pi	love
Β β	v	as in 'vine'	βήμα	*vi*ma	step
Γ γ	gh	like a rough 'g'	γάτα	*gha*ta	cat
	y	as in 'yes'	για	*ya*	for
Δ δ	dh	as in 'there'	δέμα	*dhe*ma	parcel
Ε ε	e	as in 'egg'	ένας	*e*nas	one (m)
Ζ ζ	z	as in 'zoo'	ζώο	*zoo*	animal
Η η	i	as in 'feet'	ήταν	*it*an	was
Θ θ	th	as in 'throw'	θέμα	*the*ma	theme
Ι ι	i	as in 'feet'	ίδιος	*i*dhyos	same
Κ κ	k	as in 'kite'	καλά	*ka*la	well
Λ λ	l	as in 'leg'	λάθος	*la*thos	mistake
Μ μ	m	as in 'man'	μαμά	*ma*ma	mother
Ν ν	n	as in 'net'	νερό	*ne*ro	water
Ξ ξ	x	as in 'ox'	ξύδι	*ksi*dhi	vinegar
Ο ο	o	as in 'hot'	όλα	*o*la	all
Π π	p	as in 'pup'	πάω	*pa*o	I go
Ρ ρ	r	as in 'road'	ρέμα	*re*ma	stream
		a slightly trilled *r*	ρόδα	*ro*dha	tyre
Σ σ, ς	s	as in 'sand'	σημάδι	*sima*dhi	mark
Τ τ	t	as in 'tap'	τόπι	*to*pi	ball
Υ υ	i	as in 'feet'	ύστερα	*is*tera	after
Φ φ	f	as in 'find'	φύλλο	*fi*lo	leaf
Χ χ	h	as the *ch* in Scottish *loch*, or	χάνω	*ha*no	I lose
		like a rough *h*	χέρι	*he*ri	hand
Ψ ψ	ps	as in 'lapse'	ψωμί	*pso*mi	bread
Ω ω	o	as in 'hot'	ώρα	*o*ra	time

Combinations of Letters

The combinations of letters shown here are pronounced as follows:

Greek	Pronunciation Guide		Example		
ει	i	as in 'feet'	είδα	*i*dha	I saw
οι	i	as in 'feet'	οικόπεδο	*iko*pedho	land
αι	e	as in 'bet'	αίμα	*e*ma	blood
ου	u	as in 'mood'	πού	*pou*	who/what
μπ	b	as in 'beer'	μπάλα	*ba*la	ball
	mb	as in 'amber'	κάμπος	*kam*bos	forest
ντ	d	as in 'dot'	ντουλάπα	*doula*pa	wardrobe
	nd	as in 'bend'	πέντε	*pen*de	five
γκ	g	as in 'God'	γκάζι	*ga*zi	gas
γγ	ng	as in 'angle'	αγγελία	*angeli*a	classified
γξ	ks	as in 'minks'	σφιγξ	*sfinks*	sphynx
τζ	dz	as in 'hands'	τζάκι	*dza*ki	fireplace

The pairs of vowels shown above are pronounced separately if the first has an acute accent, or the second a dieresis, as in the examples below:

γαϊδουράκι	*gaidhoura*ki	little donkey
Κάιρο	*ka*iro	Cairo

Some Greek consonant sounds have no English equivalent. The υ of the groups αυ, ευ and ηυ is generally pronounced 'v'. The Greek question mark is represented with the English equivalent of a semicolon ';'.

Small Talk

What's your name?
pos sas lene?   Πώς σας λένε;
My name is ...
me lene ...   Με λένε ...
Where are you from?
apo pou iste?   Από πού είστε;

I'm from ...
ime apo ...   Είμαι από ...
America
tin ameriki   την Αμερική
Australia
tin afstralia   την Αυστραλία
England
tin anglia   την Αγγλία
Ireland
tin irlandhia   την Ιρλανδία
New Zealand
ti nea zilandhia   τη Νέα Ζηλανδία
Scotland
ti skotia   τη Σκωτία

How old are you?
poson hronon   Πόσων χρονών
iste?   είστε;
I'm ... years old.
ime ... hronon   Είμαι ... χρονών.

Getting Around

What time does
the ... leave/arrive?
ti ora fevyi/   Τι ώρα φεύγει/
ftani to ...?   φτάνει το ...;

plane	*aeroplano*	αεροπλάνο
boat	*karavi*	καράβι
bus	*astiko*	αστικό

I'd like ...
tha ithela ...   Θα ήθελα ...
a return ticket
isitirio me   εισιτήριο με
epistrofi   επιστροφή
two tickets
dhio isitiria   δυο εισιτήρια
a student's fare
fititiko isitirio   φοιτητικό εισιτήριο
first class
proti thesi   πρώτη θέση

Signs

ΕΙΣΟΔΟΣ	ENTRY
ΕΞΟΔΟΣ	EXIT
ΩΘΗΣΑΤΕ	PUSH
ΣΥΡΑΤΕ	PULL
ΓΥΝΑΙΚΩΝ	WOMEN (toilets)
ΑΝΔΡΩΝ	MEN (toilets)
ΝΟΣΟΚΟΜΕΙΟ	HOSPITAL
ΑΣΤΥΝΟΜΙΑ	POLICE
ΑΠΑΓΟΡΕΥΕΤΑΙ	PROHIBITED
ΕΙΣΙΤΗΡΙΑ	TICKETS

economy
touristiki thesi   τουριστική θέση

timetable
dhromologio   δρομολόγιο
taxi
taxi   ταξί

Where can I hire a car?
pou boro na nikyaso ena aftokinito?
Πού μπορώ να νοικιάσω ένα
αυτοκίνητο;

Directions

How do I get to ...?
pos tha pao sto/   Πώς θα πάω στο/
sti ...?   στη ...;
Where is ...?
pou ine ...?   Πού είναι...;
Is it near?
ine konda?   Είναι κοντά;
Is it far?
ine makria?   Είναι μακριά;

straight ahead	*efthia*	ευθεία
left	*aristera*	αριστερά
right	*dexia*	δεξιά
behind	*piso*	πίσω
far	*makria*	μακριά
near	*konda*	κοντά
opposite	*apenandi*	απέναντι

Can you show me on the map?
borite na mou to dhixete sto harti?
Μπορείτε να μου το δείξετε
στο χάρτη;

Around Town

I'm looking for (the) ...
psahno ya ...
Ψάχνω για ...

bank	*trapeza*	τράπεζα
beach	*paralia*	παραλία
castle	*kastro*	κάστρο
church	*ekklisia*	εκκλησία
... embassy	*tin ... presvia*	την ... προσβεία
market	*aghora*	αγορά
museum	*musio*	μουσείο
police	*astynomia*	αστυνομία
post office	*tahydhromio*	ταχυδρομείο
ruins	*arhea*	αρχαία

I want to exchange some money.
thelo na exaryiroso lefta
Θέλω να εξαργυρώσω λεφτά.

Accommodation

Where is ...?
pou ine ...? Πού είναι ...;
I'd like ...
thelo ena ... Θέλω ένα ...

a cheap hotel
ftino xenodohio φτηνό ξενοδοχείο
a clean room
katharo dho-matio καθαρό δωμάτιο
a good hotel
kalo xenodohio καλό ξενοδοχείο
a camp site
kamping κάμπιγκ

single	*mono*	μονό
double	*dhiplo*	διπλό
room	*dhomatio*	δωμάτιο
with bathroom	*me banio*	με μπάνιο
key	*klidhi*	κλειδί

How much is it ...?
poso kani ...? Πόσο κάνει ...;
per night
ti vradhya τη βραδυά
for ... nights
ya ... vradhyez για ... βραδυές

Emergencies

Help!
voithya! Βοήθεια!
Police!
astynomia! Αστυνομία!
There's been an accident.
eyine atihima Εγινε ατύχημα.
Call a doctor!
fonaxte ena yatro! Φωνάξτε ένα ιατρό!
Call an ambulance!
tilefoniste ya asthenoforo! Τηλεφωνήστε για ασθενοφόρο!
I'm ill.
ime arostos (m) Είμαι άρρωστος
ime arosti (f) Είμαι άρρωστη
I'm lost.
eho hathi Εχω χαθεί
Thief!
klefti! Κλέφτη!
Go away!
fiye! Φύγε!
I've been raped.
me viase kapyos Με βίασε κάποιος.
I've been robbed.
meklepse kapyos Μ'έκλεψε κάποιος.
Where are the toilets?
pou ine i toualetez? Πού είναι οι τουαλέτες;

Is breakfast included?
symberilamvani ke pro-ino? Συμπεριλαμβάνει και πρωϊνό;
May I see it?
boro na to dho? Μπορώ να το δω;
Where is the bathroom?
pou ine tobanio? Πού είναι το μπάνιο;
It's expensive.
ine akrivo Είναι ακριβό.
I'm leaving today.
fevgho simera Φεύγω σήμερα.

Food

breakfast	*pro-ino*	πρωϊνό
lunch	*mesimvrino*	μεσημβρινό
dinner	*vradhyno*	βραδυνό
beef	*vodhino*	βοδινό
bread	*psomi*	ψωμί
beer	*byra*	μπύρα
cheese	*tyri*	τυρί
chicken	*kotopoulo*	κοτόπουλο
Greek coffee	*ellinikos kafes*	ελληνικός καφές
iced coffee	*frappe*	φραππέ
lamb	*arni*	αρνί
milk	*ghala*	γάλα
mineral	*metalliko*	μεταλλικό
water	*nero*	νερό
tea	*tsai*	τσάι
wine	*krasi*	κρασί

I'm a vegetarian.
ime hortofaghos   Είμαι χορτοφάγος.

Shopping

How much is it?
poso kani?
Πόσο κάνει;
I'm just looking.
aplos kitazo
Απλώς κοιτάζω.
I'd like to buy ...
thelo n'aghoraso ...
Θέλω ν´αγοράσω ...
Do you accept credit cards?
pernete pistotikez kartez?
Παίρνετε πιστωτικές κάρτες;
Could you lower the price?
borite na mou kanete mya kaliteri timi?
Μπορείτε να μου κάνετε μια καλύτερη τιμή;

Time & Dates

What time is it?
ti ora ine?   Τι ώρα είναι;

It's ...	*ine ...*	είναι ...
1 o'clock	*mia i ora*	μία η ώρα
2 o'clock	*dhio i ora*	δύο η ώρα
7.30	*efta ke misi*	εφτά και μισή
am	*to pro-i*	το πρωί
pm	*to apoyevma*	το απόγευμα
today	*simera*	σήμερα

tonight	*apopse*	απόψε
now	*tora*	τώρα
yesterday	*hthes*	χθες
tomorrow	*avrio*	αύριο

Sunday	*kyriaki*	Κυριακή
Monday	*dheftera*	Δευτέρα
Tuesday	*triti*	Τρίτη
Wednesday	*tetarti*	Τετάρτη
Thursday	*pempti*	Πέμπτη
Friday	*paraskevi*	Παρασκευή
Saturday	*savato*	Σάββατο

January	*ianouarios*	Ιανουάριος
February	*fevrouarios*	Φεβρουάριος
March	*martios*	Μάρτιος
April	*aprilios*	Απρίλιος
May	*maïos*	Μάιος
June	*iounios*	Ιούνιος
July	*ioulios*	Ιούλιος
August	*avghoustos*	Αύγουστος
September	*septemvrios*	Σεπτέμβριος
October	*oktovrios*	Οκτώβριος
November	*noemvrios*	Νοέμβριος
December	*dhekemvrios*	Δεκέμβριος

Health

I need a doctor.
hriazome yatro   Χρειάζομαι ιατρό.
Can you take me to hospital?
borite na me pate sto nosokomio?   Μπορείτε να με πάτε στο νοσοκομείο;
I want something for ...
thelo kati ya ...   Θέλω κάτι για ...
diarrhoea
dhiaria   διάρροια
insect bites
tsimbimata apo endoma   τσιμπήματα από έντομα
travel sickness
naftia taxidhiou   ναυτία ταξιδιού

aspirin
aspirini   ασπιρίνη
condoms
profylaktika (kapotez)   προφυλακτικά (καπότες)
contact lenses
faki epafis   φακοί επαφής
medical insurance
yatriki asfalya   ιατρική ασφάλεια

Numbers

0	*midhen*	μηδέν	20	*ikosi*	είκοσι
1	*enas*	ένας (m)	30	*trianda*	τριάντα
	mia	μία (f)	40	*saranda*	σαράντα
	ena	ένα (n)	50	*peninda*	πενήντα
2	*dhio*	δύο	60	*exinda*	εξήντα
3	*tris*	τρεις (m & f)	70	*evdhominda*	εβδομήντα
	tria	τρία (n)	80	*oghdhonda*	ογδόντα
4	*teseris*	τέσσερεις (m & f)	90	*eneninda*	ενενήντα
	tesera	τέσσερα (n)	100	*ekato*	εκατό
5	*pende*	πέντε	1000	*hilii*	χίλιοι (m)
6	*exi*	έξη		*hiliez*	χίλιες (f)
7	*epta*	επτά		*hilia*	χίλια (n)
8	*ohto*	οχτώ			
9	*enea*	εννέα	one million		
10	*dheka*	δέκα	*ena ekatomyrio*	ένα εκατομμύριο	

Glossary

Achaean civilisation – see *Mycenaean civilisation*

acropolis – highest point of an ancient city

agia (f), agios (m) – saint

amphora – large two-handled vase in which wine or oil was kept

ANEK – Anonymi Naftiliaki Eteria Kritis; main shipping line to Crete

Archaic period – also known as the Middle Age; period (800-480 BC) in which the *city-states* emerged from the 'dark age' and traded their way to wealth and power; the city-states were unified by a Greek alphabet and common cultural pursuits, engendering a sense of national identity

arekia – short song originating from Lixouri on Kefallonia

Asia Minor – the Aegean littoral of Turkey centred around İzmir but also including İstanbul; formerly populated by Greeks

aulos – wind instrument

ballos – popular dance in the Ionians

barbitos – similar to a violin cello

basilica – early Christian church

bouzouki – stringed lute-like instrument associated with rembetika music

bouzoukia – 'bouzoukis'; used to mean any nightclub where the bouzouki is played and low-grade blues songs are sung

Byzantine Empire – characterised by the merging of Hellenistic culture and Christianity and named after Byzantium, which became the capital of the Roman Empire in 324 AD; when the Roman Empire was formally divided in 395 AD, Rome went into decline and the eastern capital, renamed Constantinople after Emperor Constantine I, flourished; the Byzantine Empire dissolved after the 1453 fall of Constantinople

caïque – small, sturdy fishing boat often used to carry passengers

capital – top of a column

city-states – states comprising a sovereign city and its dependencies; the city-states of Athens and Sparta were famous rivals

classical Greece – period in which the city-states reached the height of their wealth and power after the defeat of the Persians in the 5th century BC; ended with the decline of the city-states as a result of the Peloponnesian Wars, and the expansionist aspirations of Philip II, King of Macedon (ruled 359-336 BC), and his son, Alexander the Great (ruled 336-323 BC)

Corinthian – order of Greek architecture recognisable by columns with bell-shaped *capitals* with sculpted elaborate ornaments based on acanthus leaves

Cycladic civilisation – civilisation (3000-1100 BC) which emerged following the settlement of Phoenician colonists on the Cycladic islands

dark age – period (1200-800 BC) in which Greece was under *Dorian* rule

delfini – dolphin; the common name for hydrofoil

Dimotiki – Demotic Greek language; the official spoken language of Greece

divaratikos – popular dance in the Ionians

domatio (s), domatia (pl) – room; a cheap accommodation option available in most tourist areas

Dorians – Hellenic warriors who invaded Greece around 1200 BC, demolishing the city-states and destroying the Mycenaean civilisation; heralded Greece's 'dark age', when the artistic and cultural advancements of the Mycenaeans and Minoans were abandoned; the Dorians later developed into land-holding aristocrats which encouraged the resurgence of independent city-states led by wealthy aristocrats

Doric – order of Greek architecture characterised by a column which has no base, a fluted shaft and a relatively plain capital, when compared with the flourishes evident on *Ionic* and *Corinthian* capitals

ELPA – Elliniki Leshi Periigiseon & Aftokinitou; the Greek motoring and touring club

ELTA – Ellinika Tahydromia; Greek post office

enosis – union

EOT – Ellinikos Organismos Tourismou; national tourism organisation which has offices in most major towns

estiatorio – restaurant serving ready-made food as well as a la carte dishes

ET – Elliniki Tileorasi; state TV company

felucca – old-fashioned sailing boat

Filiki Eteria – friendly society; a group of Greeks in exile; formed during Ottoman rule to organise an uprising against the Turks

frappé – iced coffee

frontistiria – intensive coaching colleges

galaktopoleio (s), galaktopoleia (pl) – a shop which sells dairy products

galiantra – an Italian dance

gelaterias – shops which sell Italian-style ice cream

Geometric period – period (1200-800 BC) characterised by pottery decorated with geometric designs; sometimes referred to as Greece's 'dark age'

girouzatos – popular dance in the Ionians

gymnasio – middle school

Hellas, Ellas or **Ellada** – the Greek name for Greece

Hellenistic period – prosperous, influential period of Greek civilisation ushered in by Alexander the Great's empire-building and lasting until the Roman sacking of Corinth in 146 BC

hora – main town (usually on an island)

iconostasis – altar screen embellished with icons

Ionic – order of Greek architecture characterised by a column with truncated flutes and capitals with ornaments resembling scrolls

kafeneio (s), kafeneia (pl) – traditionally a male-only coffee house where cards and backgammon are played

kafeteria – upmarket *kafeneio*, mainly for younger people

kalamatianos – dance originating in Kalamata in the Peloponnese

kalderimi – cobbled or flagstone paths

kamaki – slang term for foreign women travelling alone

kantades – songs descended from opera, often love songs but can also be comedies

kastro – walled-in town

Katharevousa – purist Greek language; very rarely used these days

kithara – stringed instrument

KKE – Kommounistiko Komma Elladas; Greek Communist Party

kroupeza – percussion instrument

KTEL – Kino Tamio Ispraxeon Leoforion; national bus cooperative; runs all the long-distance bus services

limenarheio – local port police

lykeio – high school or secondary school

magadio – similar to a harp

maistro – the strong north-westerly wind which blows up in the northern Ionian Sea

manfrena – Italian dance adapted by the Zakynthians

meltemi – north-easterly wind which blows throughout much of Greece during summer

mermingas – popular dance in the Ionians

meze (s), mezedes (pl) – appetiser

Middle Age – see *Archaic period*

Minoan civilisation – Bronze Age culture of Crete (3000-1100 BC) named after the mythical king Minos and characterised by pottery and metalwork of great beauty

moni – monastery or convent

Mycenaean civilisation – first great civilisation (1900-1100 BC) of the Greek mainland, characterised by powerful independent city-states ruled by kings; also known as the Achaean civilisation

nave – aisle of a church

Nea Dimokratia – New Democracy; conservative political party

necropolis – literally 'city of the dead'; ancient cemetery

OA – Olympiaki Aeroporia or Olympic Airways; Greece's national airline and major domestic air carrier

ohi – 'no'; what the Greeks said to Mussolini's ultimatum when he said surrender or be invaded; the Italians were subsequently repelled and the event is celebrated on 28 October

OSE – Organismos Sidirodromon Ellados; Greek railways organisation

OTE – Organismos Tilepikinonion Ellados, which is Greece's premier telecommunications carrier

ouranies – ceiling paintings

ouzeri (s), ouzeria (pl) – place which serves *ouzo* and light snacks

ouzo – a distilled spirit made from grapes and flavoured with aniseed

Panagia – Mother of God; name frequently used for churches

Pantokrator – a painting or a mosaic of Christ in the centre of the dome of a Byzantine church

pantopoleio – general store

PASOK – Panellinio Sosialistiko Komma; Greek Socialist Party

pediment – triangular section (often filled with sculpture) above the columns, found at the front and the back of a classical Greek temple

periptero (s), periptera (pl) – street kiosk

piktis – pipes (musical instruments)

plateia – square

Politiki Anixi – Political Spring; centrist political party

psarotaverna – *taverna* specialising in seafood

psistaria – restaurant serving grilled food

rembetika – blues songs commonly associated with the underworld of the 1920s

retsina – resinated white wine

sacristy – room attached to a church where sacred vessels etc are kept

stavrotos – lively paced dance

syrtos – ritual dance performed in ancient Greek temples

tagari – woven wool bags which hang from the shoulder by a rope

tahydromio – post offices

tambourioniakara – Greek percussion instrument

taverna – traditional restaurant which serves food and wine

tekedes – hashish dens

thema – administrative division of the Ionian islands

vaskopoules – popular Ionian dance

vaulted – having an arched roof, normally of brick or stone

volta – promenade; evening stroll

yiaryitos – variation on the Cretan crane dance

zaharoplasteio (s), zaharoplasteia (pl) – patisserie; shop which sells cakes, chocolates, sweets and, sometimes, alcoholic drinks

LONELY PLANET

Phrasebooks

onely Planet phrasebooks are packed with essential words and phrases to help travellers communicate with the locals. With colour tabs for quick reference, an extensive vocabulary and use of script, these handy pocket-sized language guides cover day-to-day travel situations.

- handy pocket-sized books
- easy to understand Pronunciation chapter
- clear & comprehensive Grammar chapter
- romanisation alongside script to allow ease of pronunciation
- script throughout so users can point to phrases for every situation
- full of cultural information and tips for the traveller

'... vital for a real DIY spirit and attitude in language learning'
– *Backpacker*

'the phrasebooks have good cultural backgrounders and offer solid advice for challenging situations in remote locations'
– *San Francisco Examiner*

Arabic (Egyptian) • Arabic (Moroccan) • Australian *(Australian English, Aboriginal and Torres Strait languages)* • Baltic States *(Estonian, Latvian, Lithuanian)* • Bengali • Brazilian • British • Burmese • Cantonese • Central Asia (Uyghur, Uzbek, Kyrghiz, Kazak, Pashto, Tadjik • Central Europe *(Czech, French, German, Hungarian, Italian, Slovak)* • Eastern Europe *(Bulgarian, Czech, Hungarian, Polish, Romanian, Slovak)* • Ethiopian (Amharic) • Fijian • French • German • Greek • Hebrew • Hill Tribes • Hindi & Urdu • Indonesian • Italian • Japanese • Korean • Lao • Latin American Spanish • Malay • Mandarin • Mediterranean Europe *(Albanian, Croatian, Greek, Italian, Macedonian, Maltese, Serbian, Slovene)* • Mongolian • Nepali • Pidgin • Pilipino (Tagalog) • Quechua • Russian • Scandinavian Europe *(Danish, Finnish, Icelandic, Norwegian, Swedish)* • South-East Asia *(Burmese, Indonesian, Khmer, Lao, Malay, Tagalog Pilipino, Thai, Vietnamese)* • South Pacific Languages • Spanish (Castilian) *(also includes Catalan, Galician and Basque)* • Sri Lanka • Swahili • Thai • Tibetan • Turkish • Ukrainian • USA *(US English, Vernacular, Native American languages, Hawaiian)* • Vietnamese • Western Europe *(Basque, Catalan, Dutch, French, German, Greek, Irish, Italian, Portuguese, Scottish Gaelic, Spanish (Castilian), Welsh)*

Lonely Planet Journeys

Journeys is a unique collection of travel writing – published by the company that understands travel better than anyone else. It is a series for anyone who has ever experienced – or dreamed of – the magical moment when they encountered a strange culture or saw a place for the first time. They are tales to read while you're planning a trip, while you're on the road or while you're in an armchair in front of a fire.

These outstanding titles explore our planet through the eyes of a diverse group of international writers. JOURNEYS books catch the spirit of a place, illuminate a culture, recount a crazy adventure or introduce a fascinating way of life. They always entertain, and always enrich the experience of travel.

MALI BLUES
Traveling to an African Beat
Lieve Joris (translated by Sam Garrett)

Drought, rebel uprisings, ethnic conflict: these are the predominant images of West Africa. But as Lieve Joris travels in Senegal, Mauritania and Mali, she meets survivors, fascinating individuals charting new ways of living between tradition and modernity. With her remarkable gift for drawing out people's stories, Joris brilliantly captures the rhythms of a world that refuses to give in.

THE GATES OF DAMASCUS
Lieve Joris (translated by Sam Garrett)

This best-selling book is a beautifully drawn portrait of day-to-day life in modern Syria. Through her intimate contact with local people, Lieve Joris draws us into the fascinating world that lies behind the gates of Damascus. Hala's husband is a political prisoner, jailed for his opposition to the Assad regime; through the author's friendship with Hala we see how Syrian politics impacts on the lives of ordinary people.

THE OLIVE GROVE
Travels in Greece
Katherine Kizilos

Katherine Kizilos travels to fabled islands, troubled border zones and her family's village deep in the mountains. She vividly evokes breathtaking landscapes, generous people and passionate politics, capturing the complexities of a country she loves.

'beautifully captures the real tensions of Greece' – *Sunday Times*

KINGDOM OF THE FILM STARS
Journey into Jordan
Annie Caulfield

Kingdom of the Film Stars is a travel book and a love story. With honesty and humour, Annie Caulfield writes of travelling in Jordan and falling in love with a Bedouin with film-star looks.

She offers fascinating insights into the country – from the tent life of traditional women to the hustle of downtown Amman – and unpicks tight-woven western myths about the Arab world.

Lonely Planet Online

Whether you've just begun planning your next trip, or you're chasing down specific info on currency regulations or visa requirements, check out Lonely Planet Online for up-to-the-minute travel information.

As well as miniguides to more than 250 destinations, you'll find maps, photos, travel news, health and visa updates, travel advisories and discussion of the ecological and political issues you need to be aware of as you travel. You'll also find timely upgrades to popular guidebooks that you can print out and stick in the back of your book.

There's an online travellers' forum (The Thorn Tree) where you can share your experience of life on the road, meet travel companions and ask other travellers for their recommendations and advice.

There's also a complete and up-to-date list of all Lonely Planet travel products including travel guides, diving and snorkeling guides, phrasebooks, atlases, travel literature and videos, and a simple online ordering facility if you can't find the book you want elsewhere.

Lonely Planet Diving & Snorkeling Guides

Beautifully illustrated with full-colour photos throughout, Lonely Planet's Pisces books explore the world's best diving and snorkeling areas and prepare divers for what to expect when they get there, both topside and underwater.

Dive sites are described in detail with specifics on depths, visibility, level of difficulty, special conditions, underwater photography tips and common and unusual marine life present. You'll also find practical logistical information and coverage on topside activities and attractions, sections on diving health and safety, plus listings for diving services, live-aboards, dive resorts and tourist offices.

Lonely Planet Travel Atlases

onely Planet has long been famous for the number and quality of its guidebook maps. Now we've gone one step further and produced a handy companion series: Lonely Planet travel atlases – maps of a country produced in book form.

Unlike other maps, which look good but lead travellers astray, our travel atlases have been researched on the road by Lonely Planet's experienced team of writers. All details are carefully checked to ensure the atlas corresponds with the equivalent Lonely Planet guidebook.

- full-colour throughout
- maps researched and checked by Lonely Planet authors
- place names correspond with Lonely Planet guidebooks
- no confusing spelling differences
- legend and travelling information in English, French, German, Japanese and Spanish
- size: 230 x 160 mm

Available now: Chile & Easter Island • Egypt • India & Bangladesh • Israel & the Palestinian Territories • Jordan, Syria & Lebanon • Kenya • Laos • Portugal • South Africa, Lesotho & Swaziland • Thailand • Turkey • Vietnam • Zimbabwe, Botswana & Namibia

---

Lonely Planet TV Series & Videos

onely Planet travel guides have been brought to life on television screens around the world. Like our guides, the programs are based on the joy of independent travel and look honestly at some of the most exciting, picturesque and frustrating places in the world. Each show is presented by one of three travellers from Australia, England or the USA and combines an innovative mixture of video, Super-8 film, atmospheric soundscapes and original music.

Videos of each episode – containing additional footage not shown on television – are available from good book and video shops, but the availability of individual videos varies with regional screening schedules.

Video destinations include: Alaska • American Rockies • Argentina • Australia – The South-East • Baja California & the Copper Canyon • Brazil • Central Asia • Chile & Easter Island • Corsica, Sicily & Sardinia – The Mediterranean Islands • East Africa (Tanzania & Zanzibar) • Cuba • Ecuador & the Galapagos Islands • Ethiopia • Greenland & Iceland • Hungary & Romania • Indonesia • Israel & the Sinai Desert • Jamaica • Japan • La Ruta Maya • London • The Middle East (Syria, Jordan & Lebanon • Morocco • New York City • Northern Spain • North India • Outback Australia • Pacific Islands (Fiji, Solomon Islands & Vanuatu) • Pakistan • Peru • The Philippines • South Africa & Lesotho • South India • South West China • South West USA • Trekking in Uganda & Congo • Turkey • Vietnam • West Africa • Zimbabwe, Botswana & Namibia

The Lonely Planet TV series is produced by: Pilot Productions
The Old Studio
18 Middle Row
London W10 5AT, UK

LONELY PLANET

Guides by Region

L onely Planet is known worldwide for publishing practical, reliable and no-nonsense travel information in our guides and on our Web site. The Lonely Planet list covers just about every accessible part of the world. Currently there are thirteen series: travel guides, shoestring guides, walking guides, city guides, phrasebooks, audio packs, city maps, travel atlases, diving & snorkeling guides, restaurant guides, first-time travel guides, healthy travel and travel literature.

AFRICA Africa on a shoestring ● Africa – the South ● Arabic (Egyptian) phrasebook ● Arabic (Moroccan) phrasebook ● Cairo ● Cape Town ● Cape Town city map● Central Africa ● East Africa ● Egypt ● Egypt travel atlas ● Ethiopian (Amharic) phrasebook ● The Gambia & Senegal ● Healthy Travel Africa ● Kenya ● Kenya travel atlas ● Malawi, Mozambique & Zambia ● Morocco ● North Africa ● South Africa, Lesotho & Swaziland ● South Africa, Lesotho & Swaziland travel atlas ● Swahili phrasebook ● Tanzania, Zanzibar & Pemba ● Trekking in East Africa ● Tunisia ● West Africa ● Zimbabwe, Botswana & Namibia ● Zimbabwe, Botswana & Namibia travel atlas
Travel Literature: The Rainbird: A Central African Journey ● Songs to an African Sunset: A Zimbabwean Story ● Mali Blues: Traveling to an African Beat

AUSTRALIA & THE PACIFIC Auckland ● Australia ● Australian phrasebook ● Bushwalking in Australia ● Bushwalking in Papua New Guinea ● Fiji ● Fijian phrasebook ● Healthy Travel Australia, NZ and the Pacific ● Islands of Australia's Great Barrier Reef ● Melbourne ● Melbourne city map ● Micronesia ● New Caledonia ● New South Wales & the ACT ● New Zealand ● Northern Territory ● Outback Australia ● Out To Eat – Melbourne ● Out to Eat – Sydney ● Papua New Guinea ● Pidgin phrasebook ● Queensland ● Rarotonga & the Cook Islands ● Samoa ● Solomon Islands ● South Australia ● South Pacific Languages phrasebook ● Sydney ● Sydney city map ● Sydney Condensed ● Tahiti & French Polynesia ● Tasmania ● Tonga ● Tramping in New Zealand ● Vanuatu ● Victoria ● Western Australia
Travel Literature: Islands in the Clouds ● Kiwi Tracks: A New Zealand Journey ● Sean & David's Long Drive

CENTRAL AMERICA & THE CARIBBEAN Bahamas, Turks & Caicos ● Bermuda ● Central America on a shoestring ● Costa Rica ● Cuba ● Dominican Republic & Haiti ● Eastern Caribbean ● Guatemala, Belize & Yucatán: La Ruta Maya ● Jamaica ● Mexico ● Mexico City ● Panama ● Puerto Rico
Travel Literature: Green Dreams: Travels in Central America

EUROPE Amsterdam ● Amsterdam city map ● Andalucía ● Austria ● Baltic States phrasebook ● Barcelona ● Berlin ● Berlin city map ● Britain ● British phrasebook ● Brussels, Bruges & Antwerp ● Budapest city map ● Canary Islands ● Central Europe ● Central Europe phrasebook ● Corsica ● Croatia ● Czech & Slovak Republics ● Denmark ● Dublin ● Eastern Europe ● Eastern Europe phrasebook ● Edinburgh ● Estonia, Latvia & Lithuania ● Europe on a shoestring ● Finland ● France ● French phrasebook ● Germany ● German phrasebook ● Greece ● Greek Islands ● Greek phrasebook ● Hungary ● Iceland, Greenland & the Faroe Islands ● Ireland ● Italian phrasebook ● Italy ● Krakow ● Lisbon ● London ● London city map ● London Condensed ● Mediterranean Europe ● Mediterranean Europe phrasebook ● Norway ● Paris ● Paris city map ● Poland ● Portugal ● Portugal travel atlas ● Prague ● Prague city map ● Provence & the Côte d'Azur ● Romania & Moldova ● Rome ● Russia, Ukraine & Belarus ● Russian phrasebook ● Scandinavian & Baltic Europe ● Scandinavian Europe phrasebook ● Scotland ● Slovenia ● Spain ● Spanish phrasebook ● St Petersburg ● Switzerland ● Trekking in Spain ● Ukrainian phrasebook ● Vienna ● Walking in Britain ● Walking in Ireland ● Walking in Italy ● Walking in Spain ● Walking in Switzerland ● Western Europe ● Western Europe phrasebook
Travel Literature: The Olive Grove: Travels in Greece

INDIAN SUBCONTINENT Bangladesh ● Bengali phrasebook ● Bhutan ● Delhi ● Goa ● Hindi & Urdu phrasebook ● India ● India & Bangladesh travel atlas ● Indian Himalaya ● Karakoram Highway ● Kerala ● Mumbai (Bombay) ● Nepal ● Nepali phrasebook ● Pakistan ● Rajasthan ● Read This First: Asia & India ● South India ● Sri Lanka ● Sri Lanka phrasebook ● Trekking in the Indian Himalaya ● Trekking in the Karakoram & Hindukush ● Trekking in the Nepal Himalaya
Travel Literature: In Rajasthan ● Shopping for Buddhas

LONELY PLANET

Mail Order

Lonely Planet products are distributed worldwide. They are also available by mail order from Lonely Planet, so if you have difficulty finding a title please write to us. North and South American residents should write to 150 Linden St, Oakland, CA 94607, USA; European and African residents should write to 10a Spring Place, London NW5 3BH, UK; and residents of other countries to PO Box 617, Hawthorn, Victoria 3122, Australia.

ISLANDS OF THE INDIAN OCEAN Madagascar & Comoros • Maldives • Mauritius, Réunion & Seychelles

MIDDLE EAST & CENTRAL ASIA Arab Gulf States • Central Asia • Central Asia phrasebook • Hebrew phrasebook • Iran • Israel & the Palestinian Territories • Israel & the Palestinian Territories travel atlas • Istanbul • Istanbul to Cairo • Jerusalem • Jordan & Syria • Jordan, Syria & Lebanon travel atlas • Lebanon • Middle East on a shoestring • Syria • Turkey • Turkey travel atlas • Turkish phrasebook • Yemen
Travel Literature: The Gates of Damascus • Kingdom of the Film Stars: Journey into Jordan

NORTH AMERICA Alaska • Backpacking in Alaska • Baja California • California & Nevada • Canada • Chicago • Chicago city map • Deep South • Florida • Hawaii • Honolulu • Las Vegas • Los Angeles • Miami • New England • New Orleans • New York City • New York city map • New York, New Jersey & Pennsylvania • Pacific Northwest USA • Puerto Rico • Rocky Mountain • San Francisco • San Francisco city map • Seattle • Southwest USA • Texas • USA • USA phrasebook • Vancouver • Washington, DC & the Capital Region • Washington DC city map
Travel Literature: Drive Thru America

NORTH-EAST ASIA Beijing • Cantonese phrasebook • China • Hong Kong • Hong Kong city map • Hong Kong, Macau & Guangzhou • Japan • Japanese phrasebook • Japanese audio pack • Korea • Korean phrasebook • Kyoto • Mandarin phrasebook • Mongolia • Mongolian phrasebook • North-East Asia on a shoestring • Seoul • South-West China • Taiwan • Tibet • Tibetan phrasebook • Tokyo
Travel Literature: Lost Japan

SOUTH AMERICA Argentina, Uruguay & Paraguay • Bolivia • Brazil • Brazilian phrasebook • Buenos Aires • Chile & Easter Island • Chile & Easter Island travel atlas • Colombia • Ecuador & the Galapagos Islands • Healthy Travel Central & South America • Latin American Spanish phrasebook • Peru • Quechua phrasebook • Rio de Janeiro • Rio de Janeiro city map • South America on a shoestring • Trekking in the Patagonian Andes • Venezuela
Travel Literature: Full Circle: A South American Journey

SOUTH-EAST ASIA Bali & Lombok • Bangkok • Bangkok city map • Burmese phrasebook • Cambodia • Hanoi • Healthy Travel Asia & India • Hill Tribes phrasebook • Ho Chi Minh City • Indonesia • Indonesia's Eastern Islands • Indonesian phrasebook • Indonesian audio pack • Jakarta • Java • Laos • Lao phrasebook • Laos travel atlas • Malay phrasebook • Malaysia, Singapore & Brunei • Myanmar (Burma) • Philippines • Pilipino (Tagalog) phrasebook • Singapore • South-East Asia on a shoestring • South-East Asia phrasebook • Thailand • Thailand's Islands & Beaches • Thailand travel atlas • Thai phrasebook • Thai audio pack • Vietnam • Vietnamese phrasebook • Vietnam travel atlas

ALSO AVAILABLE: Antarctica • The Arctic • Brief Encounters: Stories of Love, Sex & Travel • Chasing Rickshaws • Lonely Planet Unpacked • Not the Only Planet: Travel Stories from Science Fiction • Sacred India • Travel with Children • Traveller's Tales

FREE Lonely Planet Newsletters

We love hearing from you and think you'd like to hear from us.

Planet Talk

Our FREE quarterly printed newsletter is full of tips from travellers and anecdotes from Lonely Planet guidebook authors. Every issue is packed with up-to-date travel news and advice, and includes:

- a postcard from Lonely Planet co-founder Tony Wheeler
- a swag of mail from travellers
- a look at life on the road through the eyes of a Lonely Planet author
- topical health advice
- prizes for the best travel yarn
- news about forthcoming Lonely Planet events
- a complete list of Lonely Planet books and other titles

To join our mailing list, residents of the UK, Europe and Africa can email us at go@lonelyplanet.co.uk; residents of North and South America can email us at info@lonelyplanet.com; the rest of the world can email us at talk2us@lonelyplanet.com.au, or contact any Lonely Planet office.

Comet

Our FREE monthly email newsletter brings you all the latest travel news, features, interviews, competitions, destination ideas, travellers' tips & tales, Q&As, raging debates and related links. Find out what's new on the Lonely Planet Web site and which books are about to hit the shelves.

Subscribe from your desktop: www.lonelyplanet.com/comet

Index

Text

Boxed Text

MAP LEGEND

CITY ROUTES

Freeway .... Freeway	= = = = ... Unsealed Road
Highway .... Primary Road	.... One Way Street
Road .... Secondary Road	.... Pedestrian Street
Street .... Street	.... Stepped Street
Lane .... Lane	)= = = ... Tunnel
.... On/Off Ramp	.... Footbridge

REGIONAL ROUTES

.... Tollway, Freeway
.... Primary Road
.... Secondary Road
.... Minor Road

BOUNDARIES

.... International
.... State
.... Disputed
.... Fortified Wall

HYDROGRAPHY

.... River, Creek	Dry Lake; Salt Lake
.... Canal	Spring; Rapids
.... Lake	Waterfalls

TRANSPORT ROUTES & STATIONS

.... Train	.... Walking Trail
.... Underground Train	.... Walking Tour
.... Tramway	.... Path
.... Cable Car, Chairlift	.... Pier or Jetty

AREA FEATURES

.... Building	.... Market	.... Beach	.... Campus
.... Park, Gardens	.... Sports Ground	.... Cemetery	.... Plaza

POPULATION SYMBOLS

✪ **CAPITAL** .... National Capital	● **Town** .... Town
◉ **CAPITAL** .... State Capital	● **Village** .... Village
● **CITY** .... City	.... Urban Area

WATER TRANSPORT

.... Daily Ferry
.... Low Frequency Ferry
.... Hydrofoil
.... Excursion Boat

MAP SYMBOLS

▲ .... Place to Stay	▼ .... Place to Eat
	● .... Point of Interest

✈ .... Airport	🎬 .... Cinema	🛉 .... Monument	.... Police Station
.. Archaeological Site	.... Ferry	.... Mosque	.... Post O...
.... Bank	.... Fort	▲ .... Mountain	.... Pub or Ba...
.... Bus Terminal	✚ .... Hospital	⌁ .... Mountain Range	.... Shopping Centre
⌂ .... Cave	.... Internet Cafe	.... Museum	.... Telephone
.... Church	※ .... Lookout	P .... Parking	❶ .. Tourist Information

Note: not all symbols displayed above appear in this book

LONELY PLANET OFFICES

Australia
PO Box 617, Hawthorn, Victoria 3122
☎ 03 9819 1877 fax 03 9819 6459
email: talk2us@lonelyplanet.com.au

USA
150 Linden St, Oakland, CA 94607
☎ 510 893 8555 TOLL FREE: 800 275 8555
fax 510 893 8572
email: info@lonelyplanet.com

UK
10a Spring Place, London NW5 3BH
☎ 020 7428 4800 fax 020 7428 4828
email: go@lonelyplanet.co.uk

France
1 rue du Dahomey, 75011 Paris
☎ 01 55 25 33 00 fax 01 55 25 33 01
email: bip@lonelyplanet.fr
www.lonelyplanet.fr

World Wide Web: www.lonelyplanet.com *or* AOL keyword: lp
Lonely Planet Images: lpi@lonelyplanet.com.au